MW00353803

STUDIES IN THE LEGAL HISTORY OF THE SOUTH

Edited by Paul Finkelman and Kermit L. Hall

This series explores the ways in which law has affected the development of the southern United States and in turn the ways the history of the South has affected the development of American law. Volumes in the series focus on a specific aspect of the law, such as slave law or civil rights legislation, or on a broader topic of historical significance to the development of the legal system in the region, such as issues of constitutional history and of law and society, comparative analyses with other legal systems, and biographical studies of influential southern jurists and lawyers.

The Legal Ideology of Removal

The Legal Ideology
of Removal

The Southern Judiciary and the
Sovereignty of Native American Nations

TIM ALAN GARRISON

The University of Georgia Press
Athens & London

Paperback edition, 2009
© 2002 by the University of Georgia Press
Athens, Georgia 30602
www.ugapress.org

All rights reserved

Designed by Walton Harris
Set in 10/13 Sabon by Bookcomp, Inc.

Printed digitally in the United States of America

The Library of Congress has cataloged the hardcover
edition of this book as follows:

Garrison, Tim Alan, 1961–
The legal ideology of removal : the southern judiciary and the
sovereignty of Native American nations / Tim Alan Garrison.
xiii, 331 p. ; 25 cm. — (Studies in the legal history of the South)
ISBN 0-8203-2212-1 (alk. paper)
Includes bibliographical references (p. [291]–312) and index.
1. Indians of North America—Legal status, laws, etc.—Southern
States—History. 2. Cherokee Indians—Relocation—History. 3. Trail
of Tears, 1838–1839. 4. States' rights (American politics) 5. Sovereignty.
I. Title. II. Series.
KF8228.C5 G37 2002
323.1'19755—dc21   2001052260

Paperback ISBN-13: 978-0-8203-3417-2
ISBN-10: 0-8203-3417-0

British Library Cataloging-in-Publication Data available

An earlier version of chapter 6 appeared as "Beyond *Worcester*:
The Alabama Supreme Court and the Sovereignty of the Creek Nation"
in *Journal of the Early Republic* 19.3 (fall 1999): 423–50.
Reprinted by permission of the University of Pennsylvania Press.

For Cindy and Sam

CONTENTS

ACKNOWLEDGMENTS

In the 1830s the state of Georgia seized the land of the Cherokee Nation, divided it up into parcels, and sold it in a lottery to the citizens of the state. My ancestors lived on land they acquired in one of the Cherokee land lotteries. Since becoming familiar with the story of the Indian Removal, I have acquired a deep sense of guilt about that personal heritage. I think it essential that I first acknowledge my respect for those who suffered one of the gravest injustices in American history: the citizens of the Cherokee Nation. While we as a nation are loathe to apologize, I do not hesitate to ask for forgiveness from the descendants of those who walked the Trail of Tears.

I lost all of my grandparents during the time I wrote this book. Their passing made me understand that what we produce is not just a result of our own sweat; it is a consequence of the wisdom, help, and guidance of others. In writing this book, I have had the pleasure and fortune to have received advice from scholars and students, assistance from archivists and editors, and encouragement from mentors, friends, and family. I would like to acknowledge the contributions of just a few of the many people I badgered, bored, and begged from over the last five years.

I could not have completed this book without the research assistance I received from the library staffs at the University of Georgia, the University of Kentucky, and Portland State University. I also received valuable aid from the staffs of the Georgia Department of Archives and History, the Tennessee State Library and Archives, the Alabama State Archives, and the Gilcrease Institute. Local historians and librarians in Cleveland, Tennessee; Athens, Tennessee; and Gainesville, Georgia all unearthed vital files and documents that improved my understanding of the cases I describe herein. Any historian interested in north Georgia should acknowledge the contributions of Sybil McRay.

Paul Finkelman and Kermit L. Hall read the entire manuscript and offered extremely useful criticism. I also want to thank Professor Finkelman for his advice and encouragement over the last few years. The editorial staff at the University of Georgia was consistently supportive of this first-time author. Malcolm Call was my primary editor for most of this project. He offered a measured mixture of guidance and patience as I tried to learn to write and teach at the same time. Kristine Blakeslee, Alison Waldenberg, and Nathan

Bowden came along in the latter stages and brought me to the finish line. Jeanée Ledoux was an excellent copy editor under difficult circumstances, and I will always appreciate her courage and close direction. The anonymous reader of my manuscript offered some very valuable advice on improving the organization of the text.

I must acknowledge the continuing support of my professional mentors, Theda Perdue and Michael D. Green. I will always be grateful for their guidance. They also carefully reviewed this work in its early stages. The following scholars read the manuscript in its earliest incarnation: Robert Ireland, David Hamilton, Louise Graham, Bradley C. Canon, Richard Jefferies, and Thomas Hakansson. I also want to thank Mary Young, not only for her insightful scholarship, but for her kind letter of advice on Judge Clayton. While I never burdened them with reading this work, I still feel a tremendous debt to wonderful teachers and influences like Tom Liner, Lindsey Collins, Bobby Gruhn, Don McKale, and Don Nieman. All of them, in one way or another, influenced this work in a positive fashion.

If you look at Theda Perdue's work, you will see that she always mentions her graduate students in her acknowledgments. I never quite understood why she did that until I had been teaching for some time. Now I realize that my students at Portland State University inject me with energy and enthusiasm, and they often intelligently and courageously challenge my ideas and arguments. Some of them even laugh at my jokes. Many of them are obtaining degrees under terribly challenging circumstances, and they should know that I admire them. I also want to thank my bosses Gordon Dodds, Lois Becker, and Diane Gould; my predecessor in legal history, Tom Morris; and the rest of my colleagues at Portland State for their constant support. Dean Marvin Kaiser provided two summer fellowships to give me the time to complete the revisions. My golfing partner, Mickey Beck, and our mortal enemies, Chuck Johnson and Trae Rittenberry, offered me an occasional respite from this work.

I could not have completed this work without my family. Dorothy and Jim Lamb have always offered unconditional support for my work and unconditional love to my family. At one point, they turned over their cabin in the old Cherokee town of Ellijay so that I could work on this manuscript. My mom, Jeannine Garrison, was a schoolteacher and forfeited her career so that she could raise me and my sister, Pat. I hope she realizes that my teaching is a tribute to that sacrifice. Speaking of sacrifices, C. Talmadge Garrison made a life out of giving up his money and time for his two children. Whatever positive qualities I have are a consequence of their guidance and example. Finally, I want to express my love and appreciation to my wife, Cindy. I cannot imagine living and working without her. I also want to express my love for Samuel Wyatt Garrison, another work of mine that I expect will be far better received by posterity than this simple book. He is just about to start reading, and I hope one day he will find this, read it, and recall pleasurable memories of his old dad.

The Legal Ideology of Removal

Introduction

IN THE FALL OF 1837, John Ross, the principal chief of the Cherokee Nation, traveled to Washington to meet with Martin Van Buren, the president of the United States. Van Buren had established May 23, 1838, as the final date for the removal of the Cherokees, and Ross hoped to persuade the president either to postpone the deadline or, even better, to renegotiate the removal and cession provisions of the Treaty of New Echota. For weeks, Ross tried to obtain concessions for the Cherokees, but Van Buren and his aides consistently rebuffed the chief's entreaties. The president indicated that he had no interest in further negotiations and was resolved to carry the Cherokees' removal through to its conclusion. In April 1838, Ross wrote a final desperate missive to Van Buren: "If the evil of external exile from our sacred inheritance . . . must come upon us, I am most desirous of enabling you to accomplish the favorite purpose of your nation . . . 'peaceably and on reasonable terms.' " [1]

Van Buren responded by ordering federal troops into the Cherokee Nation. United States soldiers began rounding up Cherokee families and herding them into makeshift stockades. To prevent their escaping, the troops crept up and surrounded Cherokee homes, captured the inhabitants, and forced them to depart with barely an opportunity to collect their personal belongings. Those who witnessed the roundup described it to James Mooney, the ethnologist who studied the Cherokees in the late nineteenth century: "Families at dinners were startled by the sudden gleam of bayonets in the doorway and rose up to be driven with blows and oaths along the weary miles of trail that led to the stockade." Some of those who were marched to the stockades told Mooney that when they turned back for one last look, "they saw their homes in flames, fired by the lawless rabble that followed on the heels of the soldiers to loot and pillage." To make matters worse, they told Mooney, "systematic hunts were made by the same men for Indian graves, to rob them of the silver pendants and other valuables deposited with the dead." [2]

When Ross heard the disturbing reports of what was taking place back

in the Cherokee Nation, he decided to return home. When the chief arrived
in early July, he found the nation in disarray. Thousands of his people were
locked up and preparing to march to the Indian Territory, which Congress
had recently established west of Arkansas. When the chief visited the holding
camp at Aquohee on August 1, he discovered that several members of the
Cherokee National Council were imprisoned along with their constituents.
Ross called the council members into an impromptu meeting. He told them
that he had been unable to delay the federal government's removal plans. He
added that he had informed Winfield Scott, the commander of the American
removal troops, that the Cherokees would peacefully depart for the West if
the tribe's leadership could organize the effort. Ross reported that Scott had
consented to the arrangement, and he asked the council members to provide
him with authority to superintend the removal expeditions. After agreeing
to Ross's request, the council issued one last memorial before departing
on the Trail of Tears. "The title of the Cherokee people to their lands is
the most ancient, pure, and absolute known to man," the council said, "its
validity confirmed and illustrated by possession and enjoyment antecedent
to all pretense of claims by any other portion of the human race." As such,
"the natural, political and moral relations existing among the citizens of the
Cherokee nation toward each other and toward the body politic; cannot
in reason and justice be dissolved by the expulsion of the nation from its
territory by the power of the United States Government." With that, the
council declared that the "inherent sovereignty of the Cherokee nation,
together with the Constitution, laws and usages of the same," remained "in
full force . . . in perpetuity."[3]

This last spasm of defiance, directed at the federal and state forces that
had expropriated their national territory, concluded the Cherokees' struggle
to retain their national autonomy in the Southeast. With the exile of the
Cherokees in the winter of 1838–39, and the subsequent surrender of the
Seminoles to federal troops in 1842, the United States had expelled every
major Native American nation from the Southeast. Pulled up from their ancestral roots and forced to surrender their homes, farms, and livelihoods,
the Cherokees, Creeks, Choctaws, Chickasaws, and Seminoles marched and
rode, often under extreme conditions, to an unfamiliar territory and an uncertain future. The physical and psychological hardships of removal were
terrible; the relocation decimated the populations of the Southeastern tribes.
According to the demographer Russell Thornton, from one-quarter to one-
half of the Cherokee, Creek, and Seminole populations died as a direct consequence of their removal. The Choctaws lost perhaps 15 percent of their
population; even the Chickasaws, who lived relatively close to the Indian
Territory, suffered terrible losses. The numbers, however, do not begin to

describe the inhumanity of what we might call today the ethnic cleansing of the Southeast. Countless atrocities are described in the historical record, but the most famous comment on the relocation comes from one of the removers. Decades after the Indian exile, a Georgia man recalled his service with the federal troops that locked up the Cherokees in the internment stockades: "I fought through the civil war and have seen men shot to pieces and slaughtered by the thousands, but the Cherokee removal was the cruelest work I ever knew."[4]

The thousands who suffered and died on the removal trails were the casualties of a calculated assault by the southern states on the territorial integrity and sovereignty of the Indian tribes. In the 1820s the state of Georgia launched a relentless campaign to persuade the federal government to remove the Cherokees from its borders. When the tribe adopted a constitutional government and declared itself an independent republic in 1827, the state's legislators took matters into their own hands and extended the state's jurisdiction over the Cherokees. In the extension legislation Georgia annexed the Cherokees' lands, abolished the Cherokee government and courts, and nullified the laws promulgated by the Cherokee National Council. The extension laws repudiated the Cherokees' assertion of national sovereignty and were designed to make the lot of Indians so miserable that they would accept a relocation to the West. Not long thereafter, Alabama, Tennessee, and Mississippi extended jurisdiction over the Indians within their states. White southerners, in essence, wanted the Indian tribes removed from their midst, and the extension statutes were the legal club that the southern governments used to beat the tribes into submission.[5]

The southern states acquired important support for their campaign in 1828 when Andrew Jackson, an outspoken proponent of removal, was elected president of the United States. In his first annual message to the country Jackson declared that the Indian tribes could either remove beyond the Mississippi River or fall under state jurisdiction. Within two years Congress had adopted the Indian Removal Act of 1830, which gave Jackson the authority to negotiate cession and removal treaties with the tribes. With that power, Jackson ordered federal treaty commissioners to work expeditiously toward removal. By 1835 the Creeks, Chickasaws, and Choctaws had all surrendered to the state and federal pressures.[6]

The Cherokees and Seminoles, however, refused to accept Jackson's alternatives of removal or subjection to state jurisdiction. The Seminoles took up the sword and fought a bitter war of resistance against the U.S. Army. John Ross and the Cherokee leadership adopted another course of action; they elected to bring a constitutional challenge to Georgia's extension legislation in federal court. When Ross hired William Wirt, a prominent Washington lawyer, to represent the Cherokee Nation, Wirt told the chief that some justices on the U.S. Supreme Court were sympathetic to the Cherokees' plight and might vote to enjoin Georgia from further trespasses. The problem, Wirt warned, was finding a case that would provide the Cherokees with legal standing before the Court. An opportunity arose in the summer of 1830 when the Georgia Guard, a police outfit created specifically to harass the Cherokees, entered the nation and arrested a Cherokee man named George Tassel for the murder of another Cherokee. After Tassel was convicted by a state superior court, the Cherokees appealed his case up to the U.S. Supreme Court. Georgia mooted Tassel's appeal, however, by hanging him before the Court could hear his case.[7]

Three days later, Ross and the Cherokee Nation's attorneys amended the pleadings they had prepared in Tassel's appeal and refiled them as an original action petitioning the Supreme Court to strike down Georgia's extension legislation. The Court, in the case denominated *Cherokee Nation v. Georgia* (1831), refused to rule on the merits of the Cherokees' petition. The Cherokee Nation, the majority concluded, was not a "foreign state" that could be granted original standing under Article 3 of the Constitution. In an ambiguous opinion for a divided court, Chief Justice John Marshall wrote that the Cherokees were instead a "domestic, dependent nation" with a relationship to the federal government that "resembles that of a ward to his guardian."[8]

Marshall's characterization was not the mandate of sovereignty that Ross had hoped for, and he continued to search for a case that offered his nation a full hearing on its claim of sovereignty. He found it in July 1831 when Georgia arrested Samuel A. Worcester, Elizur Butler, and several other missionaries and agents of the American Board of Foreign Missions for violating an 1830 law that prohibited white people from entering Cherokee territory without a license from the state. In September the state convicted the missionaries and sentenced them to four years' imprisonment at hard labor. The missionaries appealed their case to the U.S. Supreme Court. In the resulting decision of *Worcester v. Georgia,* the Court dramatically struck down Georgia's extension legislation and embraced the Cherokees' contention that they were a separate, sovereign nation. The Indian nations, Marshall suggested for the majority, were akin to the small countries of Europe that existed under the protection of larger and more powerful states. Although they had surrendered elements of sovereignty to the United States, he said, the Cherokees remained a politically distinct nation, possessed a legitimate title to their national territory, and were entitled to maintain their existing political and legal institutions free from Georgia's interference.[9]

Worcester, however, proved to be a paper victory for the Cherokees. John Ross had believed that the authority of a U.S. Supreme Court decision in the

Cherokees' favor might either turn Georgia from its policy of intimidation or, more likely, persuade Congress or President Jackson to intervene on the Cherokees' behalf. Ross hoped, in other words, that a legal victory would stem the political tide toward removal. Instead, Georgia ignored *Worcester* and refused to release the missionaries. To the Cherokees' further consternation, Jackson refrained from making any effort to enforce the decision against the state. "The decision of the supreme court has fell still born," the president wrote, "and they find that they cannot coerce Georgia to yield to its mandate." Without the threat of enforcement by federal troops, the Court's decision in favor of Cherokee sovereignty was rendered meaningless.[10]

During his term as chief justice, Marshall had methodically elevated the Supreme Court's authority and established it as the ultimate interpreter and arbiter of the Constitution. But ironically, at the end of his term, the word of the Court received almost unanimous disapprobation from the president and the legislatures and courts of the southern states. Scholars have never adequately explained how the Court's authority, so richly expanded during the Marshall era, could have been so completely repudiated by such a broad segment of the American legal and political community. Histories of the Removal Crisis usually state that Jackson and Georgia did not agree with *Worcester,* so they simply ignored it. But the nonenforcement of *Worcester* was less a clash of personality—between Jackson and Marshall or between the Georgia government and Ross—than it was a conflict of competing legal arguments; and the president and the radical removal proponents, as independent as they were, might not have so openly disavowed the decision without some semblance of legal authority to do so. Indeed, the southern position, that the Indian tribes held no political or property rights worthy of recognition by American courts, was not without legal foundation. In fact, elements of the southern removal ideology dated back well into the legal and political history of Europe and the United States.

Between 1830 and 1835, three state supreme courts in the South percolated the threads of the long tradition of anti-Indian legal prejudice into a formal legal position that justified the expropriation of Native American land. The decisions of the southern tribunals filled the legal vacuum created by the general disavowal of *Worcester* and provided legal legitimacy to the state legislative assault on Indian rights. In *Georgia v. Tassels* (1830), *Caldwell v. Alabama* (1831), and *Tennessee v. Forman* (1835), the southern courts produced analyses that countered those espoused by Marshall in *Cherokee Nation* and *Worcester.* The tribes were not sovereign nations, the southern courts held; Indians were simply, as individuals, subjects of the states in which they lived. Each state, the southern judges said, held the authority to extend its jurisdiction to the reaches of its territorial limits, regardless of federal-Indian treaties or national legislation to the contrary. Hence, each state possessed the power to abolish the government and laws, and the right to extinguish competing property claims, of any tribe residing within its borders.

Historically, legal scholars have quite naturally tended to focus on the decisions of the U.S. Supreme Court. As a result, the state courts are a relatively unexploited and fertile ground for historical research, and I suspect that in the future we will find that the attention to the federal courts has seriously distorted our understanding of the manner in which law developed in the United States.[11] Historical concentration on the Supreme Court's decisions in *Cherokee Nation* and *Worcester,* for example, has tended to overshadow the role the southern state courts played in the Removal Crisis and the important influences the southern judiciary had in the origins of American Indian law. The southern courts' repudiation of tribal sovereignty, and their position on the relative power of the state and federal governments over Indian affairs, perhaps influenced the development of that law as much as Marshall's recognition of tribal sovereignty in *Worcester.*

Scholars have also generally overlooked the interplay that occurred between the state and federal courts, and the impact of those remote conversations on the issues of import. For instance, when read in chronological order of decision, the federal and southern state cases offer a lengthy and concentrated debate on the place of the Native American and the Indian tribe in the American constitutional system. Issued before the Supreme Court became entangled in the dispute between Georgia and the Cherokees, *Georgia v. Tassels* initiated the conversation by directly challenging the principle of tribal sovereignty established in the previous four decades of U.S.-Indian relations. The subsequent state case, *Caldwell v. Alabama,* provided the southern judiciary's reaction to *Cherokee Nation.* The Alabama supreme court's three turgid opinions in that case, spanning 117 pages of the Alabama Reports, represented the most comprehensive explication of the southern position on Indian tribal and individual rights; we cannot appreciate the true radicalism of *Worcester v. Georgia* without placing it into the context of the southern position. *Tennessee v. Forman,* the final case of the southern triumvirate, repudiated Marshall's bold recognition of tribal sovereignty in *Worcester.*

The *Forman* case also ended the Cherokees' hopes of maintaining a national status in the Southeast. In 1832, the Cherokees had moved their government from New Echota (in the area annexed by Georgia) across the border to Red Clay in present-day Tennessee to escape Georgia's persecution. From time to time, the Cherokee leadership had considered surrendering its territory in Georgia and reestablishing the nation permanently in what is now western North Carolina and eastern Tennessee. Since the courts of Georgia and Alabama had upheld their respective legislatures' extension laws, *Forman* made the Cherokees political outlaws in almost every part of their once expansive domain. Not long after the publication of the Tennessee court's opinion, a dissident faction of Cherokees signed a removal treaty with federal officials at New Echota; and on May 8, 1838, U.S. troops arrived to round up the Cherokees and march them to the Indian Territory.[12]

The Indian Removal was the consequence of the great economic, political, and intellectual forces that transformed the South in the early decades of the nineteenth century. The explosion of cotton agriculture made arable Indian land an obsession for southern speculators, yeoman farmers, and opportunistic politicians. At the same time, the political center of power in the United States had moved distinctly westward and southward with the country's expanding and migratory population. Expansionist politicians such as George Gilmer and George Troup of Georgia seized office and suggested to their constituencies that Indians were not exploiting their land in the way that Providence had intended. Hence, they argued, white people were within their rights when they took land away from the Indian tribes. The southern courts subsequently sanctioned this justification for expropriation. In the years leading up to the Removal, southern whites also became increasingly concerned with the putative racial distinctions between themselves and blacks and Indians. As American intellectuals and scientists offered purported evidence of the biological inferiority of nonwhites, they made it easier for southern whites to reconcile their abject discrimination. As a result, discussions of assimilating the Native population, which had long been an announced objective of U.S. Indian policy, faded out of political consideration in the South.

By the late 1820s removal was a plan popular among a vast majority of the southern citizenry and a useful position for ambitious politicians. The most obdurate of the southern elite demanded removal without any real regard for its moral or constitutional implications, and although its more subtle architects cleverly marketed it as a way to provide Indians with time to prepare for assimilation, the policy was essentially a ruse to confiscate Indian land. Elias Boudinot, the editor of the *Cherokee Phoenix* newspaper, recognized as much: "Cupidity and self-interest are at the bottom of all these difficulties," he wrote in describing the removal policy. "[A] desire to possess the Indian land is paramount to a desire to see him established on the soil as a civilized man." In a society so recently grounded upon the rule of law and natural rights, however, a policy as brazenly unjust as removal required rationalization. The judges of the southern state courts offered the justifications that salved the consciences of removal advocates.[13]

The extension law cases are significant for several reasons beyond their relevance to the Indian Removal. First, they complement the body of southern state decisions involving slavery and provide a broader understanding of the racial views of the southern legal elite in the conceptual period of the proslavery ideology. The judges in these cases clearly feared that a state abdication over Indian-white relations would entice the national government into intruding into a realm in which their states claimed absolute rule—the relationship between slaveholders and bondsmen. At the same time, these cases forced southern judges to think about race in a context beyond the master-slave relationship, and when the time came to defend slavery against the attacks of abolitionists, southern judges and proslavery ideologues were prepared to counter northern moral suasion with reasoning and cant formulated in *Tassels, Caldwell,* and *Forman.*

Second, the southern courts' affirmation of the extension laws challenged the federal government's authority over Indian affairs. Since the Constitutional Convention, the construction of the Commerce Clause and the appropriate extent of federal power over Indian relations had been issues of contention between federalists and southern states' rights partisans. The latter bridled at the idea that the treaties between the federal government and the tribes superseded state jurisdictional authority. *Cherokee Nation* and *Worcester,* which reaffirmed that principle, simply gave the federal government more authority over Indian affairs than southern judges could bear. The southern courts consequently formulated a states' rights interpretation of the Commerce Clause that attempted to keep the federal government out of almost every aspect of Indian-white relations beyond economic exchange. The framers intended to endow the federal government only with the power to regulate trade with the Indian tribes, the southern courts maintained; the states possessed jurisdiction over every other aspect of Indian affairs. Included within the states' sphere of authority, they added, was the right to extinguish the Indian land title. The southern judiciary thus injected the principle of state police power into an area that the framers and early Congresses had apparently set aside solely for federal and Indian determination. Since the Removal Crisis the states and local authorities have remained reluctant to cede authority over matters involving Indians within their borders, and the southern theory of concurrent state jurisdiction over Indian territory influenced the development of American Indian law to a degree that has yet to be broadly appreciated. The Indian Removal cases were, for these reasons, an important legal laboratory for the states' rights interpretation of the Constitution.

Third, when viewed within the context of the legislation and court decisions that followed the Removal Crisis, the position of the southern courts on the constitutionality of extending state jurisdiction over the Indian tribes appears more influential in the nineteenth century than was Marshall's repudiation of that notion in *Worcester*. The southern courts declared that the idea of an autonomous Indian nation was a historical anachronism. The rest of the country's state courts and legislatures subsequently seemed to agree. While the reception of *Worcester* in the nineteenth century was, in Charles F. Wilkinson's words, "checkered," the southern affirmation of extension quickly garnered a following throughout the country. By the end of the nineteenth century every state with a material Indian population east of the Mississippi, except for Minnesota, had extended, at the least, its criminal jurisdiction over its resident Native Americans.[14]

Fourth, the Indian Removal cases demonstrate the contempt that the southern states occasionally held for federal legal authority. More specifically, the extension law decisions continued a pattern of southern suspicion for the U.S. Supreme Court that began with *Chisholm v. Georgia*. Article 6 of the Constitution made the decisions of the Supreme Court part of the "supreme law of the land." Without any effort to enforce *Worcester* on the South, federal officials allowed a southern indifference to national law to become even more entrenched. At the least, with Jackson's threat of federal force in the South Carolina nullification crisis, southerners received ambiguous and confusing signals about the supremacy of federal law. At the worst, the federal equivocation in the face of southern rambunctiousness informed many southerners that they could pick and choose the federal statutes and decisions with which they were to comply.[15]

Fifth, the cases illuminate the logical inconsistencies that characterized southern law and politics. Despite their republican philosophy of limited central government and their claim of jurisdiction over the tribes, southern leaders were not embarrassed to ask for federal assistance in the rounding up and removal of Native Americans. In that sense, as it was in the subsequent fugitive slave controversies, southern condemnations of federal power were relative and opportunistic. Similarly, though southern judges denied that the Indian tribe was a political unit capable of concluding treaties, they did not reject the federal-Indian accords that called for land cessions or removal. In other words, these cases add further evidence to the theory that for some southern leaders and judges the states' rights interpretation of the Constitution was more tactical rhetoric than heartfelt ideology. In the extension cases, southern judges portrayed the theories of tribal sovereignty, federal authority over Indian affairs, and federal legal supremacy as direct and dastardly threats to their states. Their opinions exemplified the theoretical opposition to Marshall's fundamental interpretation of the Constitution and the chief justice's understanding of the relationship between the federal government, the states, and the Indian tribes. The southern appellate courts offered a competing construction of the Constitution that made the states ascendant in the federal system and placed the states, rather than the federal government, in control of Indian affairs. But when push came to shove, the southern states were more interested in economic expansion and racial separation than consistent constitutional theory. The economic objective of acquiring cheap productive land and the racial objective of cleansing the region of Native Americans motivated the southern judges more than any constitutional or ideological principle.

Finally, these motivations, and Marshall's rather tardy conversion to tribal sovereignty, offer interesting contrasts in the contemporary personalities behind jurisprudence and the manner in which scholars have interpreted those personalities. Take John Marshall, for instance. *Worcester* was the conclusion to a meandering and troubled effort by the chief justice to sort out the anomalous status of the Indian tribes within the federal framework. To reach that terminus Marshall had to abandon positions enunciated in *Fletcher v. Peck* (1810) and *Johnson v. McIntosh* (1823) that were not far afield from what the southern courts argued in the extension law cases. In fact, these decisions served as legal precedents for the southern judiciary. That Marshall was willing to admit his own fallibility and was capable of changing positions so drastically reflected considerable courage on his part. Many students of Marshall and the Cherokee cases have not been as willing as the chief justice to recognize his humanity. Some, for example, point to Marshall's opinion in *Cherokee Nation* as an ingenious compromise. Soon after the decision, however, Marshall quickly admitted that the decision was rushed and improvidently drafted. He was right. The seemingly clever construction of the "domestic dependent nation" concept and the "guardian and ward" metaphor were disastrous for Indian rights, for they muddied the meaning of Marshall's subsequent clear pronouncement of tribal sovereignty in *Worcester*. Marshall, it seems, quickly recognized as much. *Worcester*, moreover, does not fit the conventional depiction of Marshall as a pragmatic compromiser intent on building up the authority of the Court and the power of the federal government. Instead, in *Worcester*, Marshall abandoned political calculation. Upon careful reading, one senses that the chief justice not only had reached a point of maturation on the question of tribal sovereignty but that he had also become resigned to his own mortality. For all of their flaws, *Cherokee Nation* and *Worcester* seem to have been genuine efforts by Marshall to figure out the tribal sovereignty conundrum, and ultimately he concluded to issue a decision based on morality rather than expediency.[16]

The decisions of the southern judges, in contrast, revealed ideals and motivations more base than those held by the chief justice. As the institutional

guardians of justice and property rights, the southern appellate courts were
perhaps the one institution somewhat above the popular fray that could have
forestalled the Indian Removal. Instead, the southern judges fecklessly ac-
ceded to the will of a land-voracious and prejudiced public and surrendered
their independence to the state executives and legislatures. By upholding the
state extension statutes, they sanctified the seizure of Native American land
and dignified the presumption that Indians were inherently inferior to whites
at a time that called for courageous equanimity. Their opinions, so antithetical to Marshall's declaration in *Worcester*, were backed by legal rationale
as duplicitous and fallacious as any in American legal history. Their legal
rationalizations for extension relied on a perverted history of the European
conquest of the Americas, a distorted interpretation of the treaty relationships between the United States and the Indian nations, and cynical construc-
tions of constitutional provisions. The state appellate judges, supposedly the
keenest minds in the South, ignored significant precedents, misrepresented
pertinent laws and court decisions, and refused to address the rational arguments for tribal sovereignty. In an effort to abet the legislative attack on the
Indian nations, the southern judges also violated a basic principle of judicial
ethics: they prejudged their cases. By excusing the legislative attacks on tribal
sovereignty, the southern judiciary abdicated its role as the legal conscience
of the public and offered the politicians moral and legal cover. That is not
to say that the southern judiciary was principally responsible for the mass
exile of the Southeastern Indians. By affirming the extension laws, however,
the judges in Georgia, Alabama, and Tennessee clearly became accessories
to the tragedy.

Each tribe in the Southeast responded to the pressures of the Removal Crisis
in its own way, and to attempt to include the histories of all of their nations
would be an insult to the scholars who have dedicated their efforts to telling
the story from a tribal perspective. Instead, this book is a history of competing philosophies, arguments, and rhetoric. The Cherokees, and the Creeks to
a lesser degree, became the Native American participants in this ideological
conflict, so it is their leaders and lawyers, and the state and federal attorneys
and judges, who are the primary subjects of study. The focus on these men
requires me, for the sake of narrative clarity, to omit the many dramatic
stories that are tangential to the legal arguments.

I do not wish to diminish the significance of Marshall's decisions in
the Cherokee cases. The federal trust relationship over the Indian tribes is
grounded upon Marshall's "guardian and ward" metaphor in *Cherokee
Nation*, and *Worcester*, with its conception that the Indian tribes possess
an inherent form of national sovereignty, reemerged in the second half of

the twentieth century to become the most significant case in determining issues related to Indian tribal rights. Marshall's assertion that the Indian tribes in North America are sovereign nations, possessing the precious right of self-determination, has become the fundamental principle that controls almost every question in contemporary Indian law. As one scholar wrote, "Designation as a sovereign . . . implies a kind of dignity and respectability beyond its literal meaning." Today, therefore, the tribes use *Worcester* as a powerful legal and political tool in their relations with the state and federal governments. When the states refused to recognize the principle of tribal sovereignty in the nineteenth century, however, Native American governments found themselves unable to counter the policies—removal, reservations, and allotment—that almost resulted in the extinction of tribal autonomy. Genuine respect for Marshall's theory of tribal sovereignty by the states may have produced an intriguing American federalism that would have allowed the United States and dynamic, sovereign Native American nations to coexist in a truly multicultural international alliance. The sanction of state extension by the southern courts, however, played a prominent role in the destruction of that alternative reality.[17]

Although I doubt their spirits and descendants will appreciate the conclusions I reach in this work, I have attempted to bring southern judges into the story of the Indian Removal. When I read the opinions from the southern bench, I occasionally found intelligence, skillful legal reasoning, thoughtful constitutional analysis, genuine idealism, and heartfelt emotion. More often, however, I found calculated distortion and misrepresentation, inane logic, and mean-spirited condescension. In writing this history, I hoped to demonstrate, as so many scholars have done before me, that "the law" is not necessarily the product of the adversarial process of competing rational arguments, but rather the consequence of social, cultural, economic, and political forces. In these cases, I discovered that the law is also all too often corrupted by irrational prejudice and rhetorical artifice. This study of the southern judiciary reminds us once again that law and justice are distinct ideas, and that the law is often not what the U.S. Supreme Court declares it to be, but what the American public accepts or institutional power deems to enforce.

CHAPTER ONE

Removal

The Separation Solution

JOHN MITCHELL, an English cartographer and botanist, was perhaps the first to propose removing the Indians in eastern North America beyond the reach of white settlement. In 1767 he pointed out that the Indian tribes were the only obstacle preventing Great Britain's colonies from expanding all the way to the Mississippi River. Mitchell suggested that the British government consider relocating the Creeks and the Choctaws to Florida, which he described as noninhabitable for any people other than Indians. The tribes in the northern half of the continent, he added, could be reestablished in Canada and around the Great Lakes. A few years later, Thomas Jefferson again broached the idea of removal. In a letter to Edmund Pendleton in 1776, he condemned a Cherokee attack on white settlers in the Appalachians and added, "I hope the Cherokees will now be driven beyond the Mississippi and that this in future will be declared to the Indians the invariable consequence of their beginning a war."[1]

Other leaders also suggested the relocation of the Indian tribes during the early years of the American republic. In 1793 Timothy Pickering suggested removal over the Mississippi as a way to prevent the extinction of the Indians. Gilbert Imlay also suggested a mass exile in 1797. The crucial point in the history of removal as a federal policy was 1800, when Jefferson became president. First, he made the threat of forced relocation part of his Indian policy. In an infamous letter in 1803, Jefferson told William Henry Harrison, the territorial governor of Indiana, to run influential Indians into debt to make it easier to acquire tribal lands. He also directed Harrison to warn the Indians in his territory that the United States would drive across the Mississippi any tribe that was "foolhardy" enough to attack American settlers. Jefferson, it appears, was thus contemplating the possibility of relocating the eastern tribes at the same time that his emissaries in Paris were negotiating the Louisiana Purchase. After closing the purchase, Jefferson fretted about the constitutionality of the acquisition and drafted proposed amendments to remedy those concerns. One of them would have authorized Congress to exchange lands on the west side of the Mississippi for the territories of the eastern tribes. The Indian territory, he suggested in a private letter, could be "locked up from American settlement, and under the self-government of the Native occupants." The Louisiana Purchase would therefore afford the United States a place to relocate those Indian peoples who refused to assimilate and allow the Anglo-American population to fill out and cultivate the lands within its existing territorial borders.[2]

The United States could not unilaterally relocate the eastern tribes, however, for between Jefferson's first articulation of the idea of removal and his acquisition of Louisiana, the federal government had come to recognize that, for all intents and purposes, the Indian tribes were separate, sovereign nations possessing a legitimate title to their lands. As such, American policymakers of the late eighteenth and early nineteenth centuries agreed that the Indian tribes had to consent to any effort to remove them to the West. This acknowledgment of Indian soil and sovereignty followed the British precedent established in the colonial period and was a consequence of the United States's precarious strategic situation during and following the American Revolution. Historically, relations between the colonies and the Indian tribes had been conducted through diplomatic treaties, and the United States, out of necessity, continued the custom of treating with the Indian tribes during the war. In the earliest of these agreements the treaty commissioners appointed by the Continental Congress conceded territorial rights to the signatory tribes and indicated that they viewed them as distinct, sovereign entities rather than subjects of the Crown or the newly independent states. For example, in the United States's first Indian treaty, an accord with the Delawares in 1778, U.S. negotiators acknowledged that the Delaware people possessed title and sovereignty over their own territory, offered the tribe representation in the Continental Congress, and obtained permission for American troops to travel across Delaware land. The United States negotiated these agreements and made these concessions to obtain the alliance or neutrality of the tribes at a time when the viability of the rebellion was very much in doubt. At this early stage of U.S.-Indian relations, the bargaining leverage of the tribes and their political status were partly a function of the United States's perception of Indian military power.[3]

The United States sent mixed signals to the tribes after the Revolutionary War. Occasionally, American leaders offered conciliatory statements to the Indian peoples, professed a desire for peace, and promised to respect the tribes' territorial rights. At the same time, some of the treaty commissioners appointed by the Continental Congress attempted to dictate conditions to, and coerce cessions from, the Native American peoples who abutted the

American frontier. By defeating Great Britain, the American negotiators argued, the United States had acquired dominion by right of conquest over the Crown's American possessions and was rightfully assuming the title of Britain's Native American allies. The Indian nations that had aligned with Great Britain during the Revolutionary War complained bitterly about this treatment and rejected the idea that they were defeated peoples. Britain may have capitulated, Indian leaders said, but their tribes had never surrendered to, or begged peace from, the United States. Conflicts between the Indian tribes and the colonists who moved into their territory had always been a difficult problem for the British imperial and colonial governments, and the intrusive reconnoitering by speculators and surveyors and the provocative flow of settlers into the interior of the continent continued after the war. The attitude of conquest assumed by many Americans only exacerbated the animosities between Indians and settlers, and the postrevolutionary period was marked by continuous conflict on the young nation's western edges. The Continental Congress, for its part, was unable to do much to restrain, and even less to protect, the American settlers who wanted to move across the Appalachians onto Indian lands. The practice of attempting to overawe the Indian tribes was, in sum, an abject failure, thanks to the weak military and financial position of the confederation government.[4]

The United States's ambiguous posture toward the Indian tribes and the insecurities of the new nation were evident in the treaties negotiated in the mid-1780s. On the one hand, the treaties the United States concluded with the Cherokees, Chickasaws, and Choctaws at Hopewell, South Carolina, in late 1785 and early 1786 included language reflecting a desire to bring the Indian nations under American dominion. The three tribes agreed, for example, that they lived "under the protection of the United States and of no other sovereign whatsoever" and conceded that the Congress would "have the exclusive right of regulating the trade with the Indians, and managing all their affairs in such manner as they think proper." The Hopewell agreements also prohibited the tribes from engaging in independent diplomatic or trade relations. In these same treaties, on the other hand, the United States specifically recognized the borders of the tribes' lands, acknowledged that the tribes possessed the right to determine who could enter or live in their territory, and provided the tribal councils with the power to punish those who settled on Indian land without their consent. A year after the Hopewell treaties, the United States appeared even more conciliatory to its Native American neighbors. In the Northwest Ordinance of 1787, the Continental Congress promised, "The utmost good faith shall always be observed towards the Indians, their lands and property shall never be taken from them without their consent; and in their property, rights and liberty, they shall never be invaded or disturbed, unless in just and lawful wars authorized by Congress." Thus, while the United States continued to claim dominion over the land on which the tribes resided, the postwar treaties and the ordinance represented an admission on the part of U.S. policymakers that the Indian tribes retained, at the least, a right of occupancy and some semblance of political autonomy.[5]

Although the Continental Congress indicated a desire to implement a more magnanimous policy toward the tribes, there remained considerable confusion as to whether it was the national or the state governments that held responsibility for Indian relations. The Articles of Confederation were ambiguous on the question. The articles gave the Congress "the sole and exclusive right and power of . . . regulating the trade and managing all affairs with the Indians, not members of any of the States provided that the legislative right of any state within its own limits be not infringed or violated." The conditional clause made this article practically impossible to construe; James Madison declared it "absolutely incomprehensible." Some states, like Georgia, New York, and Pennsylvania, generally ignored the apparent intent of exclusive congressional authority over Indian relations and imposed their own treaties on the Indians within their borders.[6]

The Continental Congress's inability to establish peace in the West and its difficulties in maintaining control over Indian affairs vis-à-vis the states induced the Constitutional Convention to redefine the national government's authority. While the language describing the federal government's jurisdiction over Indian matters remained vague in the new Constitution (placed in the Commerce Clause, it simply gave Congress the authority "to regulate commerce with foreign nations, and among the several States and with the Indian tribes"), it removed the confusing wording of the articles that seemed to grant the states a right of preemption over the Indians within their territories. The question of whether the federal government possessed plenary authority over every aspect of Indian relations thus remained unresolved. And after the initial euphoria that followed the ratification of the Constitution died down, the issue of the breadth of the national government's jurisdiction over Indian affairs reemerged. Over time, the southern states became less and less willing to admit that they had ceded authority over Indian relations. The most the states had done, some southerners argued, was to relinquish control over the Indian trade. One southern court came to this view years before Georgia began asserting jurisdiction over the Cherokees in the 1820s. In 1807, the North Carolina Supreme Court held that the United States's treaty with the Cherokees at Holston, which included a Cherokee land cession, was executed for the benefit of that state. Neither the treaty nor the state's ratification of the Constitution, the court said, had abrogated North Carolina's right to exert its jurisdiction over the Indians within its borders. In the 1830s, as we will see, most appellate judges in the South would come to this view.[7]

The new Constitution was silent on how the framers thought the new government should deal with the Indian tribes. Consequently, the Indian policy of the United States was left open for determination by Congress and the president. In 1789 George Washington took office as the first president under the Constitution, and he appointed Henry Knox, his old artillery commander, as secretary of war. (In this original cabinet, and until 1849, U.S.-Indian relations fell under the auspices of the War Department.) Knox immediately reviewed the country's Indian policy and found it an unmitigated disaster. In letters to Washington and in a long memorandum to Congress, Knox outlined a comprehensive plan for remedying relations with the Indian tribes. First and foremost, he argued, the United States needed to formally acknowledge the implications raised by the treaty system and the Northwest Ordinance. The United States, he said, should treat the tribes as independent, sovereign nations. The country desperately needed to establish peace along its western frontier, he wrote, and the best way to do this was to deal squarely with the tribes, by treaty, on a nation-to-nation basis. Convinced that acquiring lands by military conquest would only prolong the unrest between Indians and white settlers, Knox suggested that the United States also recognize that the tribes held some form of title to their lands. "The Indians being the prior occupants, possess the right to soil," he wrote, "[and] it cannot be taken from them unless by their free consent." Knox added that the United States had a duty, by law and by honor, to pay value to extinguish that right of possession. "To dispossess them in any other principle," Knox said, "would be a gross violation of the fundamental laws of nature and of that distributive justice which is the glory of a nation." If the United States admitted that the Indians possessed a legitimate title to their territory and declared that it would not divest them of that title except by means of "open treaties," he concluded, "the foundation of peace and justice would be laid."[8]

Knox persuaded Washington to his point of view on these issues, and together, by executive order and legislation, they implemented the secretary's suggestions. In 1790 Congress enacted the first in a series of statutes called the Trade and Intercourse Acts, which provided, among other things, that land purchases from Indians be negotiated by tribal leaders and federal commissioners specially appointed by the president. The acts specifically prohibited the states and individuals from acquiring or speculating in Indian land and forbade non-Indians from entering Indian country without permission of the tribe in possession.[9]

Although Knox's plan revealed an enlightened concern for Indian rights, the scheme was primarily designed to promote the expansion and security of the United States. Knox believed that the sovereignty of the tribes was only a temporary condition. The United States, he said, had a duty to "civilize" the Indians and prepare them for social and political assimilation. The inevitability of American expansion and the country's moral obligation could therefore be joined into a civilization program that would be mutually beneficial for the country and for the Indians. Knox wrote that the federal government could, and should, teach Indians to read and write and provide them with training in the agricultural and mechanical arts. He also wanted Indians to convert to Christianity, abandon the communal possession of property, and adopt Anglo-American cultural practices. The transformation of the Indian, he argued, was a necessary precursor to the United States's expansion into the West. He presumed that after the federal government introduced Indians to the methods of Anglo-European agriculture and explained to them the benefits of private property ownership, Indian men would want to obtain their own individual farms and wean themselves from subsistence hunting. The United States would then be able to acquire the surplus "hunting grounds" released by this conversion and open them up for sale to, and development by, white Americans. Over time, Knox predicted, the acculturated Indians would assimilate into the white society that slowly engulfed them. In 1790, in furtherance of this logic, the United States began including articles encouraging acculturation in its treaties. For example, in the Treaty of New York (1790) with the Creeks and in its accord with the Cherokees at Holston (1791), the United States agreed to provide the tribes with "useful implements of husbandry" and offered to lead the Indians "to a greater degree of civilization" as "herdsmen and cultivators instead . . . of hunters." Pursuant to that promise, Congress appropriated money to supply Indians with plows, spinning wheels, and other tools and implements and began posting agents among the tribes to instruct individual Indians in their use. (The United States did not, however, allocate money to educate Indian children until 1819. The government entrusted that responsibility to the Christian mission societies, which in 1817 moved in among the Indians in the Southeast. The federal government's financial commitment to civilization, then, was not as deep as its paternalistic objectives required.)[10]

In the end, the civilization program did not defuse the Indian threat, and the tribes along the United States's western frontier continued to resist encroachments by white settlers in the period leading up to the War of 1812. Nor did the program result in the mass assimilation of Native Americans or prepare the way for a peaceful and orderly national expansion. Proponents of civilization underestimated the speed at which the American population would grow in the future and failed to appreciate the insatiable voracity of white Americans for Indian land. Time, in other words, was not on the side of those who favored the plan for Indian acculturation and assimilation in the East. In addition, Knox and his supporters based the program on a series of flawed presumptions. Civilization was grounded on the social environmentalism of the Enlightenment; Knox, Jefferson, and others of their conviction believed that Indians, provided with the appropriate guidance, possessed the intellectual ability to elevate themselves to the reputedly higher level of Anglo-American civilization. Setting aside the moral questions raised by eradicating the culture of another people, this transformation was much more difficult for Indians than its advocates ever imagined. The program, for example, required the Indians in the Southeast to reverse their traditional gender roles. Native women in the region were the primary caretakers of agriculture while men engaged in hunting, war, and athletics. The Anglo-American norms of the civilization program placed women in the home as domestic wives, mothers, and spinners and sent men to the fields to plow. For Indian males, acculturation led to their emasculation; they were being asked to give up the hunt, the activity that defined them as men. Civilization forced Indian women, at the same time, to abandon vegetable production, one of the characterizing traits of femininity. The proponents of acculturation were either ignorant of, or saw no evil in, the psychological consequences of these transitions.

In either case, the civilization program was based on the fundamental belief that Indian culture was not worth preserving. The program's theorists wrongly assumed that Indians would be amenable to the change. Civilization proponents also believed that those who acculturated would be rewarded with an honorable and equitable place in American society. This was not to be. Although most Native Americans in the Southeast appreciated and embraced particular elements of Anglo-European thought and technology, few of them wanted to abandon completely their traditional way of life. The popularity of the civilization program varied in degree among most towns and tribes, and as a result, factional divisions arose between those willing to embrace civilization and those who sought to continue their accustomed practices. In some cases, as demonstrated by the Creek Civil War of 1813–14 and the rebellion of the Cherokee chief White Path, these fissures threatened the internal stability of the Southeastern nations and deepened as Anglo-American settlers continued to intrude into Indian territory. Despite their differences, however, those on both sides of the assimilation debate tended to agree on one important point: they preferred to remain autonomous and independent of the United States. The failure of the civilization architects to recognize or appreciate these complex factors and feelings doomed assimilation in the East and opened the door for those who posed the alternative policy of removal.[11]

Jefferson was primarily responsible for encouraging that transition. He moved the U.S. government toward exiling the eastern tribes by merging the philanthropic elements of the civilization program with his proposal to relocate hostile tribes beyond the Mississippi. Like Knox, he expressed concern for the Indians and publicly declared a desire to protect them from the advancing settler population and the corrupting influence of unscrupulous white traders. Unlike the former secretary of war, however, Jefferson came to believe that these goals could best be achieved only after a general removal. After he concluded the Louisiana Purchase, Jefferson began attempting to persuade Indian leaders to take their people to the West. Although the Southeastern tribes generally rejected the president's overtures, in 1808 the federal government did conclude a removal and exchange treaty with a group of disaffected Cherokees. By 1810 about one thousand members of that dissident group had migrated to the Arkansas River valley. Experiments like the Cherokee migration affirmed Jefferson's belief in the viability of removal and helped foster enthusiasm for the idea among those who were itching to seize Indian land.[12]

The real seed of the movement that resulted in the wholesale removal of the Southeastern tribes, however, was planted in another agreement concluded by the Jefferson administration only months before the Louisiana Purchase. In the Compact of 1802, Georgia released its claim to the lands between the Chattahoochee and Mississippi Rivers in exchange for a promise from the federal government that it would extinguish the Indian title in the state as soon as it could be "peaceably obtained, and on reasonable terms." The land that Georgia wanted to open up for white settlement was occupied by the Cherokees and the Creeks, and the state officials who consummated the Compact of 1802 understood that the state could not unilaterally extinguish their title. The two tribes, state officials conceded on several occasions, had to surrender their land voluntarily in negotiated treaties with federal commissioners. The United States's practice of recognizing tribal sovereignty and title presumed that the states would honor the constitutional supremacy of federal-Indian treaties. So long as the states acknowledged that the federal government possessed the right to extinguish the Indian title in this fashion, the national government was free to concede aspects of sovereignty to the tribes; though it grumbled about federal interference in its affairs from time to time, Georgia, for the most part, respected that principle during the first decade after the agreement.[13]

The United States's practice of acknowledging Indian sovereignty and title, as demonstrated in the Northwest Ordinance, the treaties at Hopewell, and Knox's directives, was partly a product of the Native American military capability and a fear that the tribes might align themselves with Great Britain or Spain. The Indian tribes commanded respect for their political and territorial integrity, in other words, by remaining, singularly or in combination, a viable military threat to American security. Two major U.S.-Indian conflicts, however, were enveloped by the War of 1812, and the United States's destruction of the Native American uprisings effectively eliminated that factor in the minds of most American leaders. In the Old Northwest, the United States army of William Henry Harrison defeated the combined forces of British colonel Henry Proctor and Tecumseh, the Shawnee chief, at the Battle of the Thames (1813). Tecumseh had attempted to construct a pan-Indian confederacy that would push the United States and American settlers back toward the Atlantic. The American victory over Tecumseh's army and the Shawnee chief's death in that battle foreclosed the possibility of a grand Indian revolution. In the Southeast, General Andrew Jackson's army decimated the revivalist Redstick Creeks, who to some extent had been incited by Tecumseh, at Horseshoe Bend (1814). With these victories the United States acquired military supremacy over the Indian tribes from the Great Lakes to the Gulf of Mexico and from the Atlantic to the Mississippi. After the war John C. Calhoun characterized a noticeable change in the attitude of U.S. policymakers toward the Indian nations: "The neighboring tribes are becoming daily less warlike, and more helpless and dependent on us," he wrote. "[T]hey have, in a great measure, ceased to be an object of terror, and have become that of commiseration."[14]

The destruction of the Indian threat east of the Mississippi also prompted a reconsideration of the status of the tribes in the federal system. In the peace negotiations at Ghent, British diplomats attempted to obtain assurances that the United States would respect the rights and territory of their Indian allies. John Quincy Adams, one of the American delegates to the peace conference, replied that the United States intended to treat the Indians as "subjects" rather than independent nations. Anxious to come to terms, Britain's representatives eventually abandoned their demands on this point and terminated its Indian alliances. Soon thereafter, Spain surrendered control of Florida to the United States. With the retreat of these two imperial powers, the autonomy of the tribes east of the Mississippi became even more dependent on the indulgence of the United States.[15]

In addition, Andrew Jackson's rout of the British at New Orleans unleashed a confidence among Americans in their nation's potential and prompted a belief among some that the United States was destined to expand across the North American continent. Prominent Americans such as Jackson and Calhoun began to bemoan the fact that the federal government's policy of recognizing tribal rights stood in the way of that expansion. Months after the Treaty of Ghent, Jackson, now a national hero, called for the federal government to end the "absurdity" of treating the Indian tribes as sovereign nations. The policy of recognizing Indian rights to land by treaty, he added, was the product of a time when the United States was relatively weak and the tribes posed a serious threat to the nation's security. This period of military equilibrium was over, Jackson argued. The United States had gained an upper hand with the tribes and should begin "legislating for, rather than treating with, the Indians."[16]

Jackson's position quickly gained popularity in the southern states and encouraged those in Georgia who wanted the federal government to complete the Compact of 1802. Because of its unique position as a claimant under the compact, Georgia took the lead in condemning the United States's policy of recognizing the sovereignty of the tribes and began steering the federal government toward removal. In 1817, the Senate committee on public lands counseled a relocation of the tribes. The new president, James Monroe, agreed with the basic premise of removal and adopted it as a key objective of his Indian policy. At the same time, he maintained that cessions and removal should be voluntary on the part of the tribes. He also registered his support for the continuation of the civilization and assimilation programs and refused to overturn the practice of treaty diplomacy. He made it clear, though, that the United States reserved the right to remove the tribes if they did not submit to civilization, and he encouraged the War Department to include removal provisions in future treaties. As a result, between 1817 and 1826, the Creeks, Cherokees, Choctaws, and Chickasaws all ceded great parcels of territory to the federal government. Of these, the treaties with the Cherokees in 1817 and 1819, with the Choctaws in 1820, and with the Creeks in 1826 all provided inducements for tribal members to emigrate west of the Mississippi.[17]

Monroe's continuing commitment to the treaty policy and his measured interest in a voluntary removal frustrated those in Georgia who wanted to cleanse the state of the Creeks and the Cherokees. In the early 1820s, state and congressional leaders—such men as George M. Troup, George Gilmer, John Clark, and Wilson Lumpkin—repeatedly gave speeches, issued memorials, and sent letters to the president, secretary of war, and Congress urging the federal government to comply with the Compact of 1802. Georgia was joined in its campaign by its neighbors to the west and north. Almost from the time Congress admitted Mississippi (1817) and Alabama (1819) into the Union, the political leaders in those states had asked the federal government to extinguish the Indian title within their territories. The emergence of the southern cotton economy in those states and the resulting demand for the productive soil of the Black Belt had prompted a flood of white settlers into and around tribal lands. The combined population of Mississippi and Alabama exploded from forty thousand in 1810 to almost 450,000 in 1830. White immigrants yearned to seize Indian land that they perceived to be unexploited, and the politicians in those states naturally worked to achieve their wishes. In Tennessee, state officials such as Joseph McMinn, the governor of the state, had as far back as 1816 urged federal authorities to abolish the communal land ownership of the tribes, allot their territories to individual Indians in fee simple, and open up the remainder to settlement. With the support of these three states, Georgia was able to command considerable attention in Congress to its grievances under the compact. In 1821 the House of Representatives appointed a select committee to examine Georgia's claims. The committee, chaired by Gilmer, reported that the federal government would have to abrogate its civilization and assimilation program with the Cherokees and Creeks and allot the tribes' lands to comply with the Compact of 1802. Even the idea of abolishing the tribal title was not enough to mollify some Georgians, however, for it implied that the Creeks and Cherokees would remain in Georgia on individual tracts of land. The state's congressional delegation consequently persuaded Congress to pass resolutions urging President Monroe to extinguish not only the tribal claims of the Cherokees and Creeks, but the titles of individual Indians as well. Georgia not only wanted Indian land, it wanted every Indian out of the state. In 1823 Georgia escalated its pressure. At its legislative session in December, the state senate presented a memorial demanding that the federal government extinguish the Indian title. A year later, the state house did the same. By the end of Monroe's administration, Georgia's campaign for removal was a constant distraction for the national government.[18]

Georgia's relentless pressure, however, also began to produce sympathy for the Creeks and Cherokees among the philanthropic and missionary communities in the northeastern portion of the United States. The removal proponents consequently placed a benevolent mask on their scheme and adopted rhetoric designed to ameliorate the concerns raised by the tribes and the self-appointed defenders of their interests. Removal advocates argued, following Jefferson's logic, that the relocation of the tribes would protect Indians from unscrupulous traders and American squatters, allow Native American communities to acculturate at their own pace, and alleviate the destructive animosities that existed between whites and Indians. They promised that the United States would protect the tribes from intruders once they were removed and allow them to retain their political independence. At the same time, the removers maintained, the United States would continue to provide material and training to prepare the Indians for their eventual assimilation. Removal would be a voluntary enterprise, they also said. Those who remained on the tribal lands ceded to the United States would receive individual homesteads in fee simple and become subject to the laws of the state in which they lived.[19]

Of course, these assertions belied the real sentiments expressed in previous memorials by the racial separatists who were pulling the United States toward removal. For although the removal rhetoric was intended to exemplify concern for Indian interests, many of those responsible for its development clearly cared more about the short-range goals of territorial acquisition and racial separation than the eventual objective of assimilation. Knox and the framers of the civilization program had believed in the inherent equality of Indians and whites and had been optimistic about the ultimate ability of Native Americans to incorporate themselves into Anglo-America. Removal, however, was a dramatic and insidious departure from that policy. Knox proposed that the government civilize the Indians and then take their excess land. Removal proponents, however, planned to take the Indians' land first, remove them to the West, and then worry about their cultural elevation. Perhaps some advocates of the policy genuinely believed that removal and civilization were consistent policies. The most rabid of them, however, like George M. Troup of Georgia, publicly maintained that Indians could never be assimilated. "The utmost of rights and privileges which public opinion would concede to Indians," Troup said, "would fix them in a middle station, between the negro and white man." If they remained in the East, he added, Indians would "gradually sink to the condition of the former—a point of degeneracy below which they could not fall." For some proponents of removal, then, the civilization aspect of the proposal was, at best, delegated to a secondary objective and, at worst, cynically included to assuage moral condemnation of the suggested policy. The creation and implementation of the removal strategy, in fact, were consistently marked by deceit and false promises. As secretary of war, Calhoun gave federal treaty agents the authority to use "subterfuge and fraud" to obtain Indian cessions; time after time, the federal government's treaty commissioners strictly followed those directions. Thus many Indians understood that it was dangerous and naive to accept the sugary rhetoric of removal at face value. Even those Indians who agreed with the objectives of civilization, such as Elias Boudinot, the editor of the *Cherokee Phoenix,* doubted the removers' sincerity.[20]

Georgia's state and congressional delegations continued to pursue the state's claim under the Compact of 1802 vigorously during John Quincy Adams's administration. At its 1826 session, the state legislature called for Adams to remove the Indians from the state. The assembly also prohibited non-English-speaking Indians from testifying in Georgia courts. By 1827 Georgia had forced the federal government to acquire the Creeks' remaining lands in the state. The Creeks living in Georgia fled westward into Alabama, leaving the Cherokees to face the state alone. The Cherokee government, for its part, condemned Georgia's actions, declared its intention to exist independently as a sovereign nation, and asked federal authorities to restrain the state's aggression. Troup, now governor, warned that if the national government refused to remove the Cherokees, the state government would assume authority over the Indians and forcibly drive them out of Georgia. With that, the state's acknowledgment of the sanctity of the federal-Indian treaty relationship, an essential requirement for the continuation of the Cherokee Nation in the East, began to crumble. A frustrated Adams lamented that though the United States had endeavored to "teach them the arts of civilization and the doctrines of Christianity," the Indians were now "forming in the midst of ourselves communities claiming to be independent of ours and rivals of sovereignty within the territories of the members of our Union." A remedy was needed, he said, that would "secure to the members of our confederation their rights of sovereignty and soil." The troubles in Georgia divided Adams's cabinet, and the president's waffling on the issue reflected the distinct positions of his two most influential advisers. His first secretary of war, James Barbour, believed in the viability and morality of the civilization and assimilation program, and he encouraged Adams to reaffirm the federal government's commitment to the policy. Barbour, however, was pessimistic about the popularity of his view in Congress. He predicted that the federal legislature would not be able to withstand the pressure that the southern states were bringing to bear. Adams's secretary of state, Henry Clay, advised Adams to proceed with a general removal. Indians, he argued in the cabinet, were naturally ill suited to "civilization." The American program to acculturate the Indians was a failure and would never work, he said; Indians were "destined to extinction." Although Clay said he did not "countenance inhumanity towards [Indians]," he did not "think them, as a race, worth preserving." Indians were "essentially inferior to the Anglo-Saxon race," Clay added, "they were not an improvable breed, and their disappearance from the human family will be no great loss to the world."[21]

This comment demonstrated the extent to which many Americans in the nineteenth century had, as the historian Reginald Horsman put it, become "less concerned with the liberation of other peoples by the spreading of republicanism than with the limitless expansion of a superior American Anglo-Saxon race." Many Anglo-Americans were beginning to consider themselves biologically or racially superior to, and destined to rule over, peoples of other ethnicities. This was a marked change from the ideology pronounced by the generation that lived through the American Revolution. During the Enlightenment, the philosophical age that had heavily influenced the revolutionaries' thought and rhetoric, intellectuals interested in societal progress had attributed cultural differences and relative levels of social achievement to environmental factors. All peoples were moving up a unilinear pyramid of development, they maintained, and those of European descent, because of fortuitous environmental advantages, had simply progressed further and faster than other peoples. Theoretically, Indians could catch up culturally with Anglo-Europeans. The radical fervor of the Revolution had also made America a more egalitarian society in some respects. Property requirements for office and voting had been eliminated for white males in most states, and the country had rejected those who had attempted to fabricate an American aristocracy. Slavery had been abolished in the northern states, and laws pertaining to bonded labor had been relaxed in the South to some extent. Some southern legislatures, for example, had reinstated laws permitting manumission and reduced the severity of punishments for infractions committed by slaves. The revolutionary enlightenment had also ameliorated white attitudes about Native Americans to a degree. Patrick Henry and John Marshall, for example, had presented legislation encouraging intermarriage between Indians and whites; Marshall, Henry Knox, George Washington, and Thomas Jefferson had all, at one time or another, suggested that the United States could improve Indians and incorporate them into the greater society on a legal and social level equivalent to white Americans. In 1789 Knox wrote that all Native Americans needed to achieve the level of Western civilization was "a love for exclusive property," and he set out to instill the Indian mind with this material affinity in the civilization program. The belief that individual property ownership would be the force of improvement among Native American cultures remained prominent among intellectuals deep into the nineteenth century, even after racial explanations for cultural distinctions had taken hold among U.S. policymakers. During the Removal Crisis, for example, James Hall, a lawyer and journalist, wrote that for Indians, "insecurity of property, or rather the entire absence of all ideas of property, is the chief cause of their barbarism." To raise themselves up the societal ladder, Hall wrote, Native Americans needed to do three things: renounce their warlike tendencies, become more sedentary, and, most important, adopt Western "notions of property." By the time of Hall's observation, however, many Americans in positions of power doubted that Indians could be acculturated and refused to contemplate the idea that they could be assimilated.[22]

Beginning in the eighteenth century, a group of European philosophers had begun to challenge the Enlightenment confidence in inherent human equality. They argued that the "race" of an individual determined not only physical structure and appearance, but intelligence, personality, and capacity for achievement. These "racial determinists," as Horsman has described them, were not interested in the characteristics that defined humans as a genus, but traits that particularized people into distinct ethnic or national groups. Francis Bernier, Johann Friedrich Blumenbach, Georges Cuvier, and others of the determinist school purported to identify physical and behavioral qualities common to particular groups. The racial determinists then ordered the "races" into a hierarchy of civilizations with Europeans, of course, at the top. Each society, they argued, had its own distinctive physiology and character that originated from its racial heritage. The race of the group, as a result, determined the level of civilization to which it could aspire. Scientists attempting to prove the legitimacy of racial determinism began measuring the angles and sizes of skulls, noses, and foreheads in an effort to quantify the anatomical differences between the races. Most of them claimed that their evidence proved that the "Caucasian race" was superior to all other "races," particularly in studies that contemplated factors such as cranium volume that purportedly determined intelligence. In several obvious cases, however, these scientists either manipulated their evidence to achieve this conclusion or were so intent on reaching it that they abandoned the detached, rational analysis that was characteristic of the Enlightenment. A "fuzziness of thought" developed among many European and American scientists, Horsman wrote, that "jumble[d] race, nation, and language into a hodgepodge of rampant, racial nationalism."[23]

Some intellectuals merged the new romantic science with the existing fascination with the history and culture of the ancient Anglo-Saxon tribes. English and German racial theorists argued, not coincidentally, that the Angle and Saxon tribes of Germany comprised the greatest and purest of the ancient root races. They based their praise of the Anglo-Saxons on the writings of the Roman historian Tacitus, who in *Germania* described the bravery, morality, and racial purity of the people who had ferociously confronted the Roman Empire. Admirers of the Anglo-Saxons in Britain and on the continent of Europe, like Edward Coke, Blackstone, and Montesquieu, helped promote the theory that the fundamental concepts of parliamentarianism, liberty, and law could be traced to the Germanic tribes. English Whigs embraced these notions and used them in their critiques of the monarchy, which they portrayed as trespassing on ancient national virtues. In the colonies, American revolutionaries seized upon the Whig ideology, and the legend of a brave, liberty-loving Anglo-Saxon race became a significant component of the rhetoric of the American Revolution. Jefferson, for example, was particularly fascinated by the Teutonic tribes, and in his writings he described how the Anglo-Saxons had migrated to England in the fifth century and established governments based on the principle of popular sovereignty. By declaring their independence from England, Jefferson argued, the colonies

reestablished their historical link to the great race of representative government and liberty. In truth, Anglo-Saxon racial purity was a myth. Germans
from the area of Saxony had migrated to the British Isles before the Norman
conquest, but they were certainly not a homogeneous group; once there, they
had also integrated with Celts, Romans, Normans, Bretons, and Vikings.
The Anglo-Saxons, who were putatively so influential to the development
of liberty and popular sovereignty, were by no means the blue bloods that
British and American nationalists made them out to be.[24]

Racial determinists in Great Britain and the United States attributed
Anglo-American achievement to their common racial roots in the forests
of medieval Germany. Though English racialists saw Britain's destiny as yet
unfulfilled, Americans portrayed the empire as morally and racially corrupt
and in decline. According to the emerging class of American nationalists,
the United States, by throwing off the British yoke, had revitalized the ideals
of the ancient Anglo-Saxons and in the future would spread them to the
rest of the world. This optimism about the United States's future was also
influenced by another thread of popular racial theory that was sometimes a
part of, and sometimes distinct from, the generic Anglo-Saxon glorification.
Georg Hegel and Jules Michelet, among others, had theorized that a superior
race of "Indo-Germans" or "Indo-Europeans" (their admirers would begin
to characterize them as Aryans in the second half of the nineteenth century)
and their descendants had followed the sun west across western Asia and
Europe, carrying with them the seeds of progress and civilization. According
to American visionaries of territorial expansion, the sun was indeed setting
on the British Empire, and the United States was assuming Britain's mantle
of greatness. In 1807, for example, John Adams wrote, "There is nothing,
in my little reading, more ancient in my memory than the observation that
arts, sciences, and empire had traveled westward; and in conversation it was
always added since I was a child, that their next leap would be over the Atlantic into America." Jefferson believed that this pattern would continue and
that the United States's destiny lay to the west: "I have observed this march
of civilization advancing from the seacoast, passing over us like a cloud of
light, increasing our knowledge and improving our condition, insomuch as
that we are at this time more advanced in civilization here than the seaports
were when I was a boy. And where this progress will stop no one can say."
Proponents of what would later be denominated as America's "manifest
destiny" offered a prediction: the United States, following in the tracks of
ancient Egypt, Greece, Rome, and the modern British Empire, would be the
new force for progress and was destined for world power and influence.[25]

African Americans and Indians, of course, did not fit into the Anglo-
Saxon world order. The United States, the American racial nationalists de-

clared, was an Anglo-Saxon nation. Blacks and Indians were intellectually incapable of rising to the level of white civilization, could never successfully assimilate into white America, and were therefore to be excluded from the fulfillment of the Anglo-Saxon destiny. The identifying characteristic of Americans, they held, was the love of liberty, and it was innately carried, and solely so, by people of Anglo-Saxon descent. Africans and Indians would never be able to acquire this respect for freedom; therefore, they did not deserve equal legal status with whites. These ideas were not simply the bleats of a racist minority; rather, the theories of white racial superiority and American Anglo-Saxon exceptionalism wormed their way into scientific treatises, political philosophy, college curricula, religious sermons, literature, and legal opinions throughout the United States. By the time of *Cherokee Nation v. Georgia,* the themes of American Anglo-Saxon cultural superiority were so deeply embedded in white minds that William Wirt felt compelled to counter them before the U.S. Supreme Court: "The Cherokee Nation," he said, is "a nation far more ancient than ourselves, and, in all probability far more ancient than the mixed Saxon and Norman race that people the land of our fathers." The foundation upon which the theories of Anglo-Saxon superiority were built, he argued, was flawed. Anglo-American culture was not superior to that of the Cherokees, he implied in an early manifestation of cultural relativism, nor could its purported successes be attributed to racial purity.[26]

Racial determinism and the romanticization of the Anglo-Saxons were particularly attractive among those white southerners who were intent on preserving the institution of slavery and desirous of opening up the lands of Native Americans for settlement and agricultural exploitation. Their proximity to slavery, one scholar has suggested, made southern whites "extremely receptive to theories of inherent racial difference; indeed it helped create a scientific attitude of mind that was willing, even anxious, to develop such theories." Dr. Charles Caldwell, a North Carolina physician, was a prominent example of a southern intellectual attracted by the siren of racial science. Caldwell, the founder of the University of Louisville medical school, argued that at creation, God had produced four races—the Caucasian, the Mongolian, the American Indian, and the African. The Almighty had intentionally placed these races into a hierarchy of intellectual capability, he said, with Caucasians at the apex. This intellectual advantage, Caldwell suggested, had allowed the white race to evolve at a faster pace than the other races; this mental superiority, moreover, explained why the white race was so far advanced in civilization relative to Indian and African cultures. Caldwell focused much of his attention on what he believed to be the causes of the supposed sociological inadequacies of Native Americans. In the 1820s Caldwell examined the skulls of Indians and compared them with the crania of other "races." He concluded that Indians were inherently inferior in intellectual capacity to whites. "When the wolf, the buffalo and the panther shall have been completely domesticated, like the dog, the cow, and the household cat," he wrote, "then, and not before, may we expect to see the full-blooded Indian civilized, like the white man." Any advances that Indians had made toward the level of Western civilization, Caldwell wrote, had come from "crossbreeding" with whites: "The only efficient scheme to civilize the Indians is to cross the breed. Attempt any other and you will extinguish the race." (Another prominent southern racial scientist, Josiah Clark Nott, agreed with Caldwell's conclusion. Nott, a disciple of the noted American craniologist Samuel George Morton, wrote that blacks and Indians were biologically incapable of civilization unless they mixed their blood with that of the white races.) Caldwell believed that the American attempts to civilize the Indians by education would be fruitless, that whites would not deign to "crossbreed" voluntarily, and thus the Indians were a race doomed to extinction. "Civilization is destined to exterminate them," he said, just like the "wild animals."[27]

Southern politicians seized upon the evidence produced by racial determinists like Caldwell and applied it in their justifications for removal and slavery. White southerners were beginning to fall under moralistic attack by northern abolitionists and friends of the Indian, and southern politicians quickly gobbled up any evidence that gave scientific credence to their prejudice. In the 1830s, southern politicians and judges, encouraged by the reputed physical evidence of white superiority, predicted that the southern agrarian system would expand across the North American continent. For this to happen, they urged in their speeches, memorials, and legal opinions, the United States had to open up the lands of Indians to white farmers. So it was that southern racial ideologues tied the fates of blacks and Indians together. The theories of white racial superiority and the vision of a segregated society, with racially pure whites served by black slaves on land cleared of Indians, became commonplace in southern academic and popular literature.[28]

The new theories promoting the biological supremacy of whites affirmed their society in times of moral doubt, when before they had only personal experience and the Genesis account of Noah's degradation as justification for their prejudice. As demonstrated over and over again in the speeches of southern politicians and in the editorials of the southern press, the new scientific racial determinism helped white southerners rationalize their feelings toward Indians. Southern racial ideologues came to believe that the cultural and racial wall between Indians and whites was an impenetrable one that could never be torn down by education, acculturation, or intermarriage. In

1830, the House Committee report on the Indian Removal Act described extensively the differences between whites and Indians and pessimistically predicted that the Indians of "unmixed blood" would never, because of their race, attain the level of white civilization. George M. Troup, Wilson Lumpkin, and George Gilmer, Georgia governors during the push for removal, all at one time or another professed the same beliefs. Troup declared that it was impossible for Indians to achieve the same level of civilization as whites. Lumpkin declared that Indians were innately inferior: "A few thousand half civilized men, both indisposed and incompetent to the faithful discharge of the duties of citizenship, and scattered over a territory so extensive, can never enjoy the inestimable blessing of civil government." Gilmer closely questioned his subordinates several times on the exact blood quantum of John Ross and other Cherokee leaders in an effort to prove that they were not wholly Indian at heart. Surely, Gilmer believed, "full-blooded Indians" would never have been able to travel so expertly in American legal and political circles.[29]

With this thinking so prevalent in the calculations of southern political leaders, it is not surprising to find similar cant in the opinions of the southern judiciary. In an election in the late 1820s, John Marsh, a member of the Virginia Pamunkey tribe, attempted to vote at his home precinct in York, South Carolina. The York election managers, however, turned Marsh away from the polls. The South Carolina constitution, they said, allowed only "free white men" to vote. Disturbed by this rejection, Marsh filed suit against the local election managers, praying that he be allowed to exercise his franchise. Witnesses at his state court trial testified that Marsh was a veteran of the American Continental Army and still received a pension in appreciation for his service during the war. He had lived in York for "many years," they reported, and was known as a man of "excellent character." Despite this support, the court refused to grant Marsh the remedy he sought. Undaunted, Marsh continued to press his claim. When the South Carolina Court of Appeals received the case, the judges declared that they were sympathetic to Marsh's situation but disinclined to overrule the election managers. Presiding judge Abraham Nott wrote, "It is with regret that I find myself obliged to declare, that by the laws of this state, the applicant is not entitled to vote." Marsh, he said, had been "useful to the country, both in a military and civil capacity." But "he belongs to a race of people, who have always been considered as a separate and distinct class." It was not for the court to decide whether the law was just, Nott said; "our ancestors thought it" appropriate to maintain a separation between whites and people of color. Perhaps, he concluded, the legislature should consider making exceptions for patriotic veterans like Marsh. Unfortunately, the court could not do so.[30]

Unlike Patrick Henry and John Marshall of the revolutionary age, most white southerners of this new generation rejected the possibility of assimilating the Indian population and actually recoiled at the idea of living side by side with Native Americans. Ironically, though they disparaged the Native American peoples and their culture, whites were extremely envious of what these same Indians possessed: millions of acres of fertile farmland that was, in many places, ideal for growing short-staple cotton. So, in hindsight, it is difficult to ascertain what motivated southern whites more in the 1820s and 1830s—their prejudiced feelings toward Native Americans or their ravenous appetite for the lands on which the Indians lived. There can be no doubt, however, about what these two forces unleashed: a political and popular movement aimed at removing Native Americans beyond the ken of white southerners.

The advocates of removal planned to seize tribal lands in the East and establish the Mississippi River as a formidable wall of racial separation between whites and Indians. Removal, then, was the ultimate and logical extension of the white attitudes that had deprived John Marsh of his vote: Indians were "a separate and distinct class" of people undeserving of political or social equality. The policy of separation also confirmed what George Troup had had the audacity to announce: that no matter how well Native Americans were educated, were "improved," or performed, southerners would not accord them a meaningful and equivalent place in their society. For years the United States had asked Indians to acculturate and assimilate; now the federal government was beginning to fall under the power of a generation of people who would not genuinely countenance a broad Indian assimilation. At a very early stage in the removal movement, a contributor to a Georgia newspaper testified to the depth of the racial antipathy that coursed through many southern minds: "until it shall please God to bleach [their] skin," he wrote, "the prejudices of the whites against the color of both Indians and negroes are absolutely incurable." The idea of Indians residing around and among whites was not acceptable to citizens in Georgia, the writer made clear. Whites wanted separation from Indians. By the late 1820s, years of papers and politicians inflaming this kind of prejudice toward Indians had made the white southern public ravenous for that solution.[31]

Ironically, Indian leaders such as the Cherokee principal chief John Ross also wanted a form of separation; he wanted his people to be politically separated from the United States so that they could enjoy a measure of tribal autonomy in their traditional homeland. In hindsight, then, the objectives of Indians and white southerners were actually compatible. Racial separation did not necessarily preclude the continued existence of separate, sovereign Indian nations in the East. White southerners and the southern state governments, however, wanted more than racial separation; they wanted Indian land and the products that could be drawn from it. We will never accurately know the extent that lust played in the dehumanization of the Indian people in white minds. We can know, however, that land and race were inextricably connected in the advent of the Indian Removal.

The Cherokees, however, simply refused to wilt under Georgia's pressure. Much to the dismay of Georgia's raging removal advocates, the civilization program had produced some unforeseen consequences. The architects of civilization had theorized that as Indians acculturated, they would repudiate their tribal ties and assimilate as individuals into American society. Instead, as John C. Calhoun recognized, as Indian leaders had become comfortable with Anglo-American ideas and practices in economics, politics, and law, they had turned them to uses to which U.S. civilization proponents had never expected. Native American officials had become especially adroit at lobbying the federal government and adept at raising awareness of their difficulties with the American public. In the Cherokee Nation, John Ross and the National Council had embraced the Anglo-European concept of national sovereignty and had used it to fend off encroachments on their territory and autonomy. While other Native American politicians adopted the concept of tribal sovereignty during the Removal Crisis, Ross pushed it harder and more eloquently than any Indian leader of the era. He understood that the Indian peoples' only chance of survival in the East was to force the United States to abide by its treaty commitments to protect the tribes from external threats, and he consistently reminded federal leaders of their nation's long-standing recognition of tribal rights. In an effort to bolster that argument with the world, Ross and his cadre of advisers had accelerated the Cherokee Nation's movement toward centralized republican government; under his leadership, the Cherokees became the pivotal tribe in the Native American resistance to removal.[32]

CHAPTER TWO

Spiritual Sovereignty
The Emergence of the Cherokee Nation

ON JULY 4, 1827, a convention of twenty-four delegates from the eight districts of the Cherokee Nation met in New Echota to draft a national constitution. Though the convention implemented a number of civil reforms, it essentially left the existing legal and political structure in place. The nation was already governed by a chief executive called the principal chief and a bicameral legislature. Legal disputes were already heard and resolved by an independent, hierarchical judiciary. What the convention did was to pull these institutions, created separately over the previous two decades, into the rubric of a republican constitution. More important, the decision to draft and ratify a constitution was a symbolic statement to those in the United States who were attempting to seize the Cherokees' homeland. The Cherokees were again proclaiming to the world that they considered themselves an independent, sovereign nation of people beyond the reach and jurisdiction of the federal and state governments of the United States. The Cherokees were declaring that they expected to live free from harassment and territorial trespasses and that they intended to continue wielding the principle of national sovereignty against those who sought to usurp Cherokee land and political autonomy. In the 1810s and 1820s, the Cherokees had skillfully used the concept of sovereignty to foist off several removal proposals. They had also recently used the principle to garner support for their resistance from segments of the American missionary and philanthropic community. Though the Cherokees had artfully argued their political status in public memorials and negotiations with the United States, ultimately they had been unable to silence the demands of those Americans who sought to exile the Indian nations to the West. Consequently, in 1830, the Cherokees and their legal counsel resolved to seek recognition of their sovereign status from the United States Supreme Court.[1]

The word "sovereignty" must have evoked different connotations to Indians under the threat of removal than it did for the European political theorists who devised the concept. The origins of the idea of sovereignty dated back, at least, to the ancient Greeks, but concentrated philosophical scholarship on the concept began during the Crusades when canonical legal scholars attempted to discern whether non-Christian peoples possessed legal and political rights under biblical and natural law. The European discovery of "infidel" civilizations in Africa and the Americas also encouraged debate on the comparative rights of peoples and nations. Between the fifteenth and eighteenth centuries, several European students of the law of nations produced treatises designed to aid diplomats and monarchs in their statecraft. All of these works, by such men as Franciscus de Victoria, Hugo Grotius, Samuel Pufendorf, and Jean Bodin, adopted sovereignty as the fundamental principle for identifying and prioritizing the rights of nations. The students of the law of nations, however, had difficulty in agreeing on the definition and characteristic attributes of sovereignty. In describing the development of the concept in European thought, the political scientists Michael Ross Fowler and Julie Marie Bunck concluded that "the concept of sovereignty has been used not only in different senses by different people, or in different senses at different times by the same people, but in different senses by the same person in rapid succession." Generally speaking, though, by the nineteenth century, when European and American lawyers and political philosophers used the term "sovereignty" they were expressing the idea that there existed "a final and absolute political authority in the political community" under consideration. A sovereign nation, in other words, was one that exhibited legal supremacy over all other sources of authority within a geographical area and one that maintained enough military, diplomatic, and economic power to preserve its independence relative to other nations or governments.[2]

The lawyers for the Cherokees in the Removal Crisis cases—all white men trained in the English common law and familiar with European political philosophy—clearly had some semblance of this definition in mind when they used the word to characterize the nature of the Cherokee polity. For the Cherokees themselves, the word perhaps evoked even more complicated meanings and emotions.[3] Sovereignty implied more than political autonomy or territorial integrity; sovereignty suggested a deep spiritual connection to an ancestral homeland. In addition, sovereignty was a function of historical memory for the Cherokees. In other words, sovereignty raised recollections of traditions and "law-ways" that traced back to the time before Europeans wandered into Cherokee territory.[4] At the beginning of the eighteenth century, the time when their contacts with Europeans were becoming common, the Cherokees claimed a vast region that spread over what is now northern Georgia and Alabama, western South Carolina and North Carolina, eastern

Tennessee, southeastern Kentucky, and southwestern Virginia. Perhaps as many as twenty thousand Cherokees lived in the approximately sixty towns and villages that were scattered throughout and on both sides of the southern Appalachians. The Cherokees were not a unified nation or tribe at this time, but a conglomeration of clans and towns bound together by kinship, a belief in a common heritage, an attachment to the land of their ancestors, and a collective worldview that determined community behavior and individual thought and action. The culture of the Cherokees differed dramatically from those of the Creeks, Chickasaws, and Choctaws, their Muskogean neighbors to the south and west, but it was similarly holistic. In other words, the sociopolitical structure of the Cherokee people was not at this time differentiated into specialized corporate functions; instead, the social, legal, and political institutions of the Cherokee people were integrated into an indivisible whole. This structure promoted the commonweal, furnished a functional system of rights and duties, and provided clear parameters of acceptable and unacceptable behavior.[5]

The Cherokees' affinity for their land was a product of their conception of life and the universe. Cherokee cosmology taught that the Principal People (Ani-Yun-wiya), as the Cherokees called themselves, lived at the center of a world pervaded by spiritual power. Their universe consisted of three levels. The earth—this world—was a flat disk floating on the surface of a great body of water and suspended from the dome of heaven by cords tied at the four cardinal directions. Above the earth was the upper world, the domain of friendly and supportive spirits. The upper world was signified in Cherokee art by the color white, the hue of purity, harmony, and peace. Red symbolized the land below the earth, the lower world of war, danger, sexual fertility, and change. Things monstrous and ambiguous lived in, and sometimes emerged from, this underworld of caves, lakes, and springs. Each Cherokee individual had a part in the awesome responsibility of keeping the three worlds in balance. All rituals, all laws, and all social institutions were therefore, at some level, an effort to preserve or restore equilibrium, for disharmony invited retribution from the spirit world and threatened the structure of the Cherokee universe.[6]

The roles and responsibilities of gender also determined Cherokee attitudes about their relationship to the land. The Cherokees organized their kinship relations under the matrilineal system. Property rights, including those to land and dwelling, passed down through the woman's line. Women were primarily responsible for agriculture; they grew the corn, beans, squash, and melons that constituted the core of the Cherokee vegetable diet. Agriculture, however, was more than a means to subsistence; it defined femininity for Cherokee women and connected them to the spiritual world. The most important crop to the Cherokee diet and the most sacred vegetable in Cherokee life was corn, which was first introduced to the Cherokee people by Selu, the earth mother and spirit of the plant. Growing corn therefore represented for women a spiritual heritage and a social and familial responsibility for vegetable nutrition. Perhaps, as Theda Perdue has suggested, that powerful relationship to agriculture promoted a greater depth of feeling for the land than that felt by Cherokee men. At the same time, though, hunting defined masculinity for Cherokee men; hunters felt a close spiritual connection to the game and the process of the hunt. In sum, what defined woman was her work in the soil; what made man was his pursuit of the deer and bear that darted and trundled over it. Land, to the Cherokees, was much more than a proprietary asset or capital resource.[7]

The connection between land and sovereignty took on even greater meaning for the Cherokees because they held most of their land in common. European law differentiated between individual fee simple ownership of a tract of land and the overarching political dominion over it. Indians made no such distinction. The land used by the individual belonged to the collective community; the land of the community was available to those who chose to use it. Any family could occupy and build on lands that others were not using. A family in possession "owned" the right to the improvements established on that land, but even those fixtures reverted back to the community after a period of nonuse. After one family abandoned a dwelling, for example, another family could move in and take possession. In essence, then, the right of possession arose from use or exploitation. Ironically, that Cherokee principle, as we will see, was not necessarily inconsistent with the English common law's presumption in favor of effective use. The Cherokee conception of natural resource exploitation departed from the English view in several ways, however. Rather than seeing the environment solely as a resource to be exploited, the Cherokees applied their socio-spiritual ethic of balance and harmony to their natural surroundings. This does not mean that they did not modify or derange their environment; rather, they saw themselves as part of the natural process of change and universal equilibrium. The Cherokees thus used the land and its products in accordance with their spiritual beliefs; environmental care was not a moral directive, but a consequence of the overarching worldview.[8]

The Cherokees also maintained conceptions of land tenure and use that were distinctly different from those practiced by the white colonists who invaded their territory. Anglo-European settlers were accustomed to exclusive individual ownership and believed that it was appropriate and necessary to divide real property up into tracts for possession and exploitation by individuals and corporate groups. The Cherokees, in contrast, conceived of land as something that could be divided by space, time, and use. Several communities or kin groups, for example, could hold the usufruct rights to the same geographical or ecological area. Some land, like the bottomlands, was used by the entire community, at the same time, for growing corn and other vegetables. While it remains unclear how the Cherokees specifically conceived of notions of shared use, it is perhaps not unreasonable to extrapolate from what we know of practices of Native American cultures in New England. According to William Cronon, under the Indian notion of land use, one group could possess the right to hunt a patch of woods, another to the forest's fruits and nuts, another to the water from the stream that ran through those woods, another to the fish from that stream, and another to navigate down that stream from other lands. Some Native American peoples further subdivided the usufruct by time. One community might allow another group access to an area for the purpose of hunting or fishing, but only during a specific season. Rights in and to property, consequently, might change by ecological use, over time, and across individual, kinship, village, and tribal lines. Village councils maintained dominion over very specific areas and forms of ecological use, and peoples desiring the resource negotiated boundaries to avoid conflict, competition, and depletion. The Cherokees, for instance, and the other tribes of the Southeast and the Ohio Valley had at some time in the past agreed not to settle the game-rich region of what is now Kentucky and western Virginia so that they could share it for hunting. Because of their contrasting understandings of possession and ownership, the early land cessions from Indians to Europeans sometimes prompted misunderstandings between the two cultures over what the former had actually conveyed. Europeans assumed that they were acquiring the exclusive and perpetual right of possession and ownership, whereas Indian vendors believed that they were conveying the right for a specific use and could subsequently convey the same land to another group or individual for a different purpose. Both sides quickly recognized that they were dealing at cross-purposes and came to agree that Indian cessions required a complete quitclaim.[9]

British and American commentators during the colonial period often maintained that the Indian tribes were not territorial and did not recognize geographical boundaries. They must have been wrong. In the 1760s a Creek delegation explained what boundaries meant to the Indian councils that negotiated them. The line establishing a border, the Creeks said, was "like a stone wall or a tree which you are not to climb over." Apparently, the Cherokees had in mind this natural wall of separation when they negotiated the Treaties of Hopewell (1785) and Holston (1790). They understood that while they had surrendered land and certain powers of sovereignty to the United States, they had done so for the primary purpose of preserving forevermore their remaining territory and autonomy. A few Anglo-Americans, like Alexander Hewatt, wrote that the Cherokees certainly recognized the limits of their territorial domain. He noted in 1779 that the boundaries of the Cherokee hunting grounds were "carefully fixed." "Each tribe was tenacious of its possessions," he added, "and fired with resentment at the least encroachment of them. Each individual looked upon himself as a proprietor of all the lands claimed by the whole tribe, and bound in honor to defend them." In fact, it appears that in several of the treaties between Europeans and Indians, the negotiating parties adopted traditional Native American border markings.[10]

The Cherokees not only felt a territorial interest in their homeland, they also harbored a deep spiritual and emotional connection to specific places in it. The challenges to Cherokee sovereignty in the nineteenth century thus not only implied a loss of the place where one was born and raised, they also meant the surrender of ritual places and, concomitantly, ritual practices. The Cherokees realized that if they surrendered their homeland, they disconnected themselves from the graves of their forebears and from locales of spiritual significance. To preserve that sovereignty of spirituality, the Cherokees tried to exclude those who did not have the same appreciation for their territory. In the Treaty of Hopewell, for instance, the Cherokees demanded that they have the right to prohibit whites from entering their land. In affirming and defending their borders, Cherokee leaders were not only attempting to keep out individual trespassers, they were also trying to stave off an invasion of a people who had different ideas about how humans should live on and use their land.[11]

The expression "sovereignty" must have also suggested a sense of autonomy to the Cherokees, just as it did to European students of international law. The Cherokees' conception of autonomy, however, was based not on a concern for the sanctity of the monarch or the corporate state, as it was for political theorists, but for the individual and the community. Cherokee feelings of autonomy derived from familiarity with the two major foundations of their traditional social structure—the clan and the council. In the eighteenth century, each Cherokee individual claimed affiliation with and affinity to a clan, a kinship group that traced its origin to a common ancestor in the distant past. Without a connection to a clan, a man or woman lacked legal identity, rights, privileges, and security. The Cherokees were made up of seven clans, and each clan was represented in most of the villages throughout their domain. Sojourners away from their home thus found kin, hospitality, and lodging in almost every Cherokee town. Before the Cherokee movement toward centralized and institutional government, the clans provided a functional system of social order and the basis for feelings of tribal commonality.

The Cherokees did not establish a police force and judicial system until the nineteenth century. Instead, the clans regulated interpersonal relationships and resolved most disputes. The Cherokees, like other Southeastern societies, were exogamous; individuals were expected to marry outside of their clan to avoid violating a strongly ingrained incest taboo. Consequently, men or women did not marry or separate without counsel from their clans. The clans also determined questions of property ownership: the agricultural fields, although worked by the community of women as a whole, were divided up among the clans. Clan elders settled disputes between kin and taught youngsters about the rights and responsibilities that resulted from clan affiliation. When conflicts turned violent, the clan law of blood revenge provided a systematic means of dealing with manslaughter. Under blood revenge the killing of an individual, be it intentional or accidental, was an offense against the victim's clan. The killing created in the clan of the deceased both a legal right and a societal duty to enforce lethal revenge against the assailant or another member of his or her clan. At the same time, the killer's kin had a sacred obligation to produce a life in exchange for the victim. Again, like other aspects of Cherokee culture, blood revenge functioned to preserve natural balance. The practice also took on spiritual significance; the Cherokees believed that the soul of the deceased could not enter the spirit world to the West and continued to haunt the living until its kin had avenged the killing. While it seems that this system of order potentially could have encouraged endless bloodlettings between clans, blood revenge was so rooted in Cherokee life that even close relatives of assailants stood by passively when the victim's kin came for revenge. Though brutal in the eyes of Europeans and Americans, blood revenge encouraged order and a heightened standard of care in Cherokee society.[12]

Problems and circumstances that affected the entire community fell under the jurisdiction of the town council. The local councils were responsible for the well-being of all in the community, and the clans were subordinate to the will of the council. Each local council included the entire adult population of the town, and both men and women possessed the right to voice their opinions. The Cherokees did not have a conception of majority rule. Instead, the council practiced a process of discussion and debate that was designed to reach the objective of consensus. Council discussion was usually influenced by three sets of elders—the spiritual leaders, the elders of the clans, and a group of "beloved" men and women who had achieved notoriety and respect for their wisdom, ability, charisma, and accomplishments. Debates over the appropriate course of action sometimes continued for days, and the development of a council consensus often required that entrenched minority dissenters withdraw from the debate. These dissenters, however, were not required to adhere to the decision and could act independently of the council. This individual right of dissent, then, was an essential element of the Cherokee notion of autonomy. Even warfare was not prescriptive; individual warriors could opt out if they felt that the signs or their conscience so ordered.[13]

The council also resolved disputes among the greater community. Public punishments, though rare, included shaming, ostracism, scratching, and in the most serious cases, death. Most personal animosities and conflicts, with the exception of manslaughter, were formally renounced each year at the Green Corn Ceremony, which marked the harvest of the first corn in the fall. Over several days each community fasted and conducted rituals of spiritual cleansing. The people gave thanks for the new harvest, cleaned the public grounds, and ignited a new sacred fire. At one point in the festivities, the spiritual leaders recited the law-ways and history of the people and reminded the community of the significance of forgiveness and renewal. The Green Corn Ceremony thus offered the town an annual opportunity to restore the precious state of balance and harmony. When the Cherokees used the word "sovereignty," they perhaps contemplated their unique form of particularistic autonomy, which offered each community the right and power to punish, forgive, and renew.[14]

During the Removal Crisis, Cherokee leaders believed that recognition of the tribe's sovereign status by the United States Supreme Court would provide them with security from state attacks and settler encroachments. Security, then, was another element of the Cherokee conception of sovereignty. Before the arrival of Europeans, the Cherokees maintained a political mechanism that functioned to secure their communities when threatened from without. They conceived of the oversight of war and civil government as distinctly separate functions that required different groups of leaders. When the council resolved to go to war, a group of war leaders assumed control over the enterprise. Cherokee warriors did not go to war for land, wealth, or religion. Instead, they fought to achieve social distinction and, most important, to avenge deaths inflicted by an enemy. Wars sometimes began when young men set out to assert their identity and acquire approbation; the casualties that resulted sometimes led to long wars of vendetti prompted by the principle of blood revenge. When peace was restored, the war leaders returned to their status as common members of the town council. This system had the effect of preventing one individual warrior, or the young men as a group, from acquiring an unhealthy monopoly of power. It also ensured that while the warriors were subservient to the community as a whole, the most effective leaders were in a position to protect the interests of the community in time of conflict.[15]

The Europeans who encountered the Cherokees in the eighteenth century had terrible difficulty in understanding the functions of the clan and council. A few were observant enough to recognize that the two institutions provided social order and a means for resolving most, if not all, interpersonal disputes. William Bartram, who traveled through the Southeast in the 1770s, even suggested that the legal and political systems of the Indians were superior to those of Europe's nation-states. He wrote that though simple in form, their institutions "produce a society of peace and love, which in effect better maintain human happiness, than the most complicated system of modern politics . . . enforced by coercive means." He added, "As moral men, they certainly stand in no need of European civilization." Other visitors, like Henry Timberlake, an English soldier, were more myopic and less impressed with the Cherokees' structure than was Bartram. Upon observing them in 1754, Timberlake wrote that the Cherokees had "neither laws or power" to support their government. Another witness wrote that "the Cherokees cannot be said to have any regular system of government, laws or even permanent customs which supplies the place of laws in some nations." Other commentators looked futilely for recognizable forms of centralized power. James Adair, for example, wrote that Indians had "no such titles or persons, as emperors, or kings." After contacts between British traders and the Cherokees became extensive, colonial officials began giving cooperative Indians these appellations and accompanying indicia of rank and title in an effort to simplify diplomatic relations and foster support among the Native American population for their policies. The British, in other words, had difficulty understanding the systematic structure of Cherokee government because it functioned differently from their own. As a result, they tried to impose their own conception of government upon the Cherokees.[16]

Although the tribe generally responded with remarkable aplomb and alacrity to the changes brought about by contact with Europeans, this pressure and the sustained economic interaction with Europeans disoriented every aspect of traditional Cherokee culture. The development of the deerskin trade with merchants from Great Britain, in particular, brought cataclysmic changes to the Cherokees' way of life. Before contact with Europeans, the Cherokees were generally self-sufficient; they had grown, hunted, and made everything they needed to enjoy a contented life. While they participated in an active Indian trading network, the goods they acquired by these relations only supplemented their basic means of subsistence. Though the Cherokees voluntarily adopted useful elements of Anglo-European knowledge and adapted foreign technology and material to suit their particular needs and circumstances, the trade that developed between the Cherokees and Europeans slowly destroyed this economic self-sufficiency. By the middle of the eighteenth century, colonial traders had drawn most of the Cherokee towns into their trade and credit economy. Merchants out of Charles Town provided Cherokee clients with firearms and ammunition, iron tools and utensils, glass beads, cloth, and whiskey—all on credit. In exchange, Cherokee hunters promised to repay their debts with deerskins and other pelts. The deerskin trade thus brought new materials and new technology to the Cherokees and transformed their traditional hunting and household practices. Men abandoned the bow and blowgun for the musket and rifle; women quickly appreciated the comfort provided by cotton and wool cloth and the hardy construction of the metal hoes, pots, pans, and needles offered by the traders. Unfortunately, there was a fine line between improved utility with the new items and an unhealthy reliance on them; the Cherokees quickly fell into a state of dependency that was noted by both European and Cherokee witnesses. The naturalist James Adair commented on the impact of the new technology on traditional Cherokee skills: "The Indian[s], by reason of our supplying them so cheap with every sort of goods, have forgotten the chief part of their ancient mechanical skill, so as to be not well able now, at least for some years, to live independent of us." Prescient Cherokees recognized that the goods acquired in the deerskin trade sapped their people of their accustomed autonomy. In 1745, only a few decades after regular trade began between the Cherokees and the British, a Cherokee chief lamented, "My people cannot live independently of the English." [17]

This dependency on foreign trade did more than transform the Cherokee economy; it deranged the fragile holistic structure of their society. Cherokee sociopolitical institutions were so interrelated that a change in one aspect of life produced reverberations throughout the culture. In particular, the development of commercial exchange between Europeans and the Cherokees forced the latter to reevaluate their feelings toward the game, the land, and the spirit world. The deerskin trade, for example, undermined traditional Cherokee spiritual rituals. Whereas hunters had before been careful to apologize to the spirit of the deer they killed and endeavored to use every part of the game for a purpose, the commercial deerskin trade encouraged hunters to kill by the gross. Gradually, the special relationship between hunter and game was replaced by an ethic of production; hunters killed not for meat but to acquire goods and repay their factors. Sometimes the demand for goods outpaced the capacity of hunters to pay for them, and many Indians ran up trade debts so high they could never pay them off with skins. This overextension produced disturbances in Cherokee-white relations. Some traders captured the family members of hunter-debtors and sold them into slavery, a practice that precipitated the Yamasee War of 1715. During that war Creek and Yamasee hunters killed English traders in an effort to cancel their obligations. At times, Cherokee warriors threatened to do, and may have done, the same. Overextension also often resulted in the loss of land. The Carolina colonial government, for example, occasionally required Cherokee communities to satisfy the debts of their individual hunters with cessions. Land thus became commodified to an extent, for cessions evolved into a mechanism to rescue a community from indebtedness. The surrender of territory, moreover, became a customary element of diplomacy, for the Cherokees used land cessions to restore good relations with the Carolina government. With that revisioning, land must have lost some of its spiritual sanctity in Cherokee eyes.[18]

Recognition of the processes that encouraged dependency produced a spectrum of Cherokee responses. Some attempted to withdraw into the interior away from the foreign influence; some chose to wage war against the trespassers; some urged peaceful accommodation with the traders and settlers. Dependency also produced dramatic sociopsychological reactions. In the second half of the eighteenth century, revitalization movements flared up across North America. Prophets, usually emerging from dreams, visions, or hallucinations, implored their people to take specific measures to revitalize their lives. Some, like Neolin, the Delaware Prophet, encouraged their followers to abandon Anglo-European ways and resist settler encroachments into their territory. The Cherokees experienced several prophetic uprisings of their own, including a ghost dance movement in 1811. The emergence of the Cherokee sovereignty movement was, perhaps in its own way, a unique form of cultural revitalization.[19]

Ultimately, though, the most significant Cherokee response to the Anglo-European presence, influences, and encroachments was a gradual but manifest movement toward centralized government. In the early eighteenth century, the Cherokee towns were essentially autonomous. The Appalachians and the Great Valley divided the towns into five regional groupings: the overhill towns, the valley towns, the lower towns, the middle towns, and the out towns. Occasionally, the towns in a region held combined councils or joined together for mutual defense. The Cherokees also recognized "mother towns": Tannassie and Chota among the overhill towns; Ustanali, Estatoe, and Keowee in the lower town region; Tellico and Neyohee in the valley; and Keetoowah in the middle and out town region. The mother towns seem to have possessed considerable influence but no coercive power over the other towns in their respective region. Beyond these regional and mother town affiliations, the Cherokees did not maintain a coordinated political structure at the time of the European entry into the Cherokee homeland. This frustrated the English, who wanted to regularize the contacts they had been making sporadically with the Cherokees since the 1690s. In 1716 the colonial government of Carolina began to encourage the Cherokees to centralize all trade and diplomatic authority in the hands of one leader. That year the colony appointed the spiritual leader of Tugaloo as the Cherokees' nominal chief. Tugaloo was an especially significant town to the Cherokees, for it was the place where the Great Spirit had provided them with their sacred fire. Consequently, at that time, the spiritual leader of Tugaloo was perhaps the most revered individual among the Cherokees. He was apparently replaced in 1721 when the governor of the colony persuaded a council of thirty-seven chiefs to recognize a headman named Wrosetasatow as their principal leader.[20]

In 1730, Alexander Cuming, an envoy of King George II, appointed Moytoy of Tellico, a renowned warrior, as "emperor" of the Cherokees in exchange for his loyalty to the Crown. Cuming traveled around the Cherokee country encouraging local councils to conduct trade and diplomatic relations through their new emperor. Cuming and Moytoy then arranged for seven Cherokee representatives to travel to England to meet King George. This mission would later play a prominent place in the American cases dealing with the question of Cherokee sovereignty. Those who opposed the United States's recognition of Cherokee sovereignty argued that the seven Cherokee delegates had pledged the tribe's fealty to King George. Proponents of Cherokee sovereignty argued that Great Britain and the Cherokee Nation were separate, sovereign nations and that Moytoy's emissaries were simply establishing diplomatic relations with King George and the British government. That Moytoy came from the warrior class, however, was not necessarily an affront to traditional Cherokee leadership habits; in fact, the political status of warriors, of whom Oconostota and Old Hop were among the most prominent, remained high, and perhaps increased, among Cherokee councils in the eighteenth century. Colonial authorities tried to deal directly with these men of military repute, and the warrior chiefs therefore became the primary conduit through which the Cherokees conducted trade and diplomatic relations with the colonies. Sometimes large numbers of Cherokee towns endeavored to funnel authority into a British designate; in most cases, however, local Cherokee councils refused to cede authority to these Cherokee "emperors" and "kings." Pressure toward centralizing the Cherokee political structure did not come just from without, in any event. Several of the Cherokee warrior-chiefs, like Old Hop, understood that European colonization and trade brought novel problems and challenges to every community, and they occasionally attempted to bring the town and regional councils together into grand tribal councils to deal with issues of defense, trespass, and trade.[21]

Gradually, the town councils surrendered authority to an emerging National Council. In the 1740s the council of Chota, an overhill town, played the French and British off against each other in an effort to get both imperial powers to recognize it as the source and center of Cherokee political authority. Chota held a legitimate claim to host and lead the National Council as one of the mother towns of the Cherokee people. The British colonial government, however, encouraged the valley towns of Tellico and Hiwassee to challenge Chota's preeminence. After the lower towns, under the leadership of the Tellico and Hiwassee councils, were defeated by the Creeks in 1752, many local councils began to recognize Chota's position and allow its council to administer trade and diplomatic relations for them. The National Council, composed of representatives from all of the towns, met regularly at Chota until the American Revolution. Like the local councils, the National Council attempted to reach decisions by consensus. Though these decisions seemed to have received approbation from most town councils, there was little the National Council could do to enforce its will on recalcitrant individuals or villages; and though it theoretically included every member of the Cherokee Nation, the National Council was dominated by the chiefs and elders of the largest and historically most significant towns. These leaders, in turn, sought guidance from their own town councils. In essence, then, the National Council was moving toward a representative political system.[22]

One of the greatest challenges that the National Council faced was maintaining peaceful relations with the Carolina colony. The practice of blood revenge, which fell under the jurisdiction of the clans rather than the National Council, inhibited the development of tribal controls over violence. Under blood revenge, Cherokee warriors had customarily gone out in small war parties to avenge the deaths of slain members of their town or clan. This custom, along with the right of dissenters to go to war when the council had resolved to make peace, exacerbated the already hostile relations between the Cherokees and the settlers who were moving into their domain. When avenging warriors or malcontents attacked a British settler, Cherokee towns often suffered disproportional retaliatory invasions. The fact that small groups of dissenters could bring on such devastation persuaded some influential headmen that the Cherokees needed to centralize the decision-making process on questions of such import. The Carolina colonial government also tried to force the Cherokees to punish individuals who killed traders or settlers. Consequently, in the second half of the eighteenth century the Cherokee National Council repeatedly attempted to extend jurisdiction over blood revenge and threatened to punish towns and individuals who killed colonial traders, attacked English settlements, or endangered relations with the Carolina government. The Cherokee people, however, refused to surrender their right to revenge, and as a result, the council was unable to prevent conflicts between Cherokee warriors and British traders and settlers.

For example, in the middle of the Seven Years' War, Virginia settlers killed several Cherokee warriors who were returning from a raid on the Shawnees in the Ohio Valley. The relatives of the slain Cherokee warriors defied the National Council's admonition to refrain from retaliation and attacked the settlers to obtain blood revenge. In response, in 1760 the British army invaded Cherokee territory and destroyed all of the lower towns. Hundreds of warriors died in the conflict; with their crops and homes burned to the ground, an even greater number of Cherokee men, women, and children died from starvation and exposure. To make matters worse, another in a long series of smallpox epidemics raged through the population at around the same time. The traditional practice of blood revenge, some Cherokees believed, had brought on a national disaster. The invasion of the Cherokee homeland demonstrated the necessity of unified action to many of the former opponents of nationalization and moved the council to continue its efforts to terminate blood revenge against white settlers.[23]

Great Britain's victories in the Cherokee war of 1760 and in the greater geopolitical struggle with the French in the Seven Years' War ended the Cherokees' once powerful position in the Southeast. Before 1760, the Cherokees had been able to pit France, Britain, and the colonies against each other for their own economic and diplomatic aggrandizement. The Treaty of Paris removed the French from the region and placed the southern colonies in a position to dictate conditions to the Indians. After the war, the Cherokees offered up four major cessions totaling over twenty thousand square miles to Great Britain and the southern colonies. These cessions had the effect of exacerbating existing political differences in the National Council. Many Cherokee leaders conceived of cessions as a way to make peace and accommodate the imperial and colonial forces aligned against them. A competing group of Cherokees, however, were beginning to grow weary of surrendering land.[24]

After the Seven Years' War, King George III attempted to alleviate the tensions between settlers and the Indian tribes and bring the colonial governments under imperial control. In the Proclamation of 1763, he prohibited colonial settlement west of a line running down the Appalachian ridge. The British government also established a southern superintendent of Indian affairs to coordinate settlement, land cessions, and trade issues. The Proclamation of 1763 was also intended to reduce British expenses in North America and protect England's transatlantic commerce by keeping its consumers close to port. The British government recognized that if the inner continent became populated with settlers, distance and transportation difficulties might encourage them to develop an independent American economy free from the ties and tariffs of British regulation. George's concern for colonial independence was justified; and just as the Cherokees were beginning to recover from the British invasion of 1760, the American Revolution broke out. The Chota council determined that the nation's best hope for survival rested in neutrality. Some Cherokee towns, however, saw the Revolution as an opportunity to drive white trespassers out of Cherokee territory, and, in April 1776, their young men joined up with warriors from other tribes and colonials loyal to the Crown and attacked American settlers living on the western edges of the southern colonies. In retaliation, militia forces from Georgia, North Carolina, South Carolina, and Virginia once again tore through the Cherokee country, burning, killing, and looting as they went. More than fifty Cherokee town sites in the lower and middle towns were destroyed in the war. In 1777, the Cherokees of the lower, middle, and overhill towns made peace with the hostile colonies and surrendered two large cessions to them. Disgusted by this submission, chiefs and warriors from several towns, who became known as the Chickamauga Cherokees, migrated to the western edge of the Cherokee Nation and continued their attacks against settlers in Kentucky and Tennessee. Encouraged and supplied by Great Britain and Spain, the Chickamaugas continued to attack American settlements until 1794, when they finally came to terms with the United States. The divisions the war and the cessions provoked among the Cherokees, however, continued for years thereafter.[25]

The two wars left the Cherokees in what the historian William G. McLoughlin called a state of anomie. Before the Seven Years' War and the American Revolution, depopulation by epidemic diseases had already decimated the Cherokees. The demographer Russell Thornton estimated that the Cherokee population declined by more than 50 percent between 1690 and 1740. By the end of the two wars, the Cherokee population had perhaps been depleted again by another half. The Cherokees had also surrendered their land at an equally alarming pace. At the end of the American Revolution, the United States demanded three more cessions totaling over thirteen thousand square miles. Since 1721, the date of their first formal cession, the Cherokees had been forced to cede over one-half of their territorial holdings to Great Britain, the colonies, or the United States. The American Revolution and the rapidly increasing American settler population left the Cherokees isolated and under the constant threat of trespass and attack. The Cherokees had reached an emotional, demographic, and geopolitical nadir and were in a vulnerable position when the United States came asking for peace and cessions in 1785 at Hopewell. That the treaty reads so ambiguously in its description of the relationship between the two parties perhaps tells us more than anything the exhausted state that both sides were in when they entered the negotiations. Some have suggested that despite the disastrous events of the previous two decades, the Cherokees were still a force to be reckoned with; the United States's recognition of the Cherokees' sovereignty perhaps, however, reflected that they were not both strong nations dealing at arms' length, but fragile and damaged polities that needed peace from each other to survive.[26]

When the United States called upon the Cherokees to surrender their territory, it did so, as the British government and colonies had done, in the form of the diplomatic treaty. The notion of the treaty apparently carried a different connotation for Indians than it did for British and American treaty commissioners. Francis Jennings, the historian and critic of Anglo-American Indian policies, suggested that the British, colonial, and American governments conceived of treaties as "arrangements of necessity and convenience, to be dispensed with when circumstance would permit." Indians, in contrast, regarded treaties as binding "agreements between sovereign peers." The treaty process had traditional antecedents for the Cherokee people, and when they came to negotiate, British and American treaty commissioners followed Indian diplomatic practices. These procedures, like smoking the calumet of peace, drinking from the common bowl, and reciprocal gift giving, were traditional rituals used to cement alliances, initiate trade relations, and reestablish peace after war. In the latter case negotiations between Indian peoples usually included recitations of the historical good feelings between the parties, formal lamentations that circumstances had temporarily sundered the state of good thoughts, and symbolic rituals like the burying of the hatchet. The negotiators spoke to each other in metaphors, telling stories intended to point out grievances held against the other party or to illustrate the expected norms of the relationship. The peacemakers often referred to each other in terms that reflected some form of kin relation. And rather than the pointed negotiations that marked diplomatic relations between European states, Indian negotiators delicately avoided words or conduct that would offend the other party or violate the ethic of hospitality. The agreements that resulted from this process were not temporary contracts of strategic expedience, but sacred compacts defined in terms of kinship and universal familiarity. By concluding diplomatic accords, in other words, an Indian community ceremoniously brought another people into its fold. As Robert A. Williams Jr. has suggested, Indians perhaps conceived of diplomacy as something even greater than a simple kin or intertribal relationship. Indians, he wrote, saw the treaty as a "supreme act of commitment to create a new type of society." He added, "In the language of Indian diplomacy, the treaty itself bespoke of a divinely-inspired, universal vision of all humankind as one."[27]

Indian councils applied this conception of treaty making to their early

relations with British and colonial officials. Perhaps, as the ethnohistorian
Patricia Galloway has argued, the matrilineal structure of some Southeastern societies led Indian treaty makers to regard their European diplomatic
partners as "kind indulgent non-relatives who had no authority over them."
This was the status of the man who had married into a clan and become a
father in a matrilineal society. The spouse-father held the responsibility of
teaching and disciplining his sisters' male children. To his own offspring,
however, he took on a role akin to that of the modern American grand-
parent. He lavished love on his children and left the difficult responsibilities
of discipline and tutoring to his spouse's closest male relative. When European and American treaty makers described their governments as father
figures to the tribes, Galloway suggested, the Indian negotiators accepted
the metaphor in their own conception of benevolent and distant paternity,
not as the authoritative, patriarchal father of Western conceit. While the
British wanted to take on that latter role, the Cherokees at times preferred
to speak to their British treaty partners as an elder brother. By doing so,
the Cherokees tried to inform the British of how they were to perform in
that relationship. As with the elder brother in the household, the Cherokees
were telling the British that while they appreciated their protection, they also
expected to be treated as autonomous, although perhaps less than powerful,
relations capable of pursuing their own destiny. They could not be ordered
around by a brother; under the matrilineal system, only the man's mother's
brother possessed that authority. By applying kinship appellations to their
diplomatic partners, the Cherokees seized control of the treaty relationship:
they expected their British and American counterparts to treat them, and
respect them, as their own brother would.[28]

The Cherokees agreed to treaties with Great Britain and the United States
for economic and security reasons. First, stable diplomatic relations ensured
that the Cherokees obtained access to a reliable and consistent supply of
trade goods. More important, the Cherokee National Council used treaties
to build a wall of protection and separation around their territory. In the
Removal Crisis the Cherokees argued that their earlier treaties with Great
Britain, the colonies, and the United States had confirmed their status as an
independent nation, partly because the agreements recognized and described
the borders of Cherokee territory. The opponents of Cherokee sovereignty
pointed out that at Hopewell the tribe had also surrendered its right to
conduct foreign relations, had given up its power to regulate trade, and
had placed itself under the protection of the United States. The concessions offered in these treaties, however, must be read in conjunction with
the subsequent actions of the National Council to understand the Cherokees' conception of their political status at that time. While the Hopewell

agreement stated, for example, that the Cherokees had offered the United States Congress the "sole and exclusive right of regulating the trade with the Indians, and managing all their affairs, as they think proper," the National Council clearly continued to operate as if it considered the Cherokee Nation an independent, sovereign state.[29]

In 1788, for example, the National Council began meeting again, this time at the town of Ustanali, and moved to fend off threats to its sovereign status. In particular, the council continued to try to wrest control of blood revenge from the clans. National leaders like The Ridge argued that eliminating blood revenge was essential if the Cherokees wanted to retain their independence. The improvident exercise of blood revenge against the states or the United States, he warned, could result in the Cherokees' annihilation. In 1797 The Ridge finally convinced the National Council to modify the practice so that those who caused death accidentally would be secure from blood retaliation. In addition, he persuaded the council to amend the clan law to ensure that only killers, rather than their kin, be forced to forfeit their lives to repay a blood debt. The modification of blood revenge opened the way for the development of a separate, institutional criminal justice system. In 1799 the council formed the Cherokee Lighthorse Guard to protect individuals from robbers and horse thieves. A year later, the government prohibited blood revenge against Lighthorsemen who killed or injured while performing their duties. Finally, in 1810, the National Council formally abolished blood revenge, thus concluding its seizure of jurisdiction over manslaughter from the clans. Over the subsequent years, the council enacted a body of criminal laws, created district courts to handle the resulting cases, and provided for the right to trial by jury. In 1817, the council printed the existing Cherokee laws and distributed them throughout the nation, perhaps for the purpose of satisfying the old common law rule of publication. These were not the acts of a people living under the dominion of the United States. They were positive assertions of sovereignty that went unchallenged by the American government.[30]

The Cherokees' relationship with the United States accelerated the internal centripetal forces resulting in the further diminishment of the influence of the clan and local councils. Beginning around 1791, with the civilization provisions of the Treaty of Holston, the United States began to encourage the Cherokees to participate in its Indian civilization program. By this time the deerskin trade had already diminished in importance for the Cherokee economy. The trade had reduced the deer population to a point that hunting could no longer provide the income required to purchase the goods desired by most Cherokee families. Many Cherokee men had therefore abandoned hunting as a means of subsistence and had begun raising cattle, hogs, and horses. Some followed the exhortations of the U.S. civilization agent and began farming. Cherokee families cultivated several crops; some sold their excess in the emerging local markets. Most families lived a modified version of the traditional Cherokee life, embracing the new economy but retaining the old mores and worldview. A small but influential class of entrepreneurs and planters, however, emerged out of the general society at the end of the eighteenth and the beginning of the nineteenth century. Many of these men, but not all, were the descendants of Cherokee women and British traders. As the progeny of Cherokee mothers in a matrilineal society, they were able to use their kinship to acquire political influence in their communities. At the same time, their paternal heritage afforded them access to education and cultural relations that were unavailable to most Cherokee young men. In effect, these bicultural men became not only linguistic, but cultural interpreters. John Ross, who would serve as principal chief for just less than forty years, was the best example of this class. The son of a Scottish trader and a woman who was one-fourth Cherokee, Ross was educated at home by a white tutor and then attended a mission school and a scholastic academy. Although he was not particularly fluent in Cherokee and never mastered Sequoyah's syllabary, he was able to serve as the conduit between the American and Cherokee worlds. He considered himself a Cherokee as opposed to a white man, was often aligned with the most traditionally conservative of the Cherokee population, and understood and possessed their desire to remain forever in the Cherokee ancestral homeland. At the same time, by being conversant in English and Anglo-American culture, Ross and his cohorts were well placed to negotiate trade and territorial conditions with the United States. With the terrible defeats inflicted on the Cherokees in 1760 and 1776 and the development of the American civilization program, Ross's class naturally replaced the great warriors in the leadership positions. It was no coincidence that the Cherokees began adopting Anglo-American forms of political and legal organization in the nineteenth century; their new generation of leaders was quite familiar with the ideas that were becoming entrenched in the fabric of the United States. The Cherokees were not simply aping the United States, as some contemporary Americans thought, though; they were being led toward representative government, centralized authority, and market economics by men comfortable with the ideas of parliamentarianism, the common law, capital investment, and private accumulation. While the leadership of the entrepreneurial class was significant in moving the Cherokees toward a centralized state, however, the true political power and sovereignty of the government ultimately resided in the Cherokee people. Most Cherokees, regardless of their cultural inclinations, were adamantly opposed to further national land cessions, and their unity in this wish determined the direction of Cherokee political decision making more than any individual or class. The Cherokee people wanted to remain autonomous in the East, and if the leadership believed that centralization and civilization were the best ways to achieve that objective, many were willing to take that path.[31]

The movement toward centralized government was further invigorated in 1808 by the first Cherokee removal crisis. That year, a group of chiefs asked the United States to recognize the Chickamaugas, who remained bitterly divided from the Cherokee government, as a separate nation. Return J. Meigs, the federal agent to the Cherokees, suggested that all of the Cherokees follow President Jefferson's advice and exchange their lands for territory in what is now Arkansas. There, he said, the Cherokees could live as they pleased, free from the annoying influence and trespasses of American settlers. Those who were already acculturated or who were inclined toward civilization, Meigs said, could remain in the East, continue to farm, and become citizens of the United States. In July 1809, representatives from forty-two towns met in national council at Ustanali and rejected the removal proposal. Following the traditional right of dissent, about eight hundred to a thousand Cherokees from the lower towns, led by a chief named Taluntuskee, agreed to a separate removal agreement with the United States. When these dissidents set off for Arkansas, the Cherokees moved to bind the wounds raised by the Chickamauga crisis. In September representatives from almost all of the Cherokee towns met for a national Green Corn Ceremony at Wills Town. The National Council declared that the Cherokees were again a unified nation, that it was committed to protecting the nation's territory, and that it would reject any overtures or pressure for removal. The National Council then moved to make the government more proficient in responding to these external threats. The traditional system of consensus, which worked effectively at the local level, had begun to prove unduly problematic at the national level, particularly in managing relations with the United States. The council found it very difficult to construct positions and solutions that were satisfactory to the delegates of forty or fifty Cherokee towns. To resolve this problem, the council established a Standing Committee, composed of thirteen members selected by the National Council, and endowed it with authority to administer the day-to-day business of the nation. The National Council delegated the administration of the Lighthorse Guard, the collection and disbursement of federal annuities, and the oversight of trade and regulatory matters to the committee.[32]

The Cherokee participation in the Creek Redstick conflict during the War of 1812 and the subsequent treaty of Fort Jackson further turned the National Council against any future cessions. In the war, many Cherokee warriors joined with Andrew Jackson's U.S. forces to put down the Redstick

Creeks, who wanted to provoke a pan-Indian revolt that would clear the Native world of Anglo-American influences. After Jackson's destruction of the Redstick uprising at Horseshoe Bend, he demanded that the entire Creek Nation, most of whose population had either allied with him or remained neutral, cede an enormous tract of twenty-three million acres to the United States. More than two million acres of this shotgun cession, however, belonged to the Cherokees. When the Cherokees protested the Treaty of Fort Jackson, the United States agreed to pay them for their claim rather than annul that portion of the session. Jackson's treachery and his comments on the inevitability of removal alarmed and angered the National Council. In May 1817, the council called town representatives to meet at Amohee to consider a strategy to counter the removal and cession pressures gathering in Georgia. The council reformed the Standing Committee, which came to be known as the National Committee, by providing for the general election of its members to two-year terms. More important, the council prohibited the committee from selling national land without the unanimous consent of the National Council. This, of course, effectively proscribed future cessions.[33]

This legislation did not deter the United States from continuing its efforts to persuade the Cherokees to remove. On July 8, 1817, U.S. treaty commissioners, led by Jackson, disregarded the National Council's refusal to negotiate a removal and cession treaty and concluded an agreement with another group of dissident Cherokee chiefs. The agreement called for the Cherokees to surrender a tract in Georgia and three more parcels in Tennessee. The federal government told the Cherokee families living on this land that they could either move to Arkansas or remain in the East, accept an allotment of land, and live as individual subjects of the state in which they lived. In the summers of 1817 and 1818, about a thousand more of these dissidents joined the earlier exiles in the West. The Cherokee government immediately repudiated the treaty and began lobbying the federal government to repeal it. In 1819 a delegation to Washington convinced the United States to revise the 1817 agreement. In return for a cession of six thousand square miles, the United States guaranteed the title of and promised to protect the Cherokees' remaining territory in the East. At the time the 1817 treaty dispute was resolved, the Cherokees' representatives told President James Monroe that they hoped the United States would never again ask them for another cession. The Cherokee Nation had resolved to yield no more. The National Council again implemented specific legislative measures to prevent the further loss of Cherokee land. First, it enacted a statute that mandated death for any Cherokee who sold national land without its approval. Then, on October 23, 1822, the council passed a resolution stating that it would not meet with commissioners from the United States "on the subject of making cession[s] . . . as we are determined hereafter never to make any cessions of lands, having not more than sufficient for our nation and prosperity." The chiefs of the nation, the government added, would be glad to discuss "any other business not relating to making a treaty of cession . . . with friendship and cordiality." In 1825, the council reduced the traditional view that the land belonged to the nation in common into statutory law. By prohibiting individual land ownership, the council presumed that it could protect the nation from the piecemeal sale and loss of tribal territory. The National Council was, in essence, ingeniously using foreign ideas such as sovereignty, codification, and democracy to preserve traditional Cherokee values.[34]

In the 1820s the National Council continued to consolidate the Cherokee people and town councils into a unified, centralized nation. In 1820, the National Council and National Committee effectively ended the relationship between the national and local town councils, created eight electoral districts (which also served as judicial districts), and reorganized the government into a true bicameral legislature. After the reconstruction, the Cherokee government consisted of the National Council, a lower house of thirty-two representatives (with four each elected from the eight districts), and the National Committee, an upper house of thirteen members selected by the National Council. Each house elected a principal chief for a four-year term. All legislation had to be approved by the two houses and the two chiefs. Over the remainder of the decade, the Cherokee government legislated on all matters of national import—from economic to legal to moral concerns. The national legislature, for example, enacted specific criminal laws and punishments, passed tax and bond provisions, licensed merchants, built toll roads, regulated interest rates and slave relations, and prohibited gambling, intemperance, and Cherokee intermarriage with white Americans and black slaves. The council also surrendered judicial power to a newly constituted independent judiciary. Since the abrogation of blood revenge in 1810 the National Council and National Committee had possessed jurisdiction over all legal disputes. The 1820 act provided for a separate hierarchical trial and appellate system. Each electoral district was apportioned a judgeship with supporting marshals and constables. Four circuit judges were established, each one possessing appellate authority over two districts, to review the decisions of the district court judges. In 1822, the council created the Cherokee Supreme Court to hear appeals from the lower courts.[35]

The Cherokees' efforts to bolster their independence only antagonized the state of Georgia, which was calling for them to surrender their lands and remove. In November 1826, in a bold effort to fend off these forces, the National Council called for an election of delegates to represent the Cherokee districts at a constitutional convention. Nothing could better demonstrate their intent to remain sovereign, some Cherokee leaders believed, than the declaration of a constitutional republic. Surely, they thought, the United States would recognize the timing and symbolism of their act. On July 4, 1827, the thirty-two delegates gathered at New Echota. Even as the Cherokees drafted their constitution, Georgia officials appeared to demand another cession. The Cherokees sent them on their way. On July 26, the convention adopted the constitution and sent it to the National Council for ratification. The Cherokees' adoption and ratification of their constitution provoked an outburst of protest from the politicians and newspapers of the surrounding states. The U.S. Constitution, from which the Cherokee document drew considerable direction, stated in Article 4, Section 3: "No new state shall be formed or erected within the jurisdiction of any other state . . . without the consent of the legislature of the states concerned as well as of the Congress." The Cherokees, according to expansionists in Georgia, Alabama, and Tennessee, had clearly violated this proscription. The Cherokees, for their part, maintained that their people constituted a nation that was inherently sovereign. A few months after the Cherokee constitutional convention, John Ross, the first principal chief under the new government, explained the significance of the document. The Cherokee Nation, Ross said, "claims for its self & always maintained sovereign jurisdiction over its Territorial limits. . . . It had no relation or connection to *a State* to ask of it, its Consent, being connected and related to the United States *alone* by Treaty. . . . This nation never surrendered her right to self Government, or the exercise of internal and domestic regulation." Ross believed that the Cherokee Nation had been a sovereign nation long before the creation of the U.S. Constitution, long before the colonial charters of the states claiming Cherokee land, and long before the fateful time when Europeans had begun invading Cherokee territory. The Cherokee constitution was not a declaration of independence, Ross and the Cherokees were saying, it was a reaffirmation of an autonomy that dated back to the creation of the Cherokee people.[36]

Ross, a planter and merchant, had held several key positions in the government. Along with serving as the president of the constitutional convention, he had been a member, and later presiding officer, of the Standing Committee. He had also served as secretary to Path Killer, the popular principal chief who died only months before the convention. Ross was clearly aligned with those Cherokees who had consistently refused to accept the possibility of removal, and as principal chief he committed his energies to preserving the Cherokee Nation, intact, in the East. Ross understood that all of the recent political adaptations and legal promulgations had been motivated by a desire to protect the Cherokees from the jurisdictional encroachments of the states, the trespasses of settlers, and the American politicians who were pushing for the enactment of a general removal bill. Upon his election, Ross and the Cherokee leadership set out to construct a legal and political strategy, based on the argument that the Cherokees were a sovereign nation, to fend off the pressures for removal.[37]

Ross knew that the Cherokee people believed they possessed an immutable relationship with the land. The traditional belief system of the Cherokees, which remained more popular than the proponents of civilization would have been willing to admit, held that the Cherokees lived at the center of the universe and that they were a unique people bound together by a common origin and history. John Ross understood this as well. In arguing for the right of the Cherokees to remain in the East, he wrote that the Cherokee lands were "consecrated in their affections from having been immemorially the property and residence of their ancestors, and from containing now the graves of their fathers, relatives, and friends." By remaining on and protecting this homeland and its resources, Ross was saying, the Cherokees were perpetuating what was always meant to be. The principal chief thus understood that removal was not simply a plan for forced emigration. Removal implied blasphemy, spiritual dislocation, and the abandonment of one's culture and ancestors.[38]

By 1828 the Cherokee Nation had been reduced to an area of approximately one-third the size of its original domain. The population of the nation, which now numbered around sixteen thousand, had patiently listened as American treaty commissioners and southern state politicians had asked, cajoled, and pleaded with them to remove. The state of Georgia had even threatened to invade the nation and forcibly expel the Cherokees from their homeland. The Cherokee people, however, had just endured a century marked by wars, invasions, disease epidemics, and cultural disorientation. They had already survived a long period of civil division and two previous removal crises that had resulted in the secession of two large dissident groups. They had lost a considerable measure of their economic autonomy. They had surrendered to the United States government their right to conduct foreign relations and their authority to regulate commerce. Still, the Cherokees believed that they were and had always been, by any measure or definition, an independent, sovereign nation. They intended to remain separate and were not cowed by Georgia's threats. Though the Cherokees remained independent, however, the ultimate question of their continued residency in the East depended on external exigencies. The Cherokee people needed the United States federal government to abide by its treaty promises and protect them from the trespasses and encroachments of the states. Cherokee leaders, however, recognized that the United States government was falling into the hands of expansion-minded politicians who thought little of the political rights of the Indian tribes or the long-standing federal obligations detailed in U.S.-Indian treaties. Understanding that the elected officials of the United States were not inclined to support their position against Georgia and the other southern states, Jeremiah Evarts and other friends of the Cherokees urged John Ross to look to the American judicial system for some measure of protection. Standing in the way of that remedy was a giant monolith of precedent and scholarship that offered American judges an end run around the United States's historical practice of recognizing the political and territorial rights of the Indian tribes.[39]

CHAPTER THREE

The Precedents

Sources of Law for the Southern State
Courts during the Removal Crisis

AMERICAN JUDGES DURING the Removal Crisis had a relatively fertile literature at their disposal when they considered the question of what rights the Indian tribes possessed in the United States. They looked, for example, to the scholarship on the law of nations produced by legal and political philosophers of the colonial era. They also reviewed the English common law precedents on property rights, the histories of the European exploration and colonization of the Americas, the propaganda of European imperialists, and the statutes and cases of the colonial assemblies and courts. These diverse English and continental sources offered two schools of thought on the nature and breadth of indigenous rights. One line of argument maintained that Indians possessed the same natural rights as white Europeans and that the tribes held the same political and territorial rights as the sovereign nations of Europe. The other chain of thought held that the indigenous peoples possessed few, if any, property or political rights. Some advocates of this view contended that since the native inhabitants of the Americas were not Christians and not "civilized" in the European sense, they were not socially or politically advanced enough to claim individual natural rights or the collective rights of nationhood. Others argued that by colonizing the Americas the European imperial powers had circumscribed or even extinguished any rights to which Native American people may have been entitled under the prevailing theories of natural or international law.[1]

While the European authorities provided general guidance on the issues of Native American sovereignty and title, the peculiar origins of the United States and the unique form of government adopted by the nation in 1787 complicated the competing interpretations. The American courts in the Removal Crisis were able, however, to focus their attention on three fundamental areas of inquiry: First, did Native Americans possess property and political rights under the Constitution and American law? Second, were the Indian tribes sovereign nations independent of the United States? Third, who

held constitutional authority to conduct relations with the Indian polities—
the states or the federal government? The United States Constitution provided little direction on these questions. Article 1 referred to "Indians not
taxed" in calculating representation and direct taxes. Section 8 of the same
article gave Congress "the power to regulate commerce . . . with the Indian
tribes." Article 2 gave the president the power to enter into treaties with
the advice and consent of the Senate. Beyond these provisions, the framers
gave little indication of how they thought the states, the federal government,
and the numerous Indian peoples living in the United States should inter-
act on political terms. The traditional sources for interpreting the founders'
intent—Madison's notes, the Federalist Papers, and the other commentaries
of the time—were also of little help to the courts faced with construing these
relationships. Consequently, the courts of the Removal era closely examined
the circumstances surrounding the founding of the republic and the nation's
early treaty relations with the Indian tribes. They also reviewed a handful
of prior decisions in which the federal and state courts had considered the
question of Indian political and territorial rights. The courts, in particular,
carefully studied *Fletcher v. Peck* and *Johnson v. McIntosh*, the two major
cases in which the United States Supreme Court had considered the status
and rights of the Native American tribes. These decisions were striking, for
they introduced into American legal thought the two lines of authority promulgated earlier by the European scholars on international law.

From Victoria to Vattel:
The European Theories of Indigenous Sovereignty and Title

During the Crusades, Catholic theorists began to consider the legal status
and rights of peoples who lived beyond the realm of European civilization.
In particular, they attempted to determine whether, and to what extent, non-
Christian peoples possessed individual and communal rights. A significant
development in this scholarship was the revival of the ancient theory of natural law. Aristotle had taught that there existed in nature a system of law that
provided order in the universe. Natural law not only controlled the physical
structure of the cosmos, he said, there were basic principles of justice and political relations existing in nature. The challenge for humans was to identify
these fundamental rules. When Christian theologians rediscovered Aristotle,
they co-opted the philosopher's conception of natural law and integrated it
into canonical scholarship. Thomas Aquinas, for example, conceived of God
as the architect of natural law, and he contended that human beings could,
by using reason, identify the laws of nature that the Almighty had established
for humans.[2]

Christian philosophers presumed that these principles of legal conduct extended to the relations between peoples and nations. The underlying foundation of the laws that governed international relations, they argued, was the concept of sovereignty. Before the Crusades, the idea of national sovereignty was, in the words of one scholar, "an unthinkable thing." Instead, the idea of a completely independent and sovereign nation was subsumed under the overwhelming authority of the Catholic Church. Canonical scholars held that when Jesus Christ told Peter that he would give him the keys to the kingdom of heaven (the "Petrine Mandate"), he had intended to convey to the disciple and his papal successors supremacy over the religious *and* secular worlds. When European monarchs restricted their authority to the people and lands within their own kingdoms, the issue of sovereignty was not of burning concern for church scholars. All of them fell under the oversight of Rome. The Crusades, however, raised interest in the natural law of international conflicts and prompted inquiry into the questions of whether non-Christian political communities held the same rights as Christian nations and whether the pope held authority over the secular affairs of nonbelievers.[3]

The development of the idea that each nation deserved respect for its land, its right of self-government, and its temporal jurisdiction guided legal philosophers in the creation of models of international law. The compulsion to construct a working law of nations was revitalized in the fifteenth and sixteenth centuries by the Protestant Reformation and by the fact that the major European states were beginning to assert claims over the lands that they discovered in Africa, Asia, and North and South America. Encounters with peoples who had never heard of European civilization or Christianity again raised questions about whether non-Christians held property rights under natural law and whether their communities were nations under the European understanding of the term. This international competition for the newfound lands encouraged European legal scholars to concoct principles and theories that gave their respective nations legal priority against other claimants and prompted them to construct justifications to deny the indigenous residents rights to their own countries. In 1455 Prince Henry the Navigator appealed to Pope Nicholas V to confer to the Crown of Portugal the title to any lands that he and his countrymen discovered on their expeditions down the western coast of Africa. In return, Henry promised to spread the Christian faith to nonbelievers and bring them under the authority of the church. At that time, the papacy claimed the right under the Petrine Mandate to convey the title of a newly discovered land to a Christian nation. Nicholas, anxious to challenge Islamic hegemony in Africa, issued to the king of Portugal an unfettered claim to an area stretching from the northern coast of Africa east to India. Reports of Columbus's first voyage in 1492 immediately provoked questions from Portugal about its title to the lands assigned by Nicholas's papal donation. Columbus might have discovered a western route to Asia, the Portuguese argued, but Nicholas had already conveyed title to those lands to their king. In 1493, Spanish representatives of King Ferdinand convinced Pope Alexander VI to clarify the respective titles of Spain and Portugal. Alexander issued a series of papal bulls called the *Inter caetera divinae* that established a longitudinal line that ran from pole to pole, one hundred leagues west of the Azores. The papal decrees gave the Portuguese dominion over all of the undiscovered lands east of the imaginary line; Spain obtained papal title to the territory to the west. A few months later, in the Treaty of Tordesillas, Spain and Portugal agreed to move the line of demarcation 270 more leagues to the west. Despite this concession to Portugal, subsequent surveys revealed that Spain had acquired papal claim to almost all of the Americas. Portugal, however, acquired title in the Western Hemisphere to what turned out to be only a small portion of South America in what is now Brazil. In exchange for his territorial blessing, Alexander had required the Iberian powers to convert the indigenous inhabitants of their new realms to Christianity and educate them in the ways of European civilization. Spanish conquistadors in America convinced King Ferdinand and the pope that they could accomplish this mission only by forcing the Indian population to labor in their mines and fields. Working in the *encomienda* system, they argued, would best further the proselytization and civilization of the Crown's Indian subjects. Within a few years, thousands upon thousands of Indians had lost their lives in the Spanish wars of conquest, at the hands of the *encomenderos*, and from the diseases that the Europeans brought to the hemisphere.[4]

Along with the papal donation, Spain relied on two other sources of priority to support its claim to the Western Hemisphere. First, Spanish scholars argued that their king had acquired sovereignty over the Americas pursuant to the doctrine of discovery. Under the doctrine of discovery, they argued, a nation acquired the right to exclusive possession of newly discovered lands that were not previously the domain of a Christian monarch. Papal donation and discovery were both, of course, based on the presumption that the lands of non-Christians were open to seizure by Christians. To many theorists, however, discovery or papal donation alone did not confer sovereignty over the lands of nonbelievers. Rather, the Christian nation was legally obligated to perfect title by purchase, colonization and occupation, or conquest. The doctrine of conquest, the third prong of the Spanish title trident, held that a nation acquired sovereignty over another people when it defeated them in war, extended its civil administration over them, and incorporated their territory into its own. International legal scholars such as Samuel Pufendorf contended that a war of conquest could be conducted only to perfect priority created by discovery or papal donation or to defend or assert natural legal rights. Other contemporary scholars maintained that a nation could acquire a superior title to a land by defeating in war those who held contrary or existing claims.[5]

The doctrine of conquest dated back at least to Roman law, but it was the Christian church that had transformed the theory into a principle of international conduct. In the fifth century St. Augustine had introduced the concept of a Christian war of conquest; such a war, he wrote, had to be executed for a "just" cause. The only just wars, he added, were those fought in self-defense and those conducted to recover stolen church property. In the eleventh century Pope Gregory incorporated the doctrine of conquest into the Christian evangelical mission. God, he proclaimed, sanctioned crusades against nonbelievers and enemies of the church. In the thirteenth century Pope Innocent IV dramatically expanded upon and complicated Gregory's legitimization of Christian violence, but in refining the doctrine of conquest, he opened the vault of natural rights to non-Christians. Non-Christians, he declared, possessed the same rights as Christians under natural law. He then asked, "Is it licit to invade a land that infidels possess, or which belongs to them?" Innocent concluded that infidel violations of natural law, as interpreted by the church, created a papal duty to force the miscreants to admit missionaries into their lands. If the nonbelievers did not convert to Christianity, he continued, the papacy could then authorize Christian monarchs to wage war on its behalf and force the recalcitrants to accept the faith. Innocent's contemplations established two alternative paths for future students of indigenous rights. On the one hand, Innocent admitted that natural law endowed non-Christian peoples with property rights and political sovereignty. On the other hand, he declared that under certain conditions Christian nations could encroach upon and extinguish those rights. This ambiguity, which essentially gave non-Christians natural rights with one hand and then took them back with the other, controlled philosophical discussions of Native American rights during the Spanish Conquest.[6]

This dichotomous view of indigenous people's rights also prevailed in the first treatises on international law. One of the earliest and most influential scholars to consider the legal rights of Indians in any detail was Franciscus de Victoria, a Dominican professor of theology at the University of Salamanca. Victoria came to the question of indigenous rights in the sixteenth century, when King Charles V asked for an opinion on the Spanish Crown's policies in America. Charles had been troubled by the sermons and writings of Bartolomé de Las Casas and the other Dominicans who condemned the Spanish treatment of the Indian population and urged the Crown to intercede on the

Native Americans' behalf. Las Casas argued that the Indians he had encountered in America were not savages but peoples possessing a distinct culture and functional institutions of their own. These Indians held the same natural rights as Europeans, Las Casas argued, and the Spanish were violating natural law by usurping their land and encroaching on their rights.[7]

Victoria used the opportunity to prepare a series of lectures on the rights of nations, which in 1557 he published as a treatise on international law. In a chapter titled "On the Indians Lately Discovered," he wrote that indigenous non-Christian peoples possessed a bundle of natural rights as free and rational people. Individual Indians possessed the same inherent rights of property as Europeans, he asserted, and indigenous polities could claim the same powers as the nations of Christian Europe. Victoria added that the papacy had not possessed the authority to appropriate the title of Indian lands; the papal donation to Spain, he wrote, had no effect on the individual and communal rights of the Native American population. Victoria, however, believed that non-Christians could lose their natural rights by committing unnatural acts. By declaring this principle, he acknowledged the legality of the Spanish Conquest. Indians were required to abide by the natural law of nations, he wrote, and certain practices, like cannibalism, idolatry, and human sacrifice, were abhorrent to that law. When a people violated these prohibitions, they forfeited their rights under natural law. Victoria added that Christians had a natural duty to civilize the Indians and convert them to their faith. Though the pope could not capriciously hand out the title of indigenous lands to Christian monarchs, he could grant the Spanish Crown an exclusive guardianship over specific groups of Indians for the purpose of converting them to Christianity. Non-Christians, at the same time, were bound by a doctrine of "natural society and fellowship" that obligated them to admit Christian missionaries into their communities. In effect, he argued, Indians had a duty to listen to the gospel, as put forth by the church's emissaries. He also wrote that natural law required Indians to admit merchants from civilized nations into their lands for the purpose of "free and open commerce." Failure to provide such hospitalities, Victoria maintained, could result in a forfeiture of the Indians' natural rights.[8]

Victoria also contended that an indigenous non-Christian community possessed political rights only if it was truly capable of governing itself. Although Indians were intellectually inferior to Europeans, he wrote, they were rational beings and possessed a right to political autonomy. But, Victoria added, some Indian peoples were so culturally inept, and their political structures so debased, that they could not adequately administer their own affairs. In that situation, Victoria contended, a "civilized" Christian nation had the right to claim sovereignty over the deficient people and teach them the benefits and methods of Christian civilization. If the Indian group opposed this guardianship, violated any part of the natural law, or refused to remedy its reprobate behavior, he concluded, a Christian nation had the right to conquer it and impose Christian order and civilization upon the recalcitrants.[9]

Victoria did not really attempt to deduce law from nature; instead, he worked backward to achieve a predetermined result. The ambiguity of Victoria's doctrine resulted from a conflict over his admiration for his Dominican brothers, his respect for Pope Innocent IV's commentary, and a pragmatic need to please the royal will. In his original lectures on Indian rights in the early 1530s, Victoria generally adopted Las Casas's humanitarian arguments, and he brazenly defended the sanctity of the natural rights of non-Christians. His rationalizations for the Spanish Conquest appeared only in the lectures dating after 1539. Victoria frankly explained in subsequent writings that Charles V had taken considerable exception to his early pronouncements recognizing Indian rights and that his treatise on the law of nations was partly an effort to accommodate the Crown. These two clearly incongruous threads of Innocent's original argument, as a result, remained bound together in Victoria's law of nations and persisted thereafter in the writings of the international legal scholars who succeeded him.[10]

When France and England joined the competition for empire, their advocates refused to accept the idea that papal donation or simple discovery entitled Spain to outright possession of the Western Hemisphere. For example, in 1540, Spain's ambassador to France reported that Francis I, the French king, had remarked that the pope did not have the power to divide the New World between Portugal and Spain, especially inasmuch as representatives of the other Christian nations had not been party to the negotiations. Francis supposedly asked the Spanish diplomat to show him the clause of Adam's will that devised the Americas to Spain. Francis ignored Alexander VI's bulls and authorized his nation's agents to trade and settle in North America.[11]

Protestants, of course, were by this time also directly repudiating the spiritual and secular authority of the papacy. Nevertheless, imperialists and speculators in England recognized the legal dilemma posed by Spain's claim of priority by first discovery and searched to find arguments that might preempt the Spanish title. In 1582, Richard Hakluyt, the English nationalist and adventurer, cited the legend of Madoc, the prince of Wales, as evidence that the English had preceded Columbus's discovery. He wrote that Madoc led an expedition that established a colony in Florida in 1170. These settlers mingled with the local Indians and spawned descendants who spread throughout North America. The purpose of the story of Madoc, of course, was to establish the chronological priority of discovery that would leapfrog

England ahead of Spain. Hakluyt, however, was unable to provide any convincing evidence of Madoc's voyage, nor could he point to a permanent
colony in America. This failure was significant because Hakluyt's monarch,
Queen Elizabeth, argued that only notorious possession and occupation established title. Elizabeth told the Spanish ambassador to her court that Spain
could not acquire possession of the Americas simply by "touching here and
there," erecting temporary shelters, or naming rivers. All nations had the
right to explore and colonize the Americas, she contended, and only actual
occupation legitimated title. On this basis, Elizabeth ordered her charges to
establish colonies in North America.[12]

England's advocates also attacked the geographical scope of the Spanish
discovery claim. The Spanish title by discovery was limited to the West In-
dies, they argued, while the lands that England had begun to colonize to
the north were far from where the Spaniards had settled. The general repudiation of the Spanish claims under papal donation and discovery opened
most of the Western Hemisphere for seizure and colonization by other European states interested in establishing American colonies. Overlapping claims
of dominion were therefore inevitable unless some systematic way of sorting out priority was devised. Thus, while the imperial powers occasionally
treated with each other to parcel out hegemony over specific parts of North
America, ultimately a nation had to be able to defend its title by military
force. Hence England's claim to its share of colonial North America was not
perfected by legal argument and persuasion, but through a series of wars
and negotiations that culminated in territorial concessions from its rivals.
By 1768 William Blackstone summed up the arguments for English dominion with a concise declaration. "Our American plantations," he wrote, were
"obtained in the last century either by right of conquest and driving out of
the natives, or by treaties."[13]

The English not only needed to defeat the claims of their continental rivals, however, they also felt obligated to construct legal fictions that undermined the significance of the quite obvious Indian possession of the land.
Under the doctrine of *terra nullius,* the English common law presumed that
lands occupied by semisedentary or migratory peoples were vacant and subject to seizure by the Crown. In the English subjugation of the Irish in 1565,
Hugh Sidney, Queen Elizabeth's lord deputy for Ireland, used the concept to
extend English dominion over the Celtic island, and over time, the argument
became a standard theme in the justifications for the English imperial incursions into America, Africa, and India. In 1598, for example, Robert Gray, a
Puritan preacher, exhorted his listeners to undertake a colonial expedition
to America and seize the land that was open for the taking: "Some affirm,
and it is likely to be true, that these savages have no particular propriety

in any part of parcel of that country, but only a general residency there, as wild beasts in the forest; for they range and wander up and down the country without any law or government, being led only by their own lusts and sensuality. . . . So that if the whole land should be taken from them, there is not a man that can complain of any particular wrong done unto him." In 1625, in the middle of the first Powhatan war, Samuel Purchas, a Puritan preacher, published a book on the history of the Virginia colony. In describing the inhabitants of the Chesapeake, Purchas wrote that Indians "range rather than inhabite" their "unmanned wild country." In 1629 John Winthrop similarly misrepresented the manner in which the Indians of New England lived when he declared that they did not actually inhabit or exploit the land. The continent, he said, was a *vacuum domicilium* set aside by God for the Puritans. (Winthrop subsequently obtained a deed for a large tract of land from the local Indians.) By fostering the myth that Indians were no-madic hunter-gatherers in a vast, virgin wilderness, the English could then apply the common law of property doctrine that allowed owners of vacant or unexploited lands to be dispossessed by others. English imperialists and colonial entrepreneurs repeated the fiction that the lands of North America were open and unexploited so often that they ultimately made the myth a part of the Anglo-American common law.[14]

A related doctrine of English law, which traced back to the Statute of Merton in 1235, held that possessors of land had a legal obligation to im-prove and cultivate it. In 1516, Thomas More mentioned the principle in his *Utopia*. It was "perfectly justifiable," he said, "to make war on people who leave their land idle and waste yet forbid the use and possession of it to others who, by the laws of nature, ought to be supported from it." Again, the English set a precedent of relying on the common law rule without taking into account the true nature of the Native Americans' use of the land. From New England to Georgia, the Indians who occupied the territory claimed by the English colonies derived most of their subsistence from agriculture. This was obvious to any English individual who ventured out into Indian coun-try. The narratives of colonists and the artwork of John White at Roanoke confirmed that the first English settlers recognized at a very early date that the Indians of the Eastern Woodlands not only lived in organized, perma-nent settlements and under some system of sociopolitical order, but they also possessed distinct plots of land that they exploited for agricultural produc-tion. Those involved in establishing English rationalizations for conquest, however, generally ignored or misrepresented this reality.[15]

Some English colonists were actually uncomfortable with expropriations grounded on fallacious presumptions. For example, in his attempts to es-tablish an independent line of title to Salem, Roger Williams argued that

Native Americans held sovereignty over and title to their lands. The Indians, he said, hunted and farmed their lands, knew and negotiated the boundaries of their holdings, and periodically burned their fields and forests to restore nutrients to the soil. These acts, Williams said, demonstrated that the Indians exercised dominion over their lands and exploited them for productive purposes. American colonists, therefore, were foreclosed from taking Indian land; they had to obtain title by negotiation and purchase. The States General of the United Netherlands institutionalized this argument in the 1620s when it ordered the Dutch West India Company to acquire land only with the consent of the Native American inhabitants. The Dutch took this position in an effort to defeat the discovery claims of Spain and England, and by 1633 Holland was expanding into Connecticut under this theory. Massachusetts moved to protect its title by acquiring deeds from the Indians in the region, and the other English colonial governments quickly realized that they could not only bolster their title but could also ameliorate some of the conflicts between their subjects and the Indians if they paid the latter for their land.[16]

At the same time that the colonial assemblies were procuring deeds from the tribes, English individuals were buying in and speculating on lands that they acquired directly from the Native Americans. Some colonists obtained deeds from individual Indians; others procured paper titles from tribal councils. Sometimes Indian individuals or councils gave deeds for the same land to more than one purchaser and thereby created fractious title conflicts among the colonists. At the earliest stages of these conveyances, different understandings of ownership put English buyers and Indian sellers at cross-purposes. While the English purchaser believed he was buying an exclusive and perpetual right of possession, the Indian sellers assumed they were conveying a right of use. The seller logically and appropriately believed that this right could be held by more than one person. Most of the colonial legislatures centralized the land acquisition process to end these title disputes. The Massachusetts assembly, for example, enacted a statute declaring that Indians held a claim to their lands under natural law. The assembly said, however, that these title rights were strictly subject to Massachusetts law. The assembly then outlawed property transactions between individual colonists and the local indigenous residents and asserted authority over the manner in which Indian lands were acquired. The colony thus made a distinction between property rights, which the Indians retained under the law, and sovereignty or dominion, which the Massachusetts Bay Company claimed under its royal charter. This differentiation between the right of possession and an overarching dominion over the land became extremely important in the conception of tribal sovereignty and property rights under American law. Other colonies eventually moved to assert control over Indian cessions, and by the middle of the eighteenth century, ten of the thirteen colonies had passed laws prohibiting individuals from acquiring Indian lands without the permission of the government.[17]

When American judges of the nineteenth century were called upon to decide cases involving questions of Indian rights, they relied on this history of colonial expansion. They also had access to the writings of scholars such as Victoria, Hugo Grotius, Samuel Pufendorf, and Jean Bodin, all of whom had attempted to construct a working law of international relations. In the first half of that century, however, the most important source on sovereignty, international law, and the rights of Indians for American lawyers and judges was a Swiss diplomat named Emmerich de Vattel. In 1758, Vattel published *The Law of Nations,* a compendium of the previous scholarship on international law. According to one scholar, judges in American courts cited Vattel's ambitious work more than any other treatise; references to and quotations from Vattel's work, many times unattributed, can be found in the opinions of such renowned federal jurists as John Marshall and Joseph Story and throughout the law reports of the state appellate courts.[18]

Vattel revealed his conception of Indian national rights in his general scheme of international relations. Vattel understood that European commercial prosperity demanded international cooperation, and he tried to revive the idea of a binding international code of conduct that would conform to contemporary circumstances. While Vattel, like his Enlightenment contemporaries, professed a belief in the theory of natural law, his law of nations integrated the positivist customary practices of European diplomatic affairs. In many ways, Vattel could be classified as a *real politician;* he believed that the principles of international law had to be capable of implementation by practical means. According to Vattel, international peace and order could be constructed only by compromises and contracts among civilized nations. To Vattel, the secret to protecting weaker nations from more powerful and aggressive states was not an overarching international authority but the establishment and preservation of a balance of power, and he encouraged small nations to band together in security arrangements with larger and more powerful ones. Regardless of their relative powers, however, Vattel believed that a nation tied in such an alliance remained sovereign and independent if "it [continued to] govern itself by its own authority and laws." Lawyers and judges who supported the principle of tribal sovereignty in the nineteenth century, including William Wirt and John Marshall, occasionally referred to this section of Vattel's treatise as a metaphor for the unique federal-Indian relationship.[19]

Vattel was particularly influential in defining and characterizing the concepts of statehood and sovereignty. He described a nation as "a body politic,

or a society of men united together for the purpose of promoting their mutual safety and advantage by their combined strength." A nation, he wrote,
should have a "public authority, to order and direct what is to be done by
each in relation to the end of the association." This political authority, he
continued, held the "sovereignty" of the nation. The sovereign government,
regardless of its form, possessed authority over every individual within the
borders of the nation; and all citizens subjected themselves to the "authority of the entire body, in every thing that relates to the common welfare."
In essence, Vattel believed that sovereignty resided in the people and that
people delegated authority to a person or group for the purpose of effective
government. He agreed with John Locke that sovereignty implied a fiduciary
relationship in which the people placed authority in trust with a government;
the government, in turn, was obligated to serve the commonweal. Vattel also
argued that the leaders of a nation had a primary duty to ensure the country's self-preservation and a responsibility to "labor for its own perfection
and for the improvement of the circumstances in which it is placed." Each
nation had a concomitant but secondary obligation: to advance the interests
and happiness of all nations. A state's obligation to the community of nations ended, however, when a proposed action threatened to impair its own
interests or survival. Ideally, Vattel wrote, all nations were independent and
deserved to be left alone, free from the interference of other nations in their
affairs. If singular nations violated these general principles, Vattel warned,
the order provided by his international code would soon disintegrate.[20]

Along with laying out the parameters of an idealized world of sovereign
neighbors, Vattel's treatise scrutinized the doctrines that Europeans had used
to justify title to their colonial claims. He argued that the European nations
violated natural law if they tried to convert or civilize the Indians without
their consent. He rejected the doctrine of discovery, and he ridiculed the
papacy's donation in the *Inter caetera divinae*. Still, he conferred legitimacy
on the theories that the English had devised for encroaching on Indian rights.
"The Law of Nations," he said, "will only recognize the ownership and
sovereignty of a Nation over unoccupied lands when the Nation, in actual
occupation of them, forms a settlement upon them or makes some actual
use of them." Vattel also accepted the English argument that the occupants
of land had a duty to exploit it for agricultural purposes. He described
agriculture as "the most useful and the most necessary" of "all arts" and
stated that the leader of a sovereign nation "should do all in his power
to have the lands under his control as well cultivated as possible." Under
natural law, he added, in what would become an infamous passage for
Native Americans, those peoples who, "though dwelling in fertile countries,
disdain in the cultivation of the soil and prefer to live by plunder . . . deserve

to be exterminated like wild beasts of prey . . . [and] may not complain if other more industrious Nations, too confined at home, should come and occupy part of their lands." Regarding the conquest of the Americas, Vattel distinguished between the tribes uprooted by the northern European nations in North America and the civilizations decimated by the Spanish Conquest: "Though the conquest of the civilized empires of Peru and Mexico was a notorious usurpation, the establishment of many colonies on the continent of North America might, on their confining themselves within just bounds, be extremely lawful. The people of those extensive tracts rather ranged through than inhabited them." He continued, "Their unsettled habitation in those immense regions cannot be accounted a true and legal possession; and the people of Europe, too pent up at home, finding land which the savages stood in no particular need, and of which they made no actual and constant use, were lawfully entitled to take possession of it, and settle it with colonies." These particular passages would haunt the Indian nations in North America in the nineteenth century as American lawyers and judges quoted them again and again to support the original expropriations of the European empires. In many cases, American judges ignored the manifest evidence of the agricultural societies that lived around them in favor of the discursive commentaries of an eighteenth-century Swiss diplomat who never saw a Native American community. Of course, be it unintentional or feigned, it was to the profound benefit of Anglo-Americans to overlook the true means of subsistence for these Indian cultures.[21]

Vattel also recognized that wars of conquest were an essential element of international law. Hugo Grotius had argued that military victory gave the conqueror absolute title over the lands and inhabitants of the conquered. Under Grotius's scheme, the conqueror could legally enslave prisoners, kill women and children, and take all of the property of the conquered nation's inhabitants. Vattel, who possessed a greater affinity for individual property rights than did Grotius, created a distinction from the latter's rule that subsequently influenced the American legal conception of the Indian title. Vattel rejected Grotius's idea that wars were all-encompassing struggles between groups of people and adopted Rousseau's conception of war as a contest between governments. Ideally, Vattel said, conquest should not affect individual property rights. While the conquering nation acquired the sovereignty over the land of the conquered, he wrote, the individual inhabitants of the vanquished country retained the right of possession and the fee title over their own private property. By bifurcating the right to land into individual ownership and an overarching national sovereignty, Vattel conformed his law of nations to the English colonial practice and made it possible for lawyers like William Wirt, who were sympathetic to the Indian cause, to argue that the United States could hold dominion over its share of the continent without disturbing the territorial rights of the Indians.[22]

Vattel admitted that the doctrine of conquest was founded on historical custom and could not be morally justified under natural law. It was "absurd and pernicious," he said, for the Catholic Church to have sustained the medieval principle of trial by battle, which gave those victorious in war a claim of righteous dominion over the vanquished. He criticized the manner in which the European empires had applied the doctrine to the Americas: "Those ambitious Europeans who attacked the American nations, and subjected them to their greedy dominion, in order, as they pretended, to civilize them, and cause them to be instructed in the true religion,—those usurpers, I say, grounded themselves on a pretext . . . unjust and ridiculous." Though Vattel despised the conquest doctrine as immoral, he accepted it as a necessary corollary of international relations. His interpretation therefore resulted in a moral anomaly; an unjust war could give rise to legal title and sovereignty. Samuel Pufendorf had earlier argued that a nation could not acquire territorial rights by simple conquest. If a belligerent nation attacked and defeated another without just cause, he said, natural law provided the victimized nation with a legal right to fight a war of reconquest to reestablish the situation to the status quo ante. The conqueror's claim could never be legally sanctified under that hypothetical condition. Pufendorf's code of international law thus naively rejected customary rules and attempted to replace them with what he believed to be pure principles deduced from nature. The international law of Vattel, in contrast, was descriptive; he recognized that there were positivist doctrines that acquired their legitimacy from practical experience. Vattel argued that Pufendorf's rule doomed nations to interminable and unnecessary wars. In his opinion, the ancient concept of just war was superseded by a greater imperative—international order. Vattel therefore held that the conquering nation, which had launched an illegitimate attack, obtained legitimate sovereignty over the land of the people victimized by the war.[23]

The Law of Nations was not only noteworthy for moral ambiguities of this sort, it was also marred by logical contradictions. Arthur Nussbaum, a student of international law, attributed these flaws to Vattel's lack of legal training. At one point, for example, Vattel declared that Indian people could lose their land to Europeans if they were not cultivating the soil. In another part of the text, he maintained that the imperial powers of Europe could reserve lands in North America for future settlement. Then, just a few paragraphs after that passage, he wrote: "No nation has a right to expel another people from the country they inhabit, in order to settle in it herself. . . . Every people ought to be contented with that which has fallen to their share."

The logic in *The Law of Nations* was so pervasively lacking in consistency that Jeremy Bentham later commented that Vattel's conception of a rational proof was a statement like "It is not just to do what is unjust."[24]

That failing did not prevent Vattel's work from becoming accepted as the preeminent treatise on Indian rights in the nineteenth century. Under Vattel's law of nations, the Indian tribes of America were inherently the sovereign equivalents of the European states. Vattel, however, adopted the legal fictions that imperialistic scholars like Victoria and English nationalists like Hakluyt had devised to justify the invasion of Native America. In essence, Vattel promoted a Machiavellian code of international self-interest. The result was an ambiguous international law that tipped its hat to Native American natural rights but subordinated those rights to the whims of the imperial powers. Though the Swiss diplomat had hoped to create a comprehensive, consistent code of international conduct, he instead left his readers with a law of nations that was so ambiguous that his work would be, as Clive Perry wrote, "quoted on every side in every dispute." This was clearly true in the Removal Crisis debates over indigenous rights. In his law of nations, Vattel had preserved the two lines of argument that had originated with Victoria's intellectual abdication to King Charles V's demands. Those sympathetic to the concept of tribal sovereignty latched on to the idealism of Vattel's natural law principles; those who rejected the idea referred to his positivist affirmation of conquest. Vattel thus provided the opportunity for American lawyers and judges to rationalize the taking of Indian land and the destruction of Native Americans' national rights. The Swiss diplomat's treatise proved particularly useful to the southern judges in the Removal Crisis cases of the 1830s. The imprimatur of language drawn from the dean of international law comforted and provisioned those judges who were looking for intellectual rationalizations to justify the expropriation of Native American land.[25]

The Natural Rights of Indians:
Justice William Johnson and *Fletcher v. Peck*

The southern state courts were also influenced by, and selectively applied, precedents established by the United States Supreme Court. The Supreme Court first examined the issues of Indian land and political rights in *Fletcher v. Peck* (1810), the case that concluded the long-running dispute over title to the Yazoo territory. Constitutional historians have traditionally marked the case for significance because of John Marshall's novel use of the Contract Clause to strike down state legislative attacks on vested property rights and for the chief justice's comments on the role of the government and the judiciary in commercial dealings. *Fletcher v. Peck* also merits a noteworthy place in the history of American Indian law, for in what some have considered *obiter dictum,* Marshall and Associate Justice William Johnson engaged in a brief but influential debate on the nature and breadth of American Indian territorial and political rights. In a sentence tucked in the last lines of his opinion, Marshall suggested that the Indian tribes living in Yazoo held a possessory title that might be extinguishable by state action. Johnson took issue with this statement. He argued that the Indian tribes were sovereign nations and possessed a full and legitimate title paramount to the preemptive rights of the states. Proponents of Indian rights have long pointed to *Worcester v. Georgia* as the foundation of tribal sovereignty, but the genesis of that principle in American law is laid out in Johnson's separate opinion in *Fletcher v. Peck.*[26]

The Yazoo territory, so called for the river that meanders through western Mississippi, was bounded by the Alabama, Coosa, and Chattahoochee Rivers in the east, the Mississippi River in the west, and the thirty-first and thirty-fifth parallels to the north and south. At various times in the colonial era, Spain, France, and England claimed sovereignty over the thirty-five million acres that constituted the Yazoo area. Their paper titles and legal arguments, however, meant little to the Choctaws, Cherokees, Creeks, and Chickasaws who occupied the greater portion of the region. In 1785 the state of Georgia, which had succeeded to the British claim to Yazoo after the American Revolution, initiated efforts to sell the territory. The state's treasury was empty and the legislature needed money to pay the salaries of militia troops it posted on the Creek-Georgia frontier.[27] For the next ten years, Georgia offered the territory to various groups of speculators. Some of the syndicates approached Alexander McGillivray, the most influential Creek leader of the era, about investing in enterprises to purchase the Yazoo. They understood that McGillivray's support would be essential, for only he, they believed, could convince the Creek Nation to surrender its claim to the territory. McGillivray rightly suspected, however, that Georgia's efforts to sell the Yazoo were part of a plan to coerce the Creeks into outright cessions of their tribal lands. By creating a class of purchasers eager to resell the land at a profit, he understood, the Georgia legislature would generate a powerful lobby for extinguishing the Indian title in the state. In responding to the overtures, McGillivray said that he was unwilling to invest in a venture that was dependent on the extinguishment of the outstanding claims of the other tribes living in the Yazoo and that he would not jeopardize the sovereignty of the Creek Nation. McGillivray's opposition ultimately did not thwart the sale of the territory. Eventually, in 1795, the Georgia legislature completed contracts with several syndicates for sales of large chunks of the Yazoo territory. In the enabling act authorizing the sales, the state claimed in a fit of redundancy that it held "full possession" of the Yazoo and that it owned "the jurisdiction and territorial right," "the fee simple," and "the right of preemption" over the region. At the same time, however, its officials were quietly begging the federal government to extinguish the title of the Indians who were living there.[28]

The Georgia public soon learned that the sale of the Yazoo was a massive political fraud. Well-connected federal and state officials owned considerable interests in the various syndicates that purchased parts of the territory, and all but one of the state legislators received a bribe in exchange for a vote to authorize the grants. Outraged opponents of the scheme and rival politicians on the make exposed the deals behind the Yazoo legislation, and when Georgia voters discovered that the sales price for the Yazoo averaged one and half cents an acre, far below fair market value, and that the sale had been facilitated by bribes, they threw out most of the legislature in protest.[29] The anti-Yazooists, as they came to be called, campaigned on a promise to rescind the sale, and in the election of 1795 they took control of the Georgia assembly. On February 13, 1796, the new legislature repealed the enabling act and nullified the 1795 grants. The reformers declared Yazoo to be the "sole property of the state" and ordered the clerk to strike the conveyance documents from its minutes. The conquering reformers took the offensive papers out to the capitol square and ceremoniously burned them with a flame sparked by the purifying rays of the sun focused through a magnifying glass. On the same day as the rescission act, however, the Georgia Mississippi Company, one of the original purchasers, conveyed one of the largest tracts (about eleven million acres) in the Yazoo to the New England Mississippi Land Company. The latter group quickly claimed to be a bona fide third-party purchaser completely ignorant of the corruption behind the original sale. Since it was innocent to the fraudulent transaction, the company claimed, it deserved to have its title recognized or receive compensation for the loss.

The purchasers, however, were limited in their remedies. The Eleventh Amendment prohibited suits against the state in federal court, and the rescission legislation denied potential claimants standing before Georgia's tribunals. Consequently, for several years the Yazoo purchasers fought their battle to have the sale confirmed, or to be reimbursed, in the United States Congress. Supporters of the Yazooists presented several bills awarding compensation to the New England Mississippi Company investors, but each time the legislation was defeated on party and sectional lines. Federalists tended to support compensation on the grounds that property rights created by government contracts were vested and sacrosanct. Republicans, who by 1800 held enough seats to rebuff Federalist compensation efforts, argued that the people of Georgia had the right to nullify a transaction that would not have occurred but for the wholesale corruption of the state's political system. The dispute also fomented sectional divisions. Congressmen from the North tended to support compensation because most of the investors were their Federalist constituents, while those from the South generally stood firmly on popular ground with the Republican anti-Yazooists in Georgia. Unable to construct a majority in favor of compensation, the Yazooists moved the fight to the courtroom. A legal decree recognizing the validity of the original state conveyance, they believed, would increase congressional support for their compensation claims. In a collusive case that used the diversity of citizenship rule to avoid the Eleventh Amendment problem, on June 1, 1803, Robert Fletcher of New Hampshire filed suit against John Peck of Massachusetts for a "covenant broken" in his purchase of Yazoo land. Fletcher claimed that the Georgia rescission and nullification act placed a cloud on the title of the fifteen thousand acres of Yazoo land that Peck sold him and that Peck never held title to convey. He asked the court to order Peck to return the purchase price. At issue was the character of the title held by the New England Mississippi Company, the effect on that title of Georgia's repeal of the original grant, and the propriety of the New England Mississippi Company's claim for compensation. In 1806 the United States Circuit Court for Massachusetts found for Peck, upheld the validity of the 1795 sale, and struck down the Georgia legislature's subsequent repeal. Fletcher appealed for a writ of error to the Supreme Court, which heard arguments on the case in 1809 and again a year later.[30]

Only Marshall and Johnson issued opinions in the decision; they thus continued a polite confrontation that began with Johnson's appointment to the Court. In the elections of 1800, the Republican Party took control of Congress, and its leader, Thomas Jefferson, won the presidency. The Federalists feared that the Republicans would roll back their efforts to empower the central government, and they took several steps to forestall the Republican revolution in their last weeks in office. In February 1801, the Federalists pushed a new judiciary act through Congress, hoping that judges sympathetic to their cause would safeguard their principles of vested property interests, strong executive authority, and federal supremacy. The legislation broadened the jurisdiction of the federal courts and added sixteen seats to the lower federal bench. The departing president, John Adams, immediately filled these new judgeships with Federalists. Adams and the Federalists also hoped to preserve their political philosophy by maintaining influence on the Supreme Court. The best way to do that, they believed, was to appoint a strong-willed and persuasive Federalist as chief justice. When Oliver

Ellsworth retired as chief in the fall of 1800, Adams asked John Jay to fill the opening. Jay declined, and Adams turned to John Marshall, a Virginia lawyer, a staunch Federalist, and, most recently, the secretary of state.[31]

Marshall immediately set out to consolidate his position and impose the will of the Federalists on the Court. Before Marshall's appointment, each justice had prepared his own opinion in most of the Court's cases, a practice that projected indecision to the public. The new chief justice urged his brothers on the Court to issue unified opinions that clearly declared the conclusions of the majority. Marshall wrote these opinions in almost every case, and he implemented an organic process of judicial compromise that marks the Court's operating procedure to this day. Keenly aware of the Court's feeble position relative to the executive and legislative branches, Marshall understood that a unified Court would slowly garner respect from the public, the states, the Congress, and the president. From that fountain of respect, Marshall believed, flowed authority. Moreover, by strengthening the Court, the chief justice knew that he could better promote the Federalists' nationalist agenda. Because the Constitution provided for life terms for the justices, the Federalist philosophy could then be perpetuated and passed down in precedents to succeeding generations of lawyers and judges.[32]

The Federalists' midnight reformation of the judiciary sparked immediate reaction from the Republicans. In 1801, Jefferson wrote, "The Federalists have retired into the judiciary as a stronghold . . . and from that battery all the works of republicanism are to be beaten down and erased." Jefferson's party did what it could to besiege the Federalist fortress. Along with repealing the Judiciary Act of 1801, the Republicans secured the removal of the Federalist district judge John Pickering and brought impeachment proceedings against Samuel Chase, a Federalist on the Supreme Court. In the midst of this partisan acrimony, an ill Alfred Moore of Georgia retired from the bench. Jefferson selected William Johnson, a young South Carolina legislator and judge, as Moore's replacement and charged him with asserting a Republican force to counter Marshall's powerful presence.[33]

To his supporters, Johnson appeared to be the remedy to Marshall's contagious centralism. While the chief justice was willing to compromise for the sake of unanimity, Johnson was stubbornly independent and idealistic. The South Carolina judge was the son of a radical blacksmith who had been a leader of the Liberty Tree Party in Charleston, a group of mechanics and artisans who fomented antagonism toward Great Britain. One witness recalled that Johnson's father, who served on the city's committee of correspondence, was the first person in Charleston to call for independence. During the Revolutionary War, the British seized Charleston, captured Johnson's father, and shipped him with sixty-six other rebels to a St. Augustine jail. Though

he was eventually released in an exchange of prisoners, the episode left a
deep impression on the younger Johnson. As for many of his generation, the
Revolution became the central event in his intellectual development and the
struggle for liberty the ideological core of his political and judicial philosophy. Looking back at his childhood, Johnson wrote that the Revolution was
"a pillar of fire" that had the effect of "conduct[ing] man to that high destiny
for which his powers are calculated." Johnson's opinions, consequently, reflected a suspicion of arbitrary power, a fervent respect for democracy, and
an affinity for natural rights theory. As a jurist, he attempted to preserve
the constitutional supremacy of the legislature, and he constantly preached
that courts should refrain from infringing on the prerogatives of elected
assemblies. At the same time, Johnson viewed the judiciary as a bulwark
against encroachments on individual rights. "The basis of individual security
and the bond of union between the ruler and the citizen," he wrote, "must
ever be found in a judiciary sufficiently independent to disregard the will of
power, and sufficiently energetic to secure to the citizen the full enjoyment
of his rights." [34]

Johnson apprenticed with Charles Cotesworth Pinckney in Charleston,
was admitted to the city bar in 1793, and achieved what one biographer
called "almost unparalleled success." Though Pinckney was emerging as a
prominent national voice for the Federalists, his second cousin, also named
Charles Pinckney, was the leader of a group of discontented politicians that
developed into the Republican Party of South Carolina. The Republican philosophy appealed to Johnson, and he became active in the state organization.
Johnson could not have announced his loyalties at a more propitious time,
and he rapidly ascended up the pyramid of influence. In 1794 he was elected
to the state legislature, by 1798 he was Speaker of the South Carolina house,
and a year later the legislature appointed him to the state court of common pleas. Senator Thomas Sumter and Congressman Wade Hampton, the
state's two most influential politicians, advised Jefferson to select Johnson
for the Supreme Court. They described Johnson as "an excellent lawyer,
prompt, eloquent, of irreproachable character, Republican connections, and
of good nerves in his political principles." He was the kind of judge, they
implied, who could act as a countervailing force to the willful Marshall. Just
as his contemporaries, students of Johnson's work have invariably compared
him to the chief justice. William Johnson, said one of his biographers, "approached constitutional decisions with an acute sense of history . . . [and]
felt that human experience not only shaped law, but should be a guiding
principle in its enunciation." Marshall, in contrast, "tended to see law as a
controlling element in human society." Johnson was also not as attuned to
the political implications of his decisions as the chief justice, most scholars

agree, and he typically voted his conscience with relative disregard for party ties and sectional interests.[35]

This was abundantly clear in the Yazoo decision, for Johnson's opinion ran counter to the interests of his native South. Moreover, if Johnson's position on Indian rights had been adopted as the majority view, he would have established a difficult obstacle for his party's scheme for western agrarian expansion. Unlike Marshall, Johnson believed that every justice should write his own opinion in cases involving constitutional issues, and he refused to be coerced into joining the chief justice's majorities. This pugnacity, however, came at a cost. In 1822, Johnson wrote of the isolation that he felt on the Court. His years as the only consistent opponent of Marshall, he complained to Jefferson, had been "no bed of roses." He agreed with Marshall's desires to promote the authority of the Court, Johnson said, but not so much that he could put "private or party feeling" above the country's interests. He could not conscientiously join majorities, as he believed Marshall did, that were "contrary to his own judgment and vote." It was this independence of thought that earned Johnson the moniker of "the First Dissenter" from early chroniclers of the Court. Johnson described to Jefferson the treatment he received from Marshall and Bushrod Washington when he brought to the Court from the South Carolina bench his belief in separate opinions: "Some case soon occurred in which I differed from my brethren, and I thought it a thing of course to deliver my opinion. But, during the rest of the session I heard nothing but lectures on the indecency of judges cutting at each other, and the loss of reputation which the Virginia appellate court had sustained by pursuing such a course." Johnson wrote that he soon learned to join majority opinions occasionally to "ben[d] to the current." Johnson joined Marshall's majorities more frequently, however, than he let on, and he proved to be an early example of how unpredictable the Supreme Court nomination process could be and how a judge with a seemingly firm ideological philosophy could disappoint, confuse, and infuriate the president who had appointed him for partisan reasons. Johnson sat on the Court for thirty years, a period that almost spanned the entire Marshall era, but he was rarely successful in restraining Marshall's federal expansion. Still, he remained vigorously independent and positioned himself in most cases as a centrist in the debate over the appropriate size and authority of the federal government. On the one hand, the South Carolina justice authored the majority opinion in *United States v. Hudson and Goodwin* that prohibited the development of a federal common law of crimes. On the other hand, in *Cohens v. Virginia* and *Martin v. Hunter's Lessee*, Johnson added powerful rationale to support Marshall's enhancement of federal judicial authority.[36]

In *Fletcher v. Peck*, Johnson followed his independent tendencies by joining and dissenting from specific pieces of Marshall's majority opinion. In affirming the lower court's holding, Marshall rendered a now famous and significant construction of the Constitution's Contract Clause, which states: "No party shall . . . pass any . . . law impairing the obligations of contracts." The chief justice concluded that the original Georgia grant was a contract that merited the protection of the clause, thereby extending its application to agreements, conveyances, and grants executed by the state governments. The federal courts, he added, had the authority to strike down state laws, like the Georgia rescission, that impaired the obligations of private and public contracts. *Fletcher,* therefore, reduced the states in this instance to the status of a private party and foreshadowed the famous Marshall cases—*McCulloch v. Maryland, Dartmouth College v. Woodward, Gibbons v. Ogden,* and *Worcester v. Georgia*—in which his Court voided constitutionally offensive state enactments. Marshall thereby gave Supreme Court sanction to the doctrine of vested property rights and furthered the Federalist agenda of protecting business and property interests from popular legislation. Marshall believed it was of utmost importance to the commercial progress of the nation to protect the sanctity of land titles. Consequently, he upheld the common law principle of bona fide purchaser, a theory that protected innocent third-party buyers from loss by fraud in a conveyance earlier in the chain of title, even in a situation where the public's revulsion to the agreement seemed reasonable. After *Fletcher,* as a result, American commercial transactions enjoyed a measure of constitutional protection against governmental interference. On this logic, the chief justice ended the fifteen-year-old conflict over the Yazoo territory. And in 1814, with the favorable ruling in hand, the Yazooists ushered a bill through Congress that compensated those who lost their investment in the scandal.[37]

Though *Fletcher* resolved the conflict between the speculators, it did not provide clear title for the purchasers. Despite the serious issues raised by the residence of Indians in Yazoo, Marshall's comments on their rights appear to be almost an afterthought. Perhaps Marshall felt uncomfortable issuing a definitive statement on the rights of a group not party to the case. Luther Martin had raised the point on oral argument on behalf of the New England Mississippi Company and had contended that the Indian title was a "mere occupancy for the purpose of hunting." "It is not like our tenures," he said in paraphrasing Vattel. "[T]hey have no idea of a title to the soil itself. It is overrun by them, rather than inhabited. It is not a true and legal possession." Martin's argument had become commonplace among those eager to extinguish the Indian title, and his enunciation of the theory of unexploited lands in *Fletcher* may have popularized the concept even further. For instance, soon after the decision was published, Henry

Middleton, a South Carolina legislator, urged President James Madison to purchase the remaining Cherokee lands in the northwestern corner of his state. Middleton wrote that the Cherokee parcel was "cultivable," "one of the most desirable and healthful portions of our country," and would "redound to the benefit of the agricultural interests of the state." Since the Cherokees were not exploiting the land, he suggested, it could be seized by the government.[38]

Marshall, however, was not ready to break with past policy and extend American sovereignty completely over all Indian lands. He noted only that the lands involved in the Yazoo battle were also claimed by Native Americans, and he implied that addressing the claims of the Creek, Choctaw, Chickasaw, and Cherokee Nations was not as easy as passing a simple compensation bill. Apparently, the chief justice was less concerned at this time with giving judicial sanction to any particular legal doctrine than he was with promoting a course that would benefit the national interest and the authority of the Court. The future of U.S.-Indian relations revolved around the question of who held title and sovereignty to the country west of the Appalachians—the states, the federal government, or the Indian nations. Marshall was not prepared to issue a conclusive opinion on the subject and delicately noted that Georgia's claim was "subject to the Indian title." He added: "The majority of the court is of opinion that the nature of the Indian title, which is certainly to be respected by all courts, until it be legitimately extinguished, is not such as to be absolutely repugnant to seizin in fee on the part of the state." In other words, Marshall allowed that Native Americans held some vague possessory interest in their lands, but he was not yet prepared to define this interest or deny that it could be extinguished by unilateral state or federal action. He did not explain what he meant by the "Indian title" or how the competing interests of Indians, the federal government, and Georgia could be reconciled. Nor did he indicate whether the states or the federal government held the power to extinguish the Indian title. Clearly though, most with an opinion at that time, including even the most expansion-minded Georgia officials, believed that the states had surrendered that authority to the federal government at the Constitutional Convention. As part of the Compact of 1802, in fact, Georgia had patently conceded that the national government held the power to extinguish the Indian title. Marshall felt no sense of urgency on the issue, however, and left it open for future consideration.[39]

The chief justice accepted Martin's general proposition that either the states or the federal government (he did not say which) had acquired political sovereignty over the Indian tribes with the American victory in the Revolutionary War. He recounted how Georgia's chain of title descended from the

English Crown, but he noted that the Yazoo territory lay west of the line established in the Proclamation of 1763. Speculators in the Revolutionary era who wanted to purchase land directly from the Indians had argued that King George's decree, which prohibited settlement west of the Appalachians, terminated Georgia's claim and validated the title and sovereignty of the Indian nations west of George's line of demarcation. Marshall, at this time, refused to interpret the proclamation as a permanent acknowledgment of Native American title. It was only a "temporary arrangement" that "suspended" settlement of the West and was not intended to alter the western boundaries of the colonies. Nevertheless, he concluded, the Indians retained the right to occupy these lands until their rights had been extinguished.[40]

While Marshall's opinion on the rights of the Indians in Yazoo was coy and reserved, Johnson's concurring opinion was clear and typically devoid of concern for its political ramifications. The South Carolina justice tried to use the federal judicial power to preserve the political integrity of the Native American nations against the sneaking encroachment permitted by Marshall's majority opinion. Johnson encouraged his brethren to recognize the right of the unconquered and unassimilated Indian nations to exist as independent, sovereign states. He rejected the idea that Georgia possessed the right to seize Indian lands. Georgia's title to Yazoo, Johnson wrote, "amounted to nothing more than a mere possibility" that the state might acquire those lands from the Indians by purchase. As such, Georgia's sale of the Yazoo lands was only a promise to convey to the speculative companies in the event that it acquired title to those lands in the future. The question turned on the legal status of the Indian nations, and national status varied among the many tribes: "Some have totally extinguished their national fire, and submitted themselves to the laws of the states; others have, by treaty, acknowledged that they hold their national existence at the will of the state within which they reside; others retain a limited sovereignty, and the absolute proprietorship of their soil." This last situation, he said, described the tribes in the Yazoo territory. Johnson added that whites were "legislat[ing] upon the conduct of strangers or citizens" within the boundaries of Native American nations even though "innumerable" treaties acknowledged their national independence. By acquiring lands by treaty in the past, the United States had "uniformly" recognized the Native American right of sovereignty. The majority's assertion, he concluded, that one nation could hold a fee simple or reversionary title to land in which the sovereignty was held by another was ultimately irrational. The Southeastern Indians were independent peoples who retained an "absolute right of soil," and claims by the state and federal governments could be characterized only as restrictions of priority to purchase against European interlopers.[41]

Johnson never provided the countervailing leadership on the Cou[...]
Jefferson and his party so desperately sought. In this case, as with most of
the others in the Marshall era, the chief justice was able to pull the other
justices to his point of view. Johnson's voice was overwhelmed by Marshall's
popularity and forcefulness, and the South Carolina justice's tendency to
isolate himself from the majority in separate opinions left him alone on
the Court. Despite occasional moments of significance, as in the case of
Hudson and Goodwin, Johnson sank into the backwaters of American legal
history. He did, however, leave an indelible mark in Indian law as the
first advocate on the Supreme Court for the legitimacy of Native American
national sovereignty. He, in short, imported a long-standing argument in
favor of the natural rights of Indians into American legal thought. His
opinion, moreover, agreed with the principles behind the existing federal
policies toward the Indian tribes. Henry Knox had based his policy reforms
on the presumption that the tribes were sovereign nations holding title to
their land; Johnson tried to bring American law in line with that conception.
When succeeding advocates of Native American rights looked for support
for the idea that the Indian tribes possessed political and territorial rights,
they could point to Johnson's opinion in *Fletcher.*

Marshall's opinion, though, became the law of the land, and his comments on the Indian title became influential dicta, if not controlling precedent, to the state courts during the Removal Crisis. The chief justice's opinion on Indian rights was circumspect for several reasons. Primarily, he was
delicately protecting the authority of the Court. As a Federalist, he believed
that it was the federal government that had the power to extinguish the Indian title. Yet he saw no reason to incite the Indian tribes, who wanted to
retain complete dominion over their lands, or Georgia, which was beginning
to push the federal government to extinguish the rights of the Cherokees
and Creeks. Marshall acknowledged that the Indian tribes retained some
vague possessory interest in their lands and implied that Native Americans
should have a voice in future land cessions. By limiting the Indian title to
a mere right of occupancy, however, he avoided constructing a permanent
obstacle to American expansion into the West. Marshall's comments on the
Indian title offered calming assurances to both Native American leaders and
southern expansionists. But the chief justice's dangerous dicta that implied
that the southern states could perhaps extinguish the Indian usufruct or,
alternatively, sell land in spite of the Indian title, prolonged, and perhaps
exacerbated, the tribal title question. By postponing an official enunciation
of federal supremacy over Indian affairs, Marshall also unwittingly invited
southern politicians and judges to challenge Congress's authority and allowed a states' rights boil to fester into what eventually became the crisis

of the Indian Removal. In sum, the chief justice's ambiguous discussion of the "Indian title" provided temporary political quiescence rather than legal certitude and did nothing to slow down the encroachments of whites onto Indian lands.[42]

While Marshall's construction of the Contract Clause has historically been praised as a necessary precursor to American commercial expansion, his decision on the Indian title has gone relatively unnoticed by most constitutional historians. One of Marshall's biographers noted, for example, that "*Fletcher v. Peck* was one of those rare cases in which everyone profited. The original purchasers, including the members of the 1795 legislature, were generously compensated; their opponents in Georgia acquired political office; and the state resold the land to the United States for $1,250,000— which was more than double the original sales price. The federal government received territory it had long wanted . . . and was able to resell it at a substantial profit."[43]

Despite this sanguine summary, there was a distinct class of losers in the Yazoo case. The Court left the Native American nations of the Southeast to be molested by southern state expansionists and trespassed upon by white squatters. During the long litigation over Yazoo, the state of Georgia continually tried to force the Creeks and Cherokees to cede their lands in the state and encouraged settlers to move onto their lands. The Indians, in turn, constantly complained to the federal government about the trespasses. Soon after the Yazoo grant, the House of Representatives committee appointed to consider the disposition of Indian lands criticized the Yazoo sale, noted that the purchasers' titles depended on the extinguishment of the Indian title, and warned that Georgia's conveyance "threatened to embroil the government with the neighboring Indians." The committee then urged President George Washington to "use all constitutional and legal means, to prevent the infraction of the treaties made with the Indian tribes."[44]

Motivated by this admonition, the federal government moved to reconcile the differences between Georgia and the two tribes. For example, in the summer of 1796, the War Department brought the Creeks and state officials together at Coleraine, a small village on the St. Mary's River. James Jackson, the leader of the anti-Yazooist revolt, chaired the Georgia delegation. The fundamental positions of the parties, however, were wholly irreconcilable. Georgia wanted Creek land, and the Creeks refused to surrender it. At the same time, each side claimed that it was owed compensation for murders inflicted by the other on its people. The Creeks also complained that Georgians allowed their livestock to destroy their crops, fished out their streams, and hunted their game into extinction. Rather than resolving these differences, the negotiations exacerbated the enmity between the antagonists. The treaty that emerged from this conference did little to quench Georgia's demand for land free and clear of the Indian title; in essence, the Treaty of Coleraine only reaffirmed the border that had been established in the 1790 Treaty of New York. Although the treaty was practically meaningless in reordering borders or relations, it illustrated the heavy-handed tactics that Georgia used, and would continue to use, against its Indian neighbors. The arrogance of its delegates is palpable in the record, and the formal negotiations were replete with the state's efforts to cow the Creeks and subvert the federal negotiators. Before Georgia ratified the Constitution, it had concluded its own treaties with the Creeks. In three of these negotiations, the state had convinced small dissident groups, who were not formal representatives of the tribe, to sign cessions of the land that it wanted. The Georgia delegation tried the same tactic at Coleraine. When that failed, the state attempted to intimidate the Creeks and the neutral federal commissioners. At the beginning of the conference, Jackson tried to bring a platoon of the state militia to the treaty grounds. The state's representatives were clearly preparing to force the Creeks into signing a treaty if they did not do so voluntarily. When the federal commissioners refused to admit the soldiers, Jackson complained that the honor of his delegation and the state's sovereignty were being impugned. Jackson finally relented, but the episode foreshadowed a tendency toward intimidation and fraud that would become commonplace in the state's efforts to procure Indian land over the next forty years.[45]

While Georgia pressured the federal government to obtain this cession on its behalf, its delegates denied that the Indians had title to convey. They argued that the Indians were not exploiting their land and that the state was overpopulated and needed more territory: "Now when one nation has fewer people and more land than another nation, which has a great many people, and not land enough for them to live on, the earth being the nursing mother for all, white men or red men, the nation which has fewest people, and most land, ought to part with a little of it to the other nation, at a reasonable price." The Creeks, recognizing the state's disingenuous intentions, responded: "We are told that those lands are of no service to us, but still, we consider that, if we can hold our lands, there will always be a turkey or a deer, or, in the streams of water, a fish to be found, for our young generation, that will come after us. We are afraid that, if we part with any more of our lands, that at last the white people will not suffer us to keep as much as will be sufficient to bury our dead." Over and over again, the Creeks told the federal and state delegates that they would cede no more land. At the conclusion of the negotiations, the federal representatives chastised the state for its methods and confirmed the Creeks' sincerity to the governor of Georgia. Until the state could convince the Creeks that its intentions were "upright," they wrote, "we are of the opinion that all attempts to acquire land from them, by fair and open purchase, will be ineffectual." The Creeks finally acquiesced to another cession of land in Georgia in 1801. In return, federal commissioners promised that this would be the last request for their land. Efau Hadjo, a Creek chief, responded by warning, "If any man come to us after land, we shall say he has not authority for what he says; and we also put an end to all claims for property against my nation." The Creek leaders continued to remind the United States of this promise when later requests for more land were made.[46]

The movement of white settlers onto the lands of the Creeks and Cherokees continued unabated throughout the Yazoo controversy despite the federal commissioners' assurances and despite promises made in the Treaties of Hopewell and New York. For example, not long after the Supreme Court's decision in *Fletcher v. Peck*, the Creek chief Hoboithle Mico complained to President James Madison that whites were still trespassing into the Creek Nation. In *Fletcher*, Marshall had an opportunity to make a powerful statement against these encroachments but refused to do so. At this early date, a strong pronouncement from the majority in favor of Native American sovereignty, along the lines of Johnson's opinion, might have persuaded the state of Georgia that the federal government meant to abide by its treaties with the Creeks and the Cherokees and prevented Georgians from moving into their nations. Unfortunately for the Indians in Georgia, the Court was not prepared to issue that declaration as a majority. The Creeks and the Cherokees, however, knew full well the intent of the parties at New York and Hopewell and continued to push the federal government to protect their territorial integrity from the encroachments of the white trespassers. In a report to the War Department, Benjamin Hawkins, the American agent to the Creek Nation, wrote, "The Creeks are to a certain extent an independent people and treated as such by the United States. They claim and have long claimed the jurisdiction . . . over lands in their territory." The failure of the Court to confirm Hawkins's understanding of the federal-Indian relationship at this opportune time prompted Georgia officials, who were beginning to argue that the idea of Indian national sovereignty was an infringement on their state's rights, to continue to allow the state's citizens to move across the border into the Creek and Cherokee Nations. The chief justice's ambiguous comments on the Indian title thus encouraged the subsequent state attack on the sovereign rights of the Southeastern tribes. In many cases during his term, Marshall strengthened the Court and the federal government by measured compromise and judicious restraint. In *Fletcher,* this moderation was debilitating to Indian interests.[47]

The Americanization of Imperialism:
Chief Justice John Marshall and *Johnson v. McIntosh*

In 1823 the Supreme Court finally turned its full attention to the issues of Indian political status and land title. In *Johnson v. McIntosh,* the Court provided a more definitive analysis of where the Indian tribes fit into the American federal system. John Marshall's unanimous opinion, however, like his work in *Fletcher,* spawned confusion about the nature of tribal rights. On the one hand, the chief justice admitted that the Indian nations possessed a right to occupy their lands; his discussion of the Indian usufruct, in fact, is the most important elaboration of that right among the early federal cases. On the other hand, Marshall also ruled that the United States held political dominion over the Indian lands by virtue of the doctrines of discovery and conquest. According to the chief justice, the Indian tribes' right of possession and their political existence were subject to being extinguished at any time. Marshall's unfortunate choice of words and his selection of precedents also did little to protect Indian interests. By reinvigorating the outdated stereotype of Native Americans as hunter-gatherers living in communities devoid of social and political institutions, he provided dicta that the Georgia, Alabama, and Tennessee courts subsequently exploited to justify the dispossession of the Indian nations in their states.[48]

As in *Fletcher,* the question of Native American rights emerged in a land dispute in which Indians were not before the bar. In *Johnson v. McIntosh,* the Supreme Court was asked to resolve the conflicting claims to a large tract of land in the Illinois country. In 1773 two merchants named William Murray and Louis Viviat acquired two large parcels from the Illinois Indians on behalf of their investment syndicate, the Illinois-Wabash Company. The Illinois-Wabash Company investors included the plaintiff, Thomas Johnson of Maryland. The lands, one at the confluence of the Ohio and Mississippi Rivers and the other at the junction of the Mississippi and Illinois Rivers, were part of the vast territory described in the Virginia Charter of 1609. They were also within the old "Indian country" delineated in the Proclamation of 1763, the royal decree that, among other things, prohibited colonial Americans from making individual purchases from the Indians west of the Appalachians. When the British commander of Fort Gage attempted, pursuant to the proclamation, to prohibit the Illinois purchase, Murray gave the officer a copy of an opinion issued by the British jurists Lord Camden and Lord Yorke. In 1757 Camden and Yorke had considered the property rights of British colonists who acquired land directly from the native inhabitants of India. Great Britain, of course, claimed sovereignty and fee title over the entire Indian subcontinent under the doctrines of discovery and conquest. Camden and Yorke held that if lands claimed by the British Crown were unconquered in fact, British individuals could purchase them directly from the indigenous residents. British sovereignty and law, they wrote, traveled with the nation's subjects into infidel lands and were "received" by their colonists. They also added, however, that under natural law, the national sovereignty of the native residents continued and the land title remained with the native owners until they were truly subjugated by the empire. Murray and Viviat told the commander of Fort Gage that Camden and Yorke's decision controlled in North America. The American Indians possessed the title to their lands as the original occupants of the continent, they warned, and the empire's agents could not enjoin a free Englishman from buying land directly from the Indians. The commander of Fort Gage relented, and Murray and Viviat concluded their purchase from the Illinois. Two years later, Viviat secured two more tracts for the Illinois-Wabash group on the upper Ohio from the Piankashaws.[49]

The outbreak of the Revolutionary War prevented the Illinois-Wabash Company from taking possession of or developing its purchase. As the war progressed, several other events seriously complicated the syndicate's claim. In 1778 the Continental Army under George Rogers Clark seized control of the region from the British. In 1779 the Virginia legislature declared that it possessed the right of preemption to the Indian title within its borders, that individuals could no longer purchase directly from the Indians, and that any such purchases made previous to the legislation were null and void. Political developments after the war further confused the Illinois-Wabash claim. In 1784 Virginia surrendered its claims northwest of the Ohio to the United States government as part of the compromise over the landed states' (those states that possessed charters reaching to the Mississippi River or the Pacific Ocean) western holdings. In that agreement, the national government also repudiated the claims of those who had purchased land from the Indians before the war. In 1787 Congress established the Northwest Territory, surveyed it, and divided it up for sale. The Indian tribes living in the old Northwest continued to occupy the region until 1794, when American troops under "Mad" Anthony Wayne defeated a confederacy of Indian nations at the Battle of Fallen Timbers. The defeat forced the tribes to cede their claims to much of the region north of the Ohio to the United States in the Treaty of Greenville. With this cession, the United States assumed dominion over the land purchased by the Illinois-Wabash syndicate.[50]

Having had its title pulled out from under it, the Illinois-Wabash group repeatedly petitioned Congress between 1781 and 1816 to acknowledge its claim. The government consistently refused, and in 1818 Congress sold more than eleven thousand acres of the Piankashaw tract to William McIntosh.[51] All of these developments effectively produced two competing chains of title originating from nations that, at the time of original sale, claimed political sovereignty over the same land. To clarify, Johnson claimed ownership through the Illinois-Wabash Company out of the Piankashaws and the Illinois; McIntosh asserted title from his purchase, thirty years later, from the federal government. A year after the McIntosh conveyance, Thomas Johnson died and left his interest in the Illinois-Wabash lands to his son Joshua and his grandson Thomas J. Graham. Upon taking charge of their ancestor's affairs, Joshua Johnson and Graham filed suit to eject McIntosh from the contested property. The federal district court for Illinois found for McIntosh and declared the purchases from the Illinois and Piankashaws invalid. At the time they were consummated, the court said, the country was in a state of revolutionary chaos, and title to and sovereignty over the land were in general dispute. The Illinois-Wabash syndicate never took legal possession of the land, the court wrote, therefore its title claim remained too tenuous to merit recognition. Johnson and Graham appealed the case up to the U.S. Supreme Court.

At the district court trial, Johnson and Graham had presented an argument that closely followed Justice Johnson's discussion of Indian rights in *Fletcher v. Peck*. Indians, they argued, inherently possessed the same natural rights as white Americans. Before the European entry into the Americas, the tribes north of the Ohio "held, occupied, and possessed" their land "in full sovereignty." The tribes were the "absolute owners and proprietors of the soil . . . who neither acknowledged nor owed any allegiance or obedience to any European sovereign or state whatever." During the Seven Years' War, Johnson and Graham pointed out, the tribes of the Northwest were independent allies, not subjects, of France. After Great Britain's victory in the war, the northwest nations fell under the protection, but not the dominion, of the British. Despite these various diplomatic entanglements, Johnson and Graham argued, the Native American nations of the region remained "free and independent," unconquered, and with every legal right to sell their lands to the Illinois-Wabash Company.[52]

Johnson and Graham hired Daniel Webster to argue their appeal before the Supreme Court. Webster, understanding Marshall's careful obfuscation in *Fletcher,* was likewise more circumspect in his presentation. He apparently believed that continuing the argument that the Indian tribes were sovereign nations at the time of the Illinois-Wabash purchase would force Marshall to retract his comments in *Fletcher* and perhaps antagonize the justices who supported the territorial expansion of the United States. It was unnecessary, Webster said, to speculate on the character of the Indian title. The Court had already admitted that the tribes held, at the least, some right to their lands. The primary issue, Webster suggested, was whether individuals could legally acquire those rights or whether the government held the "exclusive prerogative" to do so. The answer to this question, Webster contended, depended to a great extent on the legal impact of the Proclamation of 1763 on the property rights of Native Americans.

At the trial, Johnson and Graham had suggested that the Proclamation of 1763 did not affect the territorial or national rights of the Indians because they were neither British subjects nor "bound by any authority of the British government." Moreover, they had said, even if one admitted that the Illinois and Piankashaws were British subjects, the Crown still could not simply divest an individual of property rights by proclamation. Webster's argument on appeal, again, was more restrained; he turned the point of debate into an examination of the legitimacy of the British government's efforts to extend its jurisdiction over the western territories. At this time President James Monroe was warning Britain to stay out of the Western Hemisphere, and Webster might have calibrated his remarks to fit these diplomatic sensitivities. The Proclamation of 1763, Webster argued, did not prohibit the colonists from buying from the Native American tribes because the king could not extend prerogative legislation over people who maintained an existing government. This was the case with the territory in question, which at the time of conveyance was theoretically under the jurisdiction of the colonial assembly of Virginia. The Crown, Webster continued, had authority to apply its jurisdiction only over newly conquered, unincorporated lands by martial law and could not capriciously apply new laws over the colony's territory without its consent. Webster argued that the 1779 Virginia act annulling past purchases from Indians could not be applied retroactively, that there were no laws in Virginia prohibiting purchases from Indians at the time of the Illinois-Wabash conveyance, and that the acts had been repealed *sub silentio* in the 1794 revision of the Virginia code.[53]

McIntosh countered that the Indian tribes of the Northwest, even if at one time independent, were no longer so and had fallen "under the dominion" of the French and then the British Empires. The Indians, he added, were an "inferior race" under colonial and American law and "under the protection and pupilage of the government." The European law of nations, moreover, rejected the idea that Indians were "independent communities, having a permanent property in the soil, capable of alienation to private individuals." McIntosh argued that the doctrine of discovery was a fundamental part of natural law and the "foundation of title" for the European imperial powers. The principle gave the European discoverer and its descendants in title complete dominion over the discovered territory, full sovereignty over the Indian nations residing there, and the eminent domain power to seize the lands of the inhabitants at will. The law of nations, he concluded on this point, "overlook[ed] all proprietary rights in the natives."[54]

McIntosh also argued that the Indian tribes did not use their land for agricultural purposes. Therefore, their territories were open to seizure by "a people of cultivators." The former presumption, of course, was a bald misrepresentation; the Native American peoples of the Northwest, like those in the Southeast, depended to a considerable extent on subsistence agriculture. McIntosh pointed out that the Native American vendors owned their lands communally, and he suggested that international law required the Illinois-Wabash buyers to accept title in that fashion. Consequently, since the syndicate purchased under the customs of English common law and as individual fee simple vendees, the sale was invalid. McIntosh admitted that many English colonists had purchased land directly from the Indians. These transactions, he said, were substantively meaningless and were merely ceremonial displays to "prevent hostilities" with the Native American occupants. As to the national status of the Indian tribes, McIntosh contended that Indians were subjects, but not citizens, of the United States. Since they were "destitute of the most essential rights" under natural law, they could be characterized only as "perpetual inhabitants with diminutive rights."[55]

Marshall, as was his tendency, attempted to find a compromise between the two disparate positions before the bar.[56] As he framed it, the issues to be determined were whether the Illinois and the Piankashaws had the authority to pass title to someone other than the American government and, conversely, whether a private individual under Anglo-American law could legally receive title directly from an Indian. Marshall recognized that when dealing with the distinct legal cultures of Anglo-Americans and Indians, and on the subject of a conveyance that occurred on Indian land, the Court first had to decide what law it should apply in interpreting the character of the Indian title. Marshall concluded that "the courts of the Conqueror" had the authority to enforce the conqueror's laws against a vanquished nation and that "title to lands . . . must . . . depend entirely on the law of the nation in which they lie."[57] Marshall thus began from a premise that perhaps should have been at the heart of the dispute: that the United States possessed political sovereignty over its share of the continent.[58]

Marshall refused to accept the two extreme conceptions of Native American rights. The Indians were not completely independent nations nor were they simply subjects of the American government. Instead, the chief justice declared that the United States held the ultimate sovereignty over the Indian territory within the republic's continental borders. The Indians, at the same time, retained a right to occupy, possess, and use their land, but they could sell that right only to the United States. Marshall based his decision on the history of European expansion into North and South America and explained that customary practice was more important than what seemed right or rational under natural law. The vastness of the two continents, he said, had "offered an ample field to the ambition and enterprise of all." Since the kingdoms of Europe were in competition for the newfound lands, they agreed on the doctrine of discovery as the means by which title would be distributed in the Western Hemisphere. The principle, he said, gave the "discovering" nation legal priority, or a preemptive right, against other European powers. The "character and religion of [the continent's] inhabitants," he added, gave Europeans an "apology" as a "people over whom the superior genius of Europe might claim an ascendancy." These European usurpers convinced themselves that they offered "ample compensation" for hegemony over the Native Americans' former lands, Marshall said, "by bestowing on Indians civilization and Christianity." The chief justice thus revitalized the doctrine of discovery at a time when it was under serious attack by international law theorists and when it was being repudiated by diplomats from both the United States and Europe. In 1790, for example, Spain and Great Britain had agreed to forgo their claims of discovery and allow traders from both nations into the Northwest. Soon after Marshall's decision, the United States and Britain agreed that simple discovery would not convey complete title to the Oregon territory. Howard Berman, a student of indigenous rights, contends that by the time of *Johnson v. McIntosh*, the doctrine of discovery by itself was "no longer valid as a distributional principle." Berman wrote, "Indeed, it is questionable if it ever was totally accepted as a sufficient basis for dominion." Marshall, however, attempted to make the doctrine and the subsequent settlement of the Atlantic seaboard the foundation of all land title in the United States.[59]

The European theory did not entirely disregard the rights of the Native American inhabitants, Marshall noted, but of necessity diminished them "to a considerable extent." Europeans, he said, had the options of "abandoning the country, and relinquishing their pompous claims to it, or of enforcing those claims by the sword . . . or of remaining in their neighborhood and exposing themselves and their families to the perpetual hazard of being massacred." Consequently, the European powers, faced with these choices, decided to exert their authority over the country. Britain, the United States's primary antecedent in title, had acquired hegemony over the lands "as far west as the river Mississippi," the chief justice said, and had "maintained and established" its dominion "by the sword." By treaty the English government had historically acknowledged the Indians as "the rightful occupants of the soil" in the lands beyond the Appalachians, but discovery had "necessarily diminished" their "rights to complete sovereignty." Since the doctrine of discovery gave the discovering nation "exclusive title" and "ultimate dominion" over its newfound lands, the arrival of Europeans ended the right of the Native American tribes to dispose of their lands as they pleased. "The history of America," Marshall wrote, "from its discovery to the present day, proves, we think, the universal recognition of these principles."[60]

Spain, France, Great Britain, Holland, and Portugal, he said, had all recognized the rights appurtenant to discovery. Their conflicting claims to the North American continent had subsequently been resolved by diplomacy and war. For Great Britain, priority of claim had been established by the Crown's commissions to John Cabot, Humphrey Gilbert, and Walter Raleigh, who were sent to claim lands "then unknown to all Christian people." According to Marshall's history, Cabot and those who followed took possession in the name of the English monarchy and claimed superiority of title irrespective of the rights of the "heathen" natives. These early discoveries ripened into full title when Britain established permanent settlements on the continent. For example, James I conveyed to the Virginia Company lands between the thirty-fourth and forty-fifth parallels that "either belonged to that monarch, or were not possessed by any other Christian prince or people." In 1609, the Crown expanded the claim of the Virginia settlers to one of "absolute property" along the coast for four hundred miles and "from sea to sea." Marshall wrote, "These various patents cannot be considered as nullities; nor can they be limited to a mere grant of the powers of government. A charter intended to convey political power only, would never contain words expressly granting the land, the soil and the waters." Great Britain's exertion of its authority over the eastern half of North America, Marshall concluded, culminated with the Proclamation of 1763. Repudiating Webster's argument, Marshall held that the royal decree was legitimate and that since it prohibited the colonists from purchasing lands west of the line of demarcation, the Illinois-Wabash purchases were illegal, null, and void. McIntosh was therefore the rightful owner of the land in dispute.[61]

By revitalizing the doctrine of discovery, Marshall doomed the Indian title and tribal sovereignty to arbitrary circumscriptions and encouraged the subsequent efforts of the southern states to extend their jurisdiction over the Indian nations. Marshall's comments on this point were often misinterpreted, particularly by the southern courts of the 1830s. Contrary to what some southern judges would later suggest, the chief justice did not say that discovery gave the European nations complete sovereignty and title to the continent. Nor did he suggest that European discovery had completely annihilated Indian rights to their land.[62] Rather, he wrote that the discovering nation acquired the preemptive right, or what one scholar has called the "perfectible entitlement," against the other European states, to acquire the Native American interests by purchase or conquest. Once secured from its European predecessors in title through purchase or war, the discovery claim gave the United States the "exclusive right" to "appropriate the lands occupied by the Indians." Marshall insisted that the Indian right of possession had never been questioned and that the Native American peoples could continue to occupy their land and "use it according to their discretion" until such time that the United States chose to extinguish their rights. But because the Indian nations could sell their lands only to the United States, their sovereignty had, in Marshall's words, been "impaired."[63]

Marshall was certainly aware at that time of the growing popularity of the removal scenario and recognized the increasingly antagonistic claims between the southern states and the federal government over the ownership of the supposed right of preemption. He therefore resolved an issue left vague in *Fletcher v. Peck* by declaring that the federal government possessed the plenary right to extinguish the Indian title. When the landed states had surrendered their western claims at the founding of the country, he argued, they also forfeited their right of extinguishment and their interest in regulating Indian affairs to the federal government. From that point forward, Marshall exaggerated, "the exclusive right of the United States to extinguish [the Indian] title, and to grant the soil, has never, we believe, been doubted." The chief justice, however, had not been sure of this himself in *Fletcher;* and in fact, Georgia and North Carolina had often openly challenged this assertion. By the time of *Johnson v. McIntosh,* Georgia was again beginning to seriously contest the breadth of federal power over Indians and their land. Marshall surely must have been aware of these arguments but ignored them to bolster his clarification of the federal right of extinguishment.[64]

In essence, in *Fletcher* and *Johnson v. McIntosh,* Marshall imported the legal fiction of divided title into American law, with political sovereignty and fee simple residing in the United States and the right of occupancy held by the Indian nation. Berman has argued that Marshall was completing the "Americanization of the law of real property." He notes that at the time of the drafting of the Constitution there was a movement afoot to create an independent scheme of property law beyond the realm of the European feudal influence. By limiting the question of Indian title to real property terms, Berman said, "Marshall was able to create a law of real property that arose directly from territorial claims within the United States, which could be interpreted according to principles derived from the 'natural law' philosophy of John Locke." This effect was so influential, Berman wrote, that Chancellor

Kent's commentaries on the origins of American property titles were primarily based on Marshall's analysis in *Johnson v. McIntosh*.[65] To the chief justice, this bifurcation of dominion perhaps seemed a reasonable compromise that protected the Native American nations from encroachments by the states but left the federal government with the ultimate right to extinguish the Indian title when the land was required for expansion. Marshall's thinking, however, remained either confused or unfermented. On the one hand, he clearly recognized that since the Indian nations were not party to the development of the European law of nations or the doctrine of discovery, they were not bound by its strictures. On the other hand, Marshall muddied this proposition by declaring that the Indian title had been diminished to a right of occupancy. By his circumlocutions, the chief justice had fused the distinct doctrine of discovery into the theory of conquest to create an *ex post facto* rationalization for the American supersession of Indian property and territorial rights. To Marshall, discovery and conquest were not perfect and distinct corollaries, but interchangeable, alternative, and convenient excuses for expansion. If bothered by the fact that international theorists had rejected the doctrine of discovery, he implied, the American judge could always turn to the alternative of conquest.[66]

Legal scholars and historians have had a difficult time in finding a sense of consistency in *Johnson v. McIntosh* and *Worcester v. Georgia,* in which Marshall subsequently adopted William Johnson's essential position that the Indian tribe was a sovereign nation. Generally, scholars have described *Johnson v. McIntosh* as "somewhat embryonic" in Marshall's mind, or "as part of an evolving doctrine of aboriginal rights in the Marshall Court."[67] Marshall's opinion in *Worcester* is both clear and well reasoned; his argument in *Johnson v. McIntosh* seems forced and unfocused. A few reasonable explanations exist for the chief justice's confusing messages. First, and obviously, Marshall was influenced by the existing treatises on international law, which were themselves ambiguous and confusing. Although he does not cite the Swiss theorist, the chief justice's opinion generally paraphrases Vattel in many parts, a tactic that ensured only the continuation of confusion. It also seems rational to suggest, considering Marshall's mode of operation, that his opinion was the result of a compromise between extreme positions within the chambers of the Court.[68] Another possible explanation exists. In her excellent study of the Cherokee cases, Jill Norgren suggested that Marshall might have been sending a message to those nations seeking to challenge U.S. interests in the Western Hemisphere. As *Johnson v. McIntosh* was being adjudicated, the United States was embroiled in an international debate over European colonial rights in Central and South America. James Monroe had recently announced the Monroe Doctrine; Norgren construed Marshall's opinion as an argument, intended for international consumption, for the country's national interests in Latin America. The affirmation of American sovereignty over the continent also warned foreign nations against interfering with the federal-Indian relationship and perhaps enhanced American claims to the Pacific Northwest. In particular, Norgren suggests that Marshall was sending a shot across the bow of Russia, which held designs on that territory. The chief justice did make some analogies that seemed to be targeted to parties beyond the boundaries of the immediate dispute. For example, he noted that if, during the colonial period, Britain had tried to purchase lands west of the Mississippi from the resident Native American peoples, France would have considered it "an invasion of [its] territories." Likewise, he said, the lands of the Louisiana Purchase were occupied by "independent" tribes; but if a foreign power intruded into that territory, the United States would consider it an "aggression which would justify war." Finally, Marshall also might have been intent on defending the federal government's authority over Indian affairs against those in Georgia who maintained that the states held concurrent jurisdiction. By the time of *Johnson v. McIntosh,* the state was already considering the possibility of unilaterally extending its jurisdiction over the Cherokees and Creeks. The chief justice's finding that the national government possessed the exclusive right to extinguish the Indian title may have been an effort to dissuade Georgia from disputing the federal government's authority over relations with the tribes.[69]

More than likely, though, the best way to explain Marshall's opinion is to return to his intellectual core: his conception of the Constitution as an expansive, flexible framework of government, his desire to promote the authority of the federal government and the Court, and a patriotic urge to act for the greater interest of the United States. The chief justice often admitted that he acted with the national interest in mind, and he was not ashamed to make duplicitous arguments and mold precedents to fit his political vision for the territorial and commercial expansion of the United States. Marshall wanted to provide an orderly framework of land title that would foster American commercial success just as he had tried to do in his broad interpretation of the Contract Clause in *Fletcher.* He recognized the logical incongruities of the doctrines of discovery and conquest with the prevailing theory of natural law, and he admitted that his chosen precedents were inconsistent and illogical. "However extravagant the pretension of converting the discovery of an inhabited country into conquest may appear," he said, "if the principle has been asserted in the first instance, and afterwards sustained . . . it becomes the law of the land, and cannot be questioned." Marshall best summarized his belief that established principles of natural and international law could be jettisoned if the national interest demanded in this ponderous passage:

> The Indian inhabitants are to be considered merely as occupants, to be protected, indeed, while in peace, in the possession of their lands, but to be deemed incapable of transferring the absolute title to others. However this restriction may be opposed to natural right, and to the usages of civilized nations, yet, if it be indispensable to that system under which the country has been settled, and be adapted to the actual condition of the two people, it may, perhaps, be supported by reason, and certainly cannot be rejected by courts of justice.

The chief justice allowed that principles of natural law, "those principles of abstract justice which the Creator of all things has impressed on the mind of his creature man," should be taken into consideration in judicial interpretation. He argued, however, that positive law, "those principles . . . our own government has adopted in the particular case," was the ultimate authority when deciding the disputes that came before the Court. In this particular case, Marshall admitted that American strategic and political exigencies trumped universal principles.[70]

Marshall's elevation of positivism over natural law has implied to some commentators a choice of might and expediency over right. But Marshall's compromise was not that cynical. He was faced with a complicated but necessary choice between the competing interests of Americans and Indians. When forced to decide between the two, the chief justice came down on the side of his affinity for, and his oath to, the United States. He admitted that the theories of discovery and conquest were legal fictions, but legal fictions that furthered the interests of a developing nation. Marshall's Court would not impair territorial expansion by affirming for perpetuity the sanctity of an absolute Indian title. Marshall said that it was too late to reverse what had happened to the Indians; at best, he believed, the Court could only create a workable accommodation between the interests of the states, the federal government, and the Indian nations. To Marshall, this compromise was the temporary retention of the Indian usufruct with the probability of its eventual extinguishment by federal action.

Rationalization for the chief justice, however, can go only so far. It might be easy for us, as admirers of Marshall, to argue that his affirmation of the Indian right of occupancy protected their territorial interests. This may be true to some extent, but the uncharacteristic rhetoric that he used to supplement his conclusions, in hindsight, damaged Indian interests far more than this recognition of the indigenous usufruct. Marshall's reliance on outdated stereotypes was especially destructive to Native American interests because the southern state supreme courts subsequently elevated the chief justice's dicta to precedent and used them to sanction the expansion of state jurisdiction over the Indian nations. Marshall noted that the philosophers' law of nations generally required a conqueror to assimilate the conquered people. The chief justice, however, argued that Indians were too "high-spirited," too brave, and too fierce for the United States to govern as a "distinct people." Southern courts used these comments to justify the Indian Removal. Marshall also wrote that the theories of discovery and conquest were based on the "character and habits of the people whose rights have been wrested from them" and the belief that all Indians were warring hunters and "fierce savages" who could not be allowed to retain possession of the continent. The adherents to the two doctrines, he wrote, agreed that "to leave [Indians] in possession of their country was to leave the country a wilderness." Marshall said that he would not "enter into the controversy, whether agriculturists, merchants, and manufacturers, have a right, on abstract principles, to expel hunters from the territory they possess, or to contract their limits." But Marshall did give judicial sanction to the long-standing American myth that all Indians were nomadic hunter-gatherers who did not cultivate or exploit the land. In addition, rather than admitting that whites had forcibly dispossessed the Indians of the eastern seaboard, Marshall wrote, "As the white population advanced, that of the Indians necessarily receded. The country in the immediate neighborhood of agriculturists became unfit for them. The game fled into thicker and more unbroken forests, and the Indians followed." Only then, Marshall wrote, did whites move onto vacated lands. This was a rather benign description of the European dislocation of Indians during the colonial era. The chief justice concluded that these mythical aspersions were the foundation of American title, and he was not about to disturb their historical underpinnings. Though he implied that he believed that these general stereotypes were relics of a different intellectual age, Marshall's inclusion of them in the opinion was, in retrospect, a terrible miscalculation. Subsequent American judges, unfamiliar with colonial history and the civilization of the Eastern Woodlands peoples, did not read Marshall's language carefully and took his characterization of European perceptions as reliable evidence of Indian culture. These misrepresentations of Marshall's language, be they intentional or unintentional, proved to be disastrous for the tribes.[71]

Like many Americans of his era, Marshall harbored a dual conception of the Native American, as both the treacherous savage and as the noble, natural man. But still, he knew better of Woodlands people than his opinion demonstrated. Marshall had known, fought against, and legislated for Indians since early in his life. His opinion, however, did not reflect this life experience. The private comments by the chief justice on Native Americans were mostly romantic reflections about exciting experiences in his youth. Marshall grew up in Germantown and Leeds Manor, in western Virginia, and he matured during a period marked by violent conflict between Indians and western settlers. Although he did not witness Indian-settler conflict firsthand as a child, he often heard the stories about the battles between those on the westward movement and the Native American peoples threatened by their encroachment. Though that white frontier culture was rife with fear and mistrust of the Indian, the backwoodsmen of Virginia intelligently integrated Native American methods into their own ways of hunting, fighting, and farming. Marshall's deification that resulted from his service as chief justice overwhelms our ability to comprehend his humanity, and it is therefore difficult to picture this demigod of American law as a young and tough frontiersman, clad in buckskin, fighting Indians and the British army in Lord Dunmore's War. These, however, were the dominant memories of Marshall's formative years, and in recollections in his old age, he recalled his service in the Revolution with his father and the Culpeper County militia. The Culpeper Minutemen dressed in leather hunting shirts, carried bucktails in their caps, and armed themselves with tomahawks and scalping knives. One of Marshall's fellow militiamen said of their forays into more populated and "civilized" towns, "The people hearing we came from the backwoods, and seeing our savage looking equipments, seemed as much afraid of us as if we had been Indians." Marshall served with the Culpepers until 1779, was present at the American defeats at Brandywine and Germantown, and suffered through the winter at Valley Forge. His troops came into conflict several times with the British Empire's Indian allies. In his biography of George Washington, he recalled an incident in which Indian warriors captured, killed, and scalped a young Tory woman named Jane McCrea. When the Indians brought the scalp to the British, a young officer recognized the hair as that of his fiancée. Marshall commented on how the incident had been widely spread around American camps and wrote that it had "excited everywhere a peculiar degree of sensibility." These were the measured words of someone who had enjoyed complex and varied experiences with Native American people, not the reactionary language of an individual intent on depriving Indians of their rights.[72]

According to his friends, Marshall also loved to tell the story of his family's travails in their migration to the Kentucky territory. After the war, a caravan of three longboats, led by Marshall's father, Thomas, transported a group of families and their belongings and supplies down the Ohio River. On the way, they were accosted by Simon and James Girty, the notorious frontier criminals. The Girtys most recently had been conspiring with a group of Indians who were systematically robbing settlers coming down the river. But the Girtys had fallen out of favor with the Indians, and they warned the Marshall party to stay in the middle of the Ohio and ignore any pleas for help that they heard coming from whites on the shore. The Indians, the Girtys explained, captured migrating settlers and tortured them into begging for assistance to lure other passing vessels to the shore. When boats landed to assist those who called for help, the Indians would attack the boats, seize the property, and kill the passengers. The party followed the Girtys' advice and continued to float down the middle of the Ohio. Unbeknownst to the immigrants, however, the Indian assailants had recently commandeered a vessel of their own. Sighting the three well-provisioned longboats, the Indians took off after the Marshall party. After an hour of pursuit, the Marshall group decided to abandon two of the boats that were loaded with their supplies in the hopes that the Indians would be satisfied with a pecuniary gain. All of the passengers piled into one longboat and drifted on down the Ohio. Taking the decoy and satisfied with the material booty, the Indians ended their pursuit. These distant memories of the Indian as a dangerous foe were also somewhat evident in *Johnson v. McIntosh*.[73]

Over time, however, it is clear that Enlightenment philosophy, with its accordance of natural rights to all humans, became an equally significant force in Marshall's comprehension of Native Americans. For instance, in 1784, Marshall and Patrick Henry proposed a bill in the Virginia House of Burgesses that encouraged intermarriage between whites and Indians as a way to resolve the tensions between the two peoples. When it was rejected, Marshall understood why: "Our prejudices oppose themselves to our interests, and operate too powerfully for them." Early in his career, then, Marshall was evidently willing to accept Indians into American society on an equal plane at the most intimate level. That he would, for the reasons posited above, suppress his faith in assimilation, depreciate the humanity of Native Americans, and revive the stereotype of the bloodthirsty hunter-gatherer in *Johnson v. McIntosh* illustrates the complexity of the Indian sovereignty question and the difficulty the chief justice had in contemplating a question that had terrible moral, and not just strategic, economic, or political overtones. Five years after *Johnson v. McIntosh*, Marshall revealed his feelings about the history of U.S.-Indian relations in a letter to Joseph Story: "The conduct of our Fore Fathers in expelling the original occupants of the soil grew out of so many mixed motives that any censure which philanthropy may bestow upon it ought to be qualified. The Indians were a fierce and dangerous enemy, whose love of war made them sometimes the aggressors, whose numbers and habits then made them formidable, and whose cruel system of warfare served to justify every endeavour to remove them to a distance from civilized settlements." Marshall added, "It was not until after the adoption of our present government that respect for our own safety permitted us to give full indulgence to those principles of humanity and justice which ought always to govern our conduct towards the aborigines when this course can be pursued without exposing ourselves to the most afflicting calamities. This time however is unquestionably arrived; and every oppression now exercised on a helpless people depending on our magnanimity and justice for the preservation of their existence, impresses a deep stain on the American character." The chief justice then commented on the pressures that Georgia was bringing to bear on the Indians there: "I often think with indignation of our disreputable conduct—as I think it—in the affair of the Creeks of Georgia."[74]

Marshall's sympathies for what had happened to the Indians were therefore palpable, and his attempt to create dual tenancies in Indian land was perhaps well meaning. In recognizing the Indian usufruct, Marshall gave federal sanction to the idea that the tribes retained rights to their land. Also, by holding that only the federal government possessed the power to extinguish that right, Marshall strengthened the crumbling wall of constitutional theory that protected the Indian nations from the encroachments of the southern states. As a result, Marshall's compromise may have temporarily postponed the inevitable battle over Indian rights in the Southeast. In hindsight, however, his opinion in *Johnson v. McIntosh* opened a Pandora's box at a most inopportune time for Native American people in the Southeast. By limiting Indians to a right of occupancy, the chief justice forever diminished a fundamental aspect of national sovereignty—the right to control national lands without interference—for the tribes. *Johnson v. McIntosh* thus encouraged the southern states' efforts to co-opt Native Americans' land by implying that extinguishment of the Indian title was inevitable. At a time when the president and Congress were contemplating the feasibility of a general removal, the Supreme Court was again in a position to restrain attacks on the tribes with a strong defense of the United States's historical recognition of tribal sovereignty. At this still early stage, when there was a conservative president, James Monroe, who was inclined to follow historical precedent, Marshall perhaps could have established a legal firewall against the raging southern demands. Instead, the chief justice not only equivocated on the question of Indian rights, he resuscitated the doctrine of discovery. Marshall's decision to reinvest the doctrine with legal dignity gave southern politicians a powerful intellectual weapon that they could use to beat back the moral opposition of Indians, northern philanthropists, and congressional opponents of removal. When the time came for the southern courts to decide the fate of the native tribes in their midst, *Johnson v. McIntosh* was the case that they chose to cite as precedent.

In his outstanding study of the Cherokee cases, Joseph C. Burke wrote: "In reality Marshall's opinion supported neither those who considered the tribes independent nations and proprietors of the soil nor those who regarded them as subject people and tenants at will." Perhaps, then, the most enlightening fact about *Johnson v. McIntosh* is that, like Vattel's *Law of Nations*, proponents of both positions cited it in the Cherokee cases. The ambiguities of the legal precedents and the philosophical scholarship on indigenous rights thus left open two divergent paths for the United States in its policies toward the American Indian. One led to the enhancement and protection of the sovereign status of the Indian nations; the other traced inexorably down the road toward the Indian Removal.[75]

CHAPTER FOUR

The Supremacy of State Jurisdiction

Georgia v. Tassels

THE CHEROKEE NATION'S PROMULGATION of a republican constitution in the summer of 1827 enraged the removers in Georgia. Rather than fostering support for their cause with the federal government, the Cherokees had essentially unified the southern states against their position. Georgia responded to the Cherokees' declaration of independence with its own legislation. In December the state extended the criminal jurisdiction of the northern counties of Carroll and DeKalb over acts committed by or against whites within the Cherokee Nation. The legislature also forwarded a resolution to Congress denouncing the establishment of the Cherokee constitutional government as a provocative attack on the sovereignty of the state. The assembly warned that if the United States had not concluded a removal treaty with the Cherokees by the state's next legislative session, it would unilaterally extend its sovereignty over the Cherokee Nation and take possession of its land. In other words, the state was giving the federal government one more chance to fulfill its promise in the Compact of 1802. "The absolute title to the lands in controversy" belong to Georgia, "and she may rightfully possess herself of them when, and by what means, she pleases," the legislature resolved. "Georgia has the right to extend her authority and laws over her whole territory and to coerce obedience to them from all description of people be they white, red, or black." (The historian William G. McLoughlin suggested that the reference to "white" people in the state's resolution was a veiled threat to the American missionaries living in the Cherokee Nation.)[1]

By the time of the next legislative session in December 1828, Congress had not passed a removal bill. Georgia officials believed, however, that the recent presidential election would finally bring to office a president, Andrew Jackson, who sympathized with their desire to acquire the land of the Cherokees. Jackson had attracted twice as many electoral votes as John Quincy Adams in the election and brought on his coattails a force of like-minded democrats to the Congress. The southern states, in particular, voted overwhelmingly for Jackson. The proponents of removal were elated by the results; they understood that Jackson not only wanted to relocate the Indians out of the South, but that he would be obliged to reward their states for their support in the election. Presuming that it would soon no longer be obstructed by the federal government, Georgia moved to fulfill its threat from the year before. The state legislature extended the civil and criminal jurisdiction of the state over the Cherokee Nation and annexed a large tract of its land into the counties of Carroll, DeKalb, Gwinnett, Hall, and Habersham. The assembly declared that after June 1, 1830, "all laws, usages, customs made, established and enforced in the said territory by the said Cherokee Indians" would be null and void. The Cherokee Nation and its constitution, its laws, and its courts would be abolished. After that date, the legislature warned, those Cherokees who remained in Georgia would become subject to the laws and jurisdiction of the state.

The legislature also attempted to cleanse the state of any remaining Creek presence. Though the Creek Nation had ceded its remaining holdings in the state two years before, the legislature was anxious to inhibit cooperative efforts between the Cherokees and the Creeks against removal. Thus the General Assembly prohibited "any Indian, or descendant of an Indian" from entering Georgia from the Creek Nation in Alabama without written permission from the federal agent for the Creeks. Even with a pass, a visiting Indian could stay in the state no longer than ten days. The law authorized state authorities, upon affidavit by a Georgia citizen, to arrest any Indian who "interfere[d] with the private property," "interrupte[d] the peace and tranquility of any of [Georgia's] citizens," or was captured "strolling over the territory" of the state's "frontier counties" without a pass. Violators were to be imprisoned for up to ten days and then, presumably, thrown out of the state. Indians accused of violating the statute had little hope of contesting the charges against them, for in the same term the state prohibited any "Indian or descendant of any Indian, residing within the Creek or Cherokee nations of Indians" from being a party or a witness in any case in which a "white man" was involved. Consequently, if a white man accused an Indian of being in the state without permission, the Native American visitor could be imprisoned and expelled without an opportunity to testify on his or her own behalf. According to its preamble, the law was intended to purge the state of the "inconveniences and injuries" that resulted from "unlimited intercourse" with Indians. More than likely, though, the legislature enacted the statute as a way to seize control of communications between the Creek and Cherokee Nations and block consolidated opposition to removal.[2]

Elias Boudinot, the editor of the *Cherokee Phoenix* and a proponent of Cherokee acculturation, condemned the Georgia extension laws and charged that the federal government was complicit in the state's efforts to force the Cherokees to remove. He suggested that the United States had abandoned its civilization program and that it had failed to abide by its duty to protect the Cherokees from state attack. The federal government's civilization scheme, he said, was a fraud perpetrated against Indians. "It appears now . . . that the illustrious Washington, Jefferson, Madison and Monroe were only tantalizing us," he wrote, "when they encouraged us in the pursuit of agriculture and Government, and when they afforded us the protection of the United States, by which we have been preserved to this time as a nation." Georgia had always possessed the "pretext" to extend its jurisdiction over the Cherokee Nation, Boudinot added, but "nothing was said" when the Cherokees "were governed by savage laws" of clan retaliation. "After being fostered by the U. States, & advised by great and good men to establish a government of regular law . . . we, as dutiful 'children' of the President, have followed his instructions and advice." As reward for their success in the American civilization program, Boudinot wrote, the federal government and the state of Georgia had conspired to "blast all our rising hopes and expectations" and run the Cherokees off of their land. Though just as distressed by Georgia's attack on Cherokee sovereignty as Boudinot, John Ross, the principal chief of the nation, continued to reassure the Cherokee people and urge them to stand fast against Georgia's aggression. At the same time, he begged the federal government to intervene in the nation's troubles with the state.[3]

The new president, Andrew Jackson, responded in his first inaugural address. He declared his intention to resolve the Cherokee dispute in Georgia and promised to bring the long-desired Indian exile to fruition. "A portion . . . of the Southern tribes have attempted to erect an independent government within the limits of Georgia and Alabama," he said. "The question presented was whether the General Government had a right to sustain those people in their pretensions." Jackson then described his counsel to the tribes: "I informed the Indians inhabiting parts of Georgia and Alabama that their attempt to establish an independent government would not be countenanced by the Executive of the United States, and advised them to emigrate beyond the Mississippi or submit to the laws of those states." The president then urged his listeners to set aside their concerns about the legal proprieties of removal and look toward the future: "It is too late to inquire whether it was just . . . to include them and their territory within the borders of new states," he said. "[T]hat step can not be retraced." Jackson asked the Congress to set apart "an ample district west of the Mississippi, and without the limit of any state or territory now formed." This territory, he said, was "to be guaranteed to the Indian tribes as long as they shall occupy it." He added that the Indians would be better off and happier in their new home in

the West: "There they may be secured in the enjoyments of governments of
their own choice," he promised, "subject to no other control from the United
States than such as may be necessary to preserve peace on the frontier and
between the several tribes." He emphasized, however, that the concept of
the tribe as a sovereign entity in the East was at an end. Though Jackson
declared that the Indians would not be forced to relocate, "for it would be
as cruel as unjust to compel the aborigines to abandon the graves of their
fathers and seek a home in a distant land," he made it clear that separate
tribal communities or Indian nations were no longer welcome east of the
Mississippi River.[4]

In its 1829 session, the Georgia legislature added teeth to its previous extension statutes. Along with annexing the remaining lands of the Cherokee
Nation into the state, the assembly provided the state militia with authority
to arrest violators of Georgia law in the Cherokee Nation and created new
superior courts to adjudicate the cases resulting from these infringements.
The statute also prohibited Georgia judges from accepting Cherokee laws as
legal defenses or evidence of legality in criminal actions against the Cherokees. In short, combined with the provisions of the 1828 law, which were
reaffirmed in the new act, the legislature mandated that Georgia courts treat
the entire body of Cherokee law "as if the same had never existed."[5]

The state also moved against those who opposed removal. The law criminalized any action that tended to discourage the Cherokees from emigrating
or ceding their land. It declared that those found guilty of encouraging the
Cherokees to stay in Georgia would be imprisoned at hard labor for up to
four years, that those who discouraged the nation from selling lands to the
United States were subject to the same punishment for four to six years,
and that Cherokees guilty of killing advocates of cession and removal were
subject to death by hanging. In 1825 the Creek Nation had executed William
McIntosh for ceding part of the nation's land. Georgia's leaders worked dili-
gently to develop a proremoval faction among the Cherokee leadership, and
this provision was enacted to inhibit Cherokee opponents of removal from
executing any Cherokee who wanted to accommodate the state's demands.

The legislature also provided penalties for those who advised accused violators to contend that they were acting under color of Cherokee law. The
state's executive thus gained the authority to punish lawyers for the Cherokees and "all persons acting . . . as pretended executive, ministerial or judicial officers," as if they were accomplices to a crime. In essence, with this bill
the Georgia legislature attempted to intimidate the members of the Cherokee
power structure who opposed removal and tried to frighten the missionaries, friends, and legal advocates of the tribe from defending the sanctity of
Cherokee national sovereignty. Governor George Gilmer forwarded a copy

of the new laws to the U.S. War Department and encouraged the state press to publish them in the newspapers. He also held Jackson's feet to the public fire in the South by noting in his correspondence to the papers that the new president had in the past acknowledged the state's right to extend its jurisdiction over the Cherokees. Privately, Gilmer admitted that the extension laws were produced for the sole purpose of making life so miserable for the Cherokees that they would be forced to remove. The legislature also admitted as much in 1829, when it declared that its actions were "calculated to induce [the Indians] to remove."[6]

The legislation produced another outcry from the Cherokee Nation's leaders. The *Cherokee Phoenix* published a memorial that John Ross and the National Council had forwarded to Congress vehemently criticizing Georgia's "arbitrary" extension laws and the appearance of state surveyors in the nation. "We cannot admit that Georgia has the right to extend her jurisdiction over our territory nor are the Cherokee people prepared to submit to her persecuting edict," Ross wrote. "We . . . appeal to the United States' Government for justice and protection."[7]

Georgia's years of lobbying Congress culminated in February 1830 when the Senate Indian Affairs Committee recommended the adoption of a general removal act authorizing the president to conduct negotiations with the eastern tribes for the purpose of exchanging their lands for territories west of the Mississippi. Under the bill, the national government would guarantee emigrating Indians perpetual ownership of their new lands and protect them from incursions by settlers. In addition, the United States would pay the tribes for the value of the improvements on their existing lands, fund the relocation, and provide for subsistence expenses for one year to allow the Indians to acclimate to their new environment.[8]

The Indian Removal bill divided the Congress on political and sectional lines. Henry Clay's emerging Whig faction opposed the bill. Though Clay cared little for the interests of Native Americans, he was keen on becoming president and making his American System a reality. He therefore used the bill as a way to foment sympathy for the Indians' plight and, concomitantly, popular opposition to Jackson in the North. As the debate raged in Congress, the *Washington National Intelligencer* published a set of twenty-four essays, authored by a devout lawyer named Jeremiah Evarts under the pseudonym William Penn, that laid out in exacting detail the moral and legal reasons for rejecting the Indian Removal bill. God had chosen Americans to revitalize Christian virtue in the world, Evarts argued, and people of faith had a duty to ensure that their leaders made laws and policies that were just. If the United States Congress passed the bill, he said, it would bring down punishment from the Almighty for violating that mission. Evarts organized a massive

campaign against the legislation in the North. According to Georgia delegate
Wilson Lumpkin, thousands of petitions against the bill, containing more
than a million signatures, poured into Congress at Evarts's request. Evarts
also helped coordinate opposition to the bill in Congress, and prominent legislators such as Senator Theodore Frelinghuysen gave long and impassioned
speeches that reiterated how the United States would be abandoning solemn
moral and legal obligations if it enacted the legislation. Evarts died at the
tragically young age of fifty the following year. Fortunately, he did not live
to see the outcome of his crusade to preserve the Cherokees' autonomy in
the East.[9]

The opposition of Whigs and northern philanthropists was not enough
to stem the momentum in favor of the Indian Removal bill. In late April, the
Senate passed the legislation by a 28 to 19 vote and forwarded it to the House
of Representatives for consideration. After a long and acrimonious debate,
the House approved the bill the next month by a slim 102 to 97 margin.
The vote was divided sectionally in both houses of Congress. In the House
of Representatives, the South voted three to one in favor of the bill. The
western states, except for Ohio, also approved it by a relatively healthy score.
Twice as many northeastern representatives voted against the act as for it,
although New York's delegation was split. On May 28, Jackson signed into
law what was now called the Indian Removal Act of 1830. While Congress
had declared that Jackson could remove the tribes only with their consent,
it was clear to the Cherokees and to Georgia that the federal government
had given the state the prerogative to push the Cherokees off of their land.
Privately and publicly, Jackson advised the Cherokees that he would not
stand in the way of Georgia's efforts to extend its jurisdiction over their
nation. Those Indians who remained in the East, he said again, would have
to come under state jurisdiction.[10]

The Indian Removal Act seemed to foreclose any political opportunities
that the Cherokees had to avoid relocation. And with Congress and the president refusing to intervene in Georgia's attempt to eradicate the Cherokee
Nation as a political entity, John Ross chose to turn his attention, and the
Cherokees' limited resources, to litigation. Elias Boudinot explained why
Ross and the nation decided to take the case to the courts: "If we are removed . . . by the United States . . . we wish to leave in the records of her
judicial tribunals, for future generations to read, when we are gone, ample
testimony that she acted *justly* or *unjustly*." Boudinot added, "Surely, the
Supreme Court of the United States is the proper tribunal where the great
question at issue must be settled." Ross asked William Wirt to serve as the
Cherokee Nation's counsel and authorized him to prepare an opinion on the
viability of a constitutional challenge to Georgia's extension laws. Ross's se-

lection of Wirt seemed logical. The famous lawyer had served as attorney general under James Monroe and John Quincy Adams and was a renowned and effective litigator. His reputation as an advocate before the Supreme Court was unchallenged, and Daniel Webster had suggested to Ross that Wirt's style would be popular in the courtroom and in the newspapers. At first, Wirt was reluctant to take on the Cherokee cause, but he relented when Webster, Evarts, and other prominent opponents of removal convinced him of "the injustice about to be done to these people." Wirt agreed to accept a retainer if the Cherokees promised to keep the peace and "not take the law into their own hands." [11]

Wirt's prior opinions on Indian rights were inconsistent. In 1821 he filed an opinion as attorney general maintaining that the Indian tribes were sovereign nations with complete rights to their soil. Then, in 1824, he wrote that it was "fallacious" to believe that the Cherokee Nation was a sovereign nation on par with the United States. Reversing his position again in 1828, Wirt wrote that the Creeks were a sovereign and independent nation. Perhaps because of this uncertainty in his position, Wirt turned to other prominent legal scholars for advice. Over the summer Wirt obtained opinions from Webster, Ambrose Spencer (a prominent New York judge), Horace Binney (a Philadelphia lawyer and politician), and Chancellor James Kent. All of them concluded that the Georgia extension laws were unconstitutional. Based on the letters of these experts and his own research, Wirt argued that the Cherokee Nation was an independent nation foreign to the United States and that it possessed full title to its land. The only limitation on the Cherokee Nation's rights, Wirt decided, was that it could sell its lands only to the United States. The Cherokees had conceded this limitation in their treaties with the federal government. Therefore, Wirt concluded, the Georgia extension statutes were "repugnant" to the treaties between the United States and the Cherokee Nation, to the federal Trade and Intercourse Act of 1802, and to the Commerce and Contract Clauses of the Constitution. According to Wirt, the Commerce Clause, as construed by the Trade and Intercourse Acts, gave Congress complete authority over Indian affairs. State attempts to regulate the Indian nations, consequently, were both unconstitutional and violative of the acts. The Contract Clause, Wirt added, prohibited the state from enacting laws that impaired the obligations of existing contracts between the United States and the Cherokees. Wirt reported to Ross that Kent and Horace Binney were confident in his conclusions on the propriety of the Cherokees' claim of sovereignty. But he also noted that his partner in the Cherokee cases, John Sergeant of Pennsylvania, was dubious about the validity of the argument. Overall, it appears that while his consultants felt comfortable with his analysis, Wirt was doubtful about his

chances for a favorable opinion from the federal courts. In particular, he
worried that the Cherokees had surrendered their police power to the state
in the Treaty of Holston in 1791. The eleventh article of that agreement
provided that if a "citizen or inhabitant" of the United States committed a
crime against an Indian in "any town, settlement, or territory belonging to
the Cherokees," the offender would be punished in accordance with the laws
of the state in which the act was committed. In this provision, Wirt thought,
the Cherokees seemed to have conferred all police jurisdiction to the states.
The unfortunate language of Article 11, which was caused by the overlapping of Indian and state borders, was emblematic of the questions involved in
sorting out sovereignty and title. Wirt feared that the Cherokees had perhaps
given up enough in Holston to endanger their cause. He told Ross that if the
Cherokee Nation could work out a deal that gave it lands of equal value and
the assurance that it would hold title to those lands forever, he would "most
strenuously advise you to go and give up this heart breaking contest." [12]

If the Cherokees chose to proceed, Wirt said, they had four avenues to
standing before the Supreme Court. First, Ross, as principal chief, could
file an action to enjoin Georgia's actions against an officer of the state. The
Eleventh Amendment, Wirt noted, prohibited an individual from filing suit
against the state in the federal courts. Second, the Cherokees could obtain
standing by appealing a Georgia decision upholding the extension statutes
by writ of error. Third, the Cherokee Nation could make a direct appeal
as a foreign state to the original jurisdiction of the Supreme Court. Finally,
Wirt suggested that a consensual or collusive case could be brought in, in
which the nation and Georgia agreed to argue the constitutionality of the
extension laws before the high Court. Ultimately, Wirt would attempt three
of the four routes to standing. Ross was impressed with Wirt's work, and
they soon became frequent correspondents and close allies. The lawyer's
research also had an immediate effect on Ross's efforts to bolster Cherokee
morale. By July 1830, for example, Ross was citing Vattel in his speeches
and letters as authority for the proposition that a small or weak state could,
without sacrificing its sovereignty, place itself under the protection of a more
powerful nation. [13]

Wirt first tried the congenial approach. He asked Governor Gilmer of
Georgia to join the Cherokees in a case that would allow the Supreme
Court to clarify the Indians' political status in relation to the state. Gilmer
replied that Wirt's plan, "however courteous the manner, and conciliatory
the phraseology," was "exceedingly disrespectful to the Government of the
State." Gilmer added that he would "grossly violate his duty and exceed
his authority" if he agreed to submit Georgia's sovereignty to the whim
of a federal court. In any event, the governor concluded, the Constitution

prohibited the Court from ruling on the matter. With that rebuff, Wirt suggested to Ross that the Cherokee Nation go forward with an action asking the Supreme Court to accept original jurisdiction under Article 3 and enjoin the enforcement of Georgia's laws in Cherokee territory.[14]

Before they could file the suit, however, Ross and Wirt learned that state authorities in Hall County, Georgia, had arrested a Cherokee man named George Tassel for "having waylaid and killed an Indian." The killing purportedly occurred on the western side of the Chattahoochee River, within the borders of the Cherokee Nation and in that part of the nation recently annexed to Hall County by the state. This case, Wirt believed, potentially offered the Cherokee Nation the constitutional standing before the Court that he and Ross had been looking for. Wirt and his cocounsel, John Sergeant, quickly moved to make Tassel's murder defense a national cause for the Cherokees.[15]

Hall County was a transitional region between the Cherokee Nation and the well-settled portion of the state to the east. Georgia had only recently acquired the region from the Cherokees in the controversial treaty of 1817. A year later, the legislature had established Hall as one of the state's county units. In his contemporary *Gazetteer of Georgia,* Adiel Sherwood reported that the county had "some of the finest land in the state." Consequently, white farmers quickly moved into the county and settled on lots obtained in one of the state's many land lotteries. There they joined the squatting intruders who had forced the Cherokees into the cession in the first place. In 1821, Governor John Clark issued a charter to establish the city of Gainesville at a spot called Mule Camp Springs, apparently a frequent gathering place for British traders and Indians in the past. Gainesville, the county seat, was only three miles from the Chattahoochee River, which served as the eastern border of the Cherokee Nation.[16]

Under the new state laws, Cherokees were frequently arrested and detained in the Hall County jail. In August 1830, Ross appointed William Rogers, a local lawyer, to observe all of the judicial actions involving Cherokees in north Georgia. The chief also hired the local law firm of William H. Underwood and Thomas W. Harris to represent any Cherokees who came before the state's tribunals. Underwood therefore became responsible for shepherding Tassel through his proceedings at the local level.[17] At the direction of Wirt, Underwood filed a preliminary plea objecting to the court's jurisdiction over Tassel. The superior court judge, Augustin S. Clayton, said that he had already ruled on the issue of Indian sovereignty, and he "considered it unnecessary for consumption of time, again to go into the argument." Clayton had recently antagonized John Ross with comments about the Cherokees in front of a Clarke County grand jury. Georgia's extension laws were constitutional, Clayton had said; he intended to enforce the statutes and would ignore any effort by the federal Supreme Court to interfere in the state's jurisdiction. When Ross discovered who was to preside over Tassel's case, he wrote Underwood asking, "Has he not completely prejudged the question of Cherokee Rights?" Ross instructed Underwood to seek an order forcing Clayton to recuse himself from any matters involving the Cherokees. To the principal chief's disappointment, Clayton remained on the Tassel case. Aware of Ross's discomfort with his earlier statements, however, Clayton agreed to buck the case up to the Georgia tribunal of appellate judges for a hearing on the constitutionality of the state's extension laws and the validity of the court's jurisdiction. That way, he said, the court would avoid charges of "impatience and precipitation." Tassel's challenge to Georgia's jurisdiction was therefore treated as an interlocutory appeal, and the trial on the facts was tolled until the convention of superior court judges responded with an answer to the question of law.[18]

In front of the convention of judges in Milledgeville, the state capital, Underwood argued that the state's extension laws were unconstitutional and void because they violated the several federal-Cherokee treaties that had been concluded between 1785 and 1819. Those compacts, he said, presumed that the Cherokee Nation was "an independent sovereign state" and "expressly recognized" the Cherokees' "right of self-government." Underwood argued that the Treaty of Holston provided that if the federal government violated one of its treaty promises, the Cherokees could legally declare war against the United States to obtain a redress of grievances. This, he argued, was convincing evidence that the American government regarded the Cherokee Nation as an independent, sovereign political entity. Since federal treaties were the "supreme law of the land" under Article 6 of the Constitution, Georgia could not interfere with those agreements. Georgia's arrest of Tassel, Underwood concluded, was an unconstitutional "infringement" of the Cherokee Nation's national sovereignty.[19]

Turner Hunt Trippe, the solicitor general for the state, refused to concede that the Cherokee Nation held any national or property rights in the state. He pointed to Chancellor Kent's *Commentaries on American Law,* which he paraphrased as precedent that the American judiciary considered Indians to be "inferior, dependent, and in a state of pupilage to the whites." Trippe's representation of Kent's position, however, was particularly misleading. In his *Commentaries,* Kent was referring to the manner in which the European nations had historically viewed Native Americans, not to their legal status under natural law or in American cases. Personally, Kent believed that the Indian tribes were sovereign nations, but the Supreme Court's decision in *Johnson v. McIntosh* had forced him to reconcile his own interpretation of

Native American rights with Marshall's rather ambiguous ruling. His ambitious attempt to integrate Marshall's opinion into his hornbook tainted the clarity of logic that Kent had displayed in the Tommy Jemmy case, a decision that explained the history and reasons for the United States's recognition of tribal sovereignty. In his *Commentaries,* which were published after *Johnson v. McIntosh,* Kent wrote that the Indian nations maintained a natural right to occupy their lands. The United States, by discovery and conquest, held the legal title to and sovereignty over the lands of the Indian nations. In addition, the United States possessed "an absolute and exclusive right to extinguish the Indian title of occupancy either by purchase or conquest." Of course, the Georgia court differed with Kent's opinion on the question of which government held the right to extinguish the Indian title. Kent noted that the lower court decision rendered by Ambrose Spencer in the Tommy Jemmy case had held that New York could extend its jurisdiction over the tribes in that state. On appeal, however, Kent had overturned Spencer's ruling. In that case, Kent wrote that individual Indians were aliens in respect to New York. Consequently, the Indian tribes of New York, these communities of Indians, were foreign states. In attempting to reconcile his Tommy Jemmy opinion with *Johnson v. McIntosh,* Kent wrote that the federal government held the sole right of extinguishing the Indian title but that the Indian lands could not be "taken from them, or disturbed, without their free consent, by fair purchase, except it be by force of arms in the event of a just and necessary war." Later, Marshall's reversal on this point in *Worcester v. Georgia* would vindicate Kent's original position. In Tassel's case, however, Trippe exploited the confusion caused by Marshall's opinion in *Johnson v. McIntosh* and distorted Kent's analysis to argue that the Cherokees' rights could be terminated by the state at any time.[20]

The state's solicitor general also argued that regardless of the treaties between the United States and the Cherokees, the Compact of 1802 was a federal acknowledgment that the Indian title could be unilaterally extinguished. He rejected Underwood's argument that the Cherokee right to declare war on the United States, as provided by Holston, implied that the tribe was a sovereign nation. Finally, in a bold argument that directly challenged federal authority, the solicitor contended that the treaties between the United States and the Cherokees were void except as they related to trade relations. Congress, he said, possessed jurisdiction only over "the single subject of commerce, that being the only power granted them in the constitution."[21]

The Georgia judges tipped their hand as to their prejudices at the beginning of the opinion. They wrote that they "deem[ed] it a waste of time to pursue this examination." Opposition to the extension statutes, they suggested, had not been aroused by Tassel but by the Cherokee Nation, its advocates, and "the political, party, and fanatical feeling excited during the last session of Congress." Only after the Cherokees had failed in their political efforts to block the Indian Removal Act, they charged, did the nation and its advocates choose to make a legal challenge to the extension statutes. The political circumstances surrounding the case, the court said, would have no effect on its decision. In fact, the court was correct about the political implications involved. Followers and opponents of Jackson had turned the Cherokee protests against the extension statutes into a war between Georgia and the president on one side and Jackson's enemies on the other. The judges' plea of impartiality, however, was an obvious exercise in mendacity.[22]

The court lamented that Georgia's politicians and citizens were being singled out for unfair criticism by northern reformers and newspapers sympathetic to the Cherokees. In some ways the court was right about the hypocrisy coming out of the northern press. In that region, American settlers had long ago either destroyed the resident native tribes, pushed them to the west, or isolated them onto tracts reserved out of territorial cessions. The absence of a substantial Native American presence in the region fostered a romantic conceit that the Indians were a noble people under attack from depredating westerners and southerners. As a result, a large and vociferous phalanx of reforming missionaries and philanthropists, led by Evarts, emerged to speak out for what they thought were the best interests of Native Americans. These "friends of the Indian" remained convinced that the United States should continue its civilization and assimilation program in the East. Of particular concern to these societies were the increasingly belligerent attacks on the Southeastern nations by the southern states. States in the North, including New York, the Georgia court correctly pointed out, had also extended their criminal jurisdiction over the tribes within their borders. These usurpations had not provoked the measure of hostility leveled against Georgia, but "so soon as the State of Georgia pursues the same course, a hue and cry is raised against her, and a lawyer residing near 1000 miles from her borders has been employed to controvert her rights and obstruct her laws," the judges wrote. Specifically attacking Wirt, the court noted that the Cherokees' attorney had stated that he could find no authority that justified a denial of Cherokee national rights. "Yet by the decision of the Supreme Court, which cannot be unknown to that gentleman," the panel said, referring to Marshall's opinion in *Fletcher v. Peck,* "every acre of land in the occupancy of his sovereign, independent Cherokee Nation, is vested in fee in the State of Georgia."[23]

"It is difficult to conceive," the court continued, "how any person, who has a definite idea of what constitutes a sovereign state, can have come to the conclusion that the Cherokee Nation is a sovereign and independent state." The Indian tribes were not treated as sovereign states during the European conquest and colonization of the Americas, the court added, and no European or American government had ever recognized them as such. This, of course, was not true. The Dutch, the British, and the Americans had all purchased lands by treaty from the Indian tribes; several American policymakers, including Washington, Jefferson, and Knox, had admitted that by using treaties the United States recognized the legitimacy of the tribal governments. Fortunately for the Georgia judges, the Supreme Court had not yet issued a precedent directly supporting Underwood's argument. Justice Johnson had put forth a case similar to Underwood's in *Fletcher v. Peck,* but that opinion was only a singular dissent. Consequently, the court took advantage of Marshall's ambiguity in *Fletcher* and *Johnson v. McIntosh* and portrayed the chief justice's opinions in a light most favorable to the state. In other words, in *Georgia v. Tassels,* the court was not an impartial arbiter, but an advocate for the state.[24]

Underwood and Wirt had conceded that the Cherokees could sell lands only to the United States. The Cherokees' lawyers argued that this restriction on Cherokee sovereignty had resulted from treaties concluded with the federal government and not from any legal or philosophical doctrine of title. The Georgia court countered that the state's political dominion and ultimate title over the Cherokee lands originated from its acquisition of Britain's title by discovery. In *Johnson v. McIntosh,* the judges wrote, Marshall had "ably elucidated" the character of the relationship between the states, the federal government, and the Indian tribes. He had based his construction of the rights of the states on the theory of discovery. That doctrine gave the British an "exclusive right to the country discovered" relative to the other European powers and allowed the English thereafter to "regulate by themselves" their relationships with the native inhabitants. The rights of the Indians were not "entirely disregarded," the Georgia court quoted Marshall, but were "necessarily to a considerable extent impaired." The Natives Americans were "admitted to be the rightful occupants of the soil, with a legal as well as just claim to retain possession of it, and to use it according to their own discretion." But these rights were not perfected under Anglo-American law. Discovery, the convention of judges held, gave the Europeans "exclusive title" to and "ultimate dominion" over the Indian lands and terminated the Native Americans' right to dispose of their lands as they wished. Underwood had also suggested that the Indian right of occupancy could be extinguished only by treaty. To the contrary, the court wrote, the Indian title could be eradicated by "bargain and sale or by deed as well without the form of a treaty." Treaties, the justices continued, were nothing but "contracts for the purchase and sale of Indian lands."[25]

Though willing to cite Marshall on the sanctity of the theory of discovery, the Georgia judges disagreed with his assertion that the federal government possessed the right to extinguish the Indian title. In *Johnson v. McIntosh,* Marshall had argued that the states had surrendered their right to purchase Indian lands to the federal government by ratifying the Territory and Commerce Clauses of the Constitution. The state rejected Marshall's construction. If the Constitution already gave the federal government the power of extinguishment, Trippe argued, why would it have to obtain it by compact from the state? The convention of judges agreed. In the Compact of 1802, they wrote, the state and the federal government contracted only to place the burden of extinguishing the Indian title on the United States. The state did not surrender the right or any other political power to the federal government. Since the federal government had welched on its promise to terminate the Indian title, Georgia had every right to reexert this power and require the United States to compensate it for the costs of doing so. In reality, Article 1 of the Compact of 1802 provided, "the United States shall, at their own expense, extinguish, for the use of Georgia, as early as the same can be peaceably obtained, on reasonable terms, [specific lands of the Creeks]; . . . [and] the United States shall, in the same manner, also extinguish the Indian title to all the other lands within the State of Georgia." The compact was clear: the federal government held the power of extinguishing the Native American title in Georgia, and there was no language providing the state with a right to reexert its authority over the Indian tribes or their land.[26]

The court also overstated the degree of attention that the Supreme Court gave to this issue in *Fletcher v. Peck,* saying that "the real question presented by the [Yazoo] issue was, whether the seizin in fee was in the State of Georgia or in the United States." This question, however, was far from the central issue of *Fletcher.* Marshall had, in one sentence on the issue, stated that the Indian title was not to be "absolutely repugnant to a seizin in fee by the State." Even if Marshall thought that to be the law in 1810, he had made it fairly clear in *Johnson v. McIntosh* that the power of extinguishment was a federal right. The Georgia court, however, elevated Marshall's tentative note of dicta in *Fletcher* into a ringing endorsement in favor of the state's authority to extinguish the Indian title and disregarded his subsequent ruling in *Johnson v. McIntosh.*[27]

The three branches of the Georgia state government were now prepared to seize the prerogative of extinguishment from the federal government. The state tribunal used its discussion of this power to construct a states' rights interpretation of the Commerce Clause. The "conduct" of the British government, the judges said, had created a precedent for defining the relationship between the Indian tribes and the state governments. Georgia had succeeded to all of the rights maintained by the British Crown and was "seized in fee of all lands within its chartered limits." The court said, "That a government should be seized in fee of a territory, and yet have no jurisdiction over that country is an anomaly in the science of jurisprudence." Not only did the state have jurisdiction over the lands in the Cherokee Nation, by virtue of that power, it held personal jurisdiction over every Indian resident on those lands. The judges recognized that the Commerce Clause endowed Congress with the authority "to regulate commerce with foreign nations, and among the several states, and with the Indian tribes," but they ridiculed those advocates of Cherokee sovereignty who argued that the specific wording of the clause demonstrated that the framers placed the Indian tribes on the same political plane as the states and foreign nations. The United States, the convention of judges wrote, had never treated the Indian tribes as independent nations in the regulation of their commerce. In its legislation governing Indian trade, they wrote, Congress "directs how the citizens of the United States shall conduct towards the Indians, and how the Indians shall behave to them." Though Congress prescribed rules and regulations with which foreign merchants had to comply when they entered U.S. jurisdiction, the court said, it did not and could not attempt to regulate the manner in which foreign subjects conducted every aspect of their trade. This, however, was how the United States dealt with the Indian tribes in their commercial relations. Since the federal government controlled every facet of the Indian trade, the judges concluded, individual Indians could not be considered citizens of foreign states, and their tribes could not be considered sovereign nations.[28]

In response to Underwood's argument that the United States had recognized Cherokee sovereignty in past treaties, the judges contended that the provision relating to the Cherokee right to wage war was intended to protect American citizens by requiring the "barbarian" Cherokees to provide notice to the United States before they attacked. Moreover, the court added, though Presidents Washington, Jefferson, Madison, and Monroe had all fought wars against the Indian tribes, Congress had never issued a formal declaration of war against them. A sovereign nation, the convention said, would have received the benefit of an American declaration; rebellious subjects did not deserve one. Not only did the Indian tribes not merit declarations of war, the panel wrote, they were legally incapable of concluding treaties. The court admitted that Congress and the presidents in the past had agreed that the Indian tribes were "proper objects of the treaty making power." Remarkably, the Georgia judges responded to Underwood's recitation of the U.S.-Cherokee treaty relationship by holding that the federal executives and Congresses that had negotiated and ratified those agreements had simply been wrong in the construction of their constitutional authority. "If there are any clauses in any of the compacts between the United States and the Cherokee Indians (miscalled treaties) which give to those Indians the right of independent self-government," the convention of judges declared, "they are simply void, and cannot, and ought not to be permitted to throw any obstacle in the way of the operation of the act of Georgia, extending jurisdiction over the country in the occupancy of the Cherokee Indians." According to the convention of judges, all of the past efforts to purchase lands by treaties from the Indians were only an effort to maintain goodwill between the parties; under international law, the European discoverers and their successors, including Georgia, had a clear legal right to take Native American lands if and when they so desired.[29]

The doctrine of discovery had placed the Cherokees in a condition of "pupilage" to the state of Georgia, the judges concluded. The court made no distinction between discovery and conquest; as with Marshall, the two doctrines were legally synonymous. The "discovering or conquering" powers held the ultimate dominion over the lands of North America, and any rights that had been conceded to Native Americans were part of "the duty of the discovering, or conquering nation, to make some provision for the aborigines, who were a savage race, and of imbecile intellect." After a conquest in Europe, the court said, the vanquished people had either been assimilated into the conquering nation or allowed to exist as a "separate but dependent state."[30] The Georgia judges, however, did not agree that this practice could be applied to the lands that the Europeans had conquered in America. Instead, they wrote that the European nations had carved out a new category of social distinction for the Indian tribes based on what they deemed to be an inherent inferiority. "The habits, manners, and imbecile intellect" of these "ferocious" and "barbarous" tribes prevented the European conquerors from assimilating them with a protected right of self-determination: "They could neither sink into the common mass of their discoverers or conquerors, or be governed as a separate dependent people. They were judged incapable of complying with the obligations which the laws of civilized society imposed, or of being subjected to any code of laws which could be sanctioned by any Christian community." Necessarily, the court concluded, the Indians had been set apart by the European states and allowed to live "according to their customs and manners." Although this was itself an admission that the Europeans had recognized the Indian right of self-determination, the court steadfastly stood by its assertion that Indians were intellectually incapable of governing themselves. Though the Cherokees had "advanced in civilization," the court said, the tribe was not ripe for recognition as an independent state. Individual Cherokees were, however, now prepared to come under the jurisdiction of the state. If the Cherokees did not like that alternative, the Georgia judges added, they could remove to the West.[31]

On that note, the convention of judges overruled Tassel's challenge and returned the case to Hall County for trial. On November 22, a superior court jury in front of Judge Clayton found Tassel guilty. Clayton sentenced the Cherokee to hang on December 24. When Underwood asked Clayton to certify the record for an appeal to the U.S. Supreme Court, the judge refused. According to the *Cherokee Phoenix,* Clayton "even refused to certify that Tassel was tried."[32] (Clayton subsequently apologized for his role in Tassel's case. Four years after the trial, John Ross visited the judge. The principal chief wrote to the nation's local attorney that Clayton, a devoted member of the Troup faction, had once told a Gwinnett County grand jury that Ross "should be *taken by the horns* & led before him as *the Bull* of the Cherokee Nation." Ross was determined to face down Clayton personally, but he found the judge congenial and apologetic for his decision in the *Tassels* case. Ross's letter implies that Clayton had undergone a conversion on the issue of Indian rights. Ross wrote that Clayton said that "he must acknowledge this unfortunate fact" that his decisions were a consequence of partisan warfare. He told Ross that "the two great parties in Georgia in their struggle for power had always made [the Cherokees' fate] a party question and thereby the Cherokees were placed, as it were, between two great fires." That assessment is perhaps a bit self-serving. Very few of the Troup or anti-Troup factions professed respect for the Cherokees' position. In any event, Clayton's former antipathy toward the Cherokees must have been dissipated to some extent by the shocking denouement of the Tassel controversy, for a few weeks after Tassel's trial Clayton committed "political heresy" in the eyes of the Troup party when he declared a Georgia law that prohibited the Cherokees from mining gold on their own land unconstitutional.)[33]

Wirt took control of the case in Washington and filed an appeal with the U.S. Supreme Court. Specifically, he asked the justices to overturn Tassel's conviction and enjoin Georgia from executing and enforcing its laws in the Cherokee Nation. On December 12, Chief Justice Marshall granted the writ of error, and on the twentieth, John Ross sent Georgia governor George Gilmer a copy of the notice of appeal and a subpoena ordering him to appear before the justices on the second Monday in January. This order, the state papers reported, "created considerable excitement in the legislature, and with the public generally, as early as it became known." The *Georgia Journal,* the newspaper of Milledgeville, the state capital, had earlier predicted, "As far as we can judge, it is probable the Supreme Court of the United States will not interfere in the decision of our court on this question." The *Journal* was correct; the Supreme Court never got the opportunity to hear Tassel's case. The notice of appeal should have stayed Tassel's execution. Instead, Gilmer and the state legislature panicked. The General Assembly had already adjourned *sine die* on December 22 when Governor Gilmer reported to the members still in Milledgeville that he had received an order from John Marshall requiring the state to appear before the Supreme Court. After soliciting their advice, Gilmer immediately called the remaining representatives back into an emergency joint session.[34]

During its recent term the legislature had proceeded with the next step in its plan to take over the Cherokee Nation. It had promulgated legislation providing for the survey, division, and sale of the Cherokees' territory. In an unusual fit of restraint, however, it had postponed the actual surveys until the meeting of the next legislature to give the federal government another opportunity to conclude a removal treaty with the Cherokees. The General Assembly had also moved to eradicate the liberties of individual Cherokees. On December 18, the legislature passed a law annulling all contracts with the Cherokees "as far as the Indians are concerned." On the last day of the regular session, the legislature prohibited the Cherokees from assembling in groups except for the explicit purpose of signing a removal treaty, enacted a statute requiring all whites living in the Cherokee Nation to take an oath to the state of Georgia, and mandated that non-Indians obtain a permit to continue residency there. The Cherokees, shocked by the expansion of the state's assault, now braced for an invasion by the state's militia.[35]

More than the prospect of cheap Cherokee land tempted the Georgia public. In 1827 gold was discovered just north of Gainesville, and the region was in the midst of the United States's first gold rush. Hall County's population doubled between 1828 and 1830, and disputes between prospectors provoked claim wars just north of Gainesville. The bulk of the discovered deposits lay within the Cherokee Nation. The Georgia legislature quickly moved to confiscate these mines. By the summer of 1830, the area was in turmoil. In September prospectors from Tennessee battled miners from Georgia and South Carolina for access to the mines in the Cherokee Nation. A visitor to the region reported in December that "intruders of all colors, sexes and ages, from Tennessee, Alabama, N. Carolina and Georgia, amounting to, as estimated, between 4 and 5,000, [were] all busily employed in securing as much of the precious metal as possible." The situation was so chaotic that the Cherokee Nation asked its agent to bring in federal troops to keep out intruders and maintain order in the settlements around the gold mines. As soon as the soldiers were dispatched, Gilmer and other Georgia leaders demanded that President Jackson remove them. He did so in early December. This left the Cherokee Nation vulnerable to the depredations of trespassers and the Georgia Guard, the paramilitary police force that the legislature had established to confiscate the mines.[36]

It was in these tumultuous circumstances that Gilmer and the state legislature responded to Marshall's order requiring the state to appear before the U.S. Supreme Court. At the emergency session on the evening of the twenty-second, Gilmer declared that the Court did not possess jurisdiction over Tassel's case. "The object of [Marshall's] mandate," he said, "is to control the State in the exercise of its ordinary jurisdiction, which, in criminal cases, has been vested by the [state] constitution, exclusively in its Superior Court." If the federal Supreme Court exercised jurisdiction over Georgia's criminal cases, he said, "it must eventuate in the utter annihilation of the State governments." Clearly, Gilmer and most of the legislature feared that the Supreme Court would strike down the state's extension laws and give the Cherokees perpetual possession of the nation's lands. The executive department of the state, Gilmer threatened, would "disregard" the Supreme Court order, "and any attempt to enforce such orders, will be resisted with whatever force the laws have placed at my command." The matter was immediately delegated to a committee composed of members from both houses. By 10 P.M. the committee had passed out a resolution supporting Gilmer's position and defying Marshall's order. The full assembly agreed on the resolution minutes later. The assembly declared that it "view[ed] with deep regret, the interference by the chief justice of the Supreme Court, in the administration of the criminal laws of this State." The legislature continued, "The right to punish crimes against the peace and good order of this state is a necessary part of sovereignty, which the State of Georgia has never parted with." Marshall's actions were "a flagrant violation of that right." The legislature advised the governor "and every other officer of this State" to "disregard any and every mandate and process that has been, or shall be served upon them" from the federal Supreme Court "for the purpose of arresting the execution of any of the criminal Laws of this State." Gilmer was authorized to use "all the force and means placed at his command by the constitution and laws of the state, to resist and repel any and every invasion, from whatever quarter, upon the criminal laws of the state." The state of Georgia, the assembly declared, "would never compromit [*sic*] her sovereignty, as an independent state."[37]

The legislature instructed Governor Gilmer to "communicate to the Sheriff of Hall County by Express" the contents of the resolution and "ensure the full execution of the Laws, in the case of George Tassels." For Tassel, this meant that he was to be hanged posthaste. At midnight the governor sent a special messenger at high speed to Gainesville to deliver the order to Jacob Eberhart, the sheriff of Hall County. On Christmas Eve morning, the date originally ordered for Tassel's execution, Eberhart unlocked Tassel and walked him out of the Hall County jail. The sheriff tied the condemned man's hands and feet together, helped him into the back of an oxcart, and forced him to sit down on what was to be his own coffin. When Tassel was safely secured, the sheriff carried him out to "a large open field" just south of Gainesville. One eyewitness recalled the event: "The day of execution came, and oh! what a day; cloudy, dark, rain, hail and sleet through the entire day." Despite the adverse conditions, he said, "Every road leading to the town was thronged at an early hour with men and women and children from all parts of the county and many from adjoining counties until a vast multitude had assembled to witness the death of a human being while suspended between heaven and earth." Observers recalled that there was a large crowd present, including eighteen to twenty of Tassel's fellow Cherokees. The Cherokees were there, one witness said, "to give the brother a word of encouragement before he entered upon his journey to the fair hunting grounds of the savage tribes."

According to the witness, Sheriff Eberhart moved unceremoniously and with dispatch: "The prisoner was ordered by the sheriff to get up and stand upon his coffin on which he had for some time been sitting. The arms were tied down, the cap drawn over the face, the ox cart was driven forward leaving the body suspended in the air. A few shrugs of the shoulders, a little drawing up of the feet, and all was still, and within twenty minutes the doctors in attendance pronounced him dead." Afterward, the state authorities turned Tassel's body over to his Cherokee friends. The Cherokees placed Tassel in the coffin that he rode in on and buried him several hundred yards away. Several of the Cherokees were too distraught to go home, a witness recalled, and remained in town overnight. "Some of them got drunk," he reported, "and one of them froze to death that night on Soapstone hill, and was buried a few paces from the main road." [38]

Historians have often described how South Carolina, in the nullification crisis, threatened the life of the Union. Georgia's actions in Tassel's case, however, were as antagonistic toward the Constitution as those of its eastern neighbor. Forty miles away from Gainesville in Athens, the *Athenian* immediately recognized that the state was provoking its own constitutional crisis: "The collision of authorities portends something serious. What its effect will be is impossible to predict with any degree of certainty—perhaps His Honor, Judge Marshall, may think it incumbent on him to arraign and punish (perchance he should possess the power), the State of Georgia for contempt of the Federal Court." In hanging Tassel, Georgia had, as the paper suggested, demonstrated the contempt it held for the Supreme Court and the notion of federal supremacy. The state rejected the federal government's authority over Indian affairs, ignored the strictures of U.S.-Indian treaties, and threatened to instigate a war with the Cherokees. Georgia's citizens lusted for Cherokee gold and land and despised the reality of an Indian nation at its doorstep. The state's politicians and judges were not going to allow the Supreme Court to get in the way of distributing that bounty and cleansing the area of nonwhite competitors. The tragedy was not just that Tassel had been rashly executed with his case still pending, but that in a few short years the state's political and legal authorities had exchanged their respect for the Constitution, the Union, and their Native American neighbors for material gain, political popularity, and racial prejudice.[39]

Most of the state's newspapers praised their leaders' actions and ridiculed criticism that was cascading down from the North. The *Georgia Messenger* wrote that "the Northern prints are out in full cry against us." Criticism of Georgia's actions, the editor continued, were "mischievous in the extreme." He wrote, "They serve to engender strife and foster those sectional feelings which it should be the aim of all good men to suppress. We are characterized as impetuous, hot-headed, choleric, & c. If we be so, our Northern brethren should bear with our infirmities. . . . We cannot but wince under such unqualified abuse." At the same time, the *Messenger*'s editors claimed that some observers in the North understood Georgia's position. "We are glad to find that the most respectable of the Northern papers view the subject in its proper light," the paper reported, "and are willing to concede to us, the right of exercising criminal jurisdiction over our own territory, a right so incident to government, that without it, the *Sovereignty of the State* is a mere bye word, a sounding brass, and tinkling cymbal."[40]

The Cherokee government immediately filed a memorial of protest to Congress, and Elias Boudinot condemned Georgia's hypocrisy in the *Cherokee Phoenix*: "One day they discountenance the proceedings of the nullifiers of South Carolina—at another, they even out-do the people of South Carolina, and authorize their Governor to hoist the flag of rebellion against the United States! If such proceedings are sanctioned by the majority of the people of the U. States, the Union is but a tottering fabric, which will soon fall and crumble."[41]

The national press also commented on the developments in Georgia. Calling the relationships between the Cherokee Nation, Georgia, and the federal government "delicate and difficult," the editors of *Niles' Register* wrote that Georgia's laws were unduly provocative, "seeing that Georgia has no present use for the land, and is about to waste it by a lottery." Other newspapers criticized Georgia's interference in the due process of the law. John Quincy Adams, the former president, despaired over the developing situation in the South: "The Constitution, the laws and treaties of the United States are prostrate in the State of Georgia. Is there any remedy for this state of things? None. . . . The Executive of the United States is in League with the State of Georgia." Adams accurately predicted, "This example will be imitated by other States, and with regard to other national interests—perhaps the tariff." "The Union is in the most imminent danger of dissolution," he lamented, "the ship is about to founder."[42]

When Georgia took Tassel's life, the Cherokee Nation lost its standing before the United States Supreme Court. George Gilmer and the Georgia legislature had intended this result when their agents pulled the oxcart out from under Tassel's feet. The state's lynching of Tassel left a lasting impression on many of the participants in the case. Several years after Tassel's death, his lawyer, William Underwood, was living near the Alabama-Georgia border. Periodically, he crossed into Alabama to try cases in that state. At one hearing, Underwood attempted to analogize his present case to a previous decision in Georgia. His green adversary from Alabama told Underwood that Georgia law carried no weight in Alabama. Underwood responded dryly: "My young friend has reminded me that I could not introduce Georgia law into his state. . . . I will let him understand that of which he seems to be ignorant, to wit: that Georgia takes the liberty of extending her laws over all the adjacent savage tribes, and, what concerns the young man personally still more, with very little evidence or ceremony she hangs or sends to the penitentiary all the young savages that traduce her, or are in any manner in her way." At this point, the Cherokees remained unable and unwilling to accept the Tassel affair with that kind of detached sarcasm. John Ross and the Cherokee National Council remained determined to resist Georgia's relentless effort to bully the Cherokees into submission. Ross, in particular, refused to accept defeat on the issue of the state extension statutes. He had become accustomed to the chicanery, the intimidation, and the brutality of the state's authorities. Yet he believed that at some point in the near future the United States would place legal principle ahead of political and material expediency, and he vowed to continue the Cherokee Nation's fight to bring Georgia before the bar of national justice.[43]

CHAPTER FIVE

Domestic Dependent Nations

Cherokee Nation v. Georgia

DESPITE JOHN ROSS'S OPTIMISM, the execution of George Tassel was a devastating setback to the Cherokees' legal strategy. To make matters worse, in 1830 Andrew Jackson suspended annuity payments to the Cherokees. Jackson reportedly said that he "would not break sticks to put in other people's hands to break his own head with." He would not, in other words, subsidize the Cherokees' litigation. Consequently, Ross was having a difficult time coming up with funds to pay the nation's lawyers. The principal chief sent Elias Boudinot north to drum up financial and political support for the Cherokee cause, while he traveled around the nation encouraging his charges. Ross told his constituents that the Tassel case did not leave the Cherokees at the mercy of the southern state governments and that the United States would surely not stand by and see them dispossessed. "Whatever may be the final result of this painful controversy," he declared, "the Cherokees are prepared to meet it." The Cherokee people would never remove to the West, and "they never will live in vassalage to Georgia," Ross added. "Should the last dire extremity come," he said, "they can and will live and die as freemen."[1]

Ross was encouraged that the Supreme Court had agreed to hear Tassel's writ of error, and he authorized William Wirt to file a suit to challenge Georgia's extension laws. Weeks before Tassel's case developed, Wirt and his cocounsel John Sergeant had prepared an action asking the Court to enjoin Georgia from enforcing its laws in the Cherokee Nation. With Tassel's case rendered moot, the lawyers for the Cherokees simply returned to their original plan of attack. On December 27, 1830, three days after the state hanged Tassel, Wirt filed the suit titled *The Cherokee Nation v. The State of Georgia* with the Supreme Court and served printed copies to Georgia's governor George Gilmer and Turner Hunt Trippe, the state solicitor general. The process papers ordered the Georgia officials to appear before the Court on the fifth day of the following March for a hearing on the Cherokees' claim.[2]

In the bill for injunction, Wirt and Sergeant argued that Article 3, Section 2, of the Constitution required the justices to accept jurisdiction over the case. Section 2 offered two routes to standing. The first few lines of the first clause provide United States courts with jurisdiction in federal questions, that is, cases "arising under this Constitution, the Laws of the United States, and Treaties made, or which shall be made, under their authority." While Wirt raised this ground for standing at oral argument, the Cherokees' lawyers primarily focused their claim on the clause of Section 2 that conferred jurisdiction to the federal courts in cases "between a State, or the Citizens thereof, and foreign States, Citizens or Subjects." In short, Wirt and Sergeant argued that the Cherokee Nation was a foreign state seeking redress from one of the United States and that the controversy required an immediate hearing before the Court. They also presented the action pursuant to the second clause of Section 2, which authorizes the Supreme Court to accept original jurisdiction in cases "in which a State shall be a party."[3]

Wirt designed the suit as a broad attack that would appeal to the sympathy and sense of fairness among American voters, to the political sensibilities of national legislators, and to the morality and intelligence of the Supreme Court justices. In a sense, the case filed by the Cherokee Nation was not just a suit for a redress of grievances, it was another Cherokee declaration of independence. The Cherokee Nation, the suit proclaimed, was a "foreign state, not owing allegiance to the United States, nor to any prince, potentate, or State." From "time immemorial," the Cherokee Nation had been an independent and sovereign state, and the United States had recognized that status in fourteen treaties between 1785 and 1819. In those treaties, particularly the 1785 accord at Hopewell and the 1791 agreement at Holston, the parties had recognized that the Cherokees retained almost all of the emoluments of nationhood. In concluding the animosities that arose out of America's War of Independence, the Treaty of Hopewell demonstrated that the two parties considered each other as diplomatic equals. They exchanged prisoners, they agreed to declare war before any hostilities were resumed, and they established permanent borders between them. The Cherokees pointed out that in Hopewell the federal treaty commissioners had authorized the Cherokee government to punish American trespassers, while in the Holston treaty the parties had agreed that "the Cherokee nation is not within the jurisdiction of either of the states or territorial districts of the United States." Moreover, the federal commissioners had "solemnly guarantee[d]" title to the lands the Cherokees retained. These treaties between themselves and the United States were sacrosanct under the Constitution, the Cherokees argued; Article 6 made treaties negotiated by the United States the "supreme law of the land." Georgia's extension laws, the

Cherokees concluded on this point, were an unconstitutional trespass on that supreme law.[4]

The suit contended that federal-Cherokee treaties imposed only two limitations on the latter nation's sovereignty. First, the Cherokees had agreed that their lands could be sold only to the United States. Second, the Cherokee government had surrendered control over its foreign relations and international commerce to the American government. Beyond this, their petition stated, the Cherokees continued to possess every other sovereign power and retained complete and undiminished title to their national territory. The Cherokees had owned and occupied their lands long before Europeans had found the North American continent, and their title originated from "the Great Spirit, who is the common father of the human family, and to whom the whole earth belongs." Since their creation, the Cherokees had been the "sole and exclusive masters" of their territory and had governed it according to "their own laws, usages, and customs." Title by original and sustained possession, the Cherokees said, trumped the "wild and chimerical" European claims of title by discovery. The argument that the mere sighting of a coastline conferred title to an entire continent was logically untenable; the Indian nations, moreover, had never recognized the legitimacy of the discovery doctrine. If anything, the Cherokees contended, discovery only determined priority among the European nations for the right to purchase lands from sovereign Native American nations, "a principle settled among themselves for their own convenience, in adjusting their mutual accounts of rapine on the western world." Even if one admitted that discovery gave the United States the right to extinguish the Indian title, as the federal government contended, customary practice and the previous decisions of the Court had demanded that such cessions be "offered, accepted, rejected, or modified at the pleasure of [the Indian nations], nothing being forced upon them."[5]

The complaint added that the governor, legislature, and courts of Georgia had all unlawfully refused to respect the sovereignty of the Cherokee Nation. The state authorities had also, as demonstrated by the hanging of Tassel, conspired to prevent the Cherokees from challenging the legality of the extension statutes in a court of law. To make matters worse, the president and War Department were ignoring their government's promise, reaffirmed several times since the Treaty of Hopewell, that it would protect the Cherokees from state encroachment. The Cherokees' appeals to the president for assistance had all been rebuffed, and Jackson had told them that he had "no power to protect them against the laws of Georgia." Instead, the president had authorized federal troops to assist the Georgia Guard in enforcing the extension laws in the nation. At that minute, the suit read, the state was holding a number of Cherokees in custody under the false pretense of its criminal jurisdiction. When the Cherokees had appealed to Congress for protection from the Georgia statutes, it had responded with the Indian Removal Act of 1830. Georgia's actions and the refusal of Congress and the president to intervene had forced the nation to seek relief from the Court.[6]

The Cherokee bill also maintained that the United States had a duty to continue the civilization program for the Indians in the East. In the cession treaties of 1817 and 1819, federal negotiators had promised that those Cherokees who did not remove to the West could continue to rely on the "patronage, aid and good neighborhood" of the United States. The Cherokees had met their end of the bargain, they said. At the direction of federal agents, they had built schools and churches, adopted Anglo-American agricultural and mechanical techniques, and established, just as Jefferson had suggested, a constitutional government patterned after that of the United States. The nation had enacted and codified criminal and civil laws and organized courts to enforce them. The Cherokees were so convinced of their progress, the petition declared, that they would willingly "submit to a comparison [on their level of civilization] with their white brethren around them." In return for their efforts at acculturation, the United States was now conspiring with Georgia to exile them to the West.[7]

The Cherokee complaint noted that the Indian Removal Act of 1830 did not make emigration compulsory and did not sanction territorial violations of past treaties. The Cherokees added that they knew nothing of the nature and value of the lands in the West and wished to remain where they were: "They are fully satisfied with the country they possess—the climate is salubrious; it is convenient for commerce and intercourse." More important, the Cherokee homeland in the East was "consecrated in their affections from having been immemorially the property and residence of their ancestors, and from containing now the graves of their fathers, relatives, and friends." Those who had previously removed to the Arkansas valley, the Cherokees reminded the Court, had already been forced to move again and were constantly under the threat of attack from "hostile Indians." For all of these reasons, the Cherokees concluded, the state of Georgia needed to be restrained from its unlawful attack on the tribe's sovereignty.[8]

Georgia refused to file a response to the Cherokee Nation's petition, although Governor Gilmer ridiculed specific sections of the Cherokees' complaint in private correspondence. In letters to Jackson and Judge Augustin Clayton, Gilmer, who was almost irrationally obsessed with Ross's ancestry, wrote: "What is said of their strong desire to remain with the bones of their fathers," he said, "are but the expressions of those whose ancestors' bodies are deposited in Europe." Gilmer blamed those of mixed ancestry for stirring up the "pure-blooded" Indians. Indians without mixed blood, Gilmer said, were not intelligent or moral enough to maintain devotion to ideological principles.[9]

On the day oral arguments were scheduled, Wirt and Sergeant filed a supplementary bill that detailed Tassel's arrest and execution. The pleading also described the Georgia assembly's most recent legislative attack on the Cherokee Nation. Just before Tassel's hanging, the General Assembly had ordered preparations for the survey, division, and sale of the Cherokee Nation's lands. The legislature had also authorized the Georgia Guard to seize the gold mines in the Cherokee Nation until the state assumed control of the Indians' territory. This guard, the Cherokees reported, had committed numerous "acts of violence and injustice" against their people under the authority of Georgia law. The General Assembly had also prohibited the Cherokees from collecting tolls on their ferries, bridges, and turnpikes. Finally, on pain of imprisonment for four years at hard labor, the legislature had declared that the Cherokees were proscribed from assembling for the purpose of holding court, legislating, "or for any other purpose whatever." These laws, the suit alleged, were violations of the Cherokees' rights of property and self-government.[10]

In summing up their case, the Cherokees maintained that their nation was a foreign state under Article 3, that the Supreme Court could accept jurisdiction over the case, and that the Court could remedy the nation's injuries by striking down the state laws and enjoining their enforcement. Georgia was intentionally and systematically violating the property and assembly rights of the people of the Cherokee Nation, and its extension laws were a diabolical effort to annihilate the Cherokees, their culture, and their political and legal institutions. In addition, Georgia's actions were an unconstitutional attempt to expropriate Congress's authority over Indian affairs and an affront to the treaty-making power of the federal government. If the Supreme Court refused to hear the nation's case, the bill concluded, the Cherokees would be left with limited and disturbing alternatives. They could surrender their sovereignty, their property rights, and their civil liberties to "the rapacity and injustice of the state of Georgia" and remove to the West, or they could "arm themselves in defense of [their] sacred rights, and fall, sword in hand, on the graves of their fathers." Their only hope for a peaceful solution that allowed them to remain intact as a nation in the East, the Cherokees said, was for the Supreme Court to enjoin Georgia's illegal aggression.[11]

At oral argument on the eleventh, twelfth, and fourteenth of March, the Cherokees' lawyers repeated the points laid out in their bill for injunction and offered some preemptive strikes to questions that they expected to be raised by the justices. George Gilmer had claimed that the Cherokees' lawyers had not properly served Georgia with the action, and he refused to allow the state's solicitor general to file briefs or appear at the oral arguments. The state, he declared, would not forfeit its sovereignty to the national government by appearing before the Court. In apologizing for the length of his presentation, Wirt told the justices that since "we are without an adversary to state objections at the bar . . . we are driven to the necessity of combating such as we have seen stated elsewhere."[12]

Wirt was tired and weak after several months of exhaustive work on other matters, and he allowed Sergeant to proffer part of the nation's argument. Sergeant strongly urged the Court to enforce the treaties between the United States and the Cherokees. These treaties, he said, established that the Cherokee Nation was a foreign state. Admittedly, the nation had come under the protection of the United States and had surrendered some of its extraterritorial powers. But, he said, "a man is still a man though mutilated and deprived of some of his limbs." The treaties signed by the United States, he added, created a "deliberate and solemn . . . obligation . . . binding the national faith and honor." If the federal government abrogated its treaties with the Cherokees and allowed Georgia to enforce its extension laws, Sergeant concluded, "There will be no Cherokee boundary, no Cherokee nation, no Cherokee lands, no Cherokee treaties, no laws of the United States. . . . They will all be swept out of existence together, leaving nothing but the monuments in our history of the enormous injustice that has been practiced towards a friendly nation."[13]

Wirt's argument was clever, persuasive, and even more impassioned. He was thoroughly familiar with the Court's past decisions on Native American rights, with Vattel's *Law of Nations,* and with the arguments that Georgia's legislators and judges had developed in the past. Consequently, Wirt was prepared to destroy almost every potential contention that could be raised in support of the constitutionality of Georgia's extension laws. The Cherokees' attorney proposed a two-step process for determining whether the Cherokee Nation had standing before the Supreme Court. First, was the Cherokee Nation a state? Second, was it a foreign state as contemplated by the Constitutional Convention? Vattel, Wirt reminded the Court, characterized states as "bodies politic, societies of men united together to procure their natural safety and advantage by means of their union." Wirt said, "Such a society has its affairs and interests, it deliberates and takes resolutions in common, and thus becomes a moral person, having an understanding and a will peculiar to itself, and is susceptible of obligation and laws." Wirt pointed out that Vattel had written that a nation that governed itself "in what form soever, without any dependence on foreign power," was a sovereign state. Though it had placed itself under the protection of the United States, Wirt continued, the Cherokee Nation had not surrendered its right to self-government. At the Constitutional Convention, he noted, every state in the Union had ceded considerable substantive powers to the federal government. All of the states, including Georgia, were also under the protection of the United States. The Cherokee Nation had transferred far fewer powers to the federal government than had the states, Wirt said, but Georgia would never admit that it had forfeited its sovereignty by ratifying the Constitution. Under Vattel's test, the Cherokee Nation was a state.[14]

In *Tassels,* the Georgia court had characterized the Cherokees as conquered subjects of the state. Wirt challenged the assertion that the Cherokees were a subjugated people. "As a nation," he said, "they never bowed their necks to the yoke of a conqueror." The Indians were not dictated to at Hopewell, as some Americans liked to think—the United States had come to the Cherokees seeking conciliation. "This treaty of Hopewell," Wirt said, "far from presenting us with the picture of a people subjected by conquest, dissolved as a state, and merged into the mass of citizens of the United States; gives us, on the contrary, in every article, the image of a separate, a powerful, and a martial nation, proud and jealous of their independence." Wirt also offered an argument that Chancellor Kent had suggested to him in a recent letter on the question of the Cherokee Nation's status as a foreign state under Article 3. Not only was the Cherokee Nation a state, Wirt contended, it was a foreign state: "They owe no allegiance to your constitution; have no voice in your laws. . . . They pay you no taxes. . . . They take no part in your foreign wars, unless they choose to do so. They can make war upon you themselves, without committing treason. . . . And if they are not citizens of the United States what are they; what can they be but aliens? . . . And if they be a nation of aliens, what can they be but a foreign nation, a foreign state, in the sense of the constitution?"[15]

Georgia had made much of the fact that the Cherokee Nation was located within the recognized borders of the state. Wirt wryly noted that the Cherokees "lie exactly where they have lain for a time long antecedent to the existence of that state, and very probably, long antecedent to the existence of the monarchy from which that state derives its charter." That charter, Wirt added, was not yet one hundred years old; the Cherokees had lived on the land since "time immemorial." Georgia's legislators had also often charged that the Cherokee Nation's declaration of independence created an *imperium in imperio,* a state within a state. Such a political device clearly violated the fourth article of the Constitution, which mandates that "no new state shall be formed or erected within the jurisdiction of any other state . . . without the consent of the legislature of the states concerned as well as of the Congress." Wirt said that only "half-enlightened persons, who see men only as trees walking, seem to consider this an unanswerable objection." The principle of *imperium in imperio*, he argued, prohibited two states from claiming sovereignty over the same territory; it "has no application to two distinct governments operating at the same time on separate territories." The only *imperium in imperio* that would exist in this situation, Wirt charged, would be if the Court allowed Georgia to extend its jurisdiction over the Cherokee Nation.[16]

Wirt also attacked one of the standard justifications for the European conquest of America. Vattel and early colonial apologists had argued that an overpopulated nation of cultivators could, under the law of nations, seize the unexploited lands of another people. Wirt challenged this "law of necessity" on four grounds. First, he argued that the theory had been devised after the fact. Did Columbus, Sir Walter Raleigh, the Puritans, and the Quakers, Wirt asked, come to America to relieve the European population explosion? "No one colony can, with any colour of historical truth, be said to have been settled on [that] principle." Second, he suggested that the overpopulation of Europe was a myth; the continent during the Age of Discovery was plenty big enough to bear its population. Third, the principle of necessity was intended to provide the immigrating people with land "to such an extent as it can actually people and cultivate." If this was the primary reason for European settlement in America, Wirt asked, why had the charters of colonization offered grantees title from sea to sea? In particular, he said, why would Georgia need a charter from the Atlantic to the Pacific when other English colonies to the north held the same rights? Even now, he added, Georgia was not populous enough to reasonably occupy and cultivate the lands of the Cherokee Nation. Lastly, he argued, Vattel's doctrine of necessity was based on the presumption that the lands seized by the Europeans were either vacant or peopled by nomadic bands of hunter-gatherers. The Cherokees could certainly not be categorized in this class. The doctrine of necessity, he concluded, "has no place in the law of nations, except with regard to uninhabited and desert places."[17]

In the last hours of his presentation, Wirt made several emotional entreaties to the Court. First, he appealed to the justices' sense of national honor. The United States had solemnly vowed to protect the Cherokee Nation from the states, Wirt said. If the federal government allowed Georgia to violate the Cherokee Nation's sovereignty it would be a *"participes criminis"*: "There is no moral difference between them; and if these things shall be permitted, the faith and honor of this nation are gone. . . . If such be the point of degeneracy, to which we have already sunk since the age of Washington, farewell to the honor of the American name; happy it is for the patriot that he was called from this scene of things, before he witnessed this heart-sickening degradation of his country." Next, Wirt appealed to the justices, like Marshall, who had been educated in the Enlightenment theory of the innate equality of man. "However variously colored by difference of climate or other adventitious causes," he said, all humans were of the "same family" and possessed "from their common parent equal rights." There was a "vague idea among us," he said, that Indians were "ignorant savages, wild and wandering hordes." This was a misconception that "led Pizarro and Cortez to hunt down the Mexicans with blood hounds; and which proved them to be far worse savages than those whom they persecuted under that name." The Court should not judge a nation by the "tincture of a skin," Wirt said; the United States was already suffering from "our mistake on this ground, with regard to another unfortunate race."[18]

Echoing an argument made earlier by Elias Boudinot in the *Cherokee Phoenix,* Wirt then noted that before the American civilization program, Georgia had allowed the Cherokees to live under their own "savage" laws and government. Now, after the Cherokees had progressed to a state of civilization approximate to the level of white Americans and had established a "regular and well-balanced government," the state had responded by outlawing their nation. "So it would seem," Wirt surmised, that "their right to govern themselves diminishes in the ratio that their capacity for self-government increases, and expires entirely when that capacity becomes complete."[19]

Wirt pleaded with the Court to avoid the urge to sidestep a decision on the substantive merits of the case, for he suspected that Marshall was concerned about a potential constitutional crisis if Jackson refused to enforce a judgment in the Cherokees' favor. The justices had a duty to pronounce the law regardless of its political effect, Wirt told them; if the president "refused to perform his duty the Constitution has provided a remedy. . . . I believe that if the injunction shall be awarded, there is a moral force in the sentiment of the American community, which will, alone, sustain it, and constrain obedience." Wirt hoped that public opinion would congeal in favor of the Cherokees and forestall any presidential perfidy. "Let us do our duty," he said, "and the people of the United States will take care that others do theirs."[20]

In his closing peroration, Wirt appealed to the conscience of each justice:

I cannot believe that this honourable court . . . will stand by and see these people stripped of their property and extirpated from the earth, while they are holding up to us their treaties and claiming the fulfillment of our engagements. If truth and faith and honor and justice have fled from every other part of our country, we shall find them here. If not, our sun has gone down in treachery, blood and crime, in the face of the world; and, instead of being proud of our country, as heretofore, we may well call upon the rocks and mountains to hide our shame from earth and heaven.[21]

After this emotional closing to Wirt's argument, the justices retired to their boardinghouse to deliberate. They were in a hurry to complete the 1831 session on schedule, but by March 18 they had agreed that they could not produce a unified decision. As a result, on the last day of the session three justices read opinions from the bench. Several days later, Justice Smith Thompson of New York issued a dissent to the public. Constitutional historians have tended to divide these four opinions into three blocs. Henry Baldwin and William Johnson, the latter making a remarkable change of position, argued that the Cherokees lacked constitutional standing as a foreign state under Article 3 and rejected Wirt's argument that the Cherokees were a sovereign nation. Baldwin and Johnson maintained that the Cherokees, who lived within the territorial borders of Georgia, were, as individuals, subjects of the state. The Cherokee Nation did not exist as an independent or separate polity. Joseph Story and Thompson formed a second bloc that maintained that the Indian tribes were independent, sovereign nations. In their view, the Cherokee Nation was a foreign state, it had standing before the Court under Article 3, and it was entitled to be protected from state trespass by the United States under federal-Cherokee treaties. Thompson and Story not only argued for accepting jurisdiction over the case, they were prepared to rule that the Georgia extension laws were unconstitutional.

Marshall and John McLean were left somewhat in the middle attempting to forge a compromise between the two factions. Ultimately, they concluded that the Cherokee Nation lacked standing as a foreign state under Article 3. Though Marshall and McLean vehemently disagreed with Baldwin and Johnson on the issue of whether the tribes possessed sovereign powers, as a group they formed a four-to-two majority in favor of denying the nation access to a ruling on the merits. Marshall, now seventy-five, had consistently attempted to forge one-voice majorities. In this case, however, the interests of Georgia, the Cherokee Nation, and the federal government were too disparate, the competing interpretations of the Constitution too antagonistic, and the emotions on each side too fervent for him to construct a compromise that would have reconciled the ideas of tribal sovereignty, federal plenary power, and states' rights into an opinion acceptable to a majority of the justices. As a result, the four opinions issued by the Court produced a cacophony of rhetoric and rationale.[22]

The Cherokee petition, the chief justice wrote, alleged that Supreme Court refusal to remedy their complaint would "go directly to annihilate the Cherokees as a political society, and to seize, for the use of Georgia, the lands of the nation which have been assured to them by the United States in solemn treaties repeatedly made and still in force." Personally, Marshall said, he was taken by the Cherokee cause: "If the courts were permitted to indulge their sympathies, a case better calculated to excite them can scarcely be imagined. A people once numerous, powerful, and truly independent, found by our ancestors in the quiet and uncontrolled possession of an ample domain, gradually sinking beneath our superior policy, our arts and our arms, have yielded their lands by successive treaties, each of which contains a solemn guarantee of the residue, until they retain no more of their formerly extensive territory than is deemed necessary to their comfortable subsistence." But just as Wirt had feared, though disposed to side with the Cherokees, Marshall determined that the question involved in *Cherokee Nation v. Georgia* was political, not legal. The Court, the chief justice said, could not provide a legal remedy to the Cherokees' dilemma. The Cherokees were asking the justices to intrude into matters demanding executive or legislative attention. Marshall was cognizant that Congress was considering a resolution to repeal Section 25 of the Judiciary Act of 1789, which gave the Supreme Court the power to review and reverse state court decisions. He understood that a finding favoring the Cherokees might not only be unenforceable but would further antagonize those in Congress who wanted to circumscribe the jurisdiction of the Court. The chief justice, according to some scholars, perhaps saw no reason to render a decision that only weakened the Court and did nothing to help the Cherokees.[23]

Officially, though, Marshall used the question of standing to dispose of the case. The issue, he said, was whether the Cherokee Nation had constitutional standing to originate an action with the Supreme Court as a foreign state under Article 3. First, he asked, was the Cherokee Nation a state? This question raised an extensive debate among the justices who issued opinions. Citing the section of Vattel proffered by Wirt, Thompson wrote, "It is not perceived how it is possible to escape the conclusion that [the Cherokees] form a sovereign State." Baldwin, in contrast, refused to admit that the Indian tribes were states or nations. The American government, he said, had never accorded national status to any of the Indian tribes. For lack of a precise term, United States officials had described the Indian communities as "nations, tribes, hordes, savages, chiefs, sachems and warriors" under the numerous federal-Indian treaties. Treaty authors simply used the word "nation," Baldwin said, as a convenient term of collective reference. Moreover, he added, the Native American tribes had clearly accepted a dependent relationship with the United States. "There can be no dependence so antinational, or so utterly subversive of national existence as transferring to a foreign government the regulation of its trade, and the management of all their affairs at their pleasure." Baldwin was perhaps predisposed to reject the Cherokee position. Though he was from Pennsylvania, Justice Baldwin had close ties with the South and was inclined to adopt states' rights positions. (His half-brother Abraham had been a Georgia delegate to the Continental Congress, to the Constitutional Convention, and to the United States Senate.) Baldwin believed that slaves were private property, and he often defended the South's use of bonded labor, first as a member of Congress and later in his Supreme Court opinions. For example, Baldwin joined the majority in *Prigg v. Pennsylvania,* the case that upheld the federal fugitive slave law. While in Congress, he sought to extend slavery into the territories and had voted against the Missouri Compromise.[24]

Baldwin also argued that Article 4, Section 3, which provides Congress with the power to "dispose of, and make all needful regulations and rules" for the western territories, was a federal recognition that the Indian tribes were not sovereign states. In *Gibbons v. Ogden,* Baldwin noted, the Court held that the use of the word "regulate" meant that Congress was given "plenary" or "natural full power" over the territories. This construction "leaves the jurisdiction and sovereignty of the Indian tribes wholly out of the question." Of course, here Baldwin was using logic that could be turned against him in the states' right debate. Baldwin would never have allowed that the states had conceded plenary power over the territories to the Congress. This was the position that abolitionists were taking in trying to prevent slavery from spreading to the territories. No other justice, however, pushed Baldwin on the point. In any event, there is no evidence that the Constitutional Convention or the Court in *Gibbons* ever seriously considered the status of the Indian nations when they were contemplating the territorial issue.[25]

Baldwin was not afraid of using selective quotes in this manner to misrepresent the intent of a document. In describing the content of the Northwest Ordinance, Baldwin wrote that it "[paid] no regard to Indian jurisdiction, sovereignty, or their political rights, except providing for their protection." By organizing the Northwest Territory, Baldwin argued, the federal government had accepted full and complete dominion over the western lands of the states. The jurisdiction of "numerous and powerful nations or tribes of Indians" was thereby "contemned" and their sovereignty "overturned." Only Congress or the states, he wrote, could convey political powers to the Indian nations. To the contrary, the Northwest Ordinance provided that "The utmost good faith shall always be observed towards the Indians, their lands and property shall never be taken from them without their consent; and in their property, rights and liberty, they shall never be invaded or disturbed, unless in just and lawful wars authorized by Congress; but laws founded in justice and humanity shall from time to time be made, for preventing wrongs being done to them, and for preserving peace and friendship with them." If one takes the wording of the ordinance literally, then Baldwin was at best misinterpreting and at worst misrepresenting Congress's language and interests.[26]

Marshall constructed an arbitrary position between the extremes offered by Thompson and Baldwin. He allowed that the Cherokee Nation could be considered, by definition, a "state." The nation had proved to be a "distinct political society . . . capable of managing its own affairs and governing itself." Moreover, Marshall wrote, the Cherokees had traditionally been treated as an independent state since the European discovery of the continent, and the United States had "plainly recognized" the Cherokees to be a state capable of maintaining sovereign relations and functions. "The courts," he said, "are bound by those acts." Therefore, Marshall concluded, the Court's decision turned on whether this acknowledged state was "foreign" in the sense intended by the framers of the Constitution.[27]

The Cherokee Nation, Marshall said, was obviously not a state in the federal Union. But was it foreign relative to the United States? Again, Marshall's questions provoked disagreement among the justices. Baldwin warned that if the Court declared the Cherokees a foreign state, "countless tribes" would "rush to the federal courts in endless controversies." Congress, he said, had placed federal regulation of Indian affairs under the jurisdiction of the War Department rather than that of the Department of State. The national legislature therefore did not perceive its dealings with Native Americans to be akin to a diplomatic relationship between foreign states. Baldwin did not explain, however, why this argument would not apply in the same fashion to the War Department. Despite the fact that large segments of the public encouraged the justices to recognize the sovereignty of the Cherokee Nation, Baldwin said, he could not exercise a "judicial power so awfully responsible." To his mind, the Cherokee Nation was not a foreign state. It would be inconsistent, Baldwin added, for Congress to treat the Native Americans as Indian tribes, as they were called in the Commerce Clause, and for the judiciary to deal with them as foreign states. The issue of recognizing the national sovereignty of the Indian tribes was a matter for Congress. "Foreign states cannot be created by judicial construction; Indian sovereignty cannot be roused from its long slumber, and awakened to action by our fiat."[28]

Wirt and Sergeant had contended that the Cherokees were aliens to the United States and that the Court should consider this "aggregate of aliens," by logical extension, to be foreign as a whole. Thompson and Story concurred with this thinking. In the Cherokee treaties of 1817 and 1819,

Thompson pointed out, the United States gave Cherokee heads of households the opportunity to retain a reserve of 640 acres and become American citizens. The offer to award citizenship clearly demonstrated that the federal government did not, at that time, recognize Native Americans as citizens. If the Cherokees were not citizens, he said, they must be aliens. If the Cherokees were not a foreign nation, Thompson also asked, why did the Treaty of Hopewell allow them to send a deputy to Congress? If the Cherokee Nation was considered to have been incorporated into the state of Georgia, he contended, no provision for deputorial representation would have been provided. Thompson and Story agreed with Wirt's assertion that the Commerce Clause was evidence of the framers' intentions to treat the Indian nations as foreign states. The term "the Indian tribes," Wirt said, was set aside to avoid the confusion caused by the Indian affairs clause of the Articles of Confederation. That document granted Congress the complete authority to regulate Indian matters, "provided that the legislative right of any state within its own limits be not infringed or violated." The sole purpose of the Philadelphia Convention on this point, Wirt had suggested, was to put the power to regulate commerce with the Indian nations manifestly in Congress and eliminate the troublesome state claims of concurrent jurisdiction. The framers never intended, he said, to diminish the sovereignty of the Indian nations by their use of the word "tribe." At the time of the Philadelphia Convention, Wirt had added, there was a school of definition that held that the term "foreign," when applied to legal and political issues, implied that a nation was foreign in location, that is, geographically separate and distinct. Consequently, in the Commerce Clause, the framers added the phrase "Indian tribes" to affirm that Congress had the right to regulate commerce with the Indian nations even though they were not geographically foreign.[29]

Wirt's assertion set off an argument among the justices over the meaning of the clause. Thompson suggested that the Constitutional Convention may have used the word "tribe" simply to avoid an awkward repetition of the word "nation." There were several places in the Constitution, he wrote, where two words were used interchangeably, and the words "nation" and "tribe" had both been used without differentiation in a number of treaties. Alternatively, he said, the wording may have been devised to cover those smaller Native American groups that lacked the requisite elements of nationhood. Marshall foreclosed debate on this point by rejecting the arguments of Wirt and Thompson. If the Constitutional Convention had intended to treat the Indian tribes as foreign nations, he said, it would have provided Congress with the power "to regulate commerce with foreign nations, *including* the Indian tribes, and among the several States."[30]

Thompson offered another approach to his fellow justices. He pointed out that the Indian nations were clearly foreign to all other nations at the time of their discovery by Europeans; nothing had happened since to change that foreign status. The Cherokee Nation had never been conquered, it had never been incorporated into another government, and its rights of self-government, until now, had never been challenged. "They have always been dealt with as [an independent state] by the government of the United States," Thompson wrote, "both before and since the adoption of the present Constitution."[31] Thompson also noted that Chancellor Kent had held that the Oneidas and the other Six Nations were originally and inherently "free and independent nations." Thompson had served a three-year apprenticeship with Kent and was strongly influenced by his logic. In the Tommy Jemmy case, Kent placed the burden of proof on those who challenged the sovereignty of those nations to pinpoint exactly when and how those Native American nations lost their national status. Treaties with the United States had made the members of the Iroquois confederacy "dependent" on the American government for security, he said, but the members of that league had retained the right to maintain their own laws and government. The Iroquois nations were "subject to our coercion so far as the public safety required it," the chancellor said, "and no farther." Kent concluded on this point by remarking, "The United States have never dealt with [the Indian tribes], within our national limits, as if they were extinguished sovereignties. They have constantly treated with them as dependent nations, governed by their own usages, and possessing governments competent to make and maintain treaties."[32]

In making one of the most significant decisions in the history of American Indian law, Marshall embraced Kent's characterization of the Indian tribes as "dependent nations." The relationship of the Indians to the United States, the chief justice said, was "unlike that of any other two people in existence." Nevertheless, the Indian nations could not be described as foreign states. Foreign states owed no fundamental allegiance to each other. Many Indian nations had developed a symbiotic relationship with the federal government. The "Indian Country" was considered to be within the geographical domain of the United States; that much was demonstrated "in all our maps, geographical treatises, histories, and laws." The United States regulated foreign commerce for the Indian tribes and refused to allow them to conduct their own foreign policies. In addition, treaties between the Indian nations and the United States almost always recognized the former to be under the protection of the latter. Other foreign nations, in return, considered the Indian tribes to be "under the sovereignty and dominion of the United States." If a European nation attacked an Indian tribe, attempted to take its land, or tried to establish an alliance with it, Marshall wrote, the American government would consider such efforts an act of war against the United States.[33]

Marshall believed, in sum, that the Cherokees were involved in intertwining relationships with the United States that were anathematic to a foreign state status. Wirt and Sergeant had argued that the Court had to find that the Cherokee Nation was either a state of the Union or a foreign state for the purposes of Article 3. These, they said, were the only alternatives. Marshall, however, created a new one. The Cherokee Nation, he said, was a "domestic dependent nation." In her recent book *The Cherokee Cases: The Confrontation of Law and Politics,* Jill Norgren cogently described Marshall's intent in choosing the phrase: "For his purposes, Marshall represented Indian nations as being *domestic* in the sense that their territories were located within the exterior boundaries of the United States, *dependent* because of the limitations placed on them with respect to war and foreign negotiations, and *national* because they were distinctly separate peoples outside the American polity."[34] This characterization, Marshall believed, allowed the federal government to maintain authority over the Indian tribes but protected the Native American polities from state encroachments on their rights of property and self-government. The Cherokees retained significant characteristics of sovereignty, including the right of self-government, but were clearly dependent on the United States for protection of that right. They were also in a "state of pupilage," Marshall added, and "their relation to the United States resembles that of a ward to his guardian." Marshall wrote in another momentous passage, "They look to our government for protection; rely upon its kindness and its power; appeal to it for relief to their wants; and address the President as their great father." No completely free, foreign state, Marshall implied, would do the same. The wardship metaphor and the "domestic dependent nation" characterization would thereafter become defining conceptions in American Indian law.[35]

The majority's conclusion that the Cherokee Nation was not a foreign state might have terminated discussion of the merits of the case at that point. Instead, all the justices who wrote felt it necessary to expound on their interpretation of the Indian polity and the character of the relationship between the tribes, the states, and the federal government. Baldwin took the southern position and contended that the Constitution provided the states with jurisdiction over every aspect of Indian life except commerce. The United States therefore had no constitutional right to intervene in the dispute between Georgia and the Cherokees, for the state was acting pursuant to its powers reserved under the Tenth Amendment. Though the sparse mention of the tribes in the Commerce Clause did not necessarily preclude this interpretation, Baldwin's representation of state authority was shortsighted.

How could a state regulate every aspect of Indian life but commerce and not infringe on the federal government's exclusive Article 1 authority? Baldwin added that Articles 4 and 6 of the Constitution protected the sovereignty of the state from infringements by the federal government, and "within her boundaries there can be no other nation, community, or sovereign power." Baldwin turned Article 6, which made treaties the "supreme law of the land," on its head. He admitted that the obligations of treaties were sacred. But, Baldwin wrote, the partners to treaties were bound to meet their "reciprocal obligations." The Indians must be accorded their rights under these treaties but "must claim them in that capacity in which they received the grant or guarantee." For the Cherokees now to declare themselves sovereign and independent was in conflict with the Treaties of Hopewell and Holston, which decreed that they were under the protection of the United States. By misrepresenting their political status, Baldwin argued, the Cherokees had forfeited their right to come before the Supreme Court as a foreign state. In any event, he said, the federal government had specifically conveyed its jurisdiction over the Cherokees to Georgia in the Compact of 1802, even though in that agreement the state had conceded the power of extinguishment to the Congress.[36]

While Baldwin concentrated on the states' rights interpretation of the Constitution, Johnson attempted to build an argument on what he claimed were the differences between whites and Indians. The South Carolina justice declared that he had "no concern" for the "morality of the case." He was merely resolving a legal question. He said that he doubted that the "epithet 'State' " could be applied to "a people so low in the grade of organized society as our Indian tribes most generally are." Most treaties, he said, including Hopewell, implied that the federal government regarded the Cherokees not as a nation but as "a band of hunters, occupying as hunting-grounds just what territory we chose to allot to them." Johnson acknowledged that the Cherokees were no longer a "restless, warlike, and signally cruel" people, and he recognized that the Cherokees were a unique case because of "their present form of government, which certainly must be classed among the most approved forms of civil government." Despite their admitted progress toward Western notions of nationhood, however, Johnson still refused to acknowledge the Cherokees as a "state." Their improvement, he said, was solely attributable to the efforts of the United States, and the objective of this benevolent pupilage was not independent national status but incorporation. At some distant point in time, Johnson wrote, the Cherokees might reach a "fixed state of society" that would allow them rightfully to question the American claim to the continent. But they were not ready to be recognized as an independent government by the "community of nations."[37]

Revealing perhaps his real interest in denying Indians their national status, Johnson directed his attention to the nature of the Indian title and the
correlation between national sovereignty and property ownership. He suggested that the United States had never "recognized [the Indians] as holding
sovereignty over the territory they occupy." Consistently, he said, in completely reversing his position from two decades before, the United States
and its European forebears had "notoriously asserted and exercised" the
rights of soil and sovereignty over the North American continent. The Indian nations held no intrinsic or inherent rights in their lands, and what
occupancy rights they owned were held at the whim of Congress. The Cherokees, he wrote, obtained an occupancy interest only when Great Britain
and the United States conferred it to them by treaty. "The general policy
of the United States," Johnson concluded on this point, was that the nation
"always looked to these Indian lands as a certain future acquisition." The
Cherokees had relinquished "all power, legislative, executive and judicial,"
over their land to the United States. As evidence, Johnson referred to the
Treaty of Hopewell, which stated in its prefatory clause, "The United States
give peace to all the Cherokees, and receive them into the favor and protection of the United States." This phrasing, Johnson wrote, "is certainly
the language of sovereigns and conquerors, and not the address of equals to
equals." The United States, he added, had conceded to the Cherokees only
those rights "needed by a race of hunters." Practically, he said, it would
be a bureaucratic disaster if the United States accorded national status to
"every petty kraal of Indians." If some members of the Court believed that
the Cherokee Nation was a state, Johnson said, they should admit that it
was a polity "a grade below them all." "For not to be able to alienate without permission of the remainderman or lord," he said, placed the Indians
in "a state of feudal independence." Johnson also compared the Cherokees'
"condition" to that of the biblical "Israelites when inhabiting the deserts."
Though Moses' people had held no land that they could clearly call their
own, they retained the right of self-government. The Cherokees might arguably retain this right, Johnson said, even if they were "expelled" from or
"departed" their ancestral homeland.[38]
    Johnson ridiculed Ross's decision to entrust the Cherokees' destiny to the
American judicial system. The United States had only recently established
itself in the community of nations, he wrote, and despite having "much
stronger claims" to national sovereignty than the Cherokees, the colonies
had been required to exhibit "some earnestness and capacity in asserting our
claim to be enfranchised." If the Cherokees wanted independence, Johnson
suggested, they should fight for it. If the Cherokee Nation considered itself
a sovereign state, then Georgia's extension laws were acts of war and the

exercise of those laws an invasion. For the Cherokees to come to the United States for recognition of their claims was an admission against their interest: "[The Cherokees] allege themselves to be a sovereign independent state, and set out that another sovereign state has, by its laws, its functionaries, and its armed force, invaded their State and put down their authority. . . . In the exercise of sovereign right, the sovereign is sole arbiter of his own justice. The penalty of wrong is war and subjugation. . . . Either the Cherokee Nation are a foreign state or they are not. If they are not, then they can not come here; and if they are, then how can we extend our jurisdiction into their country?" Johnson, in other words, suggested that the Cherokees were too timid to fight for their independence and disingenuous in their appeal to the Supreme Court. Suppose Georgia had filed a suit asking the Court to rule that the Cherokee lands belonged to Georgia, Johnson asked rhetorically, would the Cherokees accept a Supreme Court decision in favor of the state?[39]

After hearing the opinions of Baldwin and Johnson, Marshall became concerned that the Court appeared overly antagonistic to the Cherokee claims. He therefore asked Smith Thompson to prepare an opinion that explained the dissenters' objections to the majority decision. As a consequence, the public did not understand the depth of disagreement on the Court until days after the announcement of its decision. Thompson's opinion embraced much of Wirt's argument and went directly to the substantive merits of the Cherokees' suit. The Court, Thompson lamented, could do nothing about Georgia's attempt to abrogate Cherokee laws and abolish the Cherokee government. He agreed with Marshall that these were political issues that could be resolved only by Congress. The Court could, however, protect Cherokee property rights. Since the Cherokees held their lands in common, every act by a Georgia citizen under the color of the state extension laws was a trespass against the entire population of the Cherokee Nation. Treaties between the nation and the United States had recognized the property rights of the Cherokees, and these rights could be protected and infringements against them remedied when Georgians violated them. Wirt and Sergeant had enumerated several undisputed violations of Cherokee property rights, Thompson noted. Georgia citizens were trespassing into the nation, settling on Cherokee lands, stealing their horses, destroying their game, and driving stock over their fields. The recent statutes that allowed the governor to seize the gold mines and land of the nation were also deliberate and gross violations of the property rights of the Cherokees. Most treaty disputes were political, Thompson said, but in this case there were manifest violations of property and personal rights. These the Court could remedy.

The Indian usufruct, Thompson added, which had been admitted for years by all but the most radical of the states' rights proponents, belonged to the Cherokees "as a matter of right." The usufruct was not a mere indulgence of the Anglo-American governments; it was a natural right inherent at the time of European discovery. (Marshall agreed with this position.) Georgia could not interfere with the Cherokees' use and enjoyment of their land except with their consent or as the result of a "just and necessary war." Thompson also commented on the *imperium in imperio* argument. The fact that the Cherokee Nation was within the borders of the state of Georgia was irrelevant to this question, he said. Suppose it was a Spanish colony that had ceded territory to the extent that it was boxed in by the state. Would it not be absurd for Georgia to extend its laws over the colony? Would it not be recognized as a "foreign" entity? "[The Cherokee Nation] may be inconvenient to the State and it may be very desirable that the Cherokees should be removed," Thompson wrote, "but it does not at all affect the political relation between Georgia and the Indians." In sum, Thompson contended that the Cherokee Nation was the appropriate party for a suit in this instance. The Cherokees had shown that their property rights were being violated and that the United States, as required by treaty and by the Trade and Intercourse Acts, had failed to remedy these constant and numerous invasions. The remedy for such trespasses was an injunction, Thompson wrote, and only an injunction issued by a brave court could protect the Cherokees' rights. In this case, however, the Court and its leader were not ready to come to the Cherokees' assistance.[40]

Cherokee Nation v. Georgia had produced some dramatic results. In particular, both John Marshall and William Johnson had dramatically reversed their positions on Native American rights. In Johnson's case, the rhetorical and logical reversals were startling. First, Johnson had scrawled the natural rights theory of tribal sovereignty into the American legal consciousness in *Fletcher;* in *Cherokee Nation* he abandoned it. Second, Johnson's rhetoric was now, unlike his egalitarian phrasing in *Fletcher,* marked by demeaning stereotypes. Third, Johnson had never shied away from issuing opinions that were unpopular at home; his *Fletcher* dissent in support of Native American sovereignty clearly ran counter to the views of most white southerners. In *Cherokee Nation,* however, Johnson decided to pacify the states' rights critics who had castigated him throughout the 1820s.[41]

For years Johnson had believed that the interests of the states could be protected and reconciled with a strong federal government. The balance was delicate, he had suggested, but in the major cases that construed issues involving federalism, Johnson had come down in favor of a preeminent Union. In the 1820s, however, Johnson came under increasingly harsh criticism in his own state because he refused to oppose Marshall's tendency toward centralization. Most southern politicians and lawyers of that era embraced the

Jeffersonian view that the United States was a confederation of independent, sovereign states. Johnson had rejected this "compact theory" in favor of Marshall's Unionist, or what one historian has called "central-supremacy," federalism. Marshall believed that the national public, not the states, had ratified the Constitution. The states, he suggested, though "distinct and perfect sovereignties," were political subdivisions of a strong national state. Johnson's agreement with Marshall on this important point disturbed the states' rights radicals in South Carolina.[42]

Johnson alienated this faction further when he struck down the Negro Seaman's Acts in 1823. South Carolina had passed the legislation the year before in reaction to the popular fears engendered by Denmark Vesey's slave revolt. The primary purpose of the law was to prohibit free blacks, who supposedly carried with them the message of insurrection, from entering the state. The Negro Seaman's Acts required free black sailors entering the port of Charleston to be detained in jail during their vessel's stay. The state would release a free black sailor only when his ship was leaving port and only if his captain had paid his cost of detention. The law also provided that black sailors in violation of the law could be sold into slavery. When South Carolina authorities in Charleston arrested and jailed Henry Elkison, a black British sailor, he challenged the constitutionality of the acts. Johnson, riding federal circuit, found the acts unconstitutional and void. He wrote that the federal government possessed the plenary right to regulate interstate and international commerce and that this authority was superior to South Carolina's police power over crime and slave relations.[43]

This affirmation of federal authority enraged the states' rights partisans in South Carolina, and the backlash forced Johnson to flee to Pennsylvania. Johnson returned to his state when the controversy subsided, but when he published a pamphlet in 1830 that labeled nullification a "folly," local animosity toward the justice again forced him to escape South Carolina for refuge in the North. These episodes and Johnson's sincere fear of disunion perhaps influenced him to turn his back on Indian rights in *Cherokee Nation v. Georgia*. The South was inflamed with talk of nullification and Indian removal; and as Johnson's biographer suggested, "It is likely that the prospect of a collision in South Carolina influenced Johnson in his treatment of the issue in *Cherokee Nation v. Georgia*." Ironically, though Jefferson had selected him for the specific purpose of counteracting Marshall's influence on the Court, Johnson appears to have concluded a Marshallian compromise with his conscience to preserve a Union that he feared was in danger of dissolution.[44]

In oral arguments, Wirt had gingerly quoted Justice Johnson's dissent in *Fletcher* to support the Cherokees' position. Smith Thompson's written attack on Johnson's inconsistency, however, was unrestrained. Thompson repeated that he believed that the Cherokee Nation was an independent, sovereign state, and he added that "this seems to be the view [of the Indian tribes] taken of them by Mr. Justice Johnson in the case of *Fletcher v. Peck.*" Thompson reminded his readers that Johnson's dissent said that the tribes, including the Cherokees, retained a "limited sovereignty and the absolute proprietorship of their soil." "Innumerable treaties formed with them," Johnson had written, "acknowledge them to be an independent people." By raising the specter of Johnson's past support for Indian sovereignty, Thompson practically destroyed the impact of the South Carolina justice's own opinion. Thompson's critical assault on Johnson, more than any other passage in the set of opinions, demonstrated how bitterly divided the Court had become over the issue.[45]

Johnson's opinion also symbolized how the American vision for the Indian had changed in the twenty years between *Fletcher v. Peck* and *Cherokee Nation.* In 1810, when he issued his dissent in *Fletcher,* many American policymakers, inspired by the Enlightenment, believed that Native Americans were inherently equal to white Americans, that they deserved recognition of the same natural rights, and that they could soon be assimilated into the general population. By 1830, however, many responsible for the United States's Indian affairs believed that there were irremediable differences between whites and Native Americans. This generational change in ideology and the state sovereigntists' acquisition of political power had pushed the federal government toward the great social experiment of removal. These transformations spanned Johnson's career, and one can see the tragic consequences of the removal movement not just in the wholesale exile of the eastern tribes to the West, but in the intellectual and ethical degeneration of men like Johnson. Many men, like the justice, began their careers espousing the ideals of the Revolution and the Enlightenment and ended them with feckless abdications to racial prejudice and the unfermented popular will. Johnson's change of heart dramatized the failure of Knox and Washington's policy of honor; for, like the justice, many the nation's leaders were never able to integrate their Revolutionary ideals, their pragmatic concern for the national interest, their personal political ambitions, and their constituents' prejudice and demand for cheap land into a policy that genuinely considered the rights and interests of Native Americans.

While Johnson's reversal was a clumsy effort to save sectional face, Marshall's transformation can perhaps best be explained in terms of moral evolution. Though the chief justice had denied the Cherokee Nation standing before the Court, he had clearly become convinced that the Indian nations retained important aspects of sovereignty that could not be violated by the states. Unfortunately for the Indian tribes in the Southeast, southern courts would subsequently ignore Marshall's comments on the sovereignty and title of the Indian nations. Instead, they would use the worst of the chief justice's stereotypical descriptions of Indian culture as precedent to deny Indian rights in their states. For example, Marshall asserted in his opinion that at the time of the Constitutional Convention "the idea of appealing to an American court of justice for an assertion of right or a redress of wrong had perhaps never entered the mind of an Indian or of his tribe." He added, "Their appeal was to the tomahawk, or the government." This was a most unfortunate misrepresentation; Native Americans had filed suits in American courts as far back as the seventeenth century. It was this kind of careless remark, though, that judges in Alabama and Tennessee exploited to depreciate Marshall's substantive comments on tribal sovereignty.[46]

Some historians have suggested that Marshall's decision was an astute compromise designed to preserve the authority of the Court. Pending federal legislation threatened to circumscribe the Court's right to strike down the unconstitutional acts of state courts and legislatures, and proponents of this compromise theory argue that Marshall worried that a decision against Georgia would encourage the southern states to push even harder for an evisceration of the federal courts' power. This, they say Marshall feared, would derange the fragile balance between the state and central governments. Moreover, these scholars hold, the chief justice was keenly aware that President Jackson was suspicious of federal judicial power, concerned about the southern states' "Indian problem," and anxious over how the rest of the South would react to South Carolina's threat to nullify the national protective tariff. These concerns supposedly led Marshall to fashion a compromise that postponed the crisis over Indian removal, calmed the states' rights fires breaking out in the South, and avoided a confrontation between the Court and Jackson, all at the expense of the Cherokees. Joseph C. Burke, in his definitive article on the Cherokee cases, holds to this view. Burke called Marshall's decision ingenious. As in *Marbury v. Madison,* he said, "when faced by the resistance of a popular President and unencumbered by the arguments of defense counsel, the chief justice had commented favorably on the plaintiff's claims, had criticized the [popular] President, and had avoided the threatened disobedience of the Court's decree by dismissing the case for want of jurisdiction."[47]

More than likely, though, Marshall genuinely believed that his decision was an appropriate interpretation of the Article 3 "foreign state" clause. The chief justice simply did not agree that the Cherokee Nation was "foreign" to the United States, nor did he believe that the constitutional framers had intended for the Supreme Court to have original jurisdiction over a case between a state and an Indian tribe. Moreover, if *Cherokee Nation* was a grand compromise as some have suggested, then Marshall surely would not have encouraged the nation, as he did at the end of his opinion, to bring another action, in a different context, before the Court. Finally, Marshall's opinion was hardly an exercise in clever political conciliation. The chief justice did not reconcile the disparate opinions of the Court; in fact, he was joined by only one other justice. Instead of permanently avoiding a constitutional crisis as he did in *Marbury v. Madison,* Marshall only temporarily set back the final conflict between the Cherokees and Georgia. In explaining Marshall's opinion, it seems more rational to suggest that the chief justice's views on Native American sovereignty were evolving in the period between *Johnson v. McIntosh* and *Worcester. Cherokee Nation v. Georgia* was only an awkward step in that conversion. Political exigencies had pushed the issue of Indian rights to the forefront of national concern during the 1820s, and it appears that the more Marshall read and thought about Indian rights, the more convinced he became that his conception of those rights in *Fletcher* and *Johnson v. McIntosh* was dead wrong. The chief justice's own comments after *Cherokee Nation* confirm this analysis. He was particularly displeased with his own opinion in the case. After reconsidering the arguments of Wirt and Thompson in *Cherokee Nation,* he realized that his opinion was not an ingenious compromise, but, for him, a substandard piece of work. Marshall later explained that he was forced to orchestrate and write a decision within only four days of the oral arguments so that the Court's session could end when scheduled. In a letter to the court reporter a few weeks after the decision, Marshall wrote, "The judge who pronounced that opinion had not time to consider the case in its various bearings." Such are the sad exigencies in which precedents are set.[48]

Marshall's final words in *Cherokee Nation v. Georgia* clearly confused the Cherokee leadership. First, he seemed to apologize that the Court could not remedy the Cherokees' misery at this time. "The mere question of right," he added, "might perhaps be decided by this court in a proper case with proper parties." A few lines later, Marshall wrote, "If it be true that the Cherokee Nation have rights, this is not the tribunal in which those rights are to be asserted. If it be true that wrongs have been inflicted, and that still greater are to be apprehended, this is not the tribunal which can redress the past or prevent the future." The Cherokee reaction to those comments and to the disposal of the case was understandably ambivalent. A majority of the justices had been persuaded that the Cherokee Nation was sovereign and was in fact being wronged, but the decision did not remedy its situation. Though the *obiter dicta* and Marshall's offer to hear another Cherokee plea offered considerable hope, Wirt and Ross knew that time was of the essence.

If Marshall died or retired, Jackson might replace him with someone like Baldwin. The Cherokees' last good chance for federal judicial support might be lost when Marshall left the bench.[49]

Southern leaders rejoiced at the majority's refusal to accept jurisdiction and attacked the Cherokee Nation for taking its claims to the Court. One Georgia editor wrote, "The views of the State, with regard to her entire jurisdiction over the Indians within her limits, are fully sustained. . . . The Cherokees, therefore, must either submit altogether to our laws or emigrate to the West of the Mississippi." Elias Boudinot responded to the exhilaration of the Georgia press in the *Cherokee Phoenix:* "Does the Court say that the Cherokees have no property in the soil, but are merely tenants at will? that they have no right of self-government, but are subjects of the states? that the treaties are not binding, and the intercourse law unconstitutional? These are the views of Georgia. Now does the opinion of the Court sustain them? Far from it. No language can be plainer than the following: 'So much of the argument,' says the Court, 'as was intended to prove the character of the Cherokees as a state, as a distinct political society, separate from others, capable of managing its own affairs and government itself, has in the opinion of the majority of the judges, been completely successful.' If this sustains the views of Georgia and General Jackson (for we are told he also considered his views sustained by the Court) then we have all along been utterly ignorant as to what these views were."[50]

Though pleased with the disposition of the case, Governor Gilmer was understandably disturbed by the dicta in the opinions of Marshall and Thompson. The only purpose behind *Cherokee Nation v. Georgia,* he said, was "to give the opponents of the Administration an elevated stand from which they might be heard by the people in their denunciations." The Supreme Court strayed from the simple question of whether the Cherokee Nation was a foreign state and "made a statement wholly irrelevant, without proof, and contrary to the truth." Gilmer excoriated Marshall and Thompson for their comments on the righteousness of the Cherokee cause, their criticism of Georgia's actions, and their contention that the Cherokees had progressed to the United States's level of civilization. True Indians, Gilmer said, were racially incapable of improvement: "Upon examination, it will be found that the Aboriginal people are as ignorant, thoughtless, and improvident, as formerly; . . . that none of them in this State, with the exception of one family, have acquired property, . . . that the chief, the president of the council, the judges, marshall and sheriffs, and most other persons concerned in the administration of the Government, are the descendants of Europeans."[51]

Gilmer was referring, in particular, to John Ross. The principal chief, though disappointed by the Court's failure to accept jurisdiction, was en-

couraged by the decision. Ross took heart that four members of the Court
had agreed that the Cherokee Nation retained significant aspects of national
sovereignty, and he read Marshall's mixed signals as a reason for guarded
optimism. Ross again traveled throughout the nation, this time explaining
the meaning of the Court's decision. He trumpeted Marshall's determination
that the Cherokee government was a "distinct political society . . . capable
of managing its own affairs," and he printed copies of the decision and distributed them to the Cherokees so that they could see that the chief justice
of the United States Supreme Court had declared them a sovereign nation.
The rejection of standing did not reflect on the legitimacy of the Cherokee cause, Ross told his people, but was only a consequence of "the limited
powers of the Supreme Court." Whenever the nation was able to bring an
appropriate action before the Court, he predicted, the justices would sustain the righteousness of the Cherokee legal crusade and strike down the
Georgia statutes. Ross also again called on Jackson to come to the aid of the
Cherokees. Jackson, however, refused even to respond to the Cherokees'
memorial when they delivered it in Washington. The principal chief was not
discouraged even by this affront. He told the Cherokees that it was "our
duty & our interest still to hold fast by [Jackson's] hand, cling to his skirts
& cry aloud for justice & protection, until it shall be extended, or our feeble
hand be shaken loose from its grip by the power of the General Government." If Jackson did not come around to their point of view, he added,
the next session of Congress would "in all probability, put an end to this
grievous controversy." He told his constituents, "Our cause will ultimately
triumph." [52]

The voice of the Cherokee Nation, Elias Boudinot, was far more realistic.
He wrote that *Cherokee Nation v. Georgia* placed the Cherokees in "a peculiar situation." While the Court "explicitly acknowledged and conceded"
the rights that the Cherokees had been claiming for years, he said, "we are
at the same time considered to be in a state of 'pupilage,' unable to sue for
those rights in the judicial tribunals. This is certainly no enviable position."
Ross's telling the nation that its only course of redress was from Jackson and
Congress, Boudinot added, was "but a broken reed which has been piercing
us to our very vitals." [53]

CHAPTER SIX

The Southern Response to Marshall

Caldwell v. Alabama

PERHAPS A CLEAR PRONOUNCEMENT in favor of Indian sovereignty by a united Court in *Cherokee Nation* would have stalled the fervor for removal. More than likely, though, it would have only pushed Georgia so far toward rebellion that the state might have joined South Carolina in its nullification challenge to the federal government. Instead, Marshall's refusal to grant standing to the Cherokees persuaded Georgia officials to give the federal government time to arrange an agreement with the tribe to effect its relocation. In the meantime, the state pressures for removal that had plagued the Cherokees for so long had spread into Alabama. The Cherokees' neighbors to the southwest, the Creeks, now faced their own attack by that state on their territorial and political autonomy.

The assault on Creek national sovereignty began with the sporadic migration of white settlers into the eastern portion of the Yazoo territory in the early nineteenth century. The United States's victory over the Creeks in 1814 and the construction of a federal road through the region opened up what would become the state of Alabama for more widespread settlement. As soon as the federal government admitted Mississippi (1817) and Alabama (1819) into the Union, the white citizens began demanding that the United States remove the resident Indians. The Creeks in Alabama, who numbered about twenty thousand, endured a constant stream of trespassers stomping through or settling in their nation. The Creeks were astonished by the voracious appetite of the whites for land and began calling them "Ecunnaunuxulgee"—the "people greedily grasping after the lands of [Indians]." When Creek officials complained to the United States about the encroachments into their nation in the late 1820s, they were unceremoniously rebuffed. President Andrew Jackson told them, just as he had advised the Cherokees, that there was nothing he could do. He told Creek leaders that they should either remove beyond the Mississippi or be prepared to fall under the jurisdiction of the state.[1]

When the Creek Nation's leaders had ceded the remainder of their territory in Georgia in 1827, they thought that they had staved off the pressure for removal. In the negotiations for the Treaty of Washington, in which the Creeks had made that cession, federal commissioners had promised tribal leaders that the United States would protect them in their remaining territory from the trespasses of white settlers. Instead, the federal government took only nominal measures to prevent American intrusions. To complicate matters further for the Creek leadership, the Treaty of Washington cession and the Cherokee crisis in Georgia produced a flood of Indian refugees into the Creek lands in Alabama. The Creeks who lived on the land surrendered to Georgia in the Washington accord had been forced to move across the Chattahoochee River, and as the Georgia legislature ratcheted up its pressure for removal, many Cherokees also escaped into the Creek Nation. The new eastern borders of the Creek Nation thus became an area of unrest, as trespassing whites and refugee Indians fought with and stole from each other along the Alabama, Georgia, and Creek frontiers. Each side naturally claimed to have been victimized by the other. The Alabama newspapers and Creek leaders both complained about the lawless nature of the area. The Creeks called for the federal government to intervene; the Alabama papers blamed the Indians for the unrest and used the situation to incite public support for removal. The editors of the state also followed the Cherokee-Georgia conflict closely and published editorials supporting Georgia's attack on Cherokee sovereignty.[2]

Georgia had used the argument that the Indian country was "lawless" to justify the extension of its jurisdiction over the Cherokees. The Alabama legislature adopted Georgia's tactic and declared in 1829 that it was responding to the unrest in the region by expanding its civil and criminal authority over the Creek Nation. The state extension statute authorized a census for counting the number of Creeks inside Alabama's borders; allowed the state to build roads, bridges, and ferries within the Indian nations; and formally abolished and criminalized Creek and Cherokee "laws, usages, and customs."[3] Creek leaders recognized the motivations behind the new law and worried that it would encourage further trespasses. They were correct; the white settlers continued to invade in increasing numbers. In February 1831, a Creek man named Tuskinihahohaw complained to federal authorities, "[The white settlers] are building houses [and] mills . . . and destroying all my timber and grains. This I have always been taught by my former Fathers and Brothers was not a right which these white children were entitled to." Until recently, he added, the federal government had attempted to limit the encroachment of settlers. He wondered why this was no longer the case and pointed out that the intruders were provoking conflicts with the local

Creeks. Recently, he said, he had witnessed his fellow Indians beating up a white whiskey peddler who was trespassing in the nation. Two Lower Creek headmen, Tuckabatchee Hadjo and Octeachee Emathla, also complained to John Eaton, Jackson's secretary of war, about the incursions. They wrote that whites simply ignored the Creek borders with Alabama and Georgia and "have abundantly moved amongst us." They asked Eaton to establish firm borders between the Creek Nation and the two states and to expel all white intruders. Two weeks later, the two men went to Washington to register their complaints personally. Denied an audience with Jackson, they left him a letter warning that federal inaction would lead to bloodshed. "We have bad red people among us we can not control," they wrote, and "you have the same characters among the whites. . . . Murders have already taken place, and we have no expectation of receiving satisfaction unless by the intervention of your authority." Eaton responded that Jackson would not interfere in the state's business and again encouraged the Creeks to remove. On April 8, 1831, the two chiefs wrote to Eaton that removal was not a viable solution to their dilemma. They demanded federal protection of their national borders.[4]

The Creek fears of ethnic violence proved well founded. A few weeks after the warnings issued by Tuckabatchee Hadjo and Octeachee Emathla, a Creek man named Fushatchee Yoholo was shot in the back while walking east of the Coosa River in an area of the Creek Nation recently annexed by Alabama. When Congress admitted Alabama as a state in 1819, its enabling legislation had made the Coosa River the eastern border between the state and the Creek Nation. The river had also served as the eastern border of Shelby County, Alabama. The 1829 extension act pushed the borders of Shelby County to the east across the Coosa, and it was in the annexed portion of the county that the killing occurred. Fushatchee Yoholo held onto life for almost two weeks but finally died in a nearby house on May 1, 1831. Two weeks after Fushatchee Yoholo's death, Creek headmen, fearing further conflict, begged Jackson to send federal troops to remove white intruders. Jackson and Eaton refused to act. Local officials in Alabama, perhaps intent on implementing the extension of jurisdiction, moved to solve the murder and bring the assailant to justice. Within a few weeks, the sheriff of Shelby County arrested James Caldwell, a sixty-nine-year-old white farmer, and charged him with responsibility for Fushatchee Yoholo's death. On September 5, 1831, a grand jury indicted Caldwell for murder. Caldwell, the indictment read, had "feloniously willfully and of his mallice aforethought" shot Fushatchee Yoholo with a rifle, leaving a "mortal wound of the breadth of one inch and of the depth of six inches . . . in and upon the right side of the back of him." Caldwell, a father of eight, was arraigned

on November 1 and pleaded not guilty.[5] At the hearing, Caldwell claimed
to be a pauper, and Judge Anderson Crenshaw appointed two lawyers, Eli
Shortridge and Daniel E. Watrous, to represent him. Watrous, who had been
in Shelby County since 1825 after immigrating from Vermont, served as the
senior attorney on the case. Shortridge, like Watrous and almost all of those
involved in the case, save Fushatchee Yoholo, was an immigrant to Alabama.
Born in Kentucky, he joined the bar there and served as a local judge. He
had just arrived in Tuscaloosa when Crenshaw appointed him to work with
Watrous. Future Alabama secretary of state William Garrett recalled that
Shortridge later became a fine lawyer known throughout the state for his
oratorical ability: "His addresses to the jury . . . were models of beauty and
eloquence. . . . He had a peculiar softness and euphony in his voice which
exerted a charm on the listeners. . . . It was like the tones of a parlor organ,
rich in melody, and gushing out in a perpetual concord of sweet sounds."
To counter Watrous and Shortridge, the Alabama Supreme Court appointed
Aaron Ready, a prominent lawyer from Wetumpka, as attorney general pro
tem to prosecute the state's case.[6]

The trial turned on the testimony of a single witness, William C. Thompson, who had overheard Caldwell confess that he had killed Fushatchee
Yoholo. If Caldwell's lawyers followed the common practice of frontier
attorneys, they likely argued that their client shot in self-defense. Joseph
Glover Baldwin, a lawyer who practiced during the territorial period in Alabama, noted sardonically that in those days, "almost anything made out
a case of self-defense—a threat—a quarrel—an insult—going armed, as almost all the wild fellows did—shooting from behind a corner, or out of a
store door, in front or from behind—it was all self-defence!" Alabama juries
often accepted that defense. About the time of Caldwell's trial, an Alabama
lawyer told Alexis de Tocqueville that jurors usually acquitted because they
empathized with the defendant. Tocqueville asked an Alabama lawyer if
"the people of Alabama are as violent as is said." The lawyer replied, in
Tocqueville's words, that in this "semi-barbarous state of society" everyone
was armed, and at the least conflict, "knife or pistol come to hand." Philip
Henry Gosse concurred. He wrote, after traveling through Alabama around
that time, "The darkest side of the southerner is his quarrelsomeness, and
recklessness of human life. The terrible bowie knife is ever ready to be drawn,
and it is drawn and used too, on the slightest provocation." The violent nature of Alabama society thus offered the possibility that the juror might one
day appear in the same dock under similar circumstances. Contrary to this
general inclination to acquit, however, and despite the common reticence of
juries to send white men to the gallows for killing Indians and slaves, the
jury brought in a verdict of guilty against Caldwell.[7]

This verdict is difficult to explain, but the specific exigencies of the facts may have pushed the jury toward its decision. First, the primary evidence of the murder—a confession—certainly dissuaded a jury from ignoring the obvious. Moreover, when faced with a confession, the jury may well have decided to punish Caldwell for exacerbating the tensions that existed between Indians and whites in the area. In a time and place where these relations were so fragile, the jurors may have seen themselves as instruments of order and civilization for the frontier. As one study has suggested, white juries were quite capable of applying severe sentences to white defendants accused of injuring or killing nonwhites. Even in a society that was becoming increasingly rigid in regard to racial boundaries, whites perhaps still recognized the essential humanity of those they perceived as inferior.[8]

The jury's decision perhaps surprised Caldwell's lawyers, and they immediately asked that the case be accepted for appeal to the Alabama Supreme Court. Awaiting the verdict, attorneys Shortridge and Watrous had learned that the jurors had called Thompson into the jury room during their deliberations to clarify his testimony. The jury had asked Thompson if he heard Caldwell's confession "in the woods or at a house." Before Thompson could answer the question, the bailiff saw what was happening, dragged Thompson out of the jury room, and told him that this was improper conduct for both the witness and the jury. At the time, Caldwell's counselors appear to have concluded that this peculiarity was their most likely route to a reversal of the verdict.[9]

Judge Crenshaw sentenced Caldwell to be hanged on the second Saturday of the following February and remanded him to the custody of the Shelby County sheriff for execution of sentence, subject to any appeal. The judge, believing the Shelby County jail to be insecure, ordered the sheriff to transfer Caldwell to the jailer of Montgomery County for safekeeping until the date of execution. On December 22, Caldwell's attorneys filed their appeal to the state supreme court, and the Shelby County clerk forwarded it to Tuscaloosa for consideration.[10]

While Caldwell sat in the Montgomery jail, his lawyers decided to shift their focus away from the jury-tampering issue and resolved to challenge Alabama's jurisdiction and the constitutionality of the state's extension law. Watrous and Shortridge, however, never suggested that Caldwell's fate should be left to a Creek court. Instead they maintained that the federal district court for Alabama should have tried the case since it entailed a federal question involving the interpretation of treaties between the United States and the Creeks. They noted that Caldwell had committed his crime inside the federally recognized borders of the Creek Nation. Therefore, Caldwell's attorneys argued, Alabama's extension of jurisdiction over the Creek Nation was an unconstitutional obstruction of the federal government's plenary authority over commerce and an illegal interference with the existing treaties between the two nations. In short, they said, the Alabama court never had jurisdiction to hear their client's case.[11]

By taking that position, Caldwell, a white man, ironically became the only person with legal standing to challenge Alabama's legislative attack on Creek sovereignty. Caldwell's lawyers must have realized that this strategy would force the supreme court into a political dilemma. On the one hand, the justices could strike down the extension statute, confirm the sovereignty of the Creek Nation, and free a confessed murderer. On the other hand, they could send a white man to the gallows for killing an Indian and repudiate the Creek claims of national sovereignty. The Creeks, for their part, were never a party to the case and apparently were never consulted as to their views. Though Creek leaders may not have agreed with the gamble of pushing the Alabama supreme court to a decision, it was the best theory that Caldwell's lawyers, acting in the interest of their client, could devise.[12]

The supreme court of Alabama was not inclined to accept Caldwell's lawyers' argument. The three judges—Abner S. Lipscomb, Reuben Saffold, and John M. Taylor—were all immigrants to Alabama, veterans of the state's political and constitutional development, and in agreement with the legislature's plans for territorial and economic expansion. Neither was the court sympathetic to the Creeks' troubles; in fact, Lipscomb and Saffold had fought against them with Jackson in the Creek War of 1813–14. The judges were in lockstep agreement with the state legislature's extension policy, and each was convinced that removal was an inevitable necessity for progress in the state.[13]

Political circumstances beyond the case also seemed to have influenced the court's decision. The press in Alabama, in particular, was obsessed with South Carolina's nullification battle, and the court's opinion resonated with states' rights rhetoric that paralleled that being pronounced in the Palmetto State. In addition, Alabama newspapers paid close attention to the ongoing dispute between Georgia and the Cherokees. The editor of the *Alabama Journal* expressed outrage at the sympathetic comments written by John Marshall and Smith Thompson about the Cherokees' position that appeared in *Cherokee Nation*. In the final sentences of his opinion in that case, Marshall had suggested that the Court might consider the constitutionality of the state extension laws if they were presented "in a proper case with proper parties." The *Journal*'s editor saw this as a veiled promise to overrule the extension laws of Georgia and Alabama. Any attempt to strike down Georgia's extension laws, he warned, endangered the sovereignty of every state.[14]

Although the Alabama papers of the time appear to have overlooked the *Caldwell* case specifically, Judge Taylor wrote in his opinion that the population of Alabama was "particularly excited" about the question of Creek national rights. For him, the *Caldwell* case was the most important decision in the court's brief history. "To Alabama," Taylor said, "these questions are peculiarly important, on account of the great proportion of her territory which is embraced within the country now occupied by Indians; and, in effect, we are now to decide whether the jurisdiction of this state is to be restricted to about two-thirds of its extent, or to be coextensive with its limits."[15]

The court was particularly eager to respond to northern reformers who were criticizing the southern states' treatment of the Creeks and the Cherokees. Lipscomb indignantly complained that philanthropists from the North "sought to instruct us in morals and the true science of government." These reformers, he said, had suggested that the southern states were attempting to strip Indians "of every right that humanity is heir to" and subject them to "the most heartless, unrestrained, and diabolical despotism." Lipscomb wrote, "These consequences have been conjured up by the overheated imaginations, of those, who deny the right of the States, to exercise jurisdiction over the Indians." Saffold also charged that the concerns raised by Indian supporters were "mingle[d] in the schemes of party strife" and were solely intended to diminish Jackson's popularity. Lipscomb and Taylor suggested that the dispute over Creek sovereignty was a political issue and that the court would defer to the will of the legislature. Indian communities were not independent sovereign nations, and individual Indians were subject to the laws of the state in which they resided. The state therefore had the right to extinguish the title claims of the Indians in the state and the constitutional authority to police its own jurisdiction. The fate of the Creeks rested with the Alabama legislature. There was nothing the court could, or would, do about it.[16]

The justices simply might have affirmed Caldwell's conviction on this strict basis. Instead, they felt obligated to construct a comprehensive legal justification for the removal of the Creeks and the concomitant extinguishment of their land titles. Each judge contributed his own personal justifications for removal. Primarily, though, the court's opinion was grounded on the international law theories identified by Vattel and on the cultural misconceptions produced by the racial determinists of the late eighteenth and early nineteenth centuries. At the beginning of the colonial period, the judges said, the relationship between Indians and the invading Europeans had quickly become one of white ascendancy. This hegemony, Saffold wrote, resulted from "the superior genius of the Europeans, founded on civilization and christianity, and . . . superiority in the means . . . [and] art of war."[17] The court then elevated the fallacious stereotype of the early discovery period to legal precedent. Indians, the judges wrote, were "indolent," "fierce," "warlike," "erratic," and "rude and uncivilized." These "sons of the forest" were infantile, ignorant, and "incapable of protecting their own interests." How could these people, Judge Taylor asked, without legal capacity to "make a binding contract to the amount of a dollar" be "intelligent enough . . . to estimate their national interests [and] to meet the learned and wily European as diplomatists"? Indians had capriciously traded "millions of acres of fertile land" for "a few strings of red beads, a hogshead or two of tobacco, [and] a bale or two of coarse cloth." These people, he contended, were not intelligent enough to lay claim to national sovereignty.[18]

The Alabama judges completely dismissed as illusory Creek government and law. To them, Creek political authority was "adventitious and temporary, passing from one warrior to another, as accident might determine." The Creeks, they said, were mentally incapable of maintaining a system of jurisprudence. According to the court, Indian inferiority demanded that Native Americans be treated differently under Anglo-American law. Taylor wrote that Indians could not be motivated to obey the law by reason; supposedly, like slaves, they responded only to the whip. When threatened with this humiliating punishment, Taylor said, they reacted differently from whites. "The Indian neither felt nor feared the disgrace [of corporal punishment], the bodily pain alone was the object of terror to him." These people, the court said, were therefore incapable of civilized government. If the court acknowledged Creek sovereignty, Taylor warned, Alabama would be blockaded from trade and communication with its neighboring states to the east. Innocent travelers and Alabama citizens would be arrested by tribal authorities, "dragged before their chiefs and other head men, and upon the most crude and unsatisfactory testimony, be consigned to ignominious or fatal punishments." It would be an "intolerable proposition," Saffold added, for whites to be adjudged by Creek justice. A decision allowing such a state of affairs, Taylor suggested, would lead to a perpetual and bloody border war between Alabama and the Creeks.[19]

Also fundamental to the Alabama court's argument for Native American inferiority was the putative transient nature of the "wildman, who has no permanent abiding place, but moves from camp to camp, as the pursuit of game may lead him." Treaties with Indians were worthless, the judges argued, because when one Indian hunting camp moved out, another moved in. Recognizable geographical boundaries were essential to a national character, and Indians had no concept of national or tribal borders until Europeans told them what and where they were. General national claims of sovereignty by the Creek Nation therefore were ridiculous, as were their claims of fee simple title. The Indian title, the court said, was at best "a mere occupancy for the purpose of hunting" that was subject to termination by the state at any time. The court quoted Vattel, who had written that "[the Indians] have no idea of a title to the soil itself. It is overrun by them rather than inhabited. . . . It is not a true and legal possession. It is a right not to be transferred, but extinguished. It is a right regulated by treaties, not by deeds of conveyance. . . . A right, not individual, but national."[20]

At the same time, though, the court rejected Creek title claims based on treaties with the United States. Taylor separated himself from Saffold and Lipscomb on this point. He did not challenge Caldwell's argument that the Creeks owned a possessory interest to their land. He wrote that the fee was held by the United States through the rights of discovery and conquest but that the right of possession remained with the Creeks. "The act of our general assembly does not take from the Creek Indians their lands or property," he wrote. "It does not disturb the possession of an individual, but leaves every member of the tribe in the enjoyment of his lands and property, be they much or little." Taylor, however, also believed that the state could extinguish that usufruct at any time. He also rejected the suggestion that the Creek people comprised a sovereign government. For the Creeks to remain in Alabama, he implied, they would have to do so as individual property owners and as individual subjects of the state. To allow an independent nation inside the territorial limits of Alabama, he said, would be an unconstitutional infringement on the sovereignty of the state.[21]

Caldwell's counsel had maintained that the Indians were the original occupants of the continent and that the European discoverers only acquired the rights that the Native American peoples had conceded to them. The Creek Nation therefore retained complete title to and dominion over its land in Alabama. Lipscomb flatly rejected "this high pretension to savage sovereignty." Despite certain knowledge of what the Cherokees were arguing before the United States Supreme Court, Taylor suggested that Indians were too ignorant to understand the issues of property ownership and national sovereignty. Even if the Indians had opinions on these questions, he admitted, the court really did not care. The judges' sympathies were not with the Creek victim, Saffold added, but with the defendant. He was a citizen of Alabama.[22]

The court went on to apply a thick veneer of Anglo-European precedent, international legal theory, and American constitutional interpretation over this racial foundation of Native American inferiority. According to the judges, Vattel's ephemeral "code of national law," as "binding and obligatory as if sanctioned by the most solemn treaties," guided their decision to deny the Creeks their sovereignty. To establish sovereignty under this code, the court said, a people had to show the continual and consistent possession of a territory, the "practice of the arts of civilization," agricultural development, a written language, and an organized government. The community of nations would respect the territorial and international rights of only such a society. The court concluded, however, that the Creek people did not meet any of these prerequisites of sovereignty. Even if they did, it added, the Anglo-European discovery and conquest of the North American continent had terminated every Indian tribe's claim to that status. Vattel's "law of nations" had recognized the legal title of the American continents claimed by the European monarchs. The state of Alabama, the court explained, had succeeded to dominion over the land through a chain of title extending down through its imperial forebears. Although some international legal theorists historically had distinguished between the rights of discovery and conquest, Taylor sarcastically quipped that what was discovery to the European was conquest to the Indian.[23]

The court said that Europeans had two choices upon their discovery of the western continents: acquire the land "according to their own canons of morality and national law" or "leave this fair continent in the rude and savage state in which they found it." Citing Vattel, the judges contended that societies had an obligation to improve or cultivate their land and that no community or nation could appropriate more land than it was able to settle and develop. Moving "nomadically" through their claimed lands did not indicate possession by the Indians, the court wrote, and Europeans had the right to move in and possess lands that were not in "actual and constant use." In this analysis, the court intentionally ignored the significant place of agriculture in the lives of the Indians of the region. Taylor wrote that Vattel's study of international rights contemplated a human hierarchy comprised of two classes of people: "Agriculturalists . . . who use the earth . . . to secure the subsistence and happiness of the greatest number of inhabitants" and "those who are erratic in their habits, who do not use the soil over which they roam, but live either by rapine and violence, or depend upon the precarious supplies afforded by hunting, fishing, and wild fruits." According to the Alabama judges, the Creeks fell into the latter category and could therefore be dispossessed under Vattel's maxim: "Those who live by the chase, must yield to the cultivator of the soil."[24]

The court also cited the colonial conquest of the Americas to justify Alabama's encroachment. The British Crown had conveyed a right to the chartered colonists "to invade and destroy the natives." This meant that the "grantor considered himself lord and rightful sovereign of these domains;" and with the sword, Europeans had obtained title as far west as the Mississippi. Caldwell's attorneys argued that most of the colonial grants intended the purchase of title from the Indians, "who were viewed as the rightful occupants, and who could not be dispossessed without their consent." The court rejected this interpretation and treated the imperial conquests as legal precedent for state extension: "The Spaniards, the Dutch, the French, the English, all took possession of great part of the countries they discovered without regard to any title in the first inhabitants, and extended their settlements and territories as their wants required. . . . A great part of Virginia, and of the other Southern States, and of Kentucky and Tennessee were taken possession of, not because the Indians agreed that it should be done, but because the whites willed to do it." Saffold rejected the idea that the Indians had to be paid for cessions of their land. He admitted that the Puritans of New England had paid for some of the lands acquired from the Indians, but "the prices given by the Puritans . . . were scarcely more than nominal, compared with the then value of the lands." Cession agreements were therefore unnecessary, he implied, for the states could simply seize any land that they desired from the Indian tribes. European and colonial allowances for the continuation of Indian government and payments for land, Saffold wrote, were merely attempts to placate the Indians and eliminate unnecessary hostility.[25]

According to the court's interpretation, Great Britain, by negotiation and military victories over its European rivals, had acquired "absolute dominion" over the Native American peoples in the era before the American Revolution. The original British charter to the Georgia lands read: "That it is our royal will and pleasure, for the present use as aforesaid, to reserve (the land aforesaid) unto our sovereignty, protection and dominion, for the use of said Indians, and we do hereby strictly forbid, on pain of our displeasure, all our loving subjects from making any purchases, or settlements whatever, or taking possession of any of the lands above reserved, without our special leave and license, for that purpose first obtained." Rather than reading this as a justification or recognition of Indian title claims, Saffold construed the charter as "a clear indication of the assumed right of the British government to grant the future license, at pleasure." In 1725, Taylor noted, Parliament had declared that the Indians of eastern North America were "in hostilities and rebellion." He argued that rebellions could not be raised by independent sovereign entities; only subjects of the Crown could foment such an uprising. "Rebellion implies allegiance," he wrote, "and if there has been no allegiance, there can be no rebellion." Taylor added that, accordingly, no president of the United States had ever asked for a declaration of war against an Indian tribe. Instead, the argument went, the executive sent out troops to quell rebellions by American subjects. Rebels were bound by the jurisdiction of the nation against which they rebelled. They did not comprise sovereign states.[26]

The court observed that with the Treaty of Paris, Georgia had inherited Britain's authority over the Creeks' lands, and, therefore, that state could have extended its jurisdiction over the Indians at any time it so desired. Alabama subsequently succeeded to Georgia's right of dominion through the Compact of 1802 and with Alabama's admission into the Union in 1819. According to the court, this chain of title, which originated out of European discovery and conquest, placed the Creeks into a "true condition of privilege" subject to Alabama's unilateral right to terminate Indian possessory and political rights.[27] Caldwell had argued that Creek treaties with Great Britain and the United States prohibited Alabama from exerting its jurisdiction over the Creek Nation. The court rejected the binding nature of Indian treaties in general and the specific contention that Creek treaties constricted Alabama action. "In what way is [the Indian] to be treated with?" Lipscomb scoffed. "[A]s well might a treaty, on terms of equality, be attempted with the beast of the same forest that he inhabits." Treaties were not admissions of Indian title to land, he continued; the Anglo-European governments executed them only to "conciliat[e] the savages." Saffold argued that the word "treaty" was a misnomer because the United States could not contract treaties with an entity that was not a foreign state. Since he had presumably proved that the Indian nations were not sovereign states, he contended that European and American agreements with the Indians could not be considered treaties. The court even used earlier treaty violations by the European powers to justify the breaching of recent agreements by the United States. By violating the strictures of treaties at will, the judges concluded, the "Christian powers" had demonstrated that they did not recognize the Indian tribes as polities that deserved respect for promises received.[28]

Taylor noted that Article 2 of the Constitution empowered the president to enter into treaties with foreign nations, with the advice and consent of the Senate, through his appointed "ambassadors, other public ministers, and consuls." He added that national ambassadors usually contracted treaties with foreign nations, and that in negotiating with the Indian tribes, the president had never appointed "ministers to an Indian court." This assertion, however, misrepresented the language of Article 2, which does not mandate that treaties be negotiated at the rank of ambassador, and the intent of the federal agents who had concluded past Indian accords. In another distortion of the history of American Indian policy, Taylor wrote that except for the express purpose of appropriations, an American president had never asked the Senate to ratify a treaty with an Indian tribe. In fact, the Senate had been ratifying federal-Indian treaties as far back as the Fort Harmar accords in 1789.[29]

The court also ignored the more recent treaties between the Creeks and the United States, focusing instead on the purported Creek renouncement of relations with the American government in the Creek War of 1813–14. The court in particular paid no attention to the subsequent rapprochement between the two nations and the renewal of treaty relations at Fort Jackson in 1814. Here, and in the more recent treaty of 1827, the federal government had promised to "guaranty to the Creek nation the integrity of all their reserved territory." Rather than reading these promises literally, Saffold contended that the treaty assurances demonstrated that the Creeks held their lands at the will of the state and federal governments. Caldwell's attorneys also raised Chancellor Kent's holding in the Tommy Jemmy case, an opinion that was pivotal to Marshall's developing conception of Native American sovereignty. In that case Kent compared the Indian tribes to small, weak states that were surrounded by and under the protection of a larger state. They retained the right of home rule but sacrificed some aspects of national sovereignty, for the sake of security, to the larger state. Similarly, Caldwell's counsel contended, the Indian tribes retained partial sovereignty and concurrent dominion over the land with the federal government. Saffold flatly refuted this theory. Partial sovereignty was "entirely incompatible" with the sovereign rights of the states, he said, and "can exist only as a matter of comity, expediency, or policy, in the discretion of the states."[30]

Caldwell's counsel had made several persuasive constitutional arguments, but the court rejected them all out of hand. Naturally, the defendant's lawyers contended that the Alabama extension statutes violated the Commerce Clause. The breadth of the power conferred upon Congress by the clause was the one issue that seemed to divide the Alabama court. Reuben Saffold simply pretended that the Commerce Clause did not exist. Nowhere, he said, "is there found in the Federal Constitution . . . any authority in the United States, to exercise the right of sovereignty over, or regulate intercourse with the Indian tribes." Lipscomb was somewhat more circumspect in his approach. He argued that the state and federal governments held concurrent jurisdiction over commerce with the Indian tribes. The state also retained all other sovereign powers not relinquished to the federal government, he wrote, and there was no doubt that Alabama possessed the police power over its own territory. The Commerce Clause was therefore irrelevant to Alabama's arrest and trial of Caldwell. To imbue the federal government with plenary jurisdiction over all Indian relations by the slender thread of that constitutional provision, Lipscomb said, would capriciously annihilate the sovereignty of the state.[31]

As in *Cherokee Nation,* the Alabama court pondered the intent of the framers' use of the term "Indian tribes" in the Commerce Clause. The phrase, if taken literally, seemed to place the Indian tribes into a relative position of sovereignty with the states and foreign nations but, at the same time, in a category distinguishable from the two. Lipscomb, however, characterized the Indian nations as an uncivilized class below the status of sovereign states. He argued that the framers used "Indian tribes" as "a description of people, not coming within any known definition of an independent sovereign nation or government." He concluded, "Hence, [the Indian polities] could not be embraced in the term, foreign nation." The framers of the Constitution therefore had to construct a third category to describe the "numerous and barbarous tribes" that surrounded the young republic. Conferring Indian communities with a status equal to that of the states would irremediably and unconstitutionally violate Alabama's sovereignty. He suggested that if the court accepted Caldwell's construction of the Commerce Clause, Indian nations could potentially declare sovereignty over the states in which they were located. Saffold concluded that since the Indian tribes were neither states nor foreign nations, "Their right to a separate existence, and that within regular constitutional states of the union, is found to be not more anomalous, than embarrassing to the states. They can have no alliances, confederation, intercourse, or commerce, with any foreign nation. They have yielded these rights, by various compacts, or treaties, with our general, or state governments." [32]

In contrast to Saffold and Lipscomb, Taylor admitted that the states *had* surrendered the right to regulate commerce with the Indian tribes to the federal government. However, in his view, commerce included only intercourse "which consists in trade or traffic." This definition of commerce, he argued, "certainly does not include [criminal] jurisdiction." In relinquishing the authority to regulate commerce with the Indian tribes, he said, the states had "no more intention to surrender their sovereignty over those tribes than they had to divest foreign nations of jurisdiction within their own territories by placing in the hands of the federal government the power to regulate commerce with them." [33]

Besides rebutting the Commerce Clause argument, the court contended that the framers, in Article 1, Section 2 (which provides that Indians subject to state taxation be included in the federal census) intended that Indians would fall under the jurisdiction of the states. Article 4, Section 3, they added, prohibited Congress from creating an *imperium in imperio,* that is a state within the jurisdiction of another state. Congress could not pass a law, the court quoted the Constitution, prejudicing "any Claims of the United States, or of any particular state." The court added that if Alabama's sovereignty was to have been limited in regard to the Indian nations, Congress would have made this express circumscription in the 1819 act authorizing the people of the Alabama territory to form a state government. [34]

Caldwell's attorneys had reminded the court that the Northwest Ordinance stated that the United States would always observe "utmost good faith" toward the Indians and would never take their lands, property, or liberty from them without their consent. Although the ordinance did not apply to Alabama, the phrasing of the resolution reflected the attitudes behind U.S.-Indian policy at the time of its promulgation. The court did not challenge the territorial application of the ordinance, but the spirit behind the law. Taylor argued that Congress intended the ordinance to be a protection of individual, as opposed to national or tribal, rights. The ordinance mentioned only "Indians," not Indian nations, Taylor said. He argued, "The word liberty has been employed in a manner which must convince the mind that it is individual liberty which is intended." Congress, moreover, had never intended in the ordinance to protect the Indian governments from attacks by the states.[35]

Ultimately, the court had to deal with John Marshall's opinion in *Cherokee Nation v. Georgia,* and the other two judges allowed Saffold to shoulder most of this burden. Marshall had characterized the Indian polities as "domestic dependent nations" that looked to the United States for protection and guidance. The tribes were not foreign states under Article 3, Marshall had concluded, but they retained important aspects of sovereignty. Saffold brushed off Marshall's comments as extraneous political dicta that had no binding authority on the court. He did admit that Marshall's ruling "left the relation of the Indian tribes to the United States in an awkward dilemma." He also vehemently criticized Wirt's contention that individual Cherokees were "aliens, not owing allegiance to the United States." Saffold then seized upon Marshall's guardian and ward analogy and argued that the states were the true trustees of Indian interests. He suggested that the states had a right to extinguish both that fiduciary relationship and the Indian claims of title. The state power of extinguishment was preeminent to any Indian rights that had accrued by treaty, Saffold contended; the authority antedated the Constitutional Convention and survived ratification. The Indians were thus in a condition of "pupilage" to the state, Saffold concluded, and only the state, as the true guardian of Indian interests, had the power to determine the future of this relationship. Until the Indians removed, Lipscomb added to Saffold's argument, the state's civil and criminal jurisdiction would be a "shield of protection" for the individual Indian, not only from other Indians but "against the lawless encroachments of the white man." Alabama was therefore extending its jurisdiction to protect the Indians "on account of their liability, . . . their ignorance, [and their tendency] to be overreached and defrauded by the white man." The state would treat the Creeks as "minors" and "wards of the state" and provide them with "that degree of care and attention which their situation, and peculiar liability to injury requires."

Without extension, Lipscomb concluded, white murderers such as Caldwell would escape punishment.[36]

Though Saffold left open the possibility of Creek assimilation into white Alabama society, Taylor revealed the true motivation behind Alabama's extension laws. "The great interest of the state," he wrote, "and the object to which she has looked with the deepest solicitude, has been the removal of the Indians, and the opening of the territory occupied by them to a valuable population." The federal government had been more than generous in offering the Creeks the opportunity to remove to the West, Saffold added, "where they can have, not only the absolute right of soil, but different and higher assurances of less restricted empire."[37]

In concluding his opinion, Taylor ridiculed those who disputed Alabama's claim of dominion over the Creeks. If Alabama was unlawfully seizing the Indians' land, he wrote, "Let these unholy acquisitions be immediately surrendered; let the remnants of the once numerous and powerful, but ignorant tribes, be collected together, and honestly told that our ancestors have used their superior knowledge to cheat and defraud them; we now wish to do them justice by giving back all that extensive domain which has been thus iniquitously occupied. Let us make restitution; the rents and profits will amply compensate us for first cost and improvements." Taylor's sarcasm demonstrated the utter disdain that the court held for the Indians' claims. With that cynical swipe at the Creeks' predicament, the court affirmed Caldwell's conviction and terminated any remaining hopes that tribal leaders may have held for national sovereignty in the East.[38]

As suggested by their opinions in *Cherokee Nation v. Georgia,* John Marshall, Smith Thompson, and Joseph Story might have considered seriously Caldwell's case for review by the United States Supreme Court. Alabama governor John Gayle, however, made an appeal unnecessary. Soon after his inauguration, Gayle received a petition for pardon from Caldwell. The condemned man begged for leniency on the basis of his age and the fact that he had a large family to support. Caldwell added that the witness who accused him was a man of "infamous character" who had "malignantly color[ed]" his testimony to show a malicious intent that Caldwell said he never felt. The killing resulted from "the sad effect of sudden passion," Caldwell explained; he was "destitute of preconceived notions or malice" on the day that he assaulted and killed Fushatchee Yoholo. His lawyers added that Caldwell had been held in irons for ten months, "during which time his health has departed from him." They added, "Now in the last period of existence, friendless, abject, and miserable, his last hope rests with your Excellency to shield his grey haired and miserable old age from the dreadful and ignominious sentence of the law." Over a hundred witnesses, including Caldwell's jailer in

Montgomery County, signed the petition; one wrote that Caldwell's "unfortunate and numerous family, his old age, his suffering and contrition" induced him to support the convict's plea for clemency.[39]

Apparently moved by the petition, Gayle pardoned Caldwell on February 9, 1832, just days before his appointment with the hangman. He cited the Alabama Supreme Court's refusal to address Caldwell's jury tampering charge as his grounds for mercy. Gayle's beneficence was not uncommon. William Garrett wrote in assessing Gayle's term as governor: "Perhaps the greatest objection laid to his charge was the too free exercise of the pardoning power," a tendency that resulted from a "warm sympathizing heart, which was easily touched by human sorrow, and by all forms of distress." Alternatively, the circumstances of the pardon suggest a plot between Gayle and the court to repress the arguments for Creek sovereignty. Gayle was familiar if not friendly with all of the judges. He had read the law, for instance, under the supervision of Abner Lipscomb. With its affirmation of Caldwell's conviction, the court placed itself into the unusual and unpopular position of sanctioning the execution of a white man for the murder of an Indian. By pardoning Caldwell, Gayle defused the potentially explosive situation in a way that allowed the court to reject the argument for Creek sovereignty. It is tempting to suggest that the court conspired with the governor to extricate itself from the dilemma. In the end, though, Gayle most likely used his pardoning power to get his friends on the supreme court and an old man off the hook.[40]

Creek leaders may have been referring to the *Caldwell* case when they wrote Jackson in March of 1832: "In coming under the laws of Alabama," they said, "occurrences will take place when white men may murder the red people, when none other except red people may be present." The Creeks complained, "In this case the white man goes unpunished with impunity. [W]e wish a provision to be insisted placing us in an equal footing with our white brethren." Despite this appeal to legal equality and the rule of law, the Creeks certainly understood the reality of their status. They might adopt the ways and means of Americans and submit to the jurisdiction of Alabama, but the law would never place them on "an equal footing" with their "white brethren."[41]

Caldwell v. Alabama symbolically extinguished the hopes for Creek national existence in the East. There had been a possibility that a decision in Caldwell's favor, recognizing the legitimacy of Creek sovereignty, might have allowed the Creeks to remain in the East as a vibrant, independent nation. Instead, the court refused to stand in the way of, and actually encouraged, the public and legislative pressures brought to bear against the tribe. Without judicial protection for their rights, the Creeks had little choice but to yield. Soon after the publication of the *Caldwell* decision, the Creek Nation signed a treaty that allowed the federal government to divide the nation's land into small tracts and assign them to individual Creeks. Some Creeks sold their lots for fair market value. Many, however, were confiscated by whites through fraudulent schemes or purchased at prices far below fair market value. The treaty left the Creeks without a substantial national territory to call their own. In 1836 the United States Army relocated over fourteen thousand citizens of the Creek Nation to the Indian Territory across the Mississippi.[42]

CHAPTER SEVEN

Sovereign Nations

Worcester v. Georgia

THE MAJOR NEWSPAPERS IN ALABAMA AND GEORGIA did not mention James Caldwell's case. Instead, editorial interest remained focused on Georgia, where a group of Congregationalist missionaries were challenging the state's authority to extend its jurisdiction over the Cherokee Nation. By the 1820s, more than thirty missionaries from several Christian denominations were attempting to win converts in the Cherokee Nation. Funded in part by the United States government, these ministers were also responsible for instructing the Cherokees in the ways and means of American culture, politics, and economics. In 1825 the American Board of Commissioners for Foreign Missions, a Congregationalist evangelical group, sent Samuel A. Worcester to their Cherokee mission in Brainerd, Tennessee. Worcester was the nephew of the founder of the American Board, the eighth generation in a long line of Congregationalist pastors, and a former student and disciple of Jeremiah Evarts. Two years later, the board ordered Worcester to the Cherokee national capital of New Echota. There, with Elias Boudinot and other missionaries and acolytes, Worcester helped translate the Bible and other Christian inspirational materials into the Cherokee language. Worcester quickly earned the trust of the Cherokee leaders and often advised the national government on its political and legal rights under the U.S. Constitution and federal-Cherokee treaties. The Congregationalist missionary was also instrumental in the establishment of the *Cherokee Phoenix* under Boudinot's editorship. By 1830 Worcester had emerged as the most important non-Indian advocate of Cherokee sovereignty in the nation. Worcester's pedigree and his record of benevolent service made him a credible voice among American Christians when he criticized Georgia's Indian policy.[1]

Since Worcester had close access to Boudinot and the *Cherokee Phoenix,* Georgia officials identified him as one of the primary instigators of the Cherokee sovereignty movement. The state also focused its attention on Elizur Butler, a physician serving the American Board at its mission and school at Haweis. Dr. Butler arrived in the Cherokee Nation soon after Worcester and became known as an advocate for Cherokee rights. George Gilmer, Wilson Lumpkin, and other Georgia politicians recognized that Worcester, Butler, and other missionaries were not just spreading the gospel, they were also encouraging the Cherokees to resist removal. Prominent removal proponents in the state suggested to the Georgia General Assembly that if it could eliminate the influence of the missionaries, the state might be more successful in forcing the Cherokees to relocate. As a result, during the Tassel tumult, the legislature promulgated a statute that prohibited "white persons" from residing within the Cherokee Nation without permission from the state and gave them until March 1, 1831, to either leave the nation or obtain a license of residency from the Georgia government. The statute required white men who wished to remain among the Cherokees to take an oath to "support and defend the constitution and laws of the state of Georgia" and provided that violators of the law would be guilty of "high misdemeanors" and subject to imprisonment at hard labor for four years. The state sent copies of the new law to all of the missionaries and to every other white person known to be residing in the Cherokee Nation. The authors of the legislation knew that they would force the evangelical troublemakers either out of the state or into prison, for Governor Gilmer intended to refuse residency permits to any person who was known to oppose removal. This law, Gilmer believed, would ultimately silence white friends of the Cherokees like Worcester and Butler.[2]

The Cherokees responded to the act with indignation. Elias Boudinot wrote that the legislation not only violated Cherokee sovereignty, it was "certainly oppressive on the whites." Why should they have to take an oath, Boudinot asked, if they were already citizens of the state? In its lust to cleanse the state of Indians, he said, Georgia was now encroaching upon the civil liberties of its own people. Moreover, he added, the law inhibited the Cherokee Nation from bringing in ministers, teachers, carpenters, blacksmiths, and mechanics to instruct the Cherokees in Anglo-American ways. "The tendency of such a law," Boudinot concluded, "forces from [the Cherokees] the very means of their improvement in religion and morals, and in the arts of civilized life."[3]

At almost the exact time that the state was passing this most recent affront to Cherokee rights, the missionaries in the nation were meeting to coordinate a strategy of opposition. On January 1, 1831, they issued a manifesto prepared by Worcester on the illegality and immorality of Georgia's extension laws. The missionaries first denied the state's charge that they were influencing the Cherokees against removal. However, Worcester wrote, "it is impossible for us not to feel a lively interest in a subject of such vital importance to their welfare. . . . We view the removal . . . as an event to be most earnestly deprecated. . . . The establishment of the jurisdiction of Georgia and other states over the Cherokee people, against their will, would be an immense and irreparable injury." Removal, Worcester added, would surely "arrest their progress" in the civilization program.[4]

Several of the missionaries, including Worcester and Butler, declared that they would test the Georgia license and oath law "for righteousness sake." Worcester declared, "Taking an oath of allegiance is out of the question." Before this time, fate had foisted the weight of the Indian sovereignty movement upon George Tassel and James Caldwell, convicted murderers. Now the Cherokee Nation had a group of paladins that could clearly obtain constitutional standing to challenge the Georgia laws before the U.S. Supreme Court and, at the same time, elicit public and philanthropic support for the Cherokee cause. After the effective date of the Georgia legislation had passed, the missionaries, with full support from the board, remained in the nation and awaited the state's next move. Jeremiah Evarts wrote to his former student offering encouragement, and his letter provides an illuminating insight into the northern philanthropic conception of the Indian. It was important for Worcester and the missionaries to stand up to Georgia, Evarts said, for as a race, Indians lacked the courage and will to endure a long legal war. "I have often said," he wrote, that " 'white men, in a high state of civilization, are alone competent and expect deliverance by the slow process of law'. . . . If you leave, I fear the Cherokees will make no stand whatever." Apparently, northerners and southerners differed only in the degree of their condescension toward the Cherokees.[5]

Just after Worcester's church service on March 12, 1831, at about the same time that the Supreme Court was considering the *Cherokee Nation* case, a band of about twenty-five armed members of the Georgia Guard arrested him for residing inside the Cherokee Nation without the permission of the state. The guard also rounded up several other missionaries and teachers and marched them south to a makeshift jail at Camp Gilmer on the Chattahoochee River. The next day, the Cherokee Nation's lawyers, William Underwood and Thomas Harris, filed for a writ of habeas corpus on the missionaries' behalf with the Gwinnett County state court. The lawyers argued that the missionaries were residents of the independent Cherokee Nation and that the state did not have jurisdiction over them. Smelling an attempt to obtain standing before the U.S. Supreme Court, Ross's old adversary, Judge Augustin S. Clayton, noted that Worcester was also the federal postmaster at New Echota. Moreover, he said, the missionaries were in the Cherokee Nation under authority provided by the president of the United States and were being paid by federal funds allocated for the purpose of civilizing the Indians. Therefore, he concluded, the missionaries were exempt from prosecution because they were employees or agents of the federal government. Clayton released the missionaries, but not before declaring the Georgia license and oath law constitutional. In adjourning, he encouraged the missionaries to leave the state.[6]

Governor Gilmer immediately complained about Clayton's decision to the U.S. secretary of war. The secretary, John Eaton, responded by issuing a letter denying that the missionaries were agents of the United States. Soon thereafter, U.S. postmaster William T. Barry relieved Worcester of his duties with the New Echota post office. Assuming that he had quashed the federal agency defense, Gilmer again moved against the missionaries. On June 1, he informed them that they had ten days to leave the state. The governor then advised the colonel of the Georgia Guard to harry the recalcitrant ministers: "Spare no exertions to arrest them. . . . If they are discharged by the Courts, or give bail, continue to arrest for each repeated act of continued residence in violation of the law. If resistance is made, call upon the militia of the counties to aid you in enforcing the laws. Although I am disposed to execute the laws with the utmost forbearance upon our Indian people, I owe it to the Sovereignty of the State, to punish with the utmost rigor the injurious and insolent conduct of the whites who deny its power and oppose its authority."[7]

A few days before Gilmer's order, the American Board had explained why its agents were challenging the Georgia law in its publication, the *Missionary Herald*. The statute was a "highly unjust and oppressive" invasion of the sovereignty of the Cherokee Nation, the *Herald* declared, and an unconstitutional attack on the liberty and property rights of the missionaries and the mission board. The board would not abandon its improvements in the nation or its work with the Cherokees without a fight. The Congregationalists' agents had a duty to God, to the Cherokees, and to their own credibility as ministers of the gospel. Those missionaries who sought to challenge the Georgia statute would remain where they were; those who did not want to pick a fight with the state were free to abandon their missions. Days later, three missionaries chose to leave the state. One of them, Daniel Butrick, complained that those who intended to defy the Georgia law "appeared to me more like suffering in a political contest, from motives of worldly policy, than in the spirit of Christian meekness." Worcester worried that "our ranks are broken," but he vowed that if necessary he was "willing to bear the burden alone." He predicted that he would win a constitutional challenge if his case made it to the Supreme Court but realized that he might have to "suffer the full penalty of the unrighteous law." Worcester told his directors that if the day came that he was locked away by the state, they should use every conceivable means to publicize his case and arouse righteous indignation among the American citizenry. The ultimate objective of his civil disobedience, Worcester said, was to defeat Jackson in the upcoming election. Only a new president, more sympathetic to the Indians' plight, might save the Cherokees from removal.[8]

After giving the missionaries a full month to abandon their cause, Gilmer sent his guard against the determined holdouts. On July 7 the state arrested Worcester, Butler, and nine other missionaries and marched them back to Gwinnett County. According to Worcester, the guard ridiculed, cursed, and beat their prisoners along the way. The troops forced Butler to walk the entire eighty-five miles while chained to the neck of a horse. At the time of Worcester's arrest, his wife and infant daughter were very ill; the soldiers forced the missionary to abandon his family and walk behind their horses to Lawrenceville. There, Gilmer's henchmen placed the missionaries in the county jail. "The floor was sufficiently dirty," Worcester wrote from the vault, "and there was little air to light, and a very unpleasant smell." Soon after their incarceration, the missionaries asked their jailer if they could hold church services in a place large enough that other prisoners, the guards, and neighbors could attend. C. H. Nelson, the colonel in command of the Georgia Guard, denied their request with this message: "We view the within request as an impertinent one. If your conduct be evidence of your character and the doctrines you wish to promulgate, we are sufficiently enlightened as to both. Our object is to restrain, not . . . facilitate their promulgation. If your object be true piety you can enjoy it where you are. Were we hearers we would not be benefitted, devoid as we are of confidence in your honesty."[9]

After several days of the missionaries' confinement, the Gwinnett County court allowed them to post a security bond of five hundred dollars. Worcester returned home to tend to his sick child and wife. However, he understood that Gilmer would arrest him over and over again to run up the length of his sentence; so he again left his family and moved across the state line to work at the board's mission in Brainerd, Tennessee. Not long after his arrival, however, Worcester received word that his daughter, his youngest child, had died. The child was buried before Worcester could make it back to New Echota. When he arrived, the Georgia Guard again arrested the missionary on the charge of entering Cherokee territory without a license from the state. Exhausted and distraught, the missionary explained to the officer in charge his reasons for returning. For the first time, the commander of the guard exhibited some sympathy for Worcester's situation and released him.[10]

In September, Turner Hunt Trippe, the state's attorney general, presented Georgia's case against the missionaries before a Gwinnett County grand jury. The jury members quickly returned with a true bill. Elisha Chester,

the missionaries' local counsel and an old friend of Worcester, filed a special plea on the defendants' behalf challenging the state's jurisdiction. The
motion followed the arguments that Wirt and Sergeant had laid out the year
before in *Cherokee Nation v. Georgia*. Georgia's extension laws, Chester
argued, violated a long line of treaties between the federal government and
the Cherokees. These treaties acknowledged that the Cherokee Nation was
a sovereign state and guaranteed that the United States would protect that
sovereignty from state encroachment. The Georgia laws were unconstitutional because they violated the Contract and Commerce Clauses of the
Constitution by interfering with Congress's exclusive authority to "regulate
and control the intercourse" with the Indian tribes. Georgia, therefore, did
not possess jurisdiction over the residents in the Cherokee Nation, Indian
or white.

On September 15 Judge Clayton overruled the motion and brought the
eleven defendants to trial. The missionaries readily admitted they were living
within the Cherokee Nation without a license from the governor. With little
dispute over the facts, the trial quickly moved toward a conclusion. The closing arguments between Trippe and Chester focused primarily on the constitutionality of the state extension statutes. These arguments continued until
after midnight. The jury, however, was not particularly moved by the missionaries' defense and came back after only fifteen minutes of deliberation
with a verdict of guilty. Clayton asked if the defendants had anything to say
before he delivered sentence. Worcester again declared that the court and the
state lacked jurisdiction over them. Clayton then announced that he would
sentence the defendants to the maximum afforded by the statute—four years
of imprisonment at hard labor in the state penitentiary in Milledgeville.

Governor Gilmer understood that the state's actions would provoke widespread criticism in the North and among constituents uncomfortable with
the prosecution of Christian preachers. As a result, he was eager to have the
missionaries either recant their protest or leave the state; he did not want
them imprisoned. Gilmer offered the convicted defendants a pardon if they
promised to swear allegiance to Georgia or agreed to depart immediately
from the state. All of the prisoners relented except for Worcester and Butler,
who replied that they were determined to either serve out their sentence or
have Georgia's laws declared unconstitutional.[11]

As Worcester had hoped, the missionaries' travails at the hands of the
state focused the attention of the American public on the Cherokees' war
for national survival. Protests against Georgia's imprisonment of the missionaries poured in from all over the United States; even some newspapers in
the South excoriated Georgia for incarcerating ministers of the gospel. "No
official act of mine occasioned so much abuse at the time, or was so little

understood," Governor Gilmer wrote, "as the punishment of the religious missionaries by imprisonment." Gilmer added, "Georgia people traveling in other States were every where subjected to the mortification of listening to the most malignant strictures upon the conduct of the authorities of the state, and particularly its Governor, who was specially abused by name." Northern editors depicted Worcester and Butler as heroic martyrs to the Cherokee cause, American John Bunyans imprisoned by tyrannical persecutors. Many of the nation's religious orders, from north and south, condemned Gilmer's handling of the matter.[12]

One reporter visited the missionaries and described the conditions of the state prison for the *Missionary Herald*. There were about one hundred prisoners, he said, locked away behind a high wall in an area about five acres in size. Worcester and Butler "were confined at night in separate rooms, each having twenty-eight or thirty others with him." The prisoners "were clad in a shirt and trowsers of coarse cotton, having the initials of their names, and the term of imprisonment painted in large characters on the breast." The missionaries were satisfactorily fed and sheltered, the reporter concluded, but they were indeed forced to manual labor as their sentence required. The guards had put them to work in the prison shop as cabinetmakers. Worcester and Butler were not demoralized by this treatment, however. Soon after their incarceration, the two missionaries went to work at their calling—witnessing to the other prisoners, leading hymns, and teaching Bible lessons. In October, Worcester reported, "I preached Sabbath before last to about twenty-six prisoners confined in the same room with me, and last Sabbath in a room to which about sixty had access." Publicly, the American Board compared Worcester and Butler to the apostle Paul, who had converted his jailer while in prison at Philippi. Privately, the mission board sent a memorial to President Jackson protesting Georgia's incarceration of the missionaries. The state, it said, did not have jurisdiction over the missionaries or the Cherokee Nation. For his part, Worcester compared himself to Nehemiah, Shadrach, and Daniel, Old Testament figures who had been imprisoned for defying the authority of the realm. "However, easy it might appear to others," he wrote, "I could not conscientiously comply with requirements which would have kept me from this confinement." He was resolved to serve out his sentence. "I am led firmly to believe," he added, "that any man contending for the rights of conscience and the liberty of spreading the gospel, will always find strength given him from above."[13]

The American Board hired William Wirt and John Sergeant to handle the missionaries' appeal. The two lawyers were obviously well versed on the constitutional issues presented by the Georgia extension laws and understood that the fates of the missionaries and the Cherokee Nation were inextricably connected. On October 27, 1831, Wirt and Sergeant filed a petition for a writ of error with the United States Supreme Court. On November 22, the lawyers served copies of the petition and an order requiring the newly inaugurated governor of Georgia, Wilson Lumpkin, and his attorney general, Charles J. Jenkins, to appear before the Court. The new gubernatorial regime had not changed the state's policy toward the Cherokees. Although they had opposed each other in the election of 1832, Gilmer and Lumpkin were both wild-eyed proponents of removal. Lumpkin, moreover, was as defiant toward federal authority as his predecessor. Seeking support, he formally referred the *Worcester* documents to the state legislature for advice and direction. The assembly responded with a resolution directing Lumpkin to ignore the appeal. Lumpkin followed this advice and issued a public statement defying the Court's order of appearance. "I will disregard all unconstitutional requisitions, of whatever character or origin they may be," he wrote, "and to the best of my ability will protect and defend the rights of the State." [14]

The *Worcester* case now took on political implications at the United States's highest levels. A presidential election was coming up in November 1832, and Jackson was seeking a reelection victory that would give public affirmation to his policies regarding the national bank, internal improvements, the tariff, and Indian removal. The National Republicans selected Henry Clay as their choice for president and Cherokee cocounsel John Sergeant as their nominee for vice president. The Anti-Masonic party nominated William Wirt, the Cherokee Nation's chief counsel, as its candidate for president. Both the Whigs and the Anti-Masons were extremely critical of Jackson's policy toward the Cherokees and specifically condemned Georgia's arrest of Worcester. To some extent, thanks in part to the political involvement of Wirt and Sergeant, the 1832 election was a referendum on the Cherokee Nation's destiny. [15]

On February 20, 1832, Wirt, Sergeant, and Chester appeared before the Court to argue the missionaries' case. Again, Georgia officials, following the state legislature's directive, refused to file briefs or attend the arguments. Wirt and Sergeant did not want to be derailed by the same issue that had plagued them in *Cherokee Nation v. Georgia,* and they emphasized that the Supreme Court had jurisdiction in the case under Section 25 of the Judiciary Act of 1789. In *Cohens v. Virginia,* they reminded the justices, the Court had held that criminal defendants could appeal state judgments against them to a federal court if they believed that a state action or state law violated the Constitution or laws of the United States. The missionaries' case, in other words, was not an action originated "against one of the United States by Citizens of another State," as prohibited by the Eleventh Amendment, but an appeal of a federal question by individual defendants pursuing review of a decision of a state's highest court. There was no doubt, the missionaries' lawyers concluded on this point, that the Court had the power, and the duty, to hear and decide the case.[16]

Wirt and Sergeant then turned to the merits of the missionaries' appeal. They repeated the same jurisdictional arguments that they had carefully delineated in *Cherokee Nation*. Moreover, they argued, the new statute under which Georgia had indicted and convicted Worcester was as "unconstitutional and void" as the original extension acts. In fact, Sergeant argued, the entire scheme of extension abrogated the Cherokee Nation's sovereignty and encroached upon the federal government's exclusive right to regulate Indian affairs. The national government exercised its plenary power over Indian matters through treaties and acts of Congress. These treaties and laws were the supreme law of the land under Article 6 of the Constitution, Sergeant said, and the Court had a duty to strike down any state act that violated or interfered with that realm of jurisdiction. Georgia's laws, he said, were therefore "void and of no effect." As John Marshall later paraphrased the Cherokees' argument, Georgia's intent was to "seize on the whole Cherokee country, parcel it out among the neighboring counties of the state, extend her code over the whole country, abolish its institutions and laws, and annihilate its political existence."[17]

By the time they had finished their argument, Wirt and Sergeant had been before the Court for most of three days. Their presentations received considerable praise from the press and from members of the Court. A New York reporter at the trial wrote: "Were I to judge from Mr. Wirt's speech today, I should say that the subject is inexhaustible. He spoke until three o'clock, and was obliged, from fatigue, to ask for the Court to adjourn. So interesting was the subject, so ably did he present it to the Court, that in addition to the number of gentlemen and ladies, who attended from curiosity, so many of the members of the House reported to the Courtroom that an adjournment [of the House] was moved." Justice Story wrote to his wife that the arguments of Sergeant and Wirt were "very able" and that Wirt's, "in particular, was uncommonly eloquent, forcible, and finished." One account said that Marshall was moved to tears by Wirt's presentation.[18]

Marshall, now seventy-six, had just buried his wife and was recovering from a life-threatening bladder operation. However, the chief justice displayed an unusual energy and interest in the case. Instead of scratching out a hasty opinion as he had in *Cherokee Nation,* Marshall took two full weeks to reduce his thoughts to writing. In that time, he was successful in pulling every able member of the Court, except Baldwin, to his majority. On March 3, in a stunning victory for the Cherokees and the missionaries,

Marshall announced that the Court, by a six to one margin, had decided to overturn the missionaries' convictions. He declared that Georgia's extension laws were "repugnant to the Constitution, laws, and treaties of the United States." In brief, Marshall held that the Cherokee Nation was a separate, sovereign nation; that the federal government had exclusive authority over Indian affairs; and that Georgia had no right to extend its laws over the Cherokee Nation.[19] Reportedly disturbed by his conscience and disappointed with the waffling obfuscation of his opinion in *Cherokee Nation*, Marshall set out in *Worcester* to provide future courts with a clear direction on the issues of Native American sovereignty and the reach of federal authority over Indian affairs. The result was powerful, unyielding, and straightforward. Borrowing from the ideas of Wirt's brief and oral argument and from Thompson's dissent in *Cherokee Nation*, Marshall abandoned his reliance on the doctrine of discovery and embraced a natural rights theory of inherent Native American sovereignty. Ironically, Marshall adopted precisely the position that Justice William Johnson had pronounced in his dissent in *Fletcher v. Peck* twenty years before. Johnson, conversely, had moved to a states' rights interpretation of the federal-Indian relationship in *Cherokee Nation* that was antithetical to Indian rights and his earlier position in *Fletcher*. Johnson, now old and often ill, did not participate in the *Worcester* decision. However, it is safe to assume that he would have held to the position he had recently announced in *Cherokee Nation*.[20]

Marshall recognized that his decision would bring down a political firestorm on the Court from the South, and he explained that he had taken southern interests into account in drawing his conclusions. He wrote that the justices were required to consider the "legislative power of a state," the "controlling power of the constitution and laws of the United States," "the rights . . . and political existence of a once numerous and powerful people," and the "personal liberty of a citizen." Balancing interests and protecting the authority of the Court, however, were not Marshall's primary motivation in *Worcester*. He had concluded that Georgia's actions were so obnoxious to the Cherokees and the Constitution that he set aside his fear that a judgment against the state might provoke a constitutional crisis and a backlash against the Court. He came down with a heavy hammer against Georgia.[21]

Marshall briefly resolved the question of the Court's jurisdiction. He wrote that in 1789, Congress, in fleshing out the Article 3 powers of the federal judiciary, had provided the Court with the authority to examine the constitutionality of a state statute or a state court decision that involved the laws or treaties of the United States. The missionaries' case maintained that Georgia's extension statutes unlawfully interfered with treaties between the United States and the Cherokees, that they violated the federal Trade and Intercourse Acts, and that they encroached upon federal powers delegated to Congress in the Commerce Clause of the Constitution. Clearly, Marshall wrote, there were federal questions at issue. The Court's duty to decide the case, he concluded on this point, "however unpleasant, cannot be avoided."[22]

In concluding that the Cherokees were a sovereign nation apart from the United States, Marshall surveyed the history of the European colonization of North America. This had now become a standard practice among the judges who considered the question of Native American sovereignty. However, this time, the chief justice radically revised the conventional interpretation of the Native American people who lived in precontact North America and rejected the stereotypes he had recited in *Johnson v. McIntosh*. At the time of the European discovery of the Americas, he wrote, the continents were "inhabited by a distinct people, divided into separate nations, independent of each other and the rest of the world." These nations had "institutions of their own, and govern[ed] themselves by their own laws." Marshall now recognized that the Native American peoples of that age were not simple bands of indiscriminate savages living in a state of anarchy, but intelligent peoples with their own political, legal, and social customs and institutions. By tacking to this more anthropological view of precontact Indian culture, the chief justice was directly challenging the southern judiciary's suggestion that Indians were biologically or inherently inferior to whites. Marshall, in other words, implied that the relationship between the United States and the Indian tribes was not one of an American hegemony based on cultural and racial superiority, but one where two independent nations came together in consensual compacts for mutual benefit. The American law of Native American sovereignty, Marshall seemed to say, had to be conformed to that fundamental fact.[23]

Marshall also scrutinized the familiar justifications for the European expropriation of Indian land. The chief justice not only jettisoned the doctrine of discovery that he had embraced in *Johnson v. McIntosh,* he now ridiculed it as absurd. "It is difficult to comprehend the proposition," he said, that "either quarter of the globe" could claim dominion over an entire continent, its lands, and its inhabitants simply by "sailing along the coast, and occasionally landing on it." How rational was it, he asked, to contend that discovery could "annul the pre-existing rights of [the continent's] ancient possessors"? During the early colonial period, the idea that "feeble settlements made on the sea coast" conferred title to all of North America was an "extravagant and absurd idea" that "did not enter the mind of any man." At best, he said, Europeans had devised the theory of discovery as an afterthought to determine priority among the many nations competing for the bounty of the American continent. The doctrine endowed the discovering nation only with the "sole right of acquiring the soil [from the Indians] and of making settlements on it." Discovery had no impact on the national or individual rights of Native Americans.[24]

The Georgia and Alabama justices had noted that the charters from King George II to James Oglethorpe and the Georgia trustees had endowed the colony with title from the Atlantic to the "South Sea." This charter was superior to all Indian claims, they had held, and provided the states of Georgia, Alabama, and Mississippi with the right to extinguish any title held by the Native American inhabitants in their states. Marshall rejected the notion that the colonial charters had superseded the natural rights of the Indians. As far as they were concerned, he wrote, the charters were simply "blank papers." Southern judges and lawyers had also argued that the royal charters gave the colonies authority to make war on and conquer the native tribes. Marshall reviewed the charters of Connecticut, Rhode Island, Pennsylvania, Maryland, and Georgia and agreed that they *did* give the colonies the right to wage war. However, he explained, the power was to be used only for defensive purposes and pursuant to a just cause. The doctrine of conquest, the chief justice said, was not intended to be a tool for the indiscriminate theft of Indian land. Marshall added snidely, "The charters contain passages showing one of their objects to be the civilization of the Indians, and their conversion to Christianity—objects to be accomplished by conciliatory conduct and good example; not by extermination."[25]

The conception of the Indian's place under American law and in American society depended to a great extent on two disparate interpretations of the historical relationship between Great Britain and the Indian tribes. Southern opponents of Indian sovereignty contended that the British government completely dominated the internal and external affairs of the Indian nations during the colonial period and therefore abrogated any national rights that the Indians might have possessed. Marshall, in opposition, wrote that the British Crown had never interfered with the internal affairs of an Indian nation except for the limited purpose of denying access to the agents of competing European powers. The advocates for the southern position also argued that the British Empire had only taken what was rightfully its own. Marshall countered that Great Britain had always obtained Indian land with their consent and at a price that was agreeable to the tribe. Great Britain, he said, had always considered the Indian tribes as "nations capable of maintaining the relations of peace and war, [and] of governing themselves, under her protection." Less than ten years before, the chief justice had written in *Johnson v. McIntosh* that Britain had conquered and seized the sovereignty of the continent as far west as the Mississippi, leaving the

Indians with only a tenuous right of possession that could be extinguished at any time.[26]

Marshall's history of the United States's relationship with the Indian nations was likewise contrary to the one concocted by the southern judges. The courts in Georgia and Alabama had held that with its victory in the Revolutionary War, the United States had succeeded to Great Britain's dominion over the Indians by inheriting the empire's right of conquest. Justice Johnson, in *Cherokee Nation,* had added that the Cherokees had affirmed that they were a subjugated people in the Treaties of Hopewell and Holston. Hopewell, Johnson had pointed out, stated that the Cherokees were received "into the favour and protection of the United States of America." This meant, he said, that they were submitting their political and legal authority to their conquerors. The chief justice strongly disagreed with this construction of the United States's treaties that renewed relations with the Indian tribes after the American Revolution. From its first treaty with the Delawares, Marshall said, the United States had contracted with the Indian nations as equals. In that compact, he pointed out, the national government guaranteed "to the nation of Delawares . . . all their territorial rights" and offered them the promise of future representation in Congress. These terms would not have been offered to mere groups of American subjects, Marshall wrote; these were the actions of two nations dealing at arms' length. The United States, he added, had treated with the Cherokees in the same fashion. (Even Marshall would have to admit that the United States interfered with the internal affairs of the Cherokees when, in the Treaty of Hopewell, the commissioners encouraged the Cherokees to abolish their law of blood revenge.)[27]

Baldwin and Johnson had also contended in *Cherokee Nation* that when the Cherokees relinquished their right to regulate international commerce to the United States at Hopewell, they had also surrendered their national sovereignty. Unfortunately for the Cherokees, the Hopewell accord stated that the United States Congress "shall have the sole and exclusive right of regulating the trade with the Indians, *and managing all their affairs,* as they think proper." Here, the southern state justices had argued, was clear and convincing evidence that the Cherokees had forfeited their sovereignty. Marshall rejected this construction of the treaty. He charged that the southern states were trying to transform the genuine efforts of the federal government to protect the Cherokees from licentious American traders into unqualified state hegemony over all Indian affairs. In reality, Marshall said, the Cherokees acquired almost all of their trade goods from Americans. It was only right and fitting then for the federal government to regulate that trade. The Cherokees never intended in the agreement to confer dominion over themselves or their lands to the federal government. The unfortunate use of the phrase "and managing all their affairs," the chief justice said, meant that the United States would have the right to manage only "all their affairs" relating to trade. The parties did not intend to provide the United States with the power to encroach upon the internal autonomy of the Cherokee government. Marshall wrote that the Treaties of Hopewell and Holston simply bound the Cherokee Nation to the United States "as a dependent ally, claiming the protection of a powerful friend and neighbor, and receiving the advantages of that protection, without involving a surrender of their national character." Vattel had written that "tributary and feudatory states" did not lose their sovereignty or independence if they retained their ability to govern and administer their internal affairs. Hence, Marshall said, the Indian nations were akin to the small states of Europe; though they were under the protection and influence of the larger powers on the continent, the small states retained their rights of self-government and sovereignty. "Protection," he wrote, "does not imply the destruction of the protected."[28]

Marshall then pointed out that under the Constitution, treaties concluded by the United States became part of the "supreme law of the land." In devising the Supremacy Clause, he said, the Constitutional Convention had reaffirmed the United States–Indian treaties existing at the time and therefore recognized the tribes as "among those powers who are capable of making treaties." He added that Congress had based the Trade and Intercourse Acts, the legislation that implemented its Indian policy, on the supposition that the Indian tribes were separate nations. The Trade and Intercourse Acts were the method by which the United States intended to "civilize" the Indians, he wrote, and the laws "furnishe[d] strong additional evidence of a settled purpose to fix the Indians in their country by giving them security at home." Judging from this legislation and its treaties with the Cherokees, the chief justice concluded, the United States had intended to recognize the Indian tribes as "distinct political communities, having territorial boundaries, within which their authority is exclusive." That the Indian nations maintained a right to "all of the lands within those boundaries," he added, was "not only acknowledged, but guaranteed by the United States."[29]

Marshall noted that Georgia had repeatedly acknowledged that the Cherokees maintained "full rights" to the lands upon which they resided and had explicitly conferred the authority to regulate Indian affairs to the federal government in the Constitution's Commerce Clause. In his concurring opinion, John McLean specifically listed several instances in which the state had acknowledged the tribes as distinct polities. In 1783 the state legislature had authorized a survey of the state; in that map, the state's surveyors had established a boundary between Georgia and the Creek and Cherokee

Nations. In 1787 the state had enacted a statute that prohibited, on pain of corporal punishment, surveys "beyond the temporary line designating the Indian hunting ground." In 1796, in the legislation that repealed the Yazoo sale, the legislature had claimed that the Yazoo territory was the "sole property of the state, subject only to the right of the treaty of the United States, to enable the state to purchase, under its pre-emption right, the Indian title to the same." The state's preemptive right, the legislature had acknowledged, was "subject only to the controlling power of the United States." In analyzing the Compact of 1802, McLean admitted that Georgia had a "strong ground of complaint" for the federal government's delay in extinguishing the Indian title and may have passed its extension laws out of "a sense of wrong." However, by entering into the compact, Georgia had conceded that the Creeks and Cherokees held a right to occupy their lands and that the federal government possessed the exclusive power to extinguish that right. In 1814, McLean pointed out, the Georgia legislature had again recognized that the Indians held title to their lands when it gave the governor of the state the authority to remove white squatters and intruders from Indian territory. In 1817 and 1819, he went on, after Cherokee cessions to the federal government, the Georgia legislature had waited to dispose of the land until after the treaties had been ratified by the national Senate. After the ratification of those federal-Cherokee accords, the legislature had again authorized the governor to establish a new border dividing Georgia from the Indian tribes. In 1819 the legislature had sent a memorial to James Monroe, asking the president to fulfill the federal government's promise of 1802. In that document, the legislature wrote that the state had a right to extend its jurisdiction to its territorial limits. "She admits, however," the assembly said, "that the right is inchoate—remaining to be perfected by the United States, in the extinction of the Indian title; the United States *pro hac vice* as their agents." Even as late as 1825, McLean wrote, Georgia's governor had issued a proclamation warning the state's citizens from trespassing on Indian lands. To do so would be a violation of federal treaties, the governor had declared, which were the "supreme law of the land." This litany of Georgia's admissions recognizing tribal sovereignty and federal plenary power was not exhaustive, McLean added, but it was sufficient to demonstrate a pattern that the state was now attempting to deny. Over and over again in the past, Georgia had acknowledged that the Indian tribes comprised independent polities and accepted the legitimacy of the Indian usufruct. Moreover, the state had often publicly acknowledged the constitutional authority of the federal government over all matters relating to the tribes and had committed several acts that demonstrated it had submitted to federal supremacy in that area of jurisdiction.[30]

The Court's determination that Congress held plenary authority over Indian affairs was a momentous rule that would impact all future relations between the states, the federal government, and the Indian nations. The courts in Georgia and Alabama had argued vehemently that the states held concurrent jurisdiction with the national government over matters involving the Indian tribes. According to their interpretation of the Constitution, Congress held authority under the Commerce Clause only to regulate trade with the Indians. The southern judiciary had also argued that the state courts had a duty to construe "commerce" very narrowly to protect state sovereignty and that all matters relating to the tribes beyond commerce remained under the jurisdiction of the states. Southern states' rights ideologues had regularly complained that the federal government was unconstitutionally usurping sovereignty from the states. For them, the idea of an expansive Commerce Clause was another weapon the federal government could use to encroach on the powers of the states. In response to these critics, Marshall methodically laid out his conception of the Indian Commerce Clause. Before American independence, he said, the individual colonies had never held authority over matters relating to the Indian tribes. The British Crown had jealously guarded this particular area of jurisdiction. (Marshall's contention on this point was misleading; only after the Seven Years' War did the British imperial authorities attempt to seize control over Indian affairs from the colonies.) After the American Declaration of Independence, the chief justice went on, delegates of the colonies gave the Continental Congress the power to deal with the affairs and problems that affected every colony. One of those areas of jurisdiction was "Indian affairs"; and in the Articles of Confederation, Marshall argued, the *people* of the unified states had invested the national congress with the authority to make peace and war with the Indian nations. The confederation prohibited the states from involving themselves in questions relating to Indian affairs except in the event of an attack that was so "imminent as not to admit of delay till the United States in congress assembled [could] be consulted." The articles, Marshall added, gave the national government the "sole and exclusive right" of "regulating the trade and managing all the affairs with the Indians, not members of any states; provided, that the legislative power of any state within its limits be not infringed or violated." The American Revolution, Marshall wrote, was a "popular movement, not perfectly organized," and the commerce clause in the articles was one example of the fallibility of the Continental Congress. The last phrase of the clause, added in a late amendment, made the entire provision indecipherable. North Carolina and Georgia argued that the amendment completely annulled Congress's power to regulate Indian affairs within their states, and some southern lawyers continued to cite the clause as evidence that the framers of the Constitution had intended for the states to have concurrent authority over Indian affairs. The Philadelphia convention had satisfactorily remedied this ambiguity in the Constitution, Marshall wrote, and had rendered moot the states' rights argument. The framers had "discarded" the "shackles imposed" on the federal government's power to regulate Indian affairs, Marshall concluded, and "the whole intercourse between the United States and [the Cherokee Nation], is, by our constitution and laws, vested in the government of the United States." McLean added that the Indian commerce provision was included in the same section of the Articles of Confederation that gave the Continental Congress the power to regulate the production of currency and the power to establish standards of weights and measures. These duties were clearly and necessarily the province of the national government. That the power to regulate commerce was included in this distribution of power implied to McLean that the national government's authority was to be plenary in this realm as well.[31]

Marshall's analysis raises the question of whether he based his ruling on his interpretation of the Constitution or on the international law or natural rights conception of Native American national sovereignty. Marshall might have believed that *Worcester* was a case in which federal authority preempted state power. Under this theory, Georgia held concurrent jurisdiction with the federal government over the Cherokees in regard to matters, other than commerce, that affected the state's interest. Under preemption theory, the exertion of federal authority supersedes state regulation of the same subject. As such, the federal treaties with the Cherokees and the Trade and Intercourse Acts were legitimate federal actions that preempted state jurisdiction. A related but quite distinct possibility is that Marshall determined that the Constitution provided authority to the federal government over every aspect of Indian affairs; as such, after ratification, Georgia was permanently and completely precluded by the Commerce Clause from interfering with the federal government's exclusive power. However, these two interpretations of *Worcester* do not comport with Marshall's declaration that the Cherokee Nation was inherently a sovereign state. The chief justice did not strike down the missionaries' convictions solely because Georgia was interfering with the federal government's Commerce Clause authority over the Indian tribes. He did so because the state was also attempting to extend its jurisdiction over a distinct and separate nation. Georgia, he might have thought, could no more extend its laws over the Cherokee Nation than it could over France. The special treaty relationship between the United States and the Indian nations thus created a burden on the federal government to protect the tribal nations from attack and encroachment by the states.[32]

This interpretation, however, produces a jurisdictional conundrum. If the

Cherokee Nation was an independent nation, what right did the federal government have to assume jurisdiction over what would seem to be essentially a political, or perhaps a diplomatic, dispute between Georgia and the Cherokees? Marshall resolved this problem of jurisdiction by finding that the United States had guaranteed Cherokee sovereignty by treaty and had historically legislated accordingly. Georgia's laws, therefore, were not just an infringement on the rights of the Cherokee Nation, they were a repugnant violation of the Trade and Intercourse Acts and the Constitution, which provided that treaties were part of "the supreme law of the land." In other words, the United States had enveloped the idea of tribal or Native American national sovereignty into its most basic law. Moreover, when the states ratified the Constitution, they sanctioned the existing treaties concluded by the confederation and entered the Union with the understanding that the Indian tribes were sovereign states. With his opinion, then, Marshall discovered an essential and perpetual link between Native American national sovereignty and the constitutionally sanctioned federal oversight of Indian interests.[33]

Justice McLean agreed with Marshall that the Georgia extension statutes unconstitutionally encroached upon federal responsibilities. However, he wrote his own opinion to distance himself from the chief justice's suggestion that the federal government was perpetually responsible to protect Native American national rights. At a time when two major states were in the preliminary stages of rebellion, McLean thought it necessary to lecture the states' rights leaders on a moderate interpretation of the Constitution. McLean wrote that the Constitution did not emanate solely from the people or the states. Instead, it emerged "by a combined power, exercised by the people, through their delegates, limited in their sanctions, to the respective states." If the framers had intended to adopt a purely nationalist view, McLean argued, they would have reduced the states to simple voting districts and the Constitution would have been ratified by popular referendum. By sending the document to state ratifying conventions, he said, the founders intended to acquire "popular suffrage and state support." The framers thus intended to construct a framework that balanced the interests of individuals, the states, and the national government. McLean was, in other words, leery of both excessive centralization and the emerging virulent states' rights interpretation. He pleaded in his opinion for interpretational temperance: "It has been asserted that the federal government is foreign to the state governments; and that it must consequently be hostile to them. Such an opinion could not have resulted from a thorough investigation of the great principles which lie at the foundation of our system. The federal government is neither foreign to the state governments, nor is it hostile to them. It proceeds from the same people, and is as much under their control as the state governments." It was "impossible," he said, to create a perfect prophylactic against the abuse of power, be it from the federal or the state governments. If power was never distributed because of fear of its misuse, it would never be distributed. Logically extended, McLean warned, the states' rights interpretation would "go to the destruction of all governments."[34]

To McLean, the United States was neither a confederation of independent governments nor a singular, centralized state. The framers, he believed, had reserved certain spheres of authority exclusively for the states. The Constitution also expressly set aside specific and important powers to the federal government and proscribed state intervention or interference with their execution. One of these areas of authority was the regulation of commerce with the Indian tribes. To McLean's judgment, Georgia's extension laws were an unconstitutional encroachment on the federal power. For this justice, the Commerce Clause was not just the fount of federal authority over Indian affairs, but the cipher that signified how the framers expected Congress to treat the Indian nations in the future. It was significant, he wrote, that the convention conferred this power on Congress in Article 1 along with the other powers set aside exclusively for the national government.[35]

Moreover, McLean said, the Commerce Clause placed the Indian tribes "on the same footing" with foreign nations. He reminded his fellow justices that since the administration of George Washington, the policy of the United States government had been to recognize the integrity of the Indian nations. Congress, in the Trade and Intercourse Acts, had confirmed this practice time and time again. The United States, in this legislation and in the treaties with the Cherokees, demonstrated its intent to guarantee the "rights" of the Cherokees, "both as it respects their territory and internal polity." Ultimately, McLean said, the question to be considered by the Court was "which shall stand, the laws of the United States, or the laws of Georgia?" The Court had a duty, he wrote, to strike down laws that were repugnant to the Constitution, treaties, and laws of the United States. If the justices "should shrink from a discharge of their duty, in giving effect to the supreme law of the land," he said, "would they not violate their oaths, prove traitors to the constitution, and forfeit all just claim to the public confidence?"[36]

McLean also examined the racial arguments that Baldwin, Johnson, and the southern courts had used to repudiate the theory of tribal sovereignty. Should the Court, he asked, take notice of or consider the existence of distinctions between "civilized" or "savage" peoples? McLean agreed with the southern judges that Indians were inherently "uncivilized." The southern courts, however, had used the premise of racial and cultural inferiority as justification for disregarding federal-Indian treaties and denying Indians their individual and national rights. McLean, announcing a novel argument, believed that Indian inferiority raised the standard of justice on which the American governments should be judged. If the United States concluded treaties with peoples who might not be able to read or completely understand them, he explained, then American judges were bound to construe the agreements in the favor of the Indian signatories.[37]

Some proponents of removal had charged that the federal government's civilization program had increased the Indians' affinity for the lands they inhabited. McLean suggested that this was probably the case and that the program had made it more difficult for the United States to acquire land cessions from the Indians. If this was a problem, though, he said, it was one that Congress would have to resolve, and when it did, the national legislature was required to respect and protect the Indians' rights. The United States government had never intended for the civilization program to open up the Indian nations to attacks by the states. McLean adopted the syllogism that Boudinot had devised and that Wirt had used in his *Cherokee Nation* argument. The southern state judges had contended that the Indians were savages and intellectually incapable of governing themselves. As such, the "community of nations" could not accept the tribes into their company. McLean pointed out, however, that until the late 1820s Georgia had allowed the Cherokees to govern themselves under their own political and legal systems. These same state judges had also admitted that the Cherokees were now "more civilized" than during the era of the Hopewell and Holston treaties. What Georgia was arguing, McLean said, was that the more civilized the Cherokees became, the less capable they were of governing themselves. Was it not illogical, he asked, to recognize Indian governments when they were ruled "by the rifle and the tomahawk" but not when they were "administered upon the enlightened principles of reason and justice?"[38]

McLean summed up his interpretation of the relationship between the states, the federal government, and the Indian tribes with this passage: "In the executive, legislative, and judicial branches of our government, we have admitted, by the most solemn sanctions, the existence of the Indians as a separate and distinct people, and as being vested with rights which constitute them a state, or separate community—not a foreign, but a domestic community—not as belonging to the confederacy, but as existing within it, and, of necessity, bearing to it a peculiar relation." The Constitution, the federal-Cherokee treaties, and the Trade and Intercourse Acts threw "a shield of protection over the Cherokee Indians," he said, and "guaranteed to them their rights of occupancy, of self-government, and the full enjoyment of those blessings which might be attained in their humble condition." The extension laws of Georgia broke this shield into pieces, he said, and "infamous punishment is denounced against them, for the exercise of those rights which have been most solemnly guaranteed them by the national faith." [39]

McLean, however, declared that the sovereignty of the tribes was only a temporary condition. Native Americans, he wrote, would not always be allowed "to roam, in the pursuit of game, over an extensive and rich country, whilst in other parts, human beings are crowded so closely together, as to render the means of subsistence precarious." The federal government, through its civilization program, through its gradual purchase of Indian lands, and by the Compact of 1802, demonstrated that the Indian nations would, at some point in the future, be "amalgamated into our political communities" or exchange their lands for those in the West. "At best," he said, "[the Indian nations] can enjoy a very limited independence within the boundaries of a state." Continued residence in the East would subject the tribes to continuing trespasses by the whites who moved in around them, and their existence as independent nations would continue to incite the state governments in which they lived. Eventually, because its existence was so at odds with "the political welfare of the states and the social advance of their citizens," each Indian nation would have to "give way to the greater power which surrounds it, or seek its exercise beyond the sphere of state authority." Emigration, or the transformation from sovereign status to assimilation, McLean said, could be peacefully and prosperously produced only by cooperation between the state and federal governments. In the end, despite McLean's defense of Cherokee sovereignty, he was also convinced of the inevitable necessity of removal. In fact, a few weeks after issuing his opinion, he wrote to John Ross and advised him that the Cherokee Nation would "be better to unburden itself of these difficulties by a removal" to the West. [40]

Marshall and McLean had measured the United States's commitment to treaty obligations against the standards pronounced by George Washington and Henry Knox almost a half-century before and found them wanting. They, and the other justices for the majority, offered a decision that attempted to remind the country of its obligations to Native Americans. The Court's decision in *Worcester* reaffirmed the long-established principle that the Indian tribes were independent nations possessing the right of self-determination. Moreover, the Court held, in passing the extension statutes and enforcing them against the missionaries, Georgia had violated the civil liberties of Samuel Worcester and Elizur Butler and had defied the Constitution, laws, and treaties of the United States. The state had illegally interfered with the relationship between the United States and the Cherokee Nation, had unlawfully trespassed on the lands of an independent state, and had "seized and abducted" citizens of the United States in an attempt to thwart resistance to its encroachments. The Court censured Georgia in the harshest of possible terms.[41]

Russell Barsh and James Y. Henderson have described Marshall's opinion as a "masterpiece." The chief justice, they wrote, set aside all thoughts of political consequences and "persuaded his fellow justices to join him in a search for fundamental principles consistent with the Constitution and American political theory." Marshall, they continued, "hoped to fashion a clear and ideologically acceptable *modus vivendi* for the tribes, states, and the Union, clearing away the thicket of piecemeal rules he had previously planted." *Worcester,* then, was the culmination of Marshall's moral and theoretical evolution. Phillip P. Frickey wrote, "*Cherokee Nation* and *Worcester* cannot be dismissed as merely further examples of the federalist agenda of the Marshall Court. . . . Contemporaneous evidence supports the proposition that chief justice Marshall and Justice Story were quite sympathetic to the plight of the tribes that were being encroached upon by states in the southeastern United States." More than likely, Frickey suggests, Marshall intended to supersede his "domestic, dependent nations" rationale and his guardian and ward metaphor in *Cherokee Nation* with a recognition of nearly unfettered Native American sovereignty in *Worcester*. Unfortunately, subsequent federal and state judges have failed to understand that Marshall's opinions represented not a conglomeration of reasoning, but an intellectual progression toward virtually complete sovereignty for the Indian tribes. Consequently, while Marshall had hoped to prune away the extraneous rhetoric and confusion that grew out of his former decisions, the judges who examined questions regarding tribal sovereignty in succeeding cases tried to draw consistency from the entire Marshall line. The courts that did so, and there were many, turned the "thicket" of federal Indian law into a "forest" of confusion.[42]

Two days after the announcement of its decision, the Supreme Court remanded the case to the Georgia trial court and ordered it to reverse the convictions of Worcester and Butler and release them from imprisonment. This set off great rejoicing at the office of the American Board in Boston. Elias Boudinot, who was visiting while on a prolonged speaking tour of the North, reported, "Mr. John Tappan came in to see us. . . . He then told us the true story of the case, and produced a paper which contained an account, and tried to read to us, but he was so agitated with joy that he could hardly proceed." Boudinot, at this point, saw the decision as a momentous turning point: "It is glorious news. . . . it is a great triumph on the part of the Cherokees." The war was no longer simply between the Cherokees and Georgia, he believed; the United States government now had to come to the Cherokees' assistance. John Ross reported that there were "rejoicings throughout the Nation. . . . Traitors and internal enemies are seeking places where to hide their heads." Major W. M. Davis of the U.S. Army wrote to the secretary of war that the announcement of the Court's ruling was "trumpeted forth among the Indians, by the chiefs, headmen, and missionaries. . . . Rejoicings, night dances, etc., were had in all parts," and there was "yelling and whooping in every direction." [43]

Georgia, on the other hand, responded to the *Worcester* decision with defiance. Lumpkin called the Court's ruling a "usurpation" of the state's sovereignty and promised to meet it "with determined resistance." He reportedly said that he would hang Worcester and Butler before he "submitted to this decision made by a few superannuated life estate Judges." [44] The editor of the *Macon Advertiser* wrote, "[The missionaries] have been placed where they deserved to be, in the State Prison, and not all the eloquence of a Wirt, or a Sergeant, nor the decision or power of the Supreme Court can take them from it unless the State chooses to give them up." George Troup predicted that Jackson would refuse to enforce the judgment against Georgia: "The chief magistrate of the United States will perform all his constitutional duties." Troup added, "He will, if I mistake not, defend the sovereignty of the states, as he would the sovereignty of the union." Troup's reaction demonstrated how closely Georgia's leaders now connected the issues of Indian removal and slavery. If the United States claimed jurisdiction "over one portion of our population," he warned, then it "may very soon be exerted over another . . . and in both cases they will be sustained by the fanatics of the north." However, he threatened, if the state's slaveholders needed defenders, "we will find them everywhere." Former governor Gilmer saw the Court's decision as part of a conspiracy to circumscribe states' rights. The actions of the missionaries, he wrote, were "swelled into great importance by being instruments used by the northern section of the union to prevent the increase of the population and consequent political strength of the South." Worcester and Butler were aided, he added, "by religious fanatics everywhere." He said at another time, "Great sympathy was evinced for the Indians by the people of those States in which there were none." [45]

The *Alabama Journal* expected *Worcester* to push Georgia to South Carolina's side in the nullification movement:

> By this decision, the Court declares the States have not the right of jurisdiction over the Indian tribes. This is the most important decision ever yet made by that Court. It involves the great principle of States Rights and will now test the efficacy of Nullification. Will Georgia submit to this decision? She cannot, and will not! What, then, will be the consequence? Nullification. A refusal to obey will be nullification, and we shall then see whether

or not any "sacred duty," will induce the President, "at all hazards," to enforce, by the sword, this decision of the Court.

The state's leadership, however, was not prepared to go down that road. Lumpkin rejected the idea of nullification, calling it "unsound, dangerous and delusive, in practice as well as theory." What South Carolina was doing in regard to the tariff, Lumpkin said, "tends directly to destroy all harmony between the Federal and State governments." However, he wrote, Jefferson himself would view Georgia's actions "by its plain, proper name, resistance to intolerable usurpation." Georgia had not nullified a federal law; it had "only nullified the arrogant assumption of sovereign power, claimed and set up by a remnant of the aboriginal race within her acknowledged chartered limits."[46]

Justice Story described the reaction in Washington: "The decision produced a very strong sensation in both houses; Georgia is full of anger and violence." He predicted, "Probably she will resist the execution of our judgement, & if she does I do not believe the President will interfere." Story added that the Court had absolved itself of the sins of the removal policy: "Thanks be to God, the Court can wash their hands clean of the iniquity of oppressing the Indians and disregarding their rights." He concluded, "The Court has done its duty. Let the Nation now do theirs."[47]

Story's nation did not perform its duty, and the joy of the Cherokees turned to despair when it became apparent that the federal government would take no action to enforce *Worcester* on Georgia. The realization that neither the president nor Congress would support the ruling of the United States's highest court destroyed the morale of many of those Cherokees who had believed that they would eventually obtain a fair recognition of their national rights. Boudinot wrote that he was "disillusioned by the obvious impotency of the Supreme Court decision." In August he resigned in disgust as editor of the *Cherokee Phoenix;* without his leadership, the Cherokee Nation lost its voice. Shortly before leaving the paper, Boudinot suggested that the "good people of the United States" were too caught up in the controversies over the tariff and the national bank to register any righteous indignation against the government's treatment of the Cherokees. A few weeks later, Boudinot's name appeared on a Cherokee petition supporting the acceptance of a removal treaty. The nonenforcement of *Worcester* crushed the will of the Cherokees who had counseled accommodation with the United States. Boudinot, John Ridge, and several other influential Cherokees now turned against Chief Ross. Ross, however, remained characteristically optimistic; he believed that a new president would take a different attitude toward the missionaries' case. Within weeks after the decision the Cherokee Nation was splintering into two factions: those like Boudinot, who advocated submission to the removal pressures, and those like Ross, who wanted to continue peaceful resistance.[48]

Why did the federal government fail to execute the *Worcester* judgment against Georgia? Horace Greeley wrote that Andrew Jackson, upon hearing of the decision, retorted, "John Marshall has made his decision, now let him enforce it." The traditional view is that the president simply refused to execute *Worcester*. While Greeley perhaps invented Jackson's remark, the statement did generally represent the president's position. However, Jackson's forbearance was a more complicated matter than Greeley suggested. Benjamin Butler, who would later become Jackson's attorney general, argued that the president did not refuse to obey the ruling of the Court; at that time, he said, Jackson did not have authority to interfere in the dispute. Under the Judiciary Act of 1789, the Court could not have issued a writ demanding execution of its judgment until the Georgia court had refused in writing to comply with Marshall's order to release the missionaries. By the time that a messenger had returned to Washington with the Georgia court's repudiation of the judgment, the Supreme Court had adjourned for the year. The justices were not scheduled to reconvene until January of 1833. The responsibility, Butler said, did not rest with Jackson.[49]

Wirt and Sergeant explained to Ross the lengthy process they would have to undertake to force Jackson to execute the judgment. After the Georgia court refused to obey the Supreme Court's mandate, the Cherokees' lawyers would have to obtain a contempt decree from the Supreme Court ordering the state to obey its original order. If Georgia refused, the missionaries then had to petition Governor Lumpkin to release them. Only when Lumpkin declined to follow the Court's order, Wirt said, could they call on the president to enforce the Supreme Court's judgment. If Jackson remained recalcitrant, the missionaries could only appeal to Congress and perhaps incite an impeachment movement against the president in the House of Representatives. This was highly unlikely considering Jackson's public popularity and his support in Congress.

In any event, Jackson could have easily short-circuited this escalation by persuading Lumpkin to pardon the missionaries. The president could then have argued that the case was moot in regard to the missionaries and burdened Congress with the responsibility of sending troops to Georgia to enforce the decision. Leaving the onus on Congress, Jackson could then tell the public that he had upheld the Constitution and the authority of the Court. At the same time, he could reassure Georgia of his sympathies and proceed apace with removal negotiations. In other words, a constitutional showdown could easily have been averted by a president as politically savvy and well counseled as Jackson. Needless to say, Jackson was not disappointed that he had legal grounds to ignore the judgment. While no one has ever confirmed Greeley's report of Jackson's challenge to Marshall, the president did certainly write the following to John Coffee: "The decision of the supreme court has fell still born, and they find that they cannot coerce Georgia to yield to its mandate." If a war developed between Georgia and the Cherokees, Jackson said, "the arm of the government is not sufficiently strong to preserve [the Cherokees] from destruction." In sum, Jackson's silence on the Court's decision appears to have been astutely planned.[50]

Even Ambrose Spencer and Daniel Webster, two of Jackson's fiercest political opponents, recognized that the failure of enforcement rested more with legal circumstances than with Jackson. However, Spencer immediately realized that Jackson's opponents could use the situation for political gain in the coming election by tagging Jackson with the charge that he had refused to enforce the law of the land. In the months following the Court's decision, however, the tariff unrest in South Carolina diverted much of the electorate's attention away from the *Worcester* imbroglio. When Congress did not drastically reduce the tariff in 1832, it invited John Calhoun and South Carolina into open rebellion. After Jackson's landslide reelection in November, South Carolina passed its Nullification Ordinance, declaring that the tariff would not be collected or paid within the state's borders after February 1. South Carolina, it seems, had been emboldened by Georgia's defiance in *Worcester*. The president, though, was not going to allow South Carolina to defy a law of Congress. He intended to put down the Palmetto rebellion by force, if necessary. Jackson, however, did not want to move against South Carolina until it had been isolated from the other southern states. Georgia, Alabama, and Mississippi all wanted the Indians in their states removed and believed, like South Carolina, that the federal government was dangerously encroaching upon their states' rights. Jackson suspected that if he moved to enforce *Worcester* against Georgia, these other southern states might join South Carolina's rebellion.[51]

Jackson's reelection, the nullification crisis, and the appearance that the executive department would never attempt to enforce *Worcester* persuaded the missionaries to rethink their position. At the same time, the public outcry against Georgia's imprisonment of the missionaries encouraged Wilson Lumpkin to try again to persuade the missionaries to accept a pardon and abandon their cause. Jackson's men advised the Georgia governor that he could help put out the nullification fires in the state by pardoning the missionaries. The key architect of this strategy was Martin Van Buren, who had partisan aspirations that would be unsettled by a sectional party split and a general southern rebellion. Following Van Buren's plan, the governor first convinced the state legislature to repeal the oath and license law under which Georgia was holding its prisoners. By repealing that act, Lumpkin could then pardon the missionaries without requiring a promise from them that they would leave the state or conform to the statute. Lumpkin then sent emissaries to Worcester and Butler to tell them that the dispute with the Cherokees, the bank war, and the nullification crisis were dividing the nation to a dangerous degree. If the missionaries forced Georgia to defy the Supreme Court, they were told, the state, along with South Carolina, Alabama, and Mississippi, might leave the Union. Lumpkin's agent then told the missionaries that they would therefore be partly responsible for inciting a civil war. Lumpkin also invited the wives of Worcester and Butler to an executive soiree and asked them to encourage their husbands to surrender for the good of the nation. He would gladly pardon their husbands, he said, if only they asked. Ann Worcester told Lumpkin that she would leave the decision to her husband. The pressure on the missionaries to surrender their campaign was now intense. In the end, even one of their lawyers deserted them. Lewis Cass, now Jackson's secretary of war, made Elisha Chester a federal agent for the purpose of negotiating a Cherokee removal treaty. As part of this process, Chester encouraged Worcester and Butler to give up the fight, an act that forever embittered John Ross against the lawyer.[52]

As late as November 26, 1832, Worcester and Butler had instructed their attorneys to file the appropriate motion asking the Supreme Court to order Georgia to enforce its ruling in *Worcester*. By this time, however, the pressure was beginning to take its toll on the missionaries. They had been in prison over a year and their cause had taken on national consequences that they had never anticipated. On December 7 Worcester and Butler agreed between themselves to give up the fight. They wrote to the American Board asking for permission to surrender. On Christmas day, the board agreed that the two missionaries should drop their case and sent them a letter advising them to request a pardon, under protest, from Lumpkin. Two days later, the board wrote to John Ross and encouraged him to end the Cherokee resistance and agree to a removal treaty with the federal government. On January 8, the day after receiving the notice of support from the board, the two prisoners told their lawyers to terminate their efforts to enforce Marshall's order. They wrote to Governor Lumpkin that they would push their case no further. Their principles had not changed, they said, and because of the Supreme Court's decision, they had a "perfect right to a legal discharge." However, they wrote, they had been advised that "the further prosecution of the controversy, under existing circumstances, might be attended with consequences injurious to our beloved country." The tone of the missionaries' request infuriated Lumpkin, and he declared it an insult to the authority of the state. Told of the governor's displeasure, Worcester and Butler sent a more compliant note the next afternoon: "We are sorry to be informed that some expressions in our communication of yesterday were regarded by your excellency as an indignity offered to the state or its authorities. Nothing could be further from our design. In the course we have now taken it has been our intention simply to forbear the prosecution of our case, and to leave the question of the continuance of our confinement to the magnanimity of the state." With this submission, Lumpkin believed that he had obtained acknowledgment from the missionaries that they were in the wrong. He could therefore pardon Worcester and Butler and demonstrate the state's beneficence:

> Taking into view the triumphant ground which the state finally occupies . . . [and] being assured . . . that the state is free from the menace of any pretended power . . . to infringe upon her rights. . . . I therefore . . . feel bound to sustain the generous and liberal character of [the state's] people. Whatever may have been the errors of these individuals—whatever embarrassments and heart-burnings they may have been instrumental in creating—however mischievous they may have been in working evil to the State, to themselves, and the still more unfortunate Cherokees. . . . They shall go free.[53]

Five days after their second message, Lumpkin ordered the keeper of the penitentiary to release Worcester and Butler. Since their arrest, they had been confined for sixteen months. A few days after their release, Worcester and Butler issued a letter to the public explaining their decision to submit to the will of the state. In the recent weeks, they said, Georgia had repealed the statute that had caused the missionaries and the Cherokee Nation so much grief. In addition, they had been advised that Jackson would not enforce the ruling in *Worcester* and that their efforts might endanger the Union and lead to violence between the Cherokees and Georgia. Finally, they wrote, they had determined that "there was no longer any hope" that their actions would benefit the Cherokees. It turns out, that in contrast to what Jeremiah Evarts expected, the Cherokees had demonstrated greater "long continued courage" than had his own missionaries.[54]

With the Georgia missionary crisis resolved, Jackson no longer had to bide his time with South Carolina. With Georgia, Alabama, and Mississippi now convinced that the president was intent on removing the Indians in their states, he could count on their support when he moved against their neighbor to the east. Two days after the release of Worcester and Butler, Jackson sent the Force Bill to Congress. The bill declared nullification tantamount to treason, made the act of nullification a federal criminal offense, and gave Jackson the authority to use military force to put down South Carolina's rebellion. On January 21, South Carolina, recognizing that it would be forced to wage its war alone, backed down and suspended its nullification ordinance. In return, Congress agreed to reduce the tariff. Within just a few weeks, Jackson had deftly avoided two major constitutional crises.[55]

In the end, the Supreme Court's bold decision failed to deter Georgia's assault on the Cherokees. *Worcester* was a ringing affirmation of the sovereignty of the American Indian nations, and John Marshall has rightly been praised for his opinion. Instead of acting out of his characteristic concern for the authority of the Court and his political vision for the country, Marshall had based his decision on purely moral and legal grounds. He issued a judgment that could have ushered in a new era of relations between Indians and whites in America. However, it was impossible for him to predict how the federal-Indian relationship might have evolved had *Worcester* been enforced. The decision could have forever changed the already fragile relationship between the sections and between the states in the Deep South and the federal government. In short, as Marshall wrote the opinion, he must have known at least one of two things. On the one hand, he perhaps understood that the decision would never be enforced. As such, he could safely and finally clear his conscience of his earlier opinions in *Fletcher, Johnson v. McIntosh,* and *Cherokee Nation v. Georgia* and place the Court in a position of high moral authority. On the other hand, Marshall must have known that he was pushing the nation close to the abyss of disunion. He could not have been comfortable with that thought.

Worcester simply went beyond what Georgia, the president, and a majority of Congress were willing to accept. Consequently, a vacuum now existed in American law. If what the United States Supreme Court declared was not binding on the government, what then exactly was the "supreme law of the land"? Unfortunately for the Cherokees and other American Indians, the law pertaining to Native American sovereignty was what the Georgia and Alabama courts had declared in *Tassels* and *Caldwell*. As of 1833, Indians were second-class subjects of the states in which they lived. As individuals, they possessed no rights that white Americans would respect; their political autonomy and rights of communal self-determination were in danger of annihilation. The southern state legislatures had abolished the Indian governments in the region, and the courts in Georgia and Alabama had upheld those laws. The states' rights removal ideology was emerging as the *de facto* law of the land. However, the southern interpretation required reaffirmation after Marshall's radical revisioning in *Worcester*. The supreme court of Tennessee would provide it in *Tennessee v. Forman*.

CHAPTER EIGHT

The Law of the Land

Tennessee v. Forman

THE GEORGIA GOVERNMENT had never allowed the Worcester controversy to deter it from its removal strategy. During the course of the case, the state had proceeded with the survey, lottery, and sale of the Cherokee Nation's lands. By the time the state released Worcester and Butler from the penitentiary, hundreds of white Georgians had purchased lots to 40- and 160-acre parcels of land that, according to the U.S. Supreme Court, were still owned by the Cherokee Nation. Although the Georgia General Assembly attempted to keep lottery winners out of the Cherokee Nation until the United States had concluded a removal treaty, the excited winners of the land lottery were not content to wait until that moment to take possession. Hordes of Georgians who held winning draws and those who had purchased them from the winners moved into the Cherokee Nation and seized Cherokee homes, farms, stores, and other improvements. Though most of the besieged Cherokees continued to look to their government for relief, many began to question their principal chief's optimism that the United States would ultimately do right by the Cherokee people.[1]

Most Cherokees, and the National Council, had been content to trust John Ross's policy of legal resistance against Georgia's aggression and had supported his efforts to obtain federal recognition and protection for the nation's independence. Though Ross continued to hold the loyalty of the majority of the Cherokees, the surrender of the missionaries, the refusal of the United States to enforce Worcester, the completion of the land lottery, and the increasing migration of Georgians into the nation convinced a substantial number of Ross's countrymen that continued opposition to removal was futile. Major Ridge, a wealthy planter and politician, his son John, and his nephew Elias Boudinot emerged as the leaders of a Treaty Party that urged the Cherokee government to negotiate for the best possible terms from the United States and move the nation intact to the West. The Ross and Ridge parties disagreed on more than removal; the two factions were ultimately competing for the leadership of the nation. After it became clear that *Worcester* was only a pyrrhic victory, John Ridge resolved to challenge Ross in the next election for principal chief. Georgia's extension laws, however, prohibited the nation from conducting elections; the younger Ridge accused Ross of using the legislation as an excuse to protect his position. Ross's followers in turn charged that the Ridge group sought to sell the Cherokee people out to the surrounding states. Some among the Ross party went so far as to label the Ridges as traitors to the nation. The rivalry between the Ridge and Ross parties, in sum, sundered the nation's long-standing unanimity against removal. American officials seized advantage of the division and began separate negotiations for a removal treaty with the Ridge group.[2]

Ross moved quickly to eliminate the Ridge challenge to his leadership. He and his supporters initiated efforts to unseat the Ridges from the National Council. In response, Elias Boudinot accused Ross of trying to impose his will on all of the Cherokee people. Boudinot resigned as editor of the *Cherokee Phoenix,* he said, because Ross allowed the paper to publish only the chief's views on removal. The Cherokees needed to hear alternative opinions, Boudinot argued, while Ross maintained that the *Phoenix* was a national organ and should present only the nation's official position. To quell the publication of dissent, Boudinot suggested that the National Council had replaced him with Elijah Hicks, a man who would do Ross's bidding. By 1834 the animosity between the Ridge and Ross families was so intense that rumors of assassination threats against both families wafted through the nation. On several occasions the adherents of the two parties became embroiled in fisticuffs and shootouts.[3]

One of the victims of this factionalism was John Walker Jr. "Chief Jack," as he was known among his friends, was from a prominent Cherokee family and had important ties with both the Cherokee leadership and the federal government. He was the great-grandson of Nancy Ward and had parents affluent enough to send him to boarding school in New England. His father, John Walker Sr., had served with Andrew Jackson in the War of 1812 and was active in the Cherokee government. Walker's contemporaries regarded him as handsome and intelligent and believed that he was destined for a position of high leadership on the National Council. Walker's two marriages also established important connections with leaders of the federal and Cherokee governments. In 1824 he married Emily Meigs, a white woman and the granddaughter of Return J. Meigs, the longtime federal agent to the Cherokees. Later, Walker took a second wife, Nancy Bushyhead, who was the sister of Jesse Bushyhead, the prominent Cherokee minister, teacher, and politician.[4]

By 1832 Walker had become disenchanted with Ross's leadership and

was convinced that a national migration to the West was the only way that
the Cherokee Nation could retain its independence. That year, he became involved with the removal negotiations with the federal government when he
accompanied a delegation from the Cherokee Nation in Arkansas to Washington. The western Cherokees were ironically trying to persuade the federal
government to remove the Osage Nation from the land that the United States
had provided the Cherokees in Arkansas, and the Cherokee delegation re-
cruited Walker and James Starr to ride with them to Washington. There
Walker met Andrew Jackson. The president told Walker that he recalled his
father from the War of 1812 and that the senior Walker had offered heroic
service to his troops. According to witnesses, Jackson took an immediate
liking to Walker.

The National Council of the eastern Cherokees also had a delegation in
Washington at the time, and it spread the rumor that Walker was there
for the purpose of negotiating a removal treaty. Whether this is true or
not remains unclear. In any event, Walker became recognized as one of the
more radical leaders of the Treaty Party. Walker took no action to disavow
those rumors and over time became even more active in his opposition to
Ross's leadership. In the spring of 1833, for example, he signed a petition
encouraging the National Council to conclude a removal treaty with the
United States. The petition also demanded that Ross provide a satisfactory
explanation for his refusal to negotiate such an agreement. At a meeting
in May to consider the petition, the council gave Ross until October to
prepare a response. According to witnesses, when Major Ridge agreed to
this compromise, Walker and several other radical Treaty Party Cherokees
stomped out of the council.[5]

By that time, John Ross's brother, Andrew, had also switched his allegiance to the Treaty Party. In February 1834, Andrew and three other members of the Treaty Party went to Washington and signed a removal treaty
with federal representative John Eaton. The treaty provided that the Cherokees would cede all of their lands in the East to the federal government.
In return, the United States would provide a large tract west of the Mississippi; personal allowances for rifles, blankets, and kettles; ten thousand
dollars per year for schools; and a lump sum of twenty-five thousand dollars
for other public needs. The proposed treaty did not, however, provide pay-
ment for Cherokee improvements. The proposed agreement was so adverse
to Cherokee interests that Major Ridge, John Ridge, and Elias Boudinot
had withdrawn from the negotiations. Opponents of removal accumulated
over fifteen thousand signatures to a petition protesting the treaty, and the
U.S. Senate's Committee on Indian Affairs ultimately refused to report the
agreement out to the whole assembly for ratification. John Walker, who

was involved in these negotiations, had also refused to sign the agreement, but back home in the Cherokee Nation he was rumored to be one of those responsible for initiating the negotiations. Consequently, he became one of the primary targets of the wrath of the Ross party adherents.[6]

In August, John Ross called the National Council into session at Red Clay to discuss the recent negotiations. Two years before, the National Council had moved its meetings from New Echota to Red Clay, a small community just across the Tennessee line, to get around Georgia's prohibitions on Cherokee assembly and political activity. Ross declared that he wanted to clear the air of the "innumerable and diversified falsehoods" that were circulating throughout the nation about the existence of a completed removal treaty. The council then addressed the Andrew Ross agreement. At that point, the meeting deteriorated into a vitriolic exchange of charges and recriminations. Even though Major Ridge had refused to sign the Andrew Ross agreement, Tom Foreman, an ally of Ross and one of the Cherokee sheriffs, blamed Ridge for the treaty and charged him with scheming to sell the nation's land for his own material gain. Foreman called Major Ridge, who had become a Cherokee national hero in the War of 1812, an enemy to his people. If Ridge and his cohorts had not been negotiating with the federal government, Foreman said, the United States would have come to the Cherokees' aid in the Georgia crisis. "Major Ridge had gone around the nation with the Chiefs & made speeches telling the people to love their land," Foreman complained, "[but] now he was talking another way." The leaders of the Treaty Party, he added, were trying to "suck for more [wealth] in the veins of their country." At that point, a Cherokee man named Parch Corn reportedly cried out, "Let's kill them!" Perhaps alarmed by the mood of the council and concerned for their safety, John Walker and Dick Jackson, Walker's friend, got up, left the council, and rode out toward Walker's home near present day Cleveland, Tennessee. According to witnesses, two men, James Foreman and his half-brother, Anderson Springston, followed them out.[7]

John Ridge attempted to defend his father and calm the percolating emotions. He reminded the council of Major Ridge's great service to the nation. His father saw a thunderstorm approaching the Cherokee people, the younger Ridge said, and only sought to warn the nation of the impending danger. Major Ridge's only desire, John added, was to preserve the Cherokee Nation as an independent government and protect its people from further trespasses. Major Ridge then asked for the floor. He noted that he was old and likely would not live to see the fate that awaited the Cherokees. However, he added, Ross's strategy was taking the Cherokee people down the wrong path. Georgia had abrogated the Cherokees' government and laws.

"The seats of your judges are overturned," he said, so further resistance was futile. Major Ridge then admonished his critics, "When I look upon you all, I hear you laugh at me. When harsh words are uttered by men who know better. . . . I feel on your account oppressed with sorrow. I mourn over your calamity."[8]

Major Ridge's words did not quiet his critics, and Tom Foreman continued his invective against the advocates of removal. The attack on the Ridge faction reached its climax when Elijah Hicks, the new editor of the *Phoenix,* offered a petition, signed by 144 Cherokees, to impeach the Ridges from the National Council for attempting to "terminate the existence of the Cherokee community on the lands of [their] fathers." The council accepted the petition and ordered the Ridges to appear in October to defend themselves against the charges.[9]

In the meantime, Walker and Jackson were riding north toward what is now Cleveland along the old Spring Place Road. Near a watering hole named Muskrat Springs, a few miles northeast of the council ground, two assailants ambushed Walker and Jackson from behind a fallen log. A shot blasted into Walker's back and came out of the right side of his chest. Walker later reported that he saw two men, James Foreman and Anderson Springston, running away from where the shots were fired. Jackson bandaged Walker's wound and the two rode on to Walker's house. When they arrived, Walker collapsed at the door. Jackson located Walker's wife, Emily, and together they carried the wounded man to his bed. The council was still in session when a Cherokee named Jack McCoy rushed in and announced that Walker had been shot. Fearing the attack was part of a general attempt on the Treaty faction's leadership, the Ridges left the meeting and returned to their homes by a roundabout route. They also dispatched an armed guard of Treaty Party men to Walker's home for his protection.[10]

Friends of the Ridges immediately blamed John Ross for the attack; Walker's father threatened to kill the principal chief. Andrew Jackson was infuriated when he was told of Walker's shooting and predicted that the assault was the beginning of a systematic attack on the Treaty faction. On September 3, the president ordered Benjamin Currey, a major in the U.S. Army, to lead a federal investigation into the shooting. He told Currey to advise Ross that the United States would hold the National Council responsible for any further attacks on Treaty Party men. In the meantime, Walker's health faltered. He had lingered on fitfully for almost three weeks after the assault, but on September 11, he succumbed to his wounds. Walker's male friends provided him with a full Masonic funeral; his two wives and seven children honored him at a traditional Cherokee ceremony.[11]

John and Major Ridge both informed Ross that rumors were circulating throughout the nation that the chief had ordered Walker's shooting. On the day after Walker's death, Ross began distancing himself and his supporters from the crime. In a letter to John Ridge, Ross denied that he had any part in the attack and assured him that there were no plans to assassinate Ridge or his father. "With the utmost sincerity and truth," he wrote, "I do assure you, that whatever may be [the] character of those reports they are false. At no time have I ever directly or indirectly expressed, insinuated nor even entertained any such feeling toward yourself or any other person." He asked Ridge to tell him where he heard the reports of his involvement. "It is high time," he wrote, "that all such mischievous tales should be silenced . . . [by] all men who are friends of peace & good order." (It is impossible to tell whether Ross was truly ignorant of the plans for Walker's assassination or was trying to ferret out the unreliable agent among his followers.)[12]

Ross also wrote to Andrew Jackson to express his "great astonishment" that the president considered him an accessory to Walker's death. The idea that he or the National Council was responsible for the crime, he said, was "too horrible to conceive." He wrote, "That wicked spirit which at times have prompted base men to create strife, commit murder or assassination among their fellow men, I can assure you, have no abiding place in my breast." Ross said that he hoped that President Jackson knew his "general deportment and character too long and too well than to be persuaded in the belief that I could, under any circumstances, be guilty of any criminal offence." Ross also noted that he had heard that Jackson's agent, Currey, had said that he was determined to implicate the principal chief in Walker's assault. In fact, Ross wrote, Currey had said in the presence of Walker's relatives that if Walker died of the wound, "he . . . was determined to have 'John Ross' killed, if he had to do it himself." Ross asked Jackson to "act on the subject as you may think proper." Ross also pleaded his innocence to the people of the Cherokee Nation. At the October council, he declared: "If differences of opinion, excitement, or strife, have arisen between individuals, or murder been committed upon each other from any cause whatsoever, whilst we lament the occurrence of events so deplorable, we have the consolation to know that we have neither perpetrated, nor instigated, nor approved them."[13]

By that time, Currey had completed his investigation and reported his findings to the secretary of war. He wrote that he had discovered that two half-brothers, James Foreman and Anderson Springston, were responsible for Walker's death. Soon thereafter, the McMinn County, Tennessee, sheriff arrested the two suspects. The two men lived near each other in the Wakia Creek area of McMinn County. Springston, who was about twenty at the time, was an itinerant laborer and mechanic and operated a small farm and fruit orchard. Foreman, an older "stout man," also farmed a small tract in McMinn County. At one time he was also a sheriff for the Cherokee Nation. One man who knew Foreman described him as "bad and dangerous"; another said years later that he was "considered a violent fighting man." Some personal antipathy between Foreman and Walker predated the 1834 attack. In December 1825, Walker, serving as a peace officer for the Cherokee Nation, caught Foreman and two men trying to smuggle a boatload of contraband whiskey across the Conasauga River. Foreman tried to push the boat off of the shore and escape with the liquor, but Walker jumped on the boat, struck Foreman in the head with his pistol, and knocked him into the river. Walker then confiscated the contraband. There is little doubt that Walker's death was a political assassination; however, Foreman might have gladly welcomed the opportunity to obtain some personal revenge.[14]

On October 31, Samuel Frazier, an attorney general for the seventh judicial district of Tennessee, presented the McMinn County grand jury with a bill of indictment for murder against the two defendants. According to the bill, on August 23, Springston and Foreman, "feloniously, wilfully, deliberately, maliciously, premeditatedly, and of their malice aforethought," assaulted John Walker Jr. Frazier named Springston as the trigger man and charged Foreman with "aiding, helping, abetting, comforting, assisting, and maintaining" Springston in the murder. The grand jury heard a number of Cherokee witnesses, including Charles Vann and Walker's brother-in-law, Jesse Bushyhead, who also acted as interpreters for the witnesses who could not speak English. The next day, the grand jury returned an indictment against the two suspects.[15]

At their arraignment, Spencer Jarnigan, representing the two defendants, challenged the 1833 Tennessee statute under which the state had charged his clients. When the Tennessee legislature realized that Congress and Andrew Jackson would take no action to enjoin the enforcement of Georgia's extension laws, it had enacted one of its own.[16] Proponents of the law promoted it as a necessary action to provide law and order for the southeastern counties of the state.[17] The Tennessee legislation was far less draconian than Georgia's extension acts. The law only extended Tennessee's law over the Cherokee Nation for the crimes of murder, rape, and larceny and allowed the Cherokee legal system to retain jurisdiction over all other crimes. The statute implicitly recognized political distinctions between the Cherokees and the citizens of the state and respected several of the Indian nation's national powers. It prohibited the state from levying taxes on residents of the Cherokee Nation, forbade the state from interfering with or invalidating Cherokee marriage customs, and allowed the Cherokees to continue other "customs and usages . . . until such time as it may be deemed necessary and proper further to abridge or abrogate them." The Tennessee statute prohibited whites from settling on, trespassing over, or appropriating the lands of the nation and declared that the Cherokees would be "secured and protected in the free and unmolested enjoyment of their improvements and all personal property." Finally, the law forbade state authorities from taking any action that might invalidate federal laws or treaties pertaining to the Cherokees.[18]

Jarnigan argued that Tennessee did not have the legal authority for even this limited expansion of jurisdiction. The shooting occurred south of the Hiwassee River, he said, and "within the limits of [the] Cherokee nation and within the jurisdiction of said nation of Indians." The nation's sovereignty over this territory, he added, had been confirmed "by sundry treaties between the United States of North America and said nation of Indians and also by the laws of the United States and the laws of the state of Tennessee." These treaties, Jarnigan contended, had all been ratified by the United States Senate and all acknowledged "the Cherokee nation of Indians to be a sovereign and independent nation authorized to govern itself by its own laws, usages and customs free from any legislative interference by the several states." If there was a crime to be prosecuted, he said, it was "committed and done by natives and resident citizens of said Cherokee nation of Indians against the laws of said Cherokee nation, upon and against the person of a native and resident citizen of said Cherokee nation, within the territorial limits of said nation, and within its jurisdiction, and not within but beyond the rightful jurisdiction of the state of Tennessee." Attorney General Frazier responded by filing a demurrer to Anderson and Foreman's plea of lack of jurisdiction.[19]

The attorneys for the state and the defendants argued the question of jurisdiction for the better part of three days. After the hearing, Charles Fleming Keith, the circuit judge for McMinn County, overruled the attorney general's demurrer. Although he did not believe that the Cherokee Nation was a sovereign, independent nation, he said, federal treaties recognized it as a nation nonetheless. The Cherokee people "were not citizens or members of the States, but members of a separate community." They had forfeited their sovereignty by placing themselves under the protection of the United States, the judge concluded, but remained free from the laws and jurisdiction of the states. The Tennessee statute of 1833, he declared, was unconstitutional and void.[20]

Before adjourning, Judge Keith ordered Springston and Foreman back to the McMinn County jail where they were being held. The next morning, Jarnigan filed a motion asking the court to release his clients from custody. Keith agreed to issue the order as requested and directed the state to pay the costs of the prosecution. However, Frazier immediately asked Keith for a writ of error to the Tennessee Supreme Court and an order remanding the defendants back to jail until the appellate court rendered an opinion on the question of jurisdiction. Keith issued the writ of error, commanded the clerk to forward the record of the case to the eastern division of the state supreme court in Knoxville, and ordered the McMinn County sheriff to deliver Springston and Foreman into the hands of the Knox County sheriff for detention until the court ruled on the appeal.[21]

As the two defendants sat in the Knoxville jail, the Cherokee National Council moved to deal with the Treaty Party insurgency. At the council scheduled to rule upon the expulsion of the Ridges, Ross refused to support an effort to prosecute them on the charges that they had attempted to sell the nation's land without the council's consent. The penalty for such a transgression, of course, was death. At the same time, however, Ross refused to allow them to speak so that they could respond to or deny the accusations being leveled against them. John and Major Ridge subsequently resigned from the National Council and began informing the Cherokee people that they intended to begin holding a separate council of their own in November. At that meeting, the Treaty Party announced that it intended to seize control of the Cherokee government.

Walker's death, the Ridge faction's defection, and the potential threat of further political assassinations and retaliations convinced Ross to step up his negotiations with the Jackson administration. He had already begun tentative discussions about a general cession with the federal government. In March 1834 he had asked Jackson if the United States would consent to a treaty in which the nation ceded a portion of its territory in Georgia. Under this proposal, the federal government would allow the Cherokees to continue their existence in the East under their own laws and government for an unspecified "definite period." After that time, the nation would fall under the jurisdiction of the state and its people would become "free citizens of the United States" and allowed to dispose of their land as they saw fit. Jackson had refused to budge from his position that the only options for the Cherokees were removal or subjection to the state. In February 1835, Ross moved a step closer to Jackson's position. On behalf of the nation, the principal chief offered to cede all of the Cherokee territory in Georgia except for "a fractional part bordering on Tennessee and Alabama." The Cherokees outside of this enclave, he added, would submit to the jurisdiction of the states in which they lived. In return, Ross wanted the United States to guarantee the Cherokees' title to the remainder of their territory that they would retain in Alabama, Tennessee, and North Carolina. Under Ross's proposal, the federal government would also expel the white intruders living in the nation and ensure that the states provided the Cherokees with "all the immunities rights & privileges belonging to the free citizens of the states." This offer of agreement, Ross suggested, would resolve the question of jurisdiction that had marred relations between the Cherokees and the states. "Would not such a community of the aboriginal descendants of this continent," he wrote, "be worthy of that common privilege which has ever been graciously conferred on the outcasts of the European shores, whose lot it has been to seek asylum under the tree of Liberty, of becoming free citizens of the United States?" Jackson again rejected Ross's overture and told the principal chief that he would accept nothing less than the removal of all of the Cherokees from the borders of the existing states. Days after receiving Jackson's rejection, Ross finally proposed a treaty that included provisions for a general removal. He offered a cession of the nation's land in the East in exchange for twenty million dollars and a like territory in the West. Under Ross's plan, the Cherokees would have five years to prepare for their departure. In the meantime, the United States would remove all white intruders from the nation, indemnify the Cherokees for the losses caused by those trespassers, and arrange to exempt the Cherokees from the jurisdiction of the southern state laws.[22]

Ross and the National Council perhaps devised this offer as a delaying tactic in the hope that the political climate would change in Washington. A five-year delay until removal would give the Whigs, who claimed to support Cherokee interests, two presidential elections in which to win the White House. Jackson considered Ross's five-year plan and the twenty-million-dollar sales price "extravagant" and asked him to come back with a better offer. Ross reminded Jackson that he had promised to arrange for the government to pay an amount that was acceptable to the U.S. Senate. As such, Jackson agreed to put the question of the cession price to the Senate for consideration. The Senate agreed upon an offer of five million dollars. Ross deemed this figure to be unreasonably low and continued to lobby for better conditions. Unbeknownst to the principal chief, as these negotiations foundered, Lewis Cass's agent, John F. Schermerhorn, was holding discussions on a removal treaty with the Ridge council. Ross, exploring other options, was working on a side deal of his own. He attempted to negotiate a deal with the Mexican government that would allow the Cherokees to move *en masse* to its country. If the Cherokee relocation to Mexico was successful, he suggested, perhaps all of the other Native American nations could join them there.[23]

It was in this fractious climate that the Tennessee Supreme Court considered the issue of whether the Cherokee people comprised a sovereign state. To some extent, the Foreman and Springston case offered a slim hope that the momentum toward removal could be reversed. In July, Spencer Jarnigan made the defendants' presentation before the Tennessee high court. Jarnigan was thoroughly familiar with the U.S. Supreme Court's line of Cherokee cases and followed the successful framework of argument established by William Wirt and John Sergeant. Unlike previously, though, this time the Cherokee parties before the bar had the powerful precedent of *Worcester v. Georgia* to lay before the court. Jarnigan repeated his contentions that Foreman and Springston were citizens of the Cherokee Nation, that the United States guaranteed the nation's sovereignty by treaty, that the crime occurred within the jurisdiction of the nation, and that the Tennessee extension law was unconstitutional. The laws of Tennessee, he concluded, had no force in the Cherokee Nation.[24]

In the cases involving Georgia, the state had refused to appear or file briefs. As such, the United States Supreme Court was required to anticipate Georgia's arguments in support of its extension law. In *Tennessee v. Forman,* however, the state of Tennessee decided to appear and present an argument in support of its statute. For that responsibility, Newton Cannon, the governor of the state, selected George S. Yerger, the state's attorney general and the official reporter for the Tennessee Supreme Court, and John Crozier, the solicitor for the state's fourth judicial circuit. Yerger suggested that the case was one "of the greatest magnitude," for it involved "not only the rights of the Cherokees, but those of a state, sovereign in all respects." He added, "It also embraces other important considerations affecting the morals and well being of the community in which we reside." If the court held that Tennessee had no jurisdiction over that portion of the Cherokee Nation lying in the state, Yerger argued, "then the melancholy fact must be admitted, that we have within the bosom of our State a small portion of territory in which crimes of all kinds may be perpetrated with impunity, and the powerful arm of the law falls nerveless in the mighty presence of 'Cherokee sovereignty.' "[25]

The judges in the *Tassels* case in Georgia had been relatively unencumbered by contrary precedent. The Alabama court in *Caldwell* simply shrugged off what it depicted as the anomaly of *Cherokee Nation v. Georgia.* Yerger, however, was forced to deal with *Worcester,* a case that was directly antithetical to the state's position. The principles of the law of nations, "so repeatedly recognized by the statesmen and jurists of this country," he said, "have been virtually abrogated and overturned by . . . *Worcester v. Georgia.*" Yerger effectively attacked *Worcester* by quoting Marshall's comments in the case and juxtaposing them with his earlier statements in *Fletcher v. Peck* and *Johnson v. McIntosh.* Yerger pointed out that Marshall had heartily embraced the doctrine of discovery in *Johnson v. McIntosh,* that he had stated that the sovereignty of the Indian tribes was subject to arbitrary defeasance by the United States, and that he had recognized that the national rights of the tribes were "to a considerable extent impaired." Marshall, Yerger said, had subsequently ruled to the contrary in *Worcester*. In *Johnson v. McIntosh*, Marshall had said that the colonial charters conveying title to Europeans could not be considered as mere "nullities"; in *Worcester* he had written that the charters were "blank papers" as far as Native Americans were concerned. In *Fletcher*, Yerger added, the chief justice had said "that the seizin in fee of lands covered by the Indian claim was in the State of Georgia." In *Worcester* he had written that the federal government had complete authority over Indian affairs. In short, Yerger said, in *Worcester* Marshall had contradicted everything that he had said before on the issues of Indian sovereignty and title. No person, he argued, could reconcile *Worcester* with the chief justice's previous opinions: "They are as diametrically opposed to each other as light is to darkness." In *Worcester*, Marshall had tried to distinguish his reasoning from the holdings in the earlier cases. This string of qualifications, Yerger said, "virtually denies" that the chief justice's previous opinions in *Fletcher* and *Johnson v. McIntosh* "ever existed."[26]

Yerger accepted, he said, that the state courts were obliged to place great weight on the opinions of the Supreme Court of the United States. However, there came a time when a state had the constitutional right to reject a decision of that Court:

> When the decision involved a political as well as a legal question, and was made at a time when high political excitement prevailed; when a particular right or power, always claimed; and denied to be surrendered by the States, is impaired or restricted by the decision. When the case was heard upon an ex parte argument; when its positions conflict with the previous determination of the same Court; when it is at variance with the opinion of the most respectable jurists and statesmen, for 200 years before; when it deprives a State of one of its principal attributes of sovereignty, and affects the rights of millions of freemen. When the decision has been assailed by many of the ablest politicians and legal characters of the age, and never has been acquiesced in by that portion of the Union, whose political rights and privileges it affects; and when it is a single isolated case, to follow which, and decide in conformity with it, would forever prevent it from being again examined and its errors corrected by the same tribunal who made it. . . . These considerations are surely sufficient for this Court to let the matter be again examined by the Supreme Court of the United States, when it can be fully and fairly argued.

If the Tennessee judges overruled Keith's decision in McMinn County, he said, the federal Supreme Court might have the opportunity to reconsider the issue, this time with the state and the Indian nation present to argue their cases. Of course, by this time Marshall had died and been replaced by Roger Brooke Taney. One can only surmise, but it is likely that Taney, a Jackson appointment, would have taken a position distinctly different from Marshall's in *Worcester*.[27]

In *Worcester*, Yerger continued, Marshall had attempted to offer judicial sanction to unconstitutional treaties: the Constitution prohibited the federal government from creating a state within a state; by recognizing the sovereignty of the Cherokees, the federal government (and Marshall) had illegally infringed on the sovereignty of the states. The framers, he argued, did not intend for the president and the Senate to use the Supremacy Clause to run roughshod over the rights of the states. The national government could no more require a part of Tennessee to fall under Cherokee jurisdiction than it could force the state, by treaty, to govern itself "by the laws of the Hindoos or Persians." He said, "A treaty cannot cede away any attribute of sovereignty reserved by the States, and if it does it cannot be regarded and enforced." The Constitution guaranteed the states the power to police the full extent of their territory, he concluded on this point; Tennessee's jurisdiction was coextensive with its borders.[28]

Yerger noted that the European nations had used the doctrine of discovery, which was sanctioned by Vattel and other students of the law of nations, to seize complete dominion over the continent and its "savage" inhabitants. When the Europeans acquired sovereignty over the land, he continued, they acquired jurisdiction over the people living on that land. By inheriting the sovereignty over the Cherokees' land, Tennessee also acquired the right to extend its jurisdiction over the Cherokee people. Yerger admitted that Marshall had recently brought the doctrine of discovery into disrepute in *Worcester*. He encouraged the Tennessee Supreme Court to simply ignore the decision and follow Marshall's reasoning in *Johnson v. McIntosh*: "If a certain and fixed rule is once established, and one upon which titles and property depend, its abstract justice cannot be enquired into. . . . A rule which was considered just and proper, and suitable to the times or generation in which it was adopted, may be deemed very unjust and oppressive in a succeeding age," he said. However, to now reject that rule on a new interpretation of morality "would unhinge society and produce interminable confusion."[29]

Yerger also concentrated on the Cherokees' putative failure to cultivate their territory, a claim that was clearly contradicted by the facts. When Europeans discovered the continent, he said, "it was inhabited by wandering and erratic tribes of Indians . . . [with] no fixed or permanent places of abode; no distinct boundaries or land marks; no known settled rules of property. Their only occupations were war, fishing and hunting. The soil was not subdued or cultivated; they were in fact, completely in a state of nature, wholly destitute of a national existence and of the arts and sciences." The Indians, he added, had historically claimed far more land than they could ever cultivate or populate. Under Vattel's *Law of Nations,* other peoples who were overcrowded in their own lands could come in and seize any unused territory. The "society of nations," Yerger added, had never recognized the Indian tribes as nations, thus there was no reason for Tennessee to accord the Cherokees that status. The Cherokees could continue to live on their land in Tennessee, he said, but if they did, they would have to come under the jurisdiction of the state. In sum, Yerger repeated the arguments espoused in *Caldwell* and *Tassels* and in the dissents issued by Justices Henry Baldwin and William Johnson in *Cherokee Nation v. Georgia.* Yerger's argument, as published in the *Nashville Republican,* was a concise summary of the southern removal ideology.[30]

Unlike in *Caldwell* and *Tassels,* however, the Tennessee court did not simply rubber-stamp the state's extension legislation. The Tennessee legislature had enacted its statute partly in reaction to the nonenforcement of *Worcester* and presumably expected that the state supreme court would ratify its authority. Instead, the U.S. Supreme Court's majority opinions in the Cherokee cases effectively splintered the Tennessee court. Ironically, each of the three judges on the state supreme tribunal embraced a different Marshall precedent.[31] John Catron, the chief judge, voted to uphold the Tennessee law, rejected the idea of Cherokee national sovereignty, and maintained that *Johnson v. McIntosh* was the controlling authority. His opinion, like Yerger's argument, was a complete repudiation of *Worcester.* Judge Nathan Green applied Marshall's doctrine in *Cherokee Nation* and described the Cherokees as a dependent nation that retained significant powers of self-government. However, he believed that the civil strife that had developed among the Cherokees required Tennessee to extend its criminal jurisdiction over the nation for capital crimes. Jacob Peck was the only judge among the judiciary of Georgia, Alabama, and Tennessee who dissented to the legislative attack on tribal sovereignty. He viewed *Worcester* as a proper interpretation of the Constitution, declared the Tennessee extension statute illegal and unconstitutional, and found the Cherokee Nation to be an independent, sovereign nation. In his dissent, Peck urged his comrades to draw their authority solely from the Constitution and American law: "The constituted authorities of my country I bow to with reverence; but as all authority emanates from the constitutions, state and federal, I make them the basis of my argument rather than recur to the law of nations, knowing that where we have the rule at home, that must govern rather than transatlantic learning, much of it growing out of feudal systems." A close inspection of even those authorities, Peck added, would "sustain me in both in the letter and the spirit" of his interpretation.[32]

Peck was described by one of his biographers as "a man of wide culture, with positive and independent character. . . . a man of large frame and extraordinary physical vigor, fond of music, painting, mineralogy and zoology." Peck was also an old line federalist, and he premised the viability of Cherokee sovereignty on his belief that the Constitution imbued Congress with plenary power over Indian affairs. The challenges to Cherokee sovereignty were a very recent phenomenon, he said, and the southern states' rights advocates were attempting to reconstrue the basic understandings between the Cherokees and the United States. In the Treaties of Hopewell and Holston, the United States recognized that the Cherokees possessed the essential elements of national sovereignty, Peck noted, and succeeding treaties between the two nations had consistently reaffirmed that admission. The treaties had guaranteed the Cherokees' national boundaries, allowed the nation to determine who could enter or live within its borders, and recognized the Cherokee Nation's jurisdiction over crimes committed by Indians and non-Indians in its territory. These articles, Peck said, were sufficient to convince him that the United States had, since its founding, accepted the Cherokee Nation as a separate and independent political entity. The Constitution's Contract Clause prohibited Tennessee from interfering with or impairing those agreements, and the Supremacy Clause put them on the "same footing" and deserving of the "same homage" as the Constitution itself. "All judges," Peck concluded on this point, "are commanded to obey" the strictures of the treaties by the Constitution.[33]

The states' rights jurists had argued that the agreements between the federal government and the Indian nations were not really treaties, but mere paper promises issued to "conciliate the savages." Peck wrote that southern judges and politicians willingly accepted the fruits of those compacts when the treaties benefited the states or endowed them with new lands. However, when Indians demanded recognition of the rights that had been guaranteed in those agreements, the southern leadership suddenly wanted to jettison them. Over the years, Peck said, Tennessee had demanded that the federal government conclude cession treaties with the Cherokees, its senators had ratified them, and its citizens had derived benefits from them. Repeatedly since Hopewell, Tennessee representatives had reaffirmed the sovereignty of the Cherokee Nation and acknowledged the special relationship that existed between the United States and the Indian nations.

"An argument from some unknown hand," he said, now put forth the idea that the Commerce Clause strictly limited the federal government's regulatory authority to the Indian trade, leaving all other aspects of civil and criminal jurisdiction over the Indians to the states. Peck urged his partners on the court to reject this analysis and construe the Commerce Clause in context with the Supremacy Clause and the history of the existing treaties with the Indian tribes. These treaties, Peck wrote, placed the Cherokee Nation under the protection of the United States and gave Congress the exclusive right to regulate Cherokee trade and manage "all their affairs in such manner as they think proper." Yerger had argued that this phrase in the Treaty of Hopewell demonstrated that the Cherokees had surrendered every aspect of their sovereignty and had fallen under the jurisdiction of the states. Peck, to the contrary, read the clause to mean that the United States had taken on a mantle as the protector of the Cherokee Nation's sovereignty. By express terms in the accords of Hopewell and Holston, he said, the Cherokees "excluded the exercise of any control by any [other] sovereignty." And since the Treaty of Hopewell, the Cherokees had with a "determined spirit . . . resist[ed] every authority except that of the United States." Anyone who had examined the history of the Cherokees and their relationships with the state governments, he said, could see why the Cherokees had invoked the protection of the federal government. The states had capriciously allowed their citizens to trample onto Indian lands without the consent of either the Indian or the federal governments. In Georgia, the state legislature had even purported to outlaw Indian government. For the survival of the Indian nations, Peck contended, it was essential for the federal government to protect them from incursions by the states.[34]

Peck recognized that the support for the extension laws came from Tennessee's powerful states' rights lobby and that the interpretational insurgency movement was beginning to affect the way southerners regarded the Constitution. Much to his dismay, the states' rights interpretation threatened Peck's romantic conception of the history of American republicanism. Until recently, he reminisced, there "existed no . . . conflict between single states and the general government." Before the emergence of the removal and nullification movements, the "bonds of union were more strong, love of country prevailed, and men were willing to sacrifice much of opinion for the sake of that harmony among sister communities." It was in this climate, Peck wrote, that for fifty years the United States had left the Cherokees to their "usages and customs." Now Tennessee had made it a "question of state pride" in taking jurisdiction over a "few specified crimes" within the nation. Peck suggested that the extension statutes were only "calculated to exalt us by becoming the hangmen or jailers of the Indians." In short, Peck said, the Tennessee act required the Cherokees to abide by the state's laws and live under its jurisdiction without affording them the rights and benefits of state citizenship. Tennessee authorities could arrest a Cherokee citizen for crimes committed in violation of Tennessee laws but did not offer the detainee standing to obtain redress for his own grievances before the state. By extending only some of its laws over the nation, Peck added, the legislature also violated the state constitution's mandate that every law apply equally throughout the state's jurisdiction. Peck wrote that the attorneys for the state and other members of the court had urged him to recognize the fact that Georgia, Alabama, North Carolina, New York, and Ohio had all extended their jurisdiction over the Native American nations within their borders. Peck refused to be coerced into siding with their new laws: "I will not sin," he said, even "if others do." If Tennessee was allowed to "cut off" a major aspect of the federal government's jurisdiction—its exclusive right to govern relations with the Indian nations—what was there to prevent the states from seizing other fundamental powers of the central government? The state extension laws, Peck concluded, were unconstitutionally adverse to the interests of the United States. The Tennessee Supreme Court did not have jurisdiction to hear the *Forman* case.[35]

Judge Nathan Green voted to uphold the constitutionality of the state's extension of jurisdiction. At the same time, though, he concluded that the Cherokees retained significant aspects of national sovereignty. Green appeared to be comfortable with Marshall's conception of Native American rights in *Cherokee Nation v. Georgia* but was ill disposed to embrace the chief justice's broad recognition of sovereignty in *Worcester*. He also disagreed with the southern interpretation of the doctrine of discovery and the theory of permanent Indian racial inferiority. The Indian tribes inherently possessed the essential elements of national sovereignty at the time of European discovery, Green said, and they retained those rights until they surrendered them to another government. Green wrote that the relationship between the individual states and the Indian nations was "very peculiar" and unlike any in Europe, where the legal philosophers had developed the law of nations. One could not divine the character of this relationship simply by reading Vattel, he added; one should consider "the natural rights of nations . . . the character of the parties, the necessities of the case, and the policy which dictated the attitude originally taken and the course since pursued by the parties." Rather than selectively choosing from the buffet of jurisdiction offered by Vattel, as the proremoval justices had done, Green attempted to synthesize the doctrine of discovery and inherent Native American sovereignty into a systematic scheme of title. This is not to say that Green rejected the ultimate consequence of discovery, that is, American hegemony over the tribes, only that he was more honest in his interpretation of the law of nations and a bit more thoughtful in his rationalization for Tennessee's expansion of jurisdiction.[36]

Green attempted in vain to find consistency in the system that the European international legal theorists had developed. He wrote that "civilized" nations could not, as the Georgia and Alabama courts had suggested, simply impose European laws of property ownership and sovereignty on the Indians. Rules of international conduct had to have logical bases in natural law, and that law did not give one nation the arbitrary right to subdue another. Green suggested that the presumption in favor of cultivation was the natural core of all Anglo-European rights to America and a legitimate premise that the states could use to defend their position. The Indian nations, Green asserted, held the inherent right to *possess* as much land as they could reasonably occupy and cultivate. Europeans, coming from a land that was "too closely pent up," had the right to "take, occupy, and exclusively enjoy" the "extensive territories" that the "rude nations" were not in "particular want." If the Indians opposed these efforts, Green added, the Europeans would have "been lawful to have used force to repel such resistance." Unfortunately for the Cherokees, Green was as purposefully oblivious to the ways Eastern Woodlands peoples had lived in the past as the judges in Georgia and Alabama. In referring to Vattel's trite description of Indian life, Green complained that "immense regions" of the United States were "inhabited by wandering tribes of savages . . . that traversed the forest in the chase and wandered up and down the streams in their fishing excursions, and that they had temporary habitations from which they removed as occasion required." These residences, he continued, "could not be taken for a true and legal possession." He concluded, "If they pursued honest labor for a support, instead of the idle life of hunting and fishing, a very small proportion of the extensive territories they usurped would have been amply sufficient for them." Green did admit that the Cherokees had made "considerable advances" in the "arts of civilization." He praised their abandonment of the "hunter life," their "living in good houses," their management of "good farms," and their facile adoption of Anglo-American styled laws, government, and courts. Still, he resolved, the Cherokees had not overcome the presumption that they were not effectively exploiting their land.[37]

Green believed that the states had succeeded to Great Britain's title with the United States's victory in the American Revolution. The states had subsequently endowed the federal government with the specific authority to regulate Indian commerce at the constitutional convention. This implied that the state and federal governments maintained concurrent jurisdiction over the Indian tribes, and both could, under certain circumstances, encroach on the rights of the Indian nations. For example, for purposes of security, the United States could lawfully intervene in the government of an Indian nation by prohibiting it from selling land, trading, or conducting diplomatic relations with another nation. If Congress did not maintain this power, Green explained, foreign enemies could construct fortresses in strategic positions in the Indian nations and incite the tribes against the United States. In exchange for this authority, Green noted, the United States provided protection to the Indian nations and brought them under its beneficent guardianship.

A state, similarly, could enforce its laws over an Indian nation if "peculiar condition[s] . . . render[ed] it necessary for the preservation of order and the suppression of crime." Therefore, Green wrote, the question of the court's authority to hear the case turned on the factual issue of whether the circumstances within the Cherokee Nation in 1833 created a right in Tennessee to extend its criminal jurisdiction. In the last ten years, he reminded readers, the Cherokees had undergone "a very great change." Though the Cherokees had made "considerable advances in the arts of civilization," they had come under attack from the state of Georgia. Georgia had, without legal cause, extended its civil and criminal laws over the Cherokee Nation, nullified the Cherokee Constitution and the Cherokee Nation's laws, and sold the Indians' land to white Georgians. When the federal government refused to come to the Cherokees' aid, Green said, Alabama had extended its dominion over the part of the nation that fell within its borders. By 1833, these attacks and the effect of hundreds of whites moving onto Cherokee lands had created a "general state of confusion" in the nation. According to his reading of the newspapers, Green believed that the general authority of the Cherokee government had broken down and left the nation lawless. Tennessee was therefore obligated to extend its capital criminal laws over the Cherokees to protect the personal safety of the people living in the area. Green noted that unlike Georgia, which unleashed a general attack on Cherokee sovereignty, the Tennessee legislature had demonstrated considerable restraint by limiting its extension to the crimes of murder, rape, and larceny. In all other cases, he said, the state left the Cherokees "in the exercise of their own customs and subject to their own laws." [38]

Green's rule of necessity both legitimated the expansion of state jurisdiction over the Indian tribes and positioned him as a defender of Indian rights and natural law. In sum, however, Green's opinion was another victory for the removal advocates. For all of its rhetorical recognition of Native American rights, the opinion left the Cherokees in no better a position than the decisions of the states' rights radicals in Georgia and Alabama. Under Green's theory, a state could enact unlawful extension statutes over an Indian nation and disturb social conditions to such an extent that it would legitimate its own illegal acts. In a way, this is what had happened to the Cherokees. Georgia's illegal and unconstitutional acts had paved the way for Tennessee and Alabama to extend their jurisdiction over the Cherokees. Peck addressed Green's argument in his opinion. He pointed out that Green's theory was unfairly self-serving for Tennessee because it allowed the state legislature to decide when circumstances required it to extend the state's jurisdiction over the Cherokees. Moreover, Peck noted, the Cherokees had not been afforded an opportunity to dispute the legislature's conclusion. Giving the state the power to decide for itself when an extension was necessary, he said, was tantamount to the Cherokees surrendering their destiny to the unrestrained whim of a despotic tyrant.[39]

The final opinion in the Tennessee set, that of chief judge John Catron, was denominated as the decision of the court. It confirmed the *de facto* constitutionality of the state extension laws after the southern states' setback in *Worcester.* The blatant refusal of the Tennessee court to follow the precedent set down by the United States Supreme Court represented the final and fatal strike against the idea of Native American sovereignty for the Cherokees and the other Southeastern tribes. *Georgia v. Tassels, Caldwell v. Alabama,* and the Baldwin and Johnson dissents in *Cherokee Nation* comprised a southern removal ideology that offered a distorted history of the Anglo-American relationship with the Indian nations and a states' rights interpretation of the Constitution's Supremacy, Commerce, and Contract Clauses. Catron strictly followed the arguments presented in these opinions and used Yerger's oral argument as the framework for his opinion. The only distinction between Catron's opinion and those of his states' rights cohorts is that he believed that the federal government was constitutionally obligated to extinguish the title of the Cherokees as agent for the state of Tennessee. The judges in Georgia and Alabama had contended that the states could do so unilaterally. On the question of the sovereignty of the Cherokees, though, Catron was in complete agreement with his fellow judges to the south. In sum, he held that the Cherokee people did not comprise a separate and sovereign nation but were, as individuals, subjects of the state in which they lived. Tennessee, therefore, possessed the right to extend its criminal jurisdiction over the Cherokees. The federal government's treaties with the Cherokees at Hopewell and Holston were not guarantees of Cherokee sovereignty, Catron wrote, but unconstitutional encroachments on the sovereign rights of the states.[40]

Catron's opinion was tediously long, disorganized, convoluted, internally inconsistent, and contrary to several of his own previous decisions. He opened with the obligatory swipe at northeastern newspapers and philanthropists and complained that outside influences were poisoning the court's well of impartiality. If the matter could be heard, he wrote, "freed from a controlling sympathy in favor of the weak and withering remnant of a people sought to be rescued from annihilation," then no one would question Tennessee's right to extend its laws over the Cherokees. Northeastern philanthropists were anxious to support the Cherokee cause, he wrote, even though their own ancestors had used the "law and the sword" to acquire dominion over the Indians and their land in that part of the country. The court must consider the interests of those who were still struggling against the "savages" in the West, Catron said, not just those of "the forensic scholar and orator of the refined city."[41]

Catron offered a defiant states' rights response to John Marshall's *Worcester* opinion. A few months after deciding the *Forman* case, Catron wrote to Martin Van Buren that he had "attempted to disencumber this cause of the authority of that of *Worcester*." The Tennessee chief judge was political enough to criticize *Worcester* without disparaging the general authority of the Supreme Court or the memory of Marshall, who had just died in July. "The correctness . . . of the judgment ordering Worcester to be discharged from the penitentiary of Georgia is not called into question," Catron said; what he objected to was Marshall's interpretation of the political character of the Cherokee Nation. In response to Marshall's assertion that the Indian nations were independent, sovereign states, Catron wrote, "To this we answer, *and we do it with unfeigned regret* [Catron's emphasis], that our political, legislative, executive, and judicial history, so far from proving the recognition of the sovereign independence of the Indian nations within our limits . . . proves, and conclusively, directly the reverse."[42]

Whereas Marshall had slowly evolved toward his position in *Worcester,* Catron's transformation to the opposing view was more dramatic. Before *Forman,* Catron had tended to uphold the rights of the Cherokees. In 1826, for example, Catron had declared in *Cornet v. Winston's Lessee* that the Cherokees "are in truth a nation of people under the tutelage of the government of the United States." He said, "I hold that the early notions of the Spaniards and others 'that the Indians were mere savage beasts without rights of any kind,' have long since been exploded." Although he described the Cherokees as a "conquered people" in *Cornet,* he added that they possessed "acknowledged rights; which rights, I am proud to say, have for the last thirty years been respected with that good faith on our part that became us as honest men and Christians, and which the courts of justice are bound to regard." Catron concluded that the state of Tennessee had a constitutional duty to recognize that federal-Cherokee treaties guaranteed those national rights. Catron's remarks inflamed the states' rights wing of the Tennessee legislature, and in 1829, the assembly adopted a resolution disavowing the chief judge's decision.[43]

A year later, Catron again considered the status of the Cherokees living in Tennessee in *Blair v. Pathkiller*. In 1806, the United States had acquired a cession of land from the Cherokees and conveyed the territory to the state of Tennessee. In the compact between the state and federal government, Tennessee had agreed that each Cherokee household residing in the ceded territory would be allowed to keep its home and a square mile of land around the residence. Federal-Cherokee treaties in 1817 and 1819 reaffirmed these Cherokee rights. In the case Blair, a Tennessee resident, argued that the state could extinguish the title of the Cherokee householders and seize the lands included within the original 1806 agreement. Catron rejected this argument and upheld the sanctity of the U.S.-Cherokee treaties. The chief judge wrote that the Cherokees were dependent on the United States but recognized that the federal-Indian relationship allowed the tribe to maintain a political system and a country of its own. The state governments, he said, could not "legislate upon [the Cherokee] title" until the federal government incorporated the Cherokees into the states.[44]

With *Forman*, Catron moved into the states' rights camp. His previous pronouncements defending Cherokee rights in *Cornet* and *Blair* caused considerable embarrassment for the judge when it came time to write his opinion. Catron's discomfort at defending a view that he had ridiculed in the past is patently evident throughout the opinion. He tried to explain *Blair v. Pathkiller* by contending that the court had "forcibly implied" that Tennessee possessed the authority to extinguish the Cherokee rights to their land. In truth, Catron had written that "the United States alone, by the Treaty of Holston, had the right to extinguish the Indian title." Catron also used an absurd circular argument to distinguish his contrary comments. In the previous cases, he said, Tennessee had not extended its laws over the Cherokees. In other words, Catron justified Tennessee's extension of jurisdiction by arguing that the state had extended its jurisdiction. This, however, was lofty reasoning compared to Catron's other rationalization. In the most revealing and embarrassing passage in all of the southern opinions, Catron excused his contradictory decisions of the past by pleading that they were "given at a time and place where aid from not a single book on the subject was had." Few judges have overruled their own decisions so pathetically.[45]

This feeble excuse did not explain his recent decision in *Tennessee v. Ross*. Only a few months before *Forman*, state officials had attempted to force Lewis Ross, John Ross's brother, to purchase a state business license to operate his general store. In denying Tennessee the right to regulate and tax residents of the Cherokee Nation, Catron had written: "Not having the benefits of our government extended to him, the Cherokee is not subjected to its burdens. The Cherokee has no vote in our elections, nor right to be a representative in our legislature, because he is no citizen; and to tax him would be practicing the same despotic power against which our ancestors so justly rebelled." At that time, Catron refused to consider the impact of Tennessee's extension law on Ross's rights. "No opinion on this highly interesting and delicate question has been called for," he wrote, "nor has the court formed any." Now, in *Forman*, Catron implied, the accumulated wisdom of Baldwin, Johnson, and the judges of Georgia and Alabama had provided him with a decade's worth of states' rights scholarship and an ideological script from which to work. He now possessed, it seems, the proper books on the subject.[46]

The best explanation for Catron's abandonment of Indian rights is his increasing concern over the states' authority over slavery and his long and close relationship with Andrew Jackson. Timothy S. Huebner argues that *Forman* represented the chief judge's "gradual adoption of a sectional consciousness." Catron's concerns had become the same as those among the Georgia and Alabama judiciary. "During the early 1830s," Huebner wrote, "political circumstances and legal disputes coalesced in such a way as to bring together in Catron's mind the issues of Indian lands, slave property, and state power. The tense political environment regarding slavery helped push Catron and the Tennessee Supreme Court toward a Native American policy that ignored Indian rights under federal treaties and supported Jackson's removal plan. Catron began to see the question of white control over Indian lands as similar to the issue of white power over African slaves. The national government—in the form of treaties with Indians or potentially restrictive legislation concerning the expansion of slavery—posed a potential threat to southern control over both of these populations."[47]

Catron also apparently felt some obligation to conform his opinion to please the president. He had served under Jackson during the War of 1812 and over time became one of the president's most devoted supporters. For example, the judge wrote several articles condemning the national bank in the *Nashville Republican* in 1829 and became a major force in organizing Jackson's support in Tennessee in the campaigns of 1828 and 1832. Perhaps, we can surmise, Catron was also carrying Jackson's water in the *Forman* case.[48] Hypothetically, if the chief judge had followed his earlier decisions, he and Peck would have comprised a majority sufficient to strike down the Tennessee extension law. Jackson, however, had clearly delineated his desires in a letter to Currey. John Walker's murder had enraged the president. Jackson believed that Ross had ordered the killing and demanded that Tennessee authorities capture, try, and punish the assassins in quick order. Catron also understood that Jackson agreed with the state's policy of extending its jurisdiction over the Cherokees. Consequently, it is not illogical to suspect that Catron, being familiar with what Jackson wanted, may have rendered his decision with the president's wishes in mind. In the months after *Forman,* Catron lost his reelection bid for another term on the supreme court and spent the next several months coordinating Martin Van Buren's 1836 campaign in Tennessee. Although Catron failed to deliver Tennessee to Van Buren, Jackson likely nominated Catron to the United States Supreme Court to repay him for his steadfast support.[49]

To follow Jackson's will, Catron had to somehow diminish the significance of *Worcester.* Fortunately for the judge, Yerger had provided him with plenty of ammunition. The courts, Catron said, should cling to the Supreme Court decision that Marshall had overruled *sub silentio:* "We are fortified by the great and well-considered case of *Johnson v. McIntosh,* the reasoning in which, by the same distinguished jurist, it must be admitted, if not in direct opposition, is greatly in conflict with Worcester's case." There was no reason to argue the logic of *Worcester,* Catron said, for *Johnson v. McIntosh* was "an authority . . . confidently believed to be of unequaled merit." What Catron wanted to preserve from *Johnson v. McIntosh* was the broad construction of the doctrine of discovery that Marshall had repudiated in *Worcester.* In the latter case, the chief justice had written that discovery determined only rights of priority among the other European nations and had no effect on the inherent title of the Indian nations. The Europeans had perfected the discovery rights they held by purchases from and treaties with the Indian nations. Catron contended that Tennessee's jurisdiction over the Cherokees emanated directly from a superior right based on the discovery of America by the state's European predecessors in title. *Worcester,* he said, was an unfortunate anomaly and "an exception" to the long-standing doctrine, recognized from "Cape Horn to Hudson's Bay," that European discovery "gave title to assume sovereignty over, and to govern, the unconverted natives of Africa, Asia, and North and South America." In a rambling history of the European exploration and settlement of the Western Hemisphere, Catron argued that Europeans had applied the doctrine "from the catholic reign of Henry VII, through every change of religion and government in England, by the colonies up to the Revolution, and the states having Indian relations since." The states, he said, had relied on discovery to extend their dominion "from the Rock of Plymouth to the Rocky Mountains." Parroting Yerger, Catron predicted that if the Supreme Court reconsidered the issue of Native American sovereignty, with legal representation from the state under a new chief justice, it might return to the logic of *Johnson v. McIntosh.*[50]

Catron acknowledged, as Marshall had in *Johnson v. McIntosh,* that he was defending a flawed principle. The idea that "all unconverted savages found [in America] were without rights," he wrote, "comes in conflict with our religion and with our best convictions of a refined and sound morality." The underlying premise of Christian hegemony was "amongst the most curious and most prominent truths in the history of man." It rested, he said, on "a papal supremacy once wonderful and overpowering . . . to which kings and emperors bowed with humblest submission." American courts accepted the theory not because of its inductive rationality, but on a "historical proof . . . which asserts the law of force as the rule of right." Catron admitted that he was using the questionable doctrine of a church with which he disagreed as legal precedent for the American conquest of the continent. "The pope claimed the right to dispose of all countries possessed by infidels," he wrote, "a right that it would have been deemed as absurd to deny before and during the fifteenth century as it would now be absurd to admit." Whether the church's doctrine was "enforced through the superstitious fears of Christendom, or by the sword, is immaterial," Catron said; the doctrine of discovery was the historical basis for American title and sovereignty. Admittedly, he said, this justification for the conquest of the Americas was a "hypocrisy" worthy of "contemn." "Its promulgation may have been a harsh fiat" and "cruelly executed by the Spaniards in Peru and Mexico." However, he said, "it is the fiat of our recognition." The taking of the continent under the doctrine of discovery was "the only rule of action possible" and "one not open to question in a legal point of view, or morally wrong."[51]

Ultimately, Catron wrote, the United States had to decide if "the country should be peopled by Europeans" or "continue the haunt of savage beasts." Without the "assertion and vigorous execution" of the doctrine of discovery, North America never would have been settled by civilized peoples. To repudiate that presumption, as Marshall had done in *Worcester,* would be an admission that Americans were "unjust usurpers" and "should in honesty abandon [the continent], return to Europe, and let the subdued parts again become a wilderness and hunting ground," Catron added. "Disgusted as we may be with its bigoted manner of assertion and indiscriminate execution," he said, the doctrine of discovery had become as much a part of American law after the Revolution as the English common law. "Our claim is based on the right to coerce obedience," he added defiantly, though "the claim may be denounced by the moralist. We answer, it is the law of the land."[52]

Even if one rejected the doctrine of discovery, Catron said, diplomatic history demonstrated that the Cherokees had long ago "surrendered their sovereign power" to Great Britain. Catron described how in 1730 a delegation of Cherokees had traveled to London to meet with the royal government. There it had an audience with the king. According to Catron, the Cherokee delegation "acknowledged King George for their sovereign lord, and, on their knees, promised fidelity and obedience to him." Sir Alexander Cuming, who had negotiated a peace treaty between the British and the Cherokees, "appointed [the chief] Moytoy commander-in-chief of the Cherokee Nation." The Cherokees then took the "crown or diadem of the nation," a headdress constructed of five eagle tails and four enemy scalps, and "laid the regalia . . . at the foot of the throne" of King George. By their actions, Catron concluded, the Cherokees had "submitted themselves and their people to the sovereignty of the king and his successors."[53]

As described by Catron, this event certainly damaged the case of Cherokee national independence. However, Catron was perhaps misinterpreting the Cherokees' motives in their meeting with King George. Catron construed the ceremony as a Cherokee admission of fealty to the English monarch. The Cherokees, conversely, probably perceived the event as an act of diplomatic hospitality. Before the transfer of the diadem, the British had lavished gifts of "cloth, guns, shot, vermillion, flints, hatchets, [and] knives" on the Cherokee delegation. Where Catron saw subservience, the Cherokees likely recognized an important ceremonial beginning to discussions of alliance. Catron's use of the anecdote also ignored the political structure of the Cherokees at the time of the exchange. In 1730 the Cherokee Nation was a loose confederation of affiliated but independent villages connected primarily by kinship, language, and culture. Moytoy likely did not have authority to speak for or surrender the sovereignty of any other Cherokee village but his own (if even that). Looking at the event from the Cherokee point of view, then, the meeting was not a surrender of national sovereignty but a diplomatic ceremony between equal sovereigns. Judge Nathan Green, Catron's brother on the court, argued as much and rejected the chief judge's interpretation. Green argued that by laying the crown at the feet of King George, the Cherokees placed themselves under British protection and attached themselves to the empire as "dependent allies." After this ceremony, he said, the Cherokees and the British treated each other as independent and separate political entities. What resulted was a dependent status not unlike that described by Marshall in *Cherokee Nation*. "One community may be bound to another by a very unequal alliance," Green wrote, "and still be a sovereign state."[54]

Catron also repeated the outdated stereotypes espoused by the judges on the Georgia and Alabama courts. The early English colonies, he wrote, were surrounded by "savages destroying each other, for mere pastime, with the fierceness of wild beasts. . . . The main business of their lives being war, and that a war of extermination." Catron, like his fellow judges in Alabama and Georgia, refused to admit that the Cherokees were primarily sedentary agriculturists and used the misrepresentation that they were nomadic hunter-gatherers to justify the taking of their land. "That mere wandering tribes of savages . . . should claim a vast extent of forest, as hunting grounds, for the nurture of wild animals, and exclude the cultivation of the earth is unreasonable and unjust," he said. "The earth belongs to all men in general," but "every nation" was obligated by natural law to cultivate the land that "has fallen to its share." He specifically recited Vattel's infamous comment that was so popular among southern proremoval lawyers: those peoples who do not cultivate the earth "deserve to be exterminated as savage and pernicious beasts."[55] These statements specifically contradicted the judge's more anthropological insight in the 1826 *Cornet* case:

> The Cherokees have at all times, since we knew anything of their history, had a government of their own; and in latter times many of their people have been the owners of considerable personal property, and cultivators of the soil, to a very considerable extent; . . . [They] were, and now are, far removed from the mere wandering and wild savage who depends upon hunting and game for the means of subsistence, and makes war a liveli-hood. Those of them who resided within the limits of this state, and on the territory ceded to us in 1819, might rather be deemed a grazing and agricultural than a hunting people, and therefore, had much use for their soil; and that they had the right to use and occupy it within their own territorial limits, unmolested by our citizens, has not been controverted for many years.[56]

Catron jettisoned these ideas in *Forman*. The time had come, Catron wrote, for the Indians to surrender their "idle life" and sacrifice the lands that they had usurped from the rest of the earth's inhabitants. The Cherokees, he continued, were inherently a "loose and straggling multitude not formed into a recognized society, . . . a people that had no government, and with whom the right of the strongest alone was respected." They were a people unworthy of being recognized as a legitimate member of the "family of nations" and racially incapable of the progress required to merit that recognition. Any advancements that the Cherokees had made, Catron contended, resulted from the influence of a "very few" "half-breeds and whites residing amongst them" and the "fostering care" of the government.[57]

Catron declared that the American efforts to acculturate and assimilate the Indians had failed. The separation of the white and Native American races, he believed, would be the only solution to the United States's Indian dilemma: "Ignorance and division cannot stand before science and combina-tion, nor can the civilized community exist by the side of a savage foe." If the United States recognized the Cherokees as a sovereign nation, Catron wrote, it would also have to concede that status to "the many savage tribes claim-ing the prairies, the Rocky Mountains, and great country beyond; tribes that subsist on the raw flesh, and are savage as the most savage beasts that infest that mighty wilderness." These tribes were fated for extinction, not sovereignty, the judge argued, and would be ground under the wheels of American progress. Catron, apparently, like so many other Americans of the era, had become enamored with the emerging Anglo-Saxon interpretation of history: "The tribes found inland have passed under the dominion, and melted away under the influence and superior powers, mental and moral, of the white man, as did the savages of Europe, Asia, and Africa pass under the dominion of the Romans, and as will him of Australasia, Africa, and the Rocky Mountains be compelled to submit to the stroke of fate sooner or later—to accept a master or perish. It is the destiny of man."[58]

Catron also attempted to legitimize the title of the white trespassers who had moved into the Cherokee Nation. He warned that settlers who had lived on their lands for over fifty years would be uprooted if the state and federal governments enforced the *Worcester* decision. The Cherokees had always been "either treacherous friends or open enemies" to whites: "Hardly a family of the early settlers but can number some of its former members amongst the slain, generally at or near their own dwellings, and far off from the Indian towns or boundary." For the United States to displace those who had established roots in the Cherokee Nation, he implied, would be an insult to their memory.[59]

Catron agreed with Green's argument of necessity. When the federal court denied the United States criminal jurisdiction over the Cherokee Nation in *United States v. Bailey,* Catron wrote, the Tennessee legislature moved to provide law and order for the whites and Indians residing in the Cherokee Nation. The Cherokees were unable to ensure personal security, Catron argued, because they were "overrun by the whites." Since then, he said, the Cherokees' government had been "broken up and suppressed by Georgia; their few people . . . so scattered and feeble as . . . to be incapable of self-government." He continued, "The Cherokees were wholly incapable of protecting themselves, or the whites among them, against individual depredation upon persons or property." If the court prohibited Tennessee from extending its jurisdiction over the Cherokee Nation, Catron warned, "there will be within the bounds of this Union a lawless territory where sanctuary is found for the murderer, the robber, and the thief, free from molestation."[60]

The national government's refusal to protect the citizens of the southern states from this lawlessness, Catron said, forced the states to take action to defend their residents. Consequently, a "controversy for jurisdiction" had developed "between the states and the general government, as momentous as any arising since we became independent." More so than any other opinion in the southern extension cases, Catron's effort demonstrated the increasing impact of the states' rights interpretation of the Constitution on the southern judicial process. Catron contended that the federal government's expanding regulation of Indian affairs since the Constitutional Convention had been a creeping encroachment on the sovereignty of the states. North Carolina, Catron noted, refused to ratify the Constitution until Congress passed the Tenth Amendment, which reserved the powers not delegated to the national government to the states or the people. When Congress satisfied this demand in 1790, North Carolina came into the Union. At the same time, the state ceded its western territory to the United States. At no point in this transaction, Catron argued, did North Carolina surrender its sovereignty over the Cherokee lands within its borders. Furthermore, the state's cession of its western lands was made on the "express condition" that the jurisdiction of the Tennessee territory would be "coextensive with its whole limits." Catron asked, "If North Carolina believed that, by the treaties and acts of Congress, the United States could erect an independent Cherokee government within her limits, would she have ratified the Constitution? . . . That she did not is manifest." In 1796, Congress admitted Tennessee into the Union. The state's original constitution declared that the people of Tennessee had the "right of exercising sovereignty and the right of soil" over all of the lands that had been ceded from North Carolina to the federal government. However, the Tennessee territory had been organized under the strictures of the Northwest Ordinance, which purported to protect the Indian tribes from the taking of their lands without their consent. Catron contended that this meant that Tennessee would recognize the Cherokees' right to occupy the soil under the Northwest Ordinance, but that the state would "assume general jurisdiction to exercise the right of sovereignty over the Indian country without restriction."[61]

Without any constitutional authority, Catron complained, the Supreme Court in *Worcester* had established an independent government within the limits of existing states. This was prohibited by Article 4 of the Constitution. He warned that if the federal government recognized the Cherokees as an independent and sovereign nation, the Cherokees might establish a monarchy inside the boundaries of Tennessee and destroy the constitutionally guaranteed right of the state to a republican form of government. The states, he concluded, had to make every effort to resist any further federal encroachment.[62]

Catron's fumbling logic and internal inconsistencies were startling at times. In several instances, he seems to have lost track of the rational order of his argument. For example, in describing the treaties between the United States and the Cherokees, he first argued what the Cherokees had been contending for years: that the earliest American treaties and legislative acts had confirmed their independence and sovereignty. Rather than directly attacking this construction, Catron admitted this point to vilify the federal government for what he deemed to be an unconstitutional seizure of state power. This was distinctively different from what the courts of Alabama and Georgia had argued; they simply denied that the United States had ever recognized Cherokee sovereignty. Catron, however, was thorough if not logical, for he then denied that the United States government had ever conceded the status of sovereignty to the Cherokees by treaty. The Articles of Confederation, he said, under which the United States had negotiated the Treaty of Hopewell, gave the Continental Congress the authority to send and receive ambassadors and enter into treaties and alliances. Likewise, Article 2 of the Constitution gave the president the power to make treaties with the advice and consent of the Senate, and for that purpose the executive could appoint "ambassadors and other public ministers . . . and all other officers of the United States." It was "notoriously true," Catron argued, that the commissioners appointed to negotiate Indian treaties "were not deemed ambassadors." Therefore, the agreements signed by the United States and the Cherokees were not constitutional treaties. Like the Alabama court, he asserted that the Constitution mandated that treaty negotiations be handled at the level of ambassador, when, in fact, any reasonable reading of Article 2 suggests otherwise.[63]

In another peculiar passage, Catron denied that the Senate had ever ratified federal-Indian treaties. He then contradicted himself in the same paragraph: "Compacts with Indians were never ratified by Congress. . . . Nor under the Constitution has a public minister, nominated to, and his appointment confirmed by, the senate, for the purpose of treating with an Indian tribe, been known to our country for thirty years, although the practice was adopted in some instances in the first administration of President Washington." Washington had in fact begun the tradition of asking the Senate to ratify Indian treaties, a process that had been followed up and through Catron's decision in *Forman.* Inexplicably, Catron undercut his own argument by quoting Washington's message to the Senate on the question of ratifying Indian treaties. Washington had declared:

> It doubtless is important that all treaties and compacts formed by the United States with other nations, whether civilized or not, should be made with caution and executed with fidelity. It is said to be the general understanding and practice of nations, as a check on the mistakes and indiscretions of ministers and commissioners, not to consider any treaty, negotiated and signed by such officer, as final and conclusive until ratified by the sovereign or government from whom they derive their powers. This

is the practice adopted by the United States respecting their treaties with
European nations, and I am inclined to think it would be advisable to
observe it in the conduct of our treaties with the Indians.[64]

Though they would typically not be ratified by the treating Indian nation,
Washington added, "it seems to be both prudent and reasonable that their
acts should not be binding on the nation until approved and ratified by the
government. It strikes me this point should be well considered and settled,
so that our national proceedings in this respect may become uniform, and
be directed by fixed and stable principles." It was bad enough that the chief
judge misrepresented the treaty process; Catron went to the point of refuting
his own argument. Strangely, Catron does not cite Washington's message
so that he can distinguish his own argument. In fact, he never explains
why he brought it up in the first place. Instead, he simply asked, "What
evidence does it furnish that the Indian tribes thus contracted with were,
as to the separate states, foreign, sovereign, and independent?" The answer
was obvious: Washington's precedents, and the Senate's early ratification of
Indian treaties, meant everything to the manner in which the United States
conducted Indian policy in the subsequent years.[65]

Catron's opinion, in its last pages, reveals perhaps his greatest concern—
that the federal government might use the precedent of its intrusion into
the state police power, the U.S. Supreme Court's repudiation of the doctrine
of discovery, and what he believed to be an outdated theory of inherent
racial equality in an attempt to extirpate slavery. Those who fostered Native American sovereignty, he believed, threatened the existence of slavery
and hence the social fabric of the South: "We dare not say the unconverted
heathen was not a perpetual enemy to the Christian, or that he had political rights independent of us, without saying to the red man of this continent: 'Take your own, we are your subjects; the country is yours, and
the right to govern it is yours;' without saying to the enslaved black man
of Africa: 'Go in peace! You was enslaved by superstition and fraud, and
are free as we are.'" If American courts did not continue to recognize the
natural superiority of whites and consistently apply the doctrine of discovery, he said, "The title of every slave in America, North and South, rests
on no better or different foundation" than that of the title to the Indian
country. The *Worcester* decision, he concluded, was one that was "impossible for the states to abide by . . . and should be solemnly reconsidered by
the distinguished tribunal asserting it." The states of Georgia, North Carolina, Alabama, Mississippi, and Tennessee had all extended their jurisdiction over the Indian nations in the South. Maine, New York, and Ohio
had done so in the North. Rethink *Worcester,* Catron warned the Supreme

Court, before you attempt to enforce a proposition that so many of the states opposed.[66]

Technically, then, Green and Catron created a majority of two in favor of upholding the constitutionality of Tennessee's extension law. The court remanded the case to the McMinn County circuit court for trial. Although the appellate court had affirmed the Tennessee extension statute, a majority of the judges believed that the Cherokees retained, at the least, political autonomy and legal jurisdiction over civil matters and noncapital criminal offenses. Despite this counting of the votes on these issues, the court presented Catron's opinion as its official ruling. Removal proponents in Tennessee embraced Catron's bewildering treatise as a victory for the states' rights interpretation of the Constitution and treated the decision as the final foreclosure of Cherokee national aspirations in Tennessee. In essence, then, the public perception of the decision overwhelmed what the court, as a whole, had actually written. There is no great reason to dispute this reception by the press and public, for less than three months after the publication of the court's opinion, the federal government orchestrated the removal Treaty of New Echota with the Ridge party. In hindsight, the decision was a greater defeat for the Cherokees than a close reading of the opinion might imply. In sum, Catron's opinion and those from the courts in Georgia and Alabama displaced the Supreme Court's decision in *Worcester*. The southern removal ideology had become the law of the land.

Foreman and Springston apparently planned to appeal the decision to the United States Supreme Court. On November 2, 1835, Catron wrote to Governor Newton Cannon and warned him of the impending appeal. He urged the governor to appoint a lawyer immediately to prepare for the case: "The Cherokee question, before that distinguished and final tribunal, has not been advocated by counsel in favor of State Sovereignty, in the controversies between Georgia and the Cherokee Nation; and there, as elsewhere, in great and doubtful questions, powerful and unanswered arguments have commanded decisions in their favor. No case in an American court has been argued with more zeal, or perhaps with more ability, than was the Cherokee case of 1831—and as was again Worcester's case in 1832, on behalf of the Cherokee claim to independent power: Foreman's case will present the same controversy."[67]

The U.S. Supreme Court never heard the appeal, however, and it remains unclear what happened to the Foreman and Springston case after the Tennessee Supreme Court remanded it back to McMinn County for trial. Somehow or another, the two defendants secured a release from custody and returned to their homes as if they had never been arrested. They appear in the Cherokee census of 1835 and are registered at their residences, not the

McMinn or Knox County jails. Subsequently, they emerged in the Indian Territory. John Walker's cousin, Jack Hilderbrand, provided a clue as to what might have happened. He said that he saw Foreman and asked him how he got out of jail. Foreman replied, "By God, sir, I was let out with a silver key." A few scholars have offered guesses as to the defendants' release. A local historian wrote that the "sensitive" McMinn County jurors believed that the Cherokees had the right to resolve the dispute themselves, but that "the United States got the judgment reversed." C. Thomas Byrum wrote, "It seems that 'frontier justice' prevailed, and that McMinn Countians found a subtle way of overruling the United States and affirming the stand that they took throughout the controversy." However, there is no record of a jury trial in the McMinn or Bradley County records. Duane H. King and E. Raymond Evans suggested that the Ross faction paid a bribe to the Knox County jailer to spring Foreman and Springston. Walker Chandler noted that the Treaty of New Echota was signed less than three months after the Tennessee court's decision. As such, the question of jurisdiction was mooted and the state was agreeable to sending the defendants on to the Indian Territory. However, it seems unlikely that the removal treaty would have prevented the local court from disposing of the case in some fashion. Since Tennessee's jurisdiction had been affirmed, the state had even more reason to try the two defendants. The Bradley County circuit court records contain shreds of a case file in which the state was attempting to serve subpoenas on Foreman and Springston around April 1836. If these documents pertained to the case, they indicate that the state had widened its prosecution to include six other Cherokees and had moved the proceedings to Bradley County, which is where Walker was shot. Generally, the laws of venue and jurisdiction require the state to try murder cases in the county where the crime was committed. In 1834, McMinn County held jurisdiction over that area. In the time between the shooting and the appellate decision, the state had endowed Bradley County with jurisdiction over the Cherokees in its territorial boundaries. It appears from the McMinn County sheriff's return of service on a subpoena that he determined Foreman and Springston were no longer available for service in McMinn County. However, there is no way of knowing for certain whether these documents were related to the Walker murder. I suspect from the sparse evidence that there was a jury trial, that the jury acquitted the defendants, and that the record of the trial was subsequently either destroyed or lost. However, the question of the disposal of the Foreman and Springston case remains a mystery. Whether it was by escape, bribery, acquittal, or a *nolle prosequi*, Foreman and Springston avoided trial and conviction and Tennessee avoided an appeal of the extension issue to the United States Supreme Court.[68]

As Catron, Green, and Peck considered the fate of Foreman and Spring-ston over the summer and fall of 1835, both the Ross and Treaty parties continued to negotiate with the United States government. Ross tried to patch the two factions back together so that they could present a united front in Washington. However, the principal chief's refusal to deal with Schermerhorn ensured that the two councils would continue to function and negotiate separately. When the United States sent Schermerhorn to the Cherokee Nation in October for the purpose of concluding a removal treaty, Ross challenged his credentials and refused to negotiate with him. This offended Schermerhorn and the subsequent dealings between the two were acrimonious. Ross told Schermerhorn that he preferred to deal directly with the president and secretary of war and was organizing a bipartisan delegation that would go to Washington to negotiate directly with Jackson. Schermerhorn replied that the president would not meet with the chief and suggested that Ross was simply stalling for time: "If the treaty is made, it must be done here in the nation, where Mr. Ross and his delegation when at Washington city last winter insisted it should be closed, for the sake of the peace and harmony among the people." Ross obstinately went forward with his plans for the trip to Washington and offered spots in the delegation to the Ridges and Elias Boudinot. Suspiciously, they refused to go with Ross. In early January, while the principal chief was in Washington attempting to meet with Jackson and Lewis Cass, he received notice that the Ridge party had signed a removal treaty, the Treaty of New Echota, with Schermerhorn on December 29. Though only seventy-five Cherokees out of a population of over sixteen thousand had approved the treaty, the United States Senate ratified the agreement. A group of about two thousand, includ-ing most of the Treaty Party adherents, left the Southeast during the two years provided for removal. Most Cherokees, however, faithfully waited for the fall of 1836, as Ross had suggested, to see if there would be a Whig victory in the presidential and congressional elections and to see if their principal chief could orchestrate an annulment of the New Echota accord. Ultimately, neither hope came to fruition; in the spring of 1838 the United States Army arrived in the Cherokee Nation and rounded up all but a tiny remnant of the Cherokee popu-lation. The Cherokees demanded the right to superintend their own removal and in the fall departed their homeland and traveled along the Trail of Tears.[69]

James Foreman and Anderson Springston moved west along with the rest of the Cherokee Nation and settled in the Delaware District of the Indian Territory. There they quickly became involved again in the bitter conflict between the Ross and Ridge parties. Acquaintances of Foreman quoted him as saying "that he would never pardon" those who signed the Treaty of New Echota and that he "had violent feelings towards the treaty party." The Cherokees had only recently arrived in the Indian Territory when Foreman, Springston, and other Ross men exacted their revenge on the Treaty Party leaders. Foreman and Springston were members of a group that killed Major Ridge, John Ridge, and Elias Boudinot in 1839. At dawn on June 22, about twenty-five Ross men pulled John Ridge out of his bed and dragged him out into the yard in front of his house. One at a time, each of the assailants stabbed Ridge. After Ridge fell, each man stomped across his body. A few hours later, a second group of about thirty men assaulted and killed Elias Boudinot with knives and tomahawks. That afternoon, ten to twelve men ambushed and shot Major Ridge. The killing of the Ridges and Boudinot unleashed a long and bitter civil war between the Ross and Treaty factions. Later, attorneys for the Ridges and Boudinot's relative, Stand Watie, labeled James Foreman as one of the leaders of the conspiracy to murder the three men.[70]

Though Ross denied knowledge of or involvement with the execution of the Treaty Party leaders, he directed his personal bodyguards to protect the members of the execution squads. When the United States asked Ross to produce the killers of the Ridges and Boudinot, he challenged the jurisdiction of the federal government. "By what right or sound policy [are] the Cherokee people to be deprived of the exercise of their own legitimate authority over the acts of one Indian against another? . . . How, if the persons charged be Cherokees, they have violated either treaty stipulations or acts of Congress, that they should be held answerable to the courts of the United States, and the military force employed for their arrest?" So soon after their arrival, the Cherokees were already feeling new encroachments on their sovereignty. Ultimately, neither the federal government nor the Cherokee Nation brought Foreman, Springston, and the other killers to trial.[71]

The Ridge family, however, did obtain a measure of blood revenge. On May 9, 1842, a white man named Mitchell, who was friends with several members of the Treaty Party and sympathetic to their views, stabbed Anderson Springston. Although he came very close to death, Springston survived the attack and lived on for many more years. His old accomplice was not so lucky. Five days after Springston's stabbing, Stand Watie, the brother of Boudinot, the nephew of Major Ridge, and the cousin of John Ridge, exacted his family's retaliation against Foreman. On May 14, Watie stopped at a Maysville, Arkansas, bar and grocery store for provisions. James Foreman spotted Watie, sarcastically drank to his health, and then began beating him with his horsewhip. When Foreman picked up a wooden board with which to inflict greater injury, Watie pulled his knife and stabbed his attacker. Foreman backed away and said, "You haven't done it yet." Watie pulled his revolver and fired at Foreman. According to testimony, Foreman died from his wounds about twenty minutes later. The Cherokee Nation ordered its officers to arrest Watie for murder, but in June he turned himself in to Arkansas state authorities. In May 1843, an Arkansas jury found that Watie had acted in self-defense and acquitted him of the murder charge. The knife fights and gun battles of the Cherokee civil war continued between the Ross and Ridge parties until 1846. Only when the United States government threatened to intervene in the Cherokee conflict did the two warring factions agree to a tenuous peace.[72]

The Triumph of the
Southern Removal Ideology

THE BITTER DIVISION BETWEEN the Ross and Treaty parties, which de-
volved into civil war in the Indian Territory, was only one of the consequences of the Indian Removal. Clearly the greatest tragedy of the Removal
was the staggering death toll produced by the forced relocation to Oklahoma.
The general consensus among scholars is that approximately four thousand
Cherokees, perhaps a quarter of the nation's population, died as a result of
starvation, malnutrition, disease, exposure, and heartbreak on the Trail of
Tears. Russell Thornton, a demographer of Indian depopulation, has argued
that the Removal impacted the Cherokee population in a far greater measure
than this number suggests. Using a contrafactual statistical formula, Thornton concluded that there would have been approximately ten thousand more
Cherokees alive in 1840 had the Removal not occurred. The Trail of Tears,
he notes, took its greatest toll on the oldest and youngest of the population.
The deaths of hundreds of young men and women stunted the natural population recovery that would have occurred but for the Removal and wiped
out much of the generation that would have taken the Cherokee national
resurrection to its second stage. These numbers are, of course, antiseptic;
behind every casualty figure was a deep personal tragedy. For instance, John
Ross, the leader of the Cherokee resistance, suffered his own devastating loss
in the Removal. His wife, Quatie, died of pneumonia in Little Rock, just a
short distance from the Cherokees' final destination in the Indian Territory.[1]

Beyond the shocking number of casualties, the forced relocation inflicted
immeasurable psychological and sociological damage on the Cherokee people. The Cherokees had been remarkably successful in adapting to dramatic
changes in their economic, political, and diplomatic situation over the previous century and a half. Removal, however, was a calamity of unparalleled
proportions for the Cherokee psyche. The Cherokees' crisis did not simply
begin with Andrew Jackson's election in 1828; the tribe had been resisting
removal overtures since at least 1808. Many of the removed Cherokees had

spent a lifetime under the threat of exile. When it finally came, it was a national defeat far more distressing and demoralizing than the wars of 1760 and 1776. Removal required an abject and degrading submission that produced desperate feelings of self and national doubt. Removal told the Cherokees that their voice meant nothing to the people of the United States and that they held no rights that any white American would respect. Removal affirmed to Indians that the treaty guarantees issued by the United States were indeed, as Judge Lipscomb had declared in *Caldwell,* issued only for the purpose of "conciliating the savages." This meant more to Indians than the obvious fact that the United States could be a deceitful and duplicitous diplomatic partner. The United States's treachery implied to Indians that they were a people held in contempt; the American people did not seem to feel a loss of honor when they welched on promises made to Indians. The implication that Indians were undeserving of respect for their contractual rights was a manifest embarrassment to a proud people, and this was particularly disturbing for those Cherokees who had worked for decades to meet the expectations placed on them by the American civilization agents. Removal told acculturated Indians that they were inherently incapable of attaining legal and social equality with Anglo-Americans. Removal was racial separation. Separation, they understood, meant inferiority.[2]

Removal was also much more than an exile to a faraway land. Removal required the Cherokees to leave behind places that fostered feelings of cultural and personal identity. They were forced to move away from the meadows, groves, streams, and mountains that produced pleasant memories of childhood, kinship, and romance. Women left the bottomlands where they and their sisters and friends had socialized while they worked the corn, beans, and squash. Men walked away from the forests where they had hunted deer with their fathers, brothers, sons, and nephews. Cherokee families and clans left behind the graves of their ancestors and rode and marched to a land holding absolutely no spiritual or personal familiarity. The Cherokees, in short, were forced to leave the center of the universe—the place where they had been planted at the beginning of time—for a land already occupied by other Native American peoples. Removal, it seems, made the Cherokees trespassers on the lands of other Indian nations. As the victims of innumerable encroachments on their own sovereignty, the Cherokees must have appreciated the irony of their situation. All of these realizations, in sum, produced pronounced feelings of anger, sadness, and disorientation for the Cherokees who survived the Trail of Tears.

Removal also destroyed the national potentiality of the Cherokee Nation. In the 1820s the Cherokees were poised on the brink of a golden age of national revival. Despite the tragedies and challenges of the eighteenth century, they had adapted to the changing circumstances brought on by the Anglo-European invasion of their territory. They had transformed their political structure and had established laws and procedures that would have promoted the future well-being and security of the Cherokee people. Beyond the political reforms that were unifying the nation, the Cherokees were creating a diversified economy that combined market capitalism and nationalized real property ownership. Those who wanted to proceed on the path toward acculturation were finding increasing opportunities for education, information, and financial prosperity. The government was preparing plans for a national academy for its young. Sequoyah's syllabary enabled the nation to translate texts and literature into the Cherokee language. The *Cherokee Phoenix* provided news to the population in both English and Cherokee. Cherokee entrepreneurs had built ferries and toll roads through the nation and were integrating themselves into the southern market economy. More than once individual Cherokees bragged that they were more advanced than the citizens of the states that surrounded them. At the same time, the Cherokee government endeavored to secure the rights and well-being of those who refused to acculturate, even as it promoted the interests of those who had. Without the obstacles raised by Georgia and the surrounding states, the Cherokee Nation may have kept pace, in terms of economic growth, with its neighbor states. Removal, however, quashed this Cherokee renascence. As whites moved onto Indian land, they expropriated Cherokee homes, farms, barns, livestock, stores, taverns, fences, orchards, and ferries. While the United States compensated Indians for the property that they were forced to abandon in the Southeast, the payments did not cover the investments in sweat equity that the Cherokees had expended to reconstruct their economies. Though the Cherokees recovered in the Indian Territory and rebuilt their homes, schools, churches, and livelihoods, it is impossible to determine how powerful and prosperous their nation might be today if they had been left alone to achieve their destiny in the Southeast.[3]

While we will never know the full costs of the Indian Removal in human and economic terms, it is not as difficult to assess responsibility for the tragedy. Many individuals and institutions were culpable for the exile; ironically, some of them later lamented their role in the process. Jefferson had initiated the idea of exiling the Indians across the Mississippi, Jackson and Calhoun had popularized it, and southern executives like Gilmer, Lumpkin, and Troup had relentlessly pushed it to fruition. Southern state legislators had recognized that they could enhance their political careers by appealing to the festering racial prejudice among their constituents and had passed the laws that extended state jurisdiction over the Indians. In doing so, they offered southern farmers fertile land at nominal prices and removed a despised racial minority that, according to their political rhetoric, provided no value to the southern economy. The removers not only took Native American real property and improvements, they eliminated the potential competition of a rising class of Indian planters and merchants and allowed whites to take over their homes, farms, and businesses. Removal thus expanded economic horizons for the southern elite, provided yeoman farmers with an opportunity to improve their own situations, and allowed southern politicians to capitalize on the prejudices and material desires of their constituents.

Responsibility for the Indian Removal did not rest solely with southern state leaders, legislators, and laymen. Southern politicians, supposedly so antagonistic toward federal power, were keen on the support for removal that they received from the national government. As president, Andrew Jackson seized the opportunity to redirect U.S.-Indian policy from assimilation to separation. Congress abided by Jackson's wishes, passed the Indian Removal Act of 1830, and ratified the illegitimate treaties, like New Echota, signed under the president's authority. Removal proponents sold the policy as the final solution to the problem of Indian-white relations in the East. In 1831 the perceptive Alexis de Tocqueville had already recognized that removal was a false panacea to the difficulties between white and Native Americans, and he noted that the policy was simply a temporary contract of expedience between the southern states and the federal government. "The Union treats the Indians with less cupidity and violence than the several States," he wrote, "but the two governments are alike deficient in good faith." Tocqueville added: "The States extend what they call the benefits of their laws to the Indians, believing that the tribes will recede rather than submit to them; and the central government, which promises a permanent refuge to these unhappy beings in the West, is well aware of its inability to secure it to them. Thus the tyranny of the States obliges the savages to retire; the Union, by its promises and resources, facilitates their retreat; and these measures tend to precisely the same end."[4] The southern state leaders did indeed welcome the federal government's assistance, but as soon as the Removal was accomplished, many of them again began to complain about federal meddling. With the Indians relocated, states' rights ideologues turned their energies to defending slavery—the region's other great realm of racial concern. When they did, they used much of the same racial rhetoric that southern judges had devised in the extension law cases. The federal judiciary, of course, also contributed to the climate that precipitated the Indian Removal. John Marshall and the United States Supreme Court offered removal proponents legal and intellectual arguments in *Johnson v. McIntosh*. By reinvigorating misinformed stereotypes of Native Americans and by reviving the doctrines of discovery, conquest, and effective use, the Supreme Court created a precedent that southern judges could use to justify the extension of state jurisdiction over the Indian nations.

The southern judges have generally escaped historical scrutiny for their legitimation of the state extension policy. Poised in a position of power as they were, with formal authority and public respect as the arbiters of the law, the southern appellate courts could have used the judicial system to stem the tide toward removal. The southern judiciary instead joined the rout against Indian rights and interests. In *Worcester,* John Marshall declared that the Indian tribes were sovereign nations, that their lands could not be confiscated without their consent, and that the federal government held the exclusive constitutional authority to conduct relations with the Native American governments. Andrew Jackson disagreed vehemently with the *Worcester* decision, for he sought to end the federal practice of recognizing the tribes as sovereign nations. For this reason, and since it was politically unwise to ignore southern demands at the same time he was putting down the South Carolina nullification movement, he chose not to impose *Worcester* on Georgia. The opinions of the southern courts thus filled the legal vacuum created by the federal government's failure to enforce *Worcester.* The southern judiciary held that the Indian tribes were not sovereign nations and that Native Americans were merely the subjects of the state in which they resided. According to southern judges, Native Americans were incapable of governing themselves like civilized humans and were disinterested in agricultural cultivation. For those reasons, the southern courts said, the states could abolish Indian governments, seize Indian land, and give it to white state citizens. To justify their conclusions, the southern judges intentionally misrepresented the character of Native American social and political culture, distorted the history of U.S.-Indian treaty relations, and ignored relevant and material arguments and precedents that might have led them to different results. The southern state judiciary fecklessly conformed to public sentiment and cleared the legal path for a forced removal of the eastern tribes. A bit of courage on the part of the southern judiciary as a whole, such as that demonstrated by Judge Jacob Peck of Tennessee, might have made a momentous difference in the destiny of all of the Indian nations. Contrary decisions consistent with the *Worcester* analysis and Peck's dissent might have postponed, or even prevented, the destruction of the Indian nations in the East. The southern courts refused to recognize the rights of the tribes, however, for tribal sovereignty obstructed the plans of those who envisioned a South ethnically cleansed of Indians, engined by African American labor, and ruled by whites.

The decisions in *Tassels, Caldwell,* and *Forman* encouraged state officials to ignore *Worcester* in the most brazen fashion. In the years between

Worcester and the removal of the Cherokees in 1838, dozens of Indians in the Southeast were arrested, convicted, and imprisoned by the state courts. In 1834, for example, in an almost identical repetition of the George Tassel execution, Georgia hanged another Cherokee to prevent him from appealing his murder conviction to the United States Supreme Court. Every one of those arrests and convictions was a repudiation of *Worcester*, every one a renunciation of the principle of tribal sovereignty, and every one a blatant challenge to the constitutional mandates of federal judicial supremacy and federal plenary authority over Indian affairs. John Ross described these encroachments, and Georgia's refusal to comply with *Worcester*, as nullifications of federal law more egregious than South Carolina's resistance to the national tariff. "The only difference in the principle as maintained by South Carolina and Georgia," the chief said, "is that the former has only asserted it in theory, when the latter has reduced it to practice."[5]

Tassels, Caldwell, and *Forman* culminated a national abdication of the sentiments and sensibilities expressed in Henry Knox's federal policy of enlightened expansion. In hindsight, it appears that the southern extension laws and the decisions that ratified them unleashed a long and relentless attack on the sovereignty of the tribes. According to Sidney L. Harring's analysis, by 1900, every state with a material Indian population east of the Mississippi, except for Minnesota, had extended its jurisdiction over its resident Native American populations. After the American Civil War, almost all of the western states moved to extend their jurisdiction over the Indians within their borders. By the end of the nineteenth century, the constitutionality of partial or complete extension of state jurisdiction was accepted at the state level throughout much of the United States, even in states that refrained from claiming that power. In 1883, for example, the Nevada Supreme Court held that the state did not inherently possess jurisdiction over the Ute reservation. However, the court said, the state's legislature clearly held the legal power to extend its jurisdiction over the Utes if it ever resolved to do so. The court cited *Tassels, Caldwell,* and *Forman* to support this position.[6]

This is not to suggest that references to the southern decisions are ubiquitous in the state case reporters. In fact, citations to *Tassels, Caldwell,* and *Forman* are relatively rare. That fact, however, should not depreciate their legal significance. State court decisions do not carry the weight of precedent beyond the borders of the state; southern decisions, in particular, generally carried little influence beyond the region. In addition, subsequent courts tended to hold up the more prominent U.S. Supreme Court precedent of *Johnson v. McIntosh* against proponents of tribal sovereignty. The number of citations, in any event, does not accurately reflect the weight of the southern argument. The southern state supreme court cases, I have tried to argue, did not change the law. Rather, the southern decisions are significant because they reflected the majority view of American lawyers and legislators and, indeed, the white American public, and that view was that the tribes were not sovereign nations. *Worcester*, in sum, though a decision that represented judicial courage and clarity, was a revolution with few adherents. Long after Marshall's ruling, the principle of tribal sovereignty enunciated in *Worcester* struggled against the legal orthodoxy demonstrated in the southern decisions.

While the U.S. Supreme Court never specifically relied on *Tassels, Caldwell,* and *Forman,* certain principles delineated in those cases appeared prominently in many of the Court's decisions in the nineteenth century. For example, in *United States v. Rogers* (1846), Roger Brooke Taney, Marshall's successor as chief justice, wrote, "The native tribes who were found on this continent at the time of its discovery have never been acknowledged or treated as independent nations by the European governments, nor regarded as the owners of the territories they respectively occupied. On the contrary, the whole continent was divided and parceled out, and granted by the governments of Europe as if it had been vacant and unoccupied land, and the Indians continually held to be, and treated as, subject to their dominion and control." Taney was clearly more attendant here to the southern line than he was to the Court's own precedent of *Worcester.* (Taney took the exact opposite position *in dicta* in the *Dred Scott* decision.) Similarly, in 1890 Justice John Marshall Harlan embraced the southern interpretation of tribal sovereignty in *Cherokee Nation v. Southern Kansas Railway Company:* "The proposition that the Cherokee Nation is sovereign in the sense that the United States is sovereign, or in the sense that the several States are sovereign . . . finds no support in the numerous treaties with the Cherokee Indians, or in the decisions of this court, or in the Acts of Congress defining the relations of that people with the United States." It is ironic that many of the same justices, judges, and lawyers who succeeded Marshall, and who helped establish the chief justice as the demigod of American law, paid so little attention to one of his most forthright and logical decisions.[7]

The removed Indians enjoyed a respite from state encroachments for a brief period after their exile. Primarily, this was because the tribes in the Indian Territory and those farther to the west were beyond the practical reach of the state governments and finally under the clear purview of federal territorial authority. So long as the tribal nations refrained from interfering with, legislating against, or adjudicating upon the interests of whites, the federal courts allowed the Indian nations to maintain distinct political and legal systems and left them free to administer their own internal affairs. However, the westward migration of settlers, the United States's conquest of the western tribes, and the creation of new states and reservatio... brought state, federal, and Indian jurisdictions into contact and conflict. The new western states were typically as antagonistic toward Indian interests as their sister states in the South had been in the run up to the Indian Removal. As one authority has noted, "In every imaginable way, using every conceivable argument, states have attempted to control reservation activities." This was particularly true when white interests were involved; in such cases, the federal courts affirmed state efforts to extend their reach over Indian territory. In doing so, the U.S. Supreme Court and the subordinate federal courts used concerns for state sovereignty and presumptions of Indian cultural inferiority to legitimize state efforts to seize power from the Indian nations and to authorize state intrusions into the treaty and compact relationships that existed between the tribes and the federal government. In *United States v. McBratney* (1882), for example, the U.S. Supreme Court affirmed Colorado's conviction of a white man accused of the murder of another white man on the Ute reservation. Like the Removal-era state courts, the nineteenth-century Supreme Court, and the American public for that matter, regarded Native American legal systems with contempt and was loath to allow Indians to sit in judgment of white defendants. For that reason, federal judges were willing to ignore *Worcester* and allow the states to cannibalize the sovereign rights of the tribes. Likewise, in 1885, the high Court allowed the states to tax the property of non-Indians living on a reservation. In *Ward v. Race Horse* (1896), the Court held that municipal laws issued under the purview of the state police power could preempt the inherent sovereign rights of a tribe and its existing agreements with the United States. Decisions like these only encouraged the states to assert their authority over the Indian nations in other areas of the law.[8]

With Congress's abrogation of the treaty system in 1871, the federal government began its own active interference in the domestic affairs of the Indian nations. In *Ex Parte Crow Dog* (1883), the Supreme Court followed *Worcester* and struck down attempts by federal authorities to exert jurisdiction over an Indian on Indian murder on Brule Sioux land. The *Crow Dog* case became pivotal in the late-nineteenth-century diminution of tribal sovereignty, for the Supreme Court declared *in dicta* that Congress held the constitutional power to extend federal criminal jurisdiction over Indian territory. In 1885 the national legislature capitalized on this language and passed the Major Crimes Act, which gave the federal government the power to prosecute certain felonies committed on Indian lands. The Supreme Court sanctioned this constriction of tribal autonomy a year later in *United States v. Kagama* (1886). In *Kagama* the Court suggested that Congress possessed complete authority over the Indian tribes, despite any treaty rights or claims of tribal sovereignty to the contrary. As the end of the nineteenth century approached, the states were no longer the singular threat to Native American sovereignty; the federal government had again joined them in that role.[9]

Kagama invited Congress to end federal recognition of Indian territorial and political rights. Under the authority of the Dawes (1887) and Curtis (1898) acts, the federal government seized the lands of the Cherokees and the other tribes in the Indian Territory, allotted them to individual Indians, and consigned the Native American owners to life under the Oklahoma territorial government. At about the same time, white philanthropic and Christian mission societies, who considered themselves "friends" of the Indians, convinced the United States to implement a neocivilization program designed to eradicate Indian culture, tribal government, and Native American communal property ideas. The grand pronouncements of tribal sovereignty in *Worcester* provided no protection against these attacks. Instead, the United States based its assault on tribal rights on the same principles of Indian cultural deficiency, American territorial hegemony, and white racial superiority enunciated in the southern extension law cases. In 1903 the Supreme Court in *Lone Wolf v. Hitchcock* completed the dismantlement of Indian sovereignty. The Court held that Congress could abrogate treaties without the consent of the Indian signatories, that it possessed plenary power over issues relating to Native Americans beyond the oversight of the judiciary, and that it could appropriate Native American lands with impunity. As one scholar noted, "Supreme Court jurisprudence at the end of the nineteenth century and in the first years of the new century was marked more than ever by colonialist and racist assumptions." These, of course, were the predominant themes of *Tassels, Caldwell,* and *Forman.* In 1907 Congress outlawed the national government of the Cherokees and placed them under the jurisdiction of the new state of Oklahoma. After a century of defending their national sovereignty, the Cherokee people in the old Indian Territory were now the individual subjects of the state in which they lived. The southern judiciary's conception of the Indian and the tribe had triumphed.[10]

The Indian nations as a whole again faced a crisis of state extension during the termination era of the 1950s and early 1960s. Termination, in fact, was of itself an effort to eventually subject all American Indians to state authority. In the infamous Public Law 280, Congress, expressing a desire to control crime on the reservations, gave California, Minnesota, Nebraska, Oregon, and Wisconsin criminal jurisdiction and some aspects of civil jurisdiction over the reservations within their borders. (Alaska was later added to the "mandatory" list requiring the extension of state jurisdiction.) Public Law 280 also gave the other states in the Union the option of extending their jurisdiction over their resident reservation Indians. Under that authority, Florida subsequently decided to extend its full jurisdiction over the Indian country in the state; nine other states extended partial jurisdiction, in geographic or substantive legal areas, over Indian territory. The federal legislature also provided some states with the power to exert authority over specific transactions or regulatory matters involving Native Americans. By the 1960s, when Native American peoples were bringing about the new age of tribal self-determination, all of the Indian nations were under the thumb or under the potential threat of state jurisdiction.[11]

Eventually, the Supreme Court revitalized the *Worcester* precedent in *Williams v. Lee* (1959) and established a firewall against the diminution of tribal rights. Generally speaking, since that case the Court has attempted to protect the tribal nations' rights of self-government, particularly in matters in which only Native American individuals are involved and in areas, like domestic relations, which were historically left to tribal jurisdiction. Since that time, the American Indian tribes have moved closer to Marshall's vision of them as Native American nations free from state encroachment and involved in a special treaty relationship with the United States. Between *Worcester* and *Williams,* however, American Indian law was as much influenced by the thought represented by the southern state removal cases as it was by *Worcester.* Even with the revival of *Worcester,* the principles of the southern removal decisions can be found in recent federal and state opinions. In the *Oliphant* case in 1978, the U.S. Supreme Court, like the Removal-era state courts of the South, again grounded its decision on *Johnson v. McIntosh* and refused to allow the Suquamish Nation to assert its criminal jurisdiction over the whites on its reservation. This was not a unique occurrence in modern times. As David E. Wilkins has pointed out, *Johnson v. McIntosh* "is still regularly cited by commentators and, more importantly, relied upon as 'good' precedent by the Supreme Court," *Worcester* to the contrary.

Worcester continues to be challenged by state courts that use the colonialist rhetoric of the southern courts. In 1992, in perhaps the most notorious use of the tactics of the Removal-era southern courts, a state court in Vermont held that the Missisquoi Abenakis had forfeited the possessory title to and sovereignty over their tribal lands. The Vermont court used, as Jill Norgren described it, "the harsh language of conquest and a self-serving description of the historical record" to repudiate Marshall's ideas in *Worcester.* That language and those rhetorical methods did not go to the grave with the southern Removal-era judges, and *Worcester* no more protects the tribes from their reasoning and misrepresentations today than it did in the 1830s. If nothing else, the southern cases demonstrate how damaging the failure of a court to appreciate the nature of Indian culture and the history of the federal-Indian treaty relationship can be for the tribe before the bar. So long as courts refuse to examine history critically and ignore biases and motives behind the precedents they cite, the tribal nations will continue to face similar assaults on their sovereignty. It is incumbent upon courts deciding questions involving Indian rights to get outside of the history included in the reporters. In these cases, the courts must carefully examine the historical record; they must, in effect, adopt and appreciate the methods of professional historians.[12]

In his study of the U.S. Supreme Court's Indian law decisions, Wilkins lamented the deterioration of Marshall's explication of tribal sovereignty in *Worcester:* "Over the past 150 years . . . the *Worcester* ruling has been modified and the once-impregnable wall shielding tribes from state jurisdictional authority can now be breached, according to the United States, by federal legislation or with Supreme Court authorization." According to Felix Cohen, the author of the preeminent treatise on American Indian law, the United States has historically allowed state encroachment when Congress "expressly delegated back to the State, or recognized in the State, some power of government respecting Indians" or when "a question involving Indians involved non-Indians to a degree which calls into play the jurisdiction of a State government." Under these theories, and under various federal statutes, many states have extended their laws pertaining to inheritance, health and environmental conditions, zoning, crime, and other police power matters over Indian country. While the states have the burden of defeating federal preemption and tribal sovereignty concerns in their efforts to regulate the Indian nations, they have been successful far more often than the original Native American signatories of treaties and federal compacts ever intended at the time of their conclusion. Without the development and survival of the southern removal ideology, these state assaults on the autonomy of the tribes would have been difficult for the federal courts to rationalize.[13]

If federal Indian law has become a "thicket," as Barsh and Henderson have described it, it is because the federal courts have failed to disconnect the two distinct theories of indigenous sovereignty that Franciscus de Victoria fused almost five hundred years ago. Faced with contradictory decisions from their judicial forebears, American judges resolving disputes involving Indian interests have had the luxury of choosing precedents that suited their ideological or political agendas. Those intent on expanding state power at the expense of the Indian nations have found and can find comfort, precedent, and rationale in the long line of ideology that dates back to the Spanish conquest. That ideology, comprised of a cant and logic designed to diminish Indian inherent rights, cascaded down in time until it was invigorated and perfected by the southern state courts in the 1830s. From there the courts of the United States time and again dredged up the rationale and rhetoric of the Indian Removal to circumscribe Indian individual and tribal rights. Even today, in a period of revived Indian autonomy, the states continue to endeavor to exert their authority and jurisdiction over the Indian nations in a myriad of ways, and just as in the days of the Removal, state officials feel a particular interest in Indian affairs whenever they see that they, or their states, can gain pecuniary or political results from an intrusion into the sovereignty of a tribal nation.

During the twentieth century, many Native American peoples not only resurrected their nations but repossessed powers of sovereignty that the states and the federal government had seized from them years before. To their credit, their governments have learned to maneuver and govern skillfully within the context of the legal miasma of American Indian law. Though they no longer hold all of the attributes of national sovereignty, the major Indian nations possess a considerable degree of internal autonomy at the beginning of the new millennium. Dangers still remain for the Native American nations, however. In the *Kagama* decision, the U.S. Supreme Court warned that "the people of the states where [Indians] are found are often their deadliest enemies." Native American councils must always remember this admonition, for they are by no means secure from the ghosts of *Tassels, Caldwell,* and *Forman.*[14]

NOTES

INTRODUCTION

1. In using the phrase "peaceably and on reasonable terms" Ross was referring to the language of the Compact of 1802. The compact required the federal government to extinguish the Indian title in Georgia as soon as it could be "peaceably obtained, and on reasonable terms." Carter, ed., *Territorial Papers*, vol. 5: 142–46; John Ross to Martin Van Buren, undated but around April 1838, RP, vol. 1: 634; Moulton, *John Ross*, 87–95; Woodward, *The Cherokees*, 198–204.

2. Mooney, *History, Myths, and Sacred Formulas*, 130; Moulton, *John Ross*, 95–96.

3. John Ross Papers, Gilcrease Institute; Woodward, *The Cherokees*, 214.

4. Russell Thornton, "Cherokee Losses," 289–300; Mooney, *History, Myths, and Sacred Formulas*, 130.

5. Norgren, *Cherokee Cases*, 35–48; *Acts of the General Assembly*, 20 December 1828, 19 December 1829, 11 December 1830, and 20 December 1830; *Records of the States, Alabama*, 223–25; *Public Acts Passed*, 10–12.

6. Andrew Jackson, Annual Message, Richardson, ed., *Messages and Papers of the Presidents*, vol. 2: 456–59; Prucha, *Great Father*, 191–208.

7. Norgren, *Cherokee Cases*, 53–60, 95–98; William Wirt to John Ross, 22 September 1830, RP, vol. 1: 199–200; *Georgia v. Tassels*; *Augusta Chronicle*, 29 December 1830; *Georgia Messenger*, 8 January 1831.

8. *Cherokee Nation v. Georgia*. Article 3 of the Constitution provides the Supreme

Court with the authority to hear "controversies . . . between a State, or the Citizens thereof, and foreign states, Citizens or Subjects."

9. *Acts of the General Assembly,* 11 and 20 December 1830; *Worcester v. Georgia;* Peters, *Case of the Cherokee Nation;* Norgren, *Cherokee Cases,* 117–22.

10. John Ross, "Public Letter to the Cherokees," 14 April 1831, RP, vol. 2: 215–19; Norgren, *Cherokee Cases,* 122–30; Andrew Jackson to John Coffee, 7 April 1832, *Correspondence of Andrew Jackson,* vol. 4: 430; Miles, "After John Marshall's Decision."

11. *Georgia v. Tassels; Caldwell v. Alabama; Tennessee v. Forman.* Most historians have simply never considered the logical import of the nonenforcement of the *Worcester* case on the concept of Native American sovereignty. Historians occasionally have alluded to *Tassels* in preliminary discussions of the Cherokee cases. However, the dramatic circumstances surrounding Tassel's hanging have generally overawed the arguments produced by the state tribunal. There are also very few references to the *Caldwell* and *Forman* decisions in the scholarly literature. Vine Deloria Jr. excerpted portions of *Caldwell* in *Of Utmost Good Faith,* 7–37. Donald W. Large mentions *Caldwell* in "This Land Is Whose Land? Changing Concepts of Land as Property," 1042. *Forman* is noted in the following books and articles: Virgil F. Carmichael, "The James Foreman Murder Case," 1–17; Reid Peyton Chambers, "Judicial Enforcement of the Federal Trust Responsibility to Indians," 1221 n. 42; Walter Chandler, *Associate Justice John Catron,* 8–9; James Franklin Corn, *Red Clay and Rattlesnake Springs,* 32–36; Edmund C. Gass, "The Constitutional Opinions of Justice John Catron," 54–59; Timothy S. Huebner, *Southern Judicial Tradition,* 59–63; Thurman Wilkins, *Cherokee Tragedy,* 264. Sidney L. Harring raised the significance of *Tassels, Caldwell,* and *Forman* in *Crow Dog's Case.* Harring's brief discussion of the impact of the decisions on Native American tribal sovereignty inspired me to examine these southern state cases in detail. In this work, I have tried to expand on Harring's analysis and place the southern decisions into the historical context of the Marshall tribal sovereignty line of cases.

12. Moulton, *John Ross,* 47; "Conference of Ross, Edward Gunter, and John Mason, Jr.," 6 November 1837, Washington, D.C., RP, vol. 1: 537–40; Thurman Wilkins, *Cherokee Tragedy,* 264–90; *Tennessee v. Forman.* See also the John Catron Papers; Circuit Court Minutes, file box 245, Tennessee Supreme Court Records. For a discussion of the reasons why the dissidents agreed to the New Echota treaty, see Boudinot's letter to John Ross, dated 25 November 1836, in Perdue, *Cherokee Editor,* 199–225.

13. Gossett, *Race: The History of an Idea,* 228–52; Horsman, *Race and Manifest Destiny,* 189–207.

14. Wilkinson, *American Indians, Time, and the Law,* 56; Harring, *Crow Dog's Case,* 44–53.

15. In *Chisholm v. Georgia,* the state refused to recognize the Supreme Court's authority to review the constitutionality of its laws. As in the Cherokee cases, the state refused to appear before the Court.

16. For those who see *Cherokee Nation* as an act of political inspiration, see

Burke, "Cherokee Cases," 514; Norgren, *Cherokee Cases,* 102; Swindler, "Politics as Law," 13; Washburn, *Red Man's Land,* 68. For a more persuasive interpretation of Marshall's motivations in *Worcester,* see Barsh and Henderson, *The Road,* 60–61.

17. Cohen, *Handbook of Federal Indian Law,* 211–12; Fowler and Bunck, *Law, Power, and the Sovereign State,* 32. The U.S. Supreme Court case that dramatically reinvigorated *Worcester's* notion of tribal sovereignty was *Williams v. Lee.* Wilkinson, *American Indians, Time, and the Law,* 1–3, 55–56. Harring also rightly points out that *Worcester* remained relevant to the issue of federal plenary authority throughout the nineteenth century. Only occasionally, however, did courts use the decision to limit state encroachments on Indian rights. Harring, *Crow Dog's Case,* 34, 52–56.

CHAPTER ONE. REMOVAL

1. Mitchell, *Present State of Great Britain and North America,* 231–32, notes; Thomas Jefferson to Edmund Pendleton, 13 August 1776, *Papers of Thomas Jefferson,* vol. 1: 494.

2. Sheehan, *Seeds of Extinction,* 244–46; Wallace, *Jefferson and the Indians,* 223–26.

3. *Statutes at Large,* vol. 7: 13–15; IA:LT, vol. 2: 3–5; Kohn, *Eagle and Sword,* 191–227; Prucha, *American Indian Treaties,* 31–32; Robert A. Williams, *Linking Arms Together,* 7–10, 20–24.

4. Prucha, *Great Father,* 42–48; Merrell, "Declarations of Independence," 197–204. In 1793, federal commissioners told a group of Indian leaders in the Ohio Valley that the United States held a primary right of preemption to the region: "As [the king] had not purchased the country of you, of course he could not give it away; he only relinquished to the United States his claim to it. That claim was founded on right acquired by treaty, with other nations, to exclude them from purchasing, or settling, in any part of your country; and it is this right which the King granted to the United States." One Indian leader responded that his people had never surrendered any form of title to Britain. "If the white people, as you say, made a treaty that none of them but the King should purchase of us, and that he has given that right to the United States, it is an affair which concerns you and him, and not us; we have never parted with such a power." ASP:IA, vol. 1: 341.

5. IA:LT, vol. 2: 8–16; JCC, vol. 32: 340–41.

6. JCC, vol. 9: 844–45. Madison believed that the framers of the articles intended to protect the states' right of preemption over the Indian lands within their borders. James Madison to James Monroe, 27 November 1784, *Papers of James Madison,* vol. 8: 156–57; *Federalist Papers,* no. 42; Prucha, *American Indian Treaties,* 48, 63–66, 68 n. 1.

7. U.S. Constitution, art. 1, sec. 8; Prucha, *Great Father,* 50–51; *Strother v. Cathey.*

8. Henry Knox to George Washington, 15 June 1789, 7 July 1789, and 4 January 1790, ASP: IA, vol. 1: 13, 52–54, 61; JCC, vol. 32: 365–69.

9. *Statutes at Large*, vol. 1: 137–38, 329–32; Prucha, *Great Father*, 115–34.

10. See the previously referenced letters from Knox and the "Report of Henry Knox on the Northwestern Indians," 5 June 1789, ASP: IA, vol. 1: 13–14; IA:LT, vol. 2: 28, 31. Robert F. Berkhofer Jr. denominated Knox's policy "expansion with honor" in light of the United States's antecedent practices. *White Man's Indian*, 134–53. Reginald Horsman, conversely, argued that the United States was simply putting a noble face on an ignominious land grab. Knox and Washington "eagerly sought" Indian lands, he argued, and used "military force, bribery, deception, and every other possible means to expand the arc of American expansion." "American Indian Policy," 20–28.

11. Sheehan, *Seeds of Extinction*, 119–47; Perdue, *Cherokee Women*, 109–84; Young, "Women, Civilization, and the Indian Question"; Martin, *Sacred Revolt*, 133–64; McLoughlin, *Cherokee Renascence*, 388–96.

12. Jefferson "To the Chiefs of the Chickasaw Nation, Minghey, Mataha, and Tishohotana," 7 March 1805; "To the Chiefs of the Upper Cherokees," 4 May 1808; and "To the Deputies of the Cherokees of the Upper and Lower Towns," 9 January 1809; in *Complete Jefferson*, 471–72, 494, 506–7; Wallace, *Jefferson and the Indians*, 226, 302; McLoughlin, *Cherokee Renascence*, 146–67. Satisfied with the success of the Cherokee-Arkansas transfer, Jefferson continued to promote removal long after he left office. In 1813, Creek warriors aligned with the Redstick movement were attacked by a group of white settlers at Burnt Corn Creek in what is now Alabama. In response the Creeks attacked Fort Mims and killed most of its American defenders. In reacting to the massacre, Jefferson proposed that the Creeks be removed to the West. The Creeks, he said, had committed "ferocious barbarities" against whites at Fort Mims that "justified extermination." Removal, he said, would put the Creeks in a place where they would no longer be able to incite similar disturbances. In response to the Fort Mims attack, the United States sent Andrew Jackson and his army into the Creek territory. In 1814, Jackson's army annihilated the Redstick resistance at Horseshoe Bend. Martin, *Sacred Revolt*, 133–68; Jefferson to David Baillie Warden, 29 December 1813, quoted in Sheehan, *Seeds of Extinction*, 244.

13. Carter, *Territorial Papers*, vol. 5: 142–46; *Worcester v. Georgia*, 556–60, 584–86, 590–91, 595.

14. Prucha, *Great Father*, 78–80; Martin, *Sacred Revolt*, 133–64; John C. Calhoun to the House of Representatives, 5 December 1818, ASP:IA, vol. 2: 183.

15. ASP: FR, vol. 3: 705–24; Barsh and Henderson, *The Road*, 39–45.

16. McLoughlin, *Cherokee Renascence*, 204–5; Andrew Jackson to James Monroe, 4 March 1817, in *Correspondence of Andrew Jackson*, vol. 2: 277–82; Andrew Jackson to John C. Calhoun, Secretary of War, 18 January 1821, "Report on Cherokee Proposals on Disputed Lands," H. R. Doc. 136, 18th Cong., 1st sess., serial number 102, 7–8.

17. Report of Committee on Public Lands, 9 January 1817, ASP:IA, vol. 2: 123–24; James Monroe to Andrew Jackson, in *Correspondence of Andrew Jackson*, 331–32; Prucha, *American Indian Treaties*, 145–52; Prucha, *Great Father*, 184.

18. John Clark, Governor of the state of Georgia, to the Secretary of War, 14

January 1823, NASP:IA, vol. 6: 248; G. M. Troup to President of the United States, 31 March 1825, NASP:IA, vol. 7: 160; Duncan G. Campbell to the Secretary of War, 4 May 1825, NASP:IA, vol. 7: 167; Report of George Gilmer, ASP:IA, vol. 2: 259–60; "Report of William H. Crawford," 13 March 1816; Joseph McMinn to William H. Crawford, 25 October 1816; both in ASP:IA, vol. 2: 26–28, 88–91, 99, 110–15; "Georgia Controversy," in *Report on Indian Land Title Dispute with Georgia*, H. R. Doc. 98, 19th Cong., 2nd sess., serial number 161, 1–22; *Annals of Congress*, 17th Cong., 1st sess., 555; *Acts of the General Assembly*, 18 December 1823, 207–11; *Journal of the Senate*, 278–80; *Acts of the General Assembly*, 27 November 1824, 190–91. For accounts explaining the state's position, see Phillips, "Georgia and States' Rights," 75–81 and Vipperman, "Forcibly If We Must," 103–9.

    19. Prucha, *Great Father*, 186–89.

    20. George M. Troup to John C. Calhoun, 28 February 1824, in ASP:IA, vol. 2: 475–76; Norgren, *Cherokee Cases*, 75; Michael D. Green, *Politics of Indian Removal*, 50; *Cherokee Phoenix*, 17 June 1829.

    21. *Acts of the General Assembly*, 4 and 26 December 1826, 68–69, 227–35; Michael D. Green, *Politics of Indian Removal*, 86–125; IA:LT, vol. 2: 214–21, 264–67; Charles Francis Adams, ed., *Memoirs of John Quincy Adams*, vol. 7: 89–92.

    22. Horsman, *Race and Manifest Destiny*, 6, 98–108; Gordon S. Wood, *Radicalism of the American Revolution*, 186–87, 236–37, 294–95; Morris, *Southern Slavery and the Law*, 171–72; Jordan, *White over Black*, 285–89, 301–11; Fehrenbacher, *Dred Scott Case*, 16–19; Jean Edward Smith, *Definer of a Nation*, 103–4; Prucha, *Great Father*, 169; Pearce, "Melancholy Fact," 19.

    23. Horsman, *Race and Manifest Destiny*, 26, 44–48, 54–61.

    24. Mosse, *Crisis of German Ideology*, 4–5, 13–17, 67–69; Horsman, *Race and Manifest Destiny*, 4–28; Gossett, *Race: The History of an Idea*, 54–88.

    25. John Adams to Benjamin Rush, 23 May 1807, quoted in Baritz, *City on a Hill*, 107; Jefferson to William Ludlow, September 6, 1824, in *Writings of Thomas Jefferson*, vol. 16: 74–75; Horsman, *Race and Manifest Destiny*, 25–42, 74–75, 82–89.

    26. Peters, *Case of the Cherokee Nation*, 66; Horsman, *Race and Manifest Destiny*, 139–57.

    27. Charles Caldwell, *Unity of the Human Race*, iii, vi–vii, 1–2, 88, 134–51, 173; Horsman, *Race and Manifest Destiny*, 116–24; Gossett, *Race: The History of an Idea*, 64–65; Jordan, *White over Black*, 506–9.

    28. Horsman, *Race and Manifest Destiny*, 151–57. For a contemporary editorial discussing the legitimacy of these theories, see the *Georgia Messenger*, 11 December 1830.

    29. "Removal of Indians," House Committee Report on the Indian Removal Act, NASP: IA, 9: 169–76; George Troup to John C. Calhoun, 28 February 1824, ASP:IA, vol. 2: 475–76; Lumpkin, *Removal of the Cherokee Indians*, vol. 1: 96; George R. Gilmer to Col. Hugh Montgomery, 31 May 1831; Gilmer to Col. John A. Sanford, 15 June 1831; both in Gilmer, *Settlers of Upper Georgia*, 312–13; Young, "Racism in Red and Black."

30. South Carolina ex rel. *John Marsh v. The Managers of Elections for the District of York.*

31. Young, "Racism in Red and Black"; "Bryan," *Georgia Journal,* 17 August 1819.

32. Charles Francis Adams, *Memoirs of John Quincy Adams,* vol. 6: 271–72.

CHAPTER TWO. SPIRITUAL SOVEREIGNTY

1. "Cherokee Constitution," in LCN, 118–30; Rennard Strickland, *Fire and the Spirits,* 64–66.

2. Fowler and Bunck, *Law, Power, and the Sovereign State,* 4–8, 37–38; Bull, *Anarchical Society,* 8–9; Hinsley, *Sovereignty,* 26, 107–22. Other definitions of sovereignty abound. Charles Burton Marshall described sovereignty as "the situation of being in charge of a domain." Marshall defined the essential attributes required of a sovereign nation to be "a scheme of authority . . . capable of maintaining dependable social order," "the allegiance of a determining portion of persons," a "capacity and a will to command means and to devote them to give effect to common preferences," the "capacity to enter into and to effectuate obligations," and an agency "able to communicate authentically and conclusively on its behalf to others beyond the span of jurisdiction." Charles Burton Marshall, *Exercise of Sovereignty,* 4–5. Raymond Aron called sovereignty the "supreme power of deciding in a case of crisis." Aron, *Peace and War,* 746. Ingrid DeLupis wrote, "Sovereignty has traditionally been used as a term to denote the collection of functions exercised by a state." Delupis, *International Law and the Independent State,* 3.

3. Scholars in American Indian law have devised their own criteria for determining whether a tribe or group of Native American people comprises a sovereign nation. Charles F. Wilkinson, for example, defined sovereignty as "the power of a people to make governmental arrangements to protect and limit personal liberty by social control." Wilkinson, *American Indians, Time, and the Law,* 54–55. Vine Deloria Jr. seems to agree with this characterization, although his definition of sovereignty is perhaps more demanding on the tribe under consideration for sovereign status. Deloria wrote that a completely sovereign nation should be able to "determine its own course of action with respect to other nations," maintain "sufficient territory and military strength," and "regulate one's own internal functions in the field of domestic relations." Vine Deloria Jr., "Concept of Sovereignty," 22. John R. Wunder asserted that regardless of what national powers have been ceded or surrendered to another nation by a group of Indian people, so long as they are a permanent population, occupying territory under a legitimate government that is capable of representing and fulfilling the needs of its people, then the Native American group should be considered a sovereign nation. Wunder's characterization is partly derived from the Montevideo Convention on the Rights and Duties of States. The Montevideo assemblage concluded that a presumptive people could be considered sovereign if it had a permanent population, a defined territory, a government that functioned adequately for its population, and the ability to conduct relations with other states. "According

to these criteria," Wunder concluded, "Native Americans have been sovereign nations for centuries and continue to be under international law." Wunder, *"Retained by the People"*, 8–9.

4. Karl Llewellyn and E. Adamson Hoebel used the term "law-ways" to distinguish between the images of Anglo-American jurisprudence raised by the word "law" and the unwritten, functional system of behavioral regulation common in preliterate Native American cultures. Llewellyn and Hoebel, *Cheyenne Way*.

5. Russell Thornton, *Population History*, 21–23; Mooney, *History, Myths, and Sacred Formulas*, 14–16. For broad views of Cherokee culture before or at the time of early contacts with Europeans, see, along with the above referenced works, Reid, *Law of Blood*; Hudson, *Southeastern Indians*, 120–46 passim. Most historians agree that the Southeastern peoples did not consider themselves "nations" until at least the eighteenth century. Rennard Strickland, *Fire and the Spirits*, 56; McLoughlin, *Cherokee Renascence*, xvii; Michael D. Green, *Politics of Indian Removal*, 4, 14–15. Guntram F. A. Werther, a political scientist, recently wrote that Native Americans "lived in, and understood themselves to belong to locally based, self-contained band-like polities having relatively loose linkages to other indigenous groups." *Self-Determination in Western Democracies*, xxvii.

6. Mooney, *History, Myths, and Sacred Formulas*, 5, 239–40; Hudson, *Southeastern Indians*, 127–28, 136–48.

7. Mooney, *History, Myths, and Sacred Formulas*, 242–49; Perdue, *Cherokee Women*, 13–59, 158.

8. Van Doren, *Travels of William Bartram*, 400–401; Reid, *Law of Blood*, 137–41.

9. Reid, *Law of Blood*, 137–41; Cronon, *Changes in the Land*, 58–70; McLoughlin, *Cherokee Renascence*, 7.

10. De Vorsey, *Indian Boundary*, 205–21; Hewatt, *Historical Account*, 67.

11. William Hicks and John Ross to Hugh Montgomery, 16 April 1828, in RP, vol. 1: 136–37; IA:LT, vol. 2: 16–18.

12. Reid, *Law of Blood*, 35–48; 73–122; Perdue, *Cherokee Women*, 18–20. At times, members of the victim's clan accepted compensation in property or the adoption of a captive as a substitute for blood revenge.

13. Persico, "Cherokee Political Organizations," 93–94; Reid, *Law of Blood*, 29–33; Champagne, *Social Order and Political Change*, 24–26; Hudson, *Southeastern Indians*, 244.

14. Samuel Cole Williams, ed., *Adair's History*, 105–15; Reid, *Law of Blood*, 242–45; Perdue, *Cherokee Women*, 25–27.

15. Persico, "Cherokee Political Organizations," 93–94. Oral tradition suggests that both civil leaders and warriors were subordinated to a group of religious priests in the era before Cherokee contact with Europeans. However, by the eighteenth century, the priestly class had apparently been overthrown and replaced by the council as a whole. Reid, *Law of Blood*, 153–61; Champagne, *Social Order and Political Change*, 39.

16. Van Doren, *Travels of William Bartram*, 45–46, 111, 385; Samuel Cole

Williams, ed., *Timberlake's Memoirs*, 93; Samuel Cole Williams, *Adair's History*, 459–60; Hewatt, *Historical Account*, vol. 2: 4; "Institutions of the Cherokee Indians," 41–42; Richard White, *Roots of Dependency*, 80–81; McLoughlin, *Cherokee Renascence*, 17.

17. Samuel Cole Williams, *Adair's History*, 407; Reid, *Better Kind of Hatchet*, 23–38, 45–52; Champagne, *Social Order and Political Change*, 50–55; Corkran, *Cherokee Frontier*, 14.

18. Reid, *Better Kind of Hatchet*, 52–54; Crane, *Southern Frontier*, 167. For the impact of the development of the European credit economy on Native Americans, see Richard White, *Roots of Dependency*, xv–xix. For discussions of relations between the Cherokees and the Carolina colonial government, see Reid, *Better Kind of Hatchet* and Hatley, *Dividing Paths*.

19. Dowd, *Spirited Resistance*, 20, 173–81; McLoughlin, *Cherokee Renascence*, 178–85; Wallace, "Revitalization Movements."

20. Hewatt, *Historical Account*, 297–98; McLoughlin, *Cherokee Renascence*, 8–9; Gearing, *Priests and Warriors*, 79–82; Champagne, *Social Order and Political Change*, 25–26, 56.

21. "Journal of Sir Alex. Cuming," in Samuel Cole Williams, ed., *Early Travels in the Tennessee Country*, 115–43; Hewatt, *Historical Account*, 3–11; Mooney, *History, Myths, and Sacred Formulas*, 35–36; Perdue, *Cherokee Women*, 92–95; Reid, *Law of Blood*, 17–27.

22. Reid, *Law of Blood*, 17–27.

23. Mooney, *History, Myths, and Sacred Formulas*, 41–45; Champagne, *Social Order and Political Change*, 56–59; Hatley, *Dividing Paths*, 119–40; Woodward, *The Cherokees*, 69–79.

24. Russell Thornton, *Population History*, 40–43; Champagne, *Social Order and Political Change*, 68–70. For general studies of the British colonial relations with the Cherokees, see Brown, *Old Frontiers*; Corkran, *Cherokee Frontier*; Hatley, *Dividing Paths*; Reid, *Better Kind of Hatchet*; and W. Stitt Robinson, *Southern Colonial Frontier*.

25. Prucha, *American Indian Policy*, 11–25; Mooney, *History, Myths, and Sacred Formulas*, 46–79; McLoughlin, *Cherokee Renascence*, 18–34. For the war between the Cherokees and the colonists, see O'Donnell, *Southern Indians in the American Revolution*, 34–53.

26. Russell Thornton, *Population History*, 35–43; McLoughlin, "Cherokee Anomie."

27. Jennings, *Founders of America*, 197–98; Robert A. Williams, *Linking Arms Together*, 45–51, 75–89, 126–31; Reid, *Better Kind of Hatchet*, 9–17; Reid, *Law of Blood*, 201–16.

28. Galloway, " 'Chief Who Is Your Father' "; Robert A. Williams, *Linking Arms Together*, 71–74; Reid, *Law of Blood*, 71–74.

29. Robert A. Williams, *Linking Arms Together*, 23–24; IA:LT, vol. 2: 8–16.

30. LCN, 3–4, 18, 28; Rennard Strickland, *Fire and the Spirits*, 56–58; Champagne, *Social Order and Political Change*, 76–77.

31. Perdue, *Cherokee Women*, 81–84; Champagne, *Social Order and Politi-*

cal Change, 91–92. Federal agents also encouraged the National Council to move toward a republican form of government. Overall, though, I think some scholars have overestimated their influence in this process.

32. Dowd, *Spirited Resistance,* 161–66; LCN, 4–5; Champagne, *Social Order and Political Change,* 91–103; Rennard Strickland, *Fire and the Spirits,* 57–62; McLoughlin, *Cherokee Renascence,* chapters 5 through 8. Those leaders who supported removal or cession proposals during these years, like Doublehead, Black Fox, and Toochelar, were repudiated by the Cherokee people and lost their positions. Doublehead, in fact, lost his life.

33. Dowd, *Spirited Resistance,* 185–90; McLoughlin, *Cherokee Renascence,* 201–17; Martin, *Sacred Revolt,* 165–66; Persico, "Cherokee Political Organizations," 100.

34. Mooney, *History, Myths, and Sacred Formulas,* 102–6; McLoughlin, *Cherokee Renascence,* xvii, 206–59, 276–78; Champagne, *Social Order and Political Change,* 92–111; IA:LT, vol. 2: 140–44, 177–81; LCN, 11–12, 14–18. The 1819 agreement allowed Cherokee families to take private allotments and become citizens of the United States. About 230 Cherokee families accepted allotments. However, the states in which the allotments were located refused to recognize them or provide the families with protection from the harassment of white settlers. Most of these Cherokees eventually returned to the Cherokee Nation. Champagne, *Social Order and Political Change,* 133–34.

35. LCN, 14–18, 12–148 passim; Persico, "Cherokee Political Organizations," 102–8.

36. LCN, 118–30; Rennard Strickland, *Fire and the Spirits,* 65–66; McLoughlin, *Cherokee Renascence,* 394–410; Hicks and Ross to Hugh Montgomery, 16 April 1828, RP, vol. 1: 136–37.

37. Moulton, *John Ross,* 15–39.

38. Peters, *Case of the Cherokee Nation,* 18–21.

39. Russell Thornton, *Population History,* 50–51.

CHAPTER THREE. THE PRECEDENTS

1. Jeremy Bentham introduced the term "international law" in 1789; before that time, most commentators commonly used the phrase "the law of nations." Janis, "Jeremy Bentham," 408–10; Onuf and Onuf, *Federal Union, Modern World,* 22.

2. Aristotle, *"Art" of Rhetoric,* book 1, chapter 13, 141 and *Nicomachean Ethics,* book 5, chapter 7, 295. Of course, the logical weakness of natural law was that individuals and nations were free to make their own deductions of what natural law was and how it was applied. The failure of its advocates to resolve the problem of relativity led to the decline and fall of natural law as a premise for justice and government in the nineteenth century. Until then, though, the theory of natural law was the cornerstone of European jurisprudence and the intellectual foundation of property rights and national sovereignty in the West. Ruddy, *International Law in the Enlightenment,* 4–7.

3. Barkum, *Law without Sanctions,* 133; Laski, *Foundations of Sovereignty,* 1; Onuf and Onuf, *Federal Union, Modern World,* 41; Matthew 16: 17–19.

4. Robert A. Williams, *American Indian in Western Legal Thought,* 83–85; Korman, *Right of Conquest,* 50; "Claims to Territory," in Green and Dickason, *Law of Nations and the New World,* 4–7.

5. Dickason, "Concepts of Sovereignty," 144–45; Korman, *Right of Conquest,* 8–9, 43–47; Werther, *Self-Determination in Western Democracies,* xxix. Francisco Suarez argued that papal donation did not simply provide for the temporal allocation of land for monarchs to use according to their own will. What the pope was doing under the doctrine, he argued, was creating spheres of mission responsibility. "Claims to Territory," in Green and Dickason, eds., *Laws of Nations and the New World,* 50–51.

6. Washburn, *Red Man's Land,* 4; Robert A. Williams, *American Indian in Western Legal Thought,* 13–58; Muldoon, ed., *Expansion of Europe,* 191–92. Under early international law there was a distinction between a just war and a holy war. Nations fought just wars to enforce a right or redress a grievance under the law of nations; according to Hedley Bull, holy wars were fought under the premise that "the true believers are right, and the infidels are to be converted or exterminated. . . . It is a religious conception, of war as the instrument of God's will, or of history." Bull, *Systems of States,* 34–35.

7. Berkhofer, *White Man's Indian,* 11–12; Robert A. Williams, *American Indian in Western Legal Thought,* 173–74.

8. Cohen, *Handbook of Federal Indian Law,* 52; Robert A. Williams, *American Indian in Western Legal Thought,* 96–103; Dickason, "Concepts of Sovereignty," 161, 195.

9. Robert A. Williams, *American Indian in Western Legal Thought,* 100–103; Washburn, *Red Man's Land,* 10–11. Of course, the idea that missionaries of other faiths should be legally admitted into Spain was not, to Victoria, a concomitant corollary of that principle.

10. Cohen, *Handbook of Federal Indian Law,* 50–52; Dickason, "Concepts of Sovereignty," 195 n. 60, 61. Timothy J. Christian described Victoria's argument as "predictably circular" and said it could be reduced to the statement, "If it was done it was lawful." Introduction to Green and Dickason, *Law of Nations and the New World,* x.

11. Dickason, "Concepts of Sovereignty," 215; Ruddy, *International Law in the Enlightenment,* 162; Washburn, *Red Man's Land,* 29–32.

12. Taylor, *Two Richard Hakluyts,* vol. 1: 280; Dickason, "Concepts of Sovereignty," 227–28; Robert A. Williams, *American Indian in Western Legal Thought,* 170–74.

13. Robert A. Williams, *American Indian in Western Legal Thought,* 204; Prucha, *Great Father,* 15–16; Blackstone, *Blackstone's Commentaries,* vol. 1: 105.

14. Purchas, *Hakluytus Posthumus,* 219–22; Takaki, "*Tempest* in the Wilderness"; Robert A. Williams, *American Indian in Western Legal Thought,* 211; Jennings, *Invasion of America,* 82, 138.

15. More, *Utopia*, 56. Dickason wrote that unlike discovery and conquest, there appears to be no mention of this theory in the Catholic canonical scholarship. However, William Cronon points out that the concept is founded upon Genesis 1:28, in which God tells Adam and Eve, "Be fruitful and multiply, and replenish the earth, *and subdue it;* and have dominion over the fish of the sea, and over the fowl, and over every living thing that move upon the earth." Cronon, *Changes in the Land,* 69; Dickason, "Concepts of Sovereignty," 221–26. The idea that uncultivated territory could be seized by outsiders was also used by Portugal to justify its conquest of the east African coast in the fifteenth century. Korman, *Right of Conquest,* 57–58.

16. Washburn, *Red Man's Land,* 41; Dickason, "Concepts of Sovereignty," 235–39; Jennings, "Virgin Land and Savage People," 521–26; Berman, "Concept of Aboriginal Rights," 655.

17. Cohen, *Handbook of Federal Indian Law,* 53–58; Prucha, *Great Father,* 15–18; Jennings, *Invasion of America,* 135–38; Robert A. Williams, *American Indian in Western Legal Thought,* 274–75. William Cronon warns that it is dangerous to speak of a common English or colonial law of property during this period: "They varied considerably depending on the region of England from which a group of colonists came, so that every New England town, like every Indian village, had idiosyncratic property customs of its own." Cronon, *Changes in the Land,* 69.

18. Some scholars have also suggested that *The Law of Nations* was a significant influence on the American constitutional framers. After receiving three copies of the book in 1775, Benjamin Franklin wrote in a thank you note to the publisher that the gift "came to us in good season where the circumstances of a rising state make it necessary frequently to consult the law of nations." Vattel, *Law of Nations;* Ruddy, *International Law in the Enlightenment,* ix; Onuf and Onuf, *Federal Union, Modern World,* 11–15; Fenwick, "Authority of Vattel," 370–424. In 1932, Edwin D. Dickinson counted the references to Grotius, Pufendorf, Vattel, and other European legal philosophers in American cases between 1789 and 1820. Citations to Vattel far outnumbered those to any other scholar. His popularity, however, was limited to Anglo-American legal scholars. Arthur Nussbaum noted that Vattel was rarely quoted outside of the United States and England and that by the twentieth century these countries' lawyers had come to terms with the ambiguities of his work. As a result, his importance to students of international law has faded with time. The Onufs contend, "Vattel's influence on contemporary thought has been negligible." Nussbaum, *Concise History,* 161–63; Onuf and Onuf, *Federal Union, Modern World,* 11 n. 18.

19. Onuf and Onuf, *Federal Union, Modern World,* 17; Nussbaum, *Concise History,* 161–63; Vattel, *Law of Nations,* 65–66, 168–69.

20. Vattel, *Law of Nations,* 65, 68–70, 78–82.

21. Vattel, *Law of Nations,* 65–66, 78–82, 102–4, 168–75.

22. Grotius, *Law of War and Peace,* 690–93; Vattel, *Law of Nations,* 173–75, 500; Rousseau, *Social Contract and Discourses,* 171.

23. Vattel, *Law of Nations,* 216, 290–91, 311–12; "Claims to Territory," in Green and Dickason, eds., *Laws of Nations and the New World,* 62–64.

24. Vattel, *Law of Nations*, 255–56; Nussbaum, *Concise History*, 160–61.

25. Clive Perry, introduction to Ruddy, *International Law in the Enlightenment*, ix.

26. According to the *American Digest*, two state courts considered the questions of Indian title and sovereignty before *Fletcher v. Peck*. In 1791, the Virginia Supreme Court held that war veterans who acquired land from the federal government did so "at the risk of the Indian claim." *Marshall v. Clark*. In 1808, a New York appellate court held that possession of a tract of land by an Indian did not impair the title received in a state grant if the vendor's tribe no longer existed as an independent entity at the time of the conveyance. *Jackson v. Hudson*.

27. In 1662, Charles II conveyed a charter to the lord proprietors of South Carolina. In 1732, King George II split off the region that now comprises much of Georgia, Alabama, and Mississippi and gave it to a charitable trust organized by James Oglethorpe. The charter said that the trustees would hold title to the lands "westerly from the heads of the [Savannah and Altamaha] rivers respectively in direct line to the south seas." Spain also claimed parts of the Yazoo territory at the time of the 1795 conveyance. Pindar, *Georgia Real Estate Law and Procedure*, 17–18.

28. Alexander McGillivray to Panton, 8 May 1790, in Caughey, *McGillivray of the Creeks*, 259–62; Milford, *Memoir*, 106; Michael D. Green, "Alexander McGillivray"; *Georgia Laws*, 7 January 1795; *Annals of the Congress of the United States*, 3rd Congress, 27 February 1795, 838–39.

29. Magrath, *Yazoo*, 1–12. Henry Adams noted, "No one could say what was the value of Georgia's title, but however good the title might be, the State would have been fortunate to make it a free gift to any authority strong enough to deal with the Creeks and Cherokees alone." Adams, *History of the United States*, vol. 1: 303.

30. Magrath, *Yazoo*, 12–20, 37–60; Jean Edward Smith, *John Marshall*, 389. Fletcher was an experienced speculator with close ties to Peck, who was himself a director of the New England Mississippi Company. Moreover, the contract between the Georgia Mississippi Company and the New England Mississippi Land Company included a clause requiring a court to make definitive rulings on the legitimacy of the Yazoo sale. This evidence, the uncommon cooperation of the opposing attorneys, and the relatively feeble efforts by Fletcher's lawyer in arguing the case indicated that the case was a scheme to promote the Federalist compensation cause.

31. Turner, "Federalist Policy," 3–32; Haskins and Johnson, *Foundations of Power*, vol. 2: 50–73, 107–37.

32. Before Marshall's appointment, only twelve of the sixty-three cases decided by the Court included unified opinions. Between the time that Marshall and William Johnson came to the bench, the Court decided twenty-six cases. All of these cases were decided unanimously, and Marshall authored all but two of these opinions. More than likely, he would have written these as well, but the chief justice recused himself from them on the grounds that he had already rendered opinions on the cases at the circuit court level. Of the first forty-six opinions issued by the Marshall court, forty-two were unanimous. Morgan, *Justice William Johnson*, 45–47; Jean Edward Smith, *Definer of a Nation*, 293.

33. Thomas Jefferson to John Dickinson, 19 December 1801, *Writings of Thomas Jefferson,* 304; Lillich, "Chase Impeachment"; Knudson, "Jeffersonian Assault."

34. Joseph Johnson, *Traditions and Reminiscences,* 30; Morgan, *Justice William Johnson,* 3–11; Morgan, "William Johnson," 355, 361; Stites, *John Marshall,* 109.

35. Johnson also helped found and served as the president of the Board of Trustees of Columbia College, the forerunner of the University of South Carolina. He also published a two-volume study of General Nathaniel Greene that many treated as a Republican response to Marshall's Federalist biography of George Washington. Belz, "South and the American Constitutional Tradition," 26; Herbert A. Johnson, "Constitutional Thought of William Johnson," 132–34, 145; Morgan, "William Johnson," 358; Morgan, *Justice William Johnson,* 15–40, 50. Morgan issued a solid endorsement of Johnson's historical scholarship in the Greene biography: "Johnson's blending of law, history and political experience with a high native intelligence helped fit him to view the constitutional trends of his time with prophetic insight."

36. Haskins and Johnson, *Foundations of Power,* 382–89; Morgan, "William Johnson," 367.

37. U.S. Constitution, art. 1, sec. 10; *Fletcher v. Peck,* 138; Magrath, *Yazoo,* 70–100.

38. *Fletcher,* 121; Vattel, *Law of Nations,* 102–4, 172–75; Robert A. Williams, *American Indian in Western Legal Thought,* 218; Henry Middleton to the President of the United States, 31 December 1810, LR: SW, 642–43.

39. *Fletcher,* 142–43.

40. Ibid., 140–43. Barsh and Henderson interpreted Marshall's position to mean that "there was no *inconsistency* between state ownership and tribal occupancy." Barsh and Henderson, *The Road,* 38.

41. *Fletcher,* 146–48. In his opinion, Justice Johnson condemned the fact that the suit was collusively intended to procure a judgment favoring the Yazooists.

42. Barsh and Henderson wrote that in *Fletcher,* Marshall held "embarrassingly . . . that the states could convey the fee in western lands without waiting for federal action." *The Road,* 47. I think that Barsh and Henderson read Marshall's brief comments too broadly on this point. I believe Marshall purposely intended to be more circumspect than this in his language.

43. Magrath's study of the case, for example, barely mentions the issue. For quote, see Jean Edward Smith, *Definer of a Nation,* 392–93.

44. "Indian Lands," 23 February 1795, NASP: IA, vol. 6: 117.

45. See "Report on Negotiations with Indians in Georgia," NASP: IA, vol. 6: 124–55; Michael D. Green, *Politics of Indian Removal,* 34–35.

46. "The Talk of the Commissioners of Georgia to the Kings, Head-men, and Warriors, of the Creek Nation," 18 June 1796; Creek Response to Georgia Proposal, 24 June 1796; and Benjamin Hawkins, George Clymer, and Andrew Pickens to James McHenry, Secretary of War, 1 July 1796; "Cherokees, Chickasaws, Choctaws, and Creeks," Presidential Message to the Senate, 23 December 1801; Talks of Efau Hadjo, 9 and 13 June 1802; Letter from James Wilkinson and Benjamin Hawkins to Henry Dearborn, Secretary of War, 15 July 1802; all in NASP: IA, vol. 6: 139–

41, 149, 154–55, 178, 186, 191–92, 197–98; Michael D. Green, *Politics of Indian Removal*, 39. Around the same time, violence between settlers and the Creeks in the Cumberland Valley also inspired Tennessee to consider action independent of federal sanction. In a letter to the secretary of war, the territorial governor William Blount reported that a party of Creeks killed and scalped three men near Nashville. "There is too little reason to hope that blood-thirsty nation will ever cease to rob and murder those citizens [in Cumberland]," he wrote. In implying that he was inclined to send the state militia against the Creeks, Blount mocked the federal government's success in maintaining order on its frontiers: "It cannot but be evident to the United States, that the Creeks, except the superannuated chiefs, who have satiated themselves with blood, pay no regard to the treaty formed between them." Governor Blount to the Secretary of War, 9 January 1795, NASP: IA, vol. 6: 114.

47. Hoboithle Mico to President of the United States, 15 May 1811; Benjamin Hawkins to Secretary of War, Creek Agency, 31 December 1810; LR: SW, 554–57, 583–88.

48. Between *Fletcher* and *Johnson v. McIntosh*, the Supreme Court considered the status of Indian land titles in *New Jersey v. Wilson*. Again, Marshall implied that Indians held a general usufruct claim to their lands. In that case, New Jersey, then a royal colony, had in 1758 issued a grant returning a large tract of land to the Delawares. Marshall wrote that the grant conveyed to the Delawares more than a "mere occupancy" and that, instead, the Indians had acquired a clear fee simple title. Strangely, the Delawares had elevated the character of their title by acquiring a grant from the very people who had dispossessed them in the first place. Beyond this narrow issue, the case did little to clarify the status of the Indian nations under the federal system. For other cases between *Fletcher* and *Johnson v. McIntosh* involving Native Americans, see *Preston v. Browder* and *Danforth's Lessee v. Thomas*. These opinions, however, do not contemplate the nature of the political status of the tribes.

49. Abernethy, *Western Lands and the American Revolution*, 122; Robert A. Williams, *American Indian in Western Legal Thought*, 275–80, 318 n. 5; Shortt and Doughty, *Constitutional History of Canada*, 163–68; Commager, ed., *Documents of American History*, 1–3.

50. Prucha, *Great Father*, 62–67; Robert A. Williams, *American Indian in Western Legal Thought*, 305–6; *Johnson v. McIntosh*, 565–66. In 1794, Virginia revised its code and silently repealed the 1779 act.

51. Some confusion exists among historians over the identity of William McIntosh. Michael D. Green, a student of the Creeks, holds that this William McIntosh is not the Creek chief who was executed by his nation for selling land to the United States in 1825. Personal correspondence.

52. *Johnson v. McIntosh*, 545–50, 560–62.

53. Ibid., 560–67. Webster also cited Lord Mansfield's opinion in the 1774 English case of *Campbell v. Hall*. Mansfield wrote that the idea that the laws of a conquering "civilized" nation abrogated the rights of the native inhabitants "would not exist before the Christian era, and in all probability arose from the mad enthusiasm of the Croisades." Robert A. Williams, *American Indian in Western Legal Thought*, 300–303.

54. *Johnson v. McIntosh,* 567–68.

55. *Johnson v. McIntosh,* 567–71. McIntosh's lawyers cited Vattel, Grotius, Locke, Pufendorf, Jefferson, Montesquieu, and Adam Smith as authority for their argument.

56. It is possible that Marshall's recognitions of the Indian usufruct in *Fletcher* and *Johnson v. McIntosh* were attempts to pull Justice Johnson into the majority opinion. In *Fletcher v. Peck,* Marshall was unsuccessful in bridling the South Carolina justice. Surprisingly, Johnson did not issue a separate opinion in *Johnson v. McIntosh.* On this possibility, see Herbert A. Johnson, "Constitutional Thought of William Johnson," 141–42. For discussions of Marshall's opinion in *Johnson v. McIntosh,* see Barsh and Youngblood, *The Road,* 45–49; Berman, "Concept of Aboriginal Rights," 642–58; Burke, "Cherokee Cases," 502–3; Frickey, "Marshalling Past and Present," 385–90; "Claims to Territory," in Green and Dickason, eds., *Laws of Nations and the New World,* 105–11; Hurley, "Aboriginal Rights," 416–23; Norgren, *Cherokee Cases,* 92–95; Swindler, "Politics as Law," 10–11; and Robert A. Williams, *American Indian in Western Legal Thought,* 308–17.

57. The progressive historian George Bryan sardonically repudiated the logic of Marshall's theory: "[Suppose] for the sake of argument, that our western coast defenses have broken down and that countless thousands of Japanese have invaded our Pacific slope, 'conquered' it and are annexing the lands of that territory. To the protest of the American freeholder, would Japan say, 'You can be heard only in the courts of the conqueror; and, having heard you, we cite, in lieu of a prolonged opinion, the decision of the Supreme Court of the United States in the case of Johnson and Graham's Lessee v. McIntosh—the basal proposition of which is that conquest gives a title which the courts of the conqueror can not deny?' Can it be doubted that the final judgment would be, 'It is not for the courts of Japan to question the validity of the title of a Japanese conqueror or to sustain one which is incompatible with it?' " *Imperialism of John Marshall,* 3–4.

58. *Johnson v. McIntosh,* 589. It is perhaps worth noting again that though national sovereignty and title to land are at face two distinct concepts, they are closely intertwined; the seizure of any aspect of a nation's property rights directly diminishes its control over its land and its people. Invariably, then, many judges fused the two concepts simply because encroachments on Indian title *were* attacks on Indian sovereignty. Swindler, "Politics as Law," 10. Russell Barsh and James Youngblood Henderson suggest that sovereignty and property began to be confused (*fused* might perhaps be a better word) by James Harrington and John Locke. Harrington argued that "the distribution of political power in society evolves naturally out of the distribution of land." Locke contended that the primary goal of civil government was the preservation of property. Barsh and Henderson, *The Road,* 35–36.

59. *Johnson v. McIntosh,* 572–73; Berman, "Concept of Aboriginal Rights," 651.

60. *Johnson v. McIntosh,* 573–74, 590.

61. Ibid., 576–80, 597–98.

62. See, for example, *Caldwell v. Alabama,* 402–3, 426.

63. Berman, "Concept of Aboriginal Rights," 637, 642; Henderson, "Unraveling the Riddle of Aboriginal Title," 90–91.

64. *Johnson v. McIntosh*, 585–88. John Hurley suggests that this conception of the right of extinguishment demonstrated that Justice Johnson's theory in *Fletcher* "was now endorsed by the full court." "Aboriginal Rights," 419. I disagree. Johnson, I believe, argued that many of the tribes retained full sovereignty over and complete title to their lands.

65. Berman, "Concept of Aboriginal Rights," 643–44, n. 31; Kent, *Commentaries on American Law*, vol. 3: 377.

66. *Johnson v. McIntosh*, 574, 588; Hurley, "Aboriginal Rights," 416–20.

67. Hurley, "Aboriginal Rights," 423; Berman, "Concept of Aboriginal Rights," 658. One could also argue that *Worcester v. Georgia* simply repudiated much of what Marshall had written in *Fletcher* and *Johnson v. McIntosh*.

68. Some historians have suggested that Marshall purposefully avoided discussing the international law theorists so that he could ground his opinion on his own revised conception of the doctrine of discovery. Berman, "Concept of Aboriginal Rights," 646. Disagreements over the clarity and intelligence of Marshall's opinion are not uncommon. Berman wrote that much of Marshall's opinion in *Johnson v. McIntosh* was "confusing and occasionally incoherent." Ibid., 647. Others appear reluctant to challenge the chief justice's conventional reputation. Nell Jessup Newton, for example, described Marshall's holding as a "brilliant compromise." "At the Whim of the Sovereign," 1223. I find Berman's characterization closer to the mark. I suspect that the decision was the product of compromise, but I am not persuaded that it merits the adjective "brilliant."

69. *Johnson v. McIntosh*, 580, 587, 596–97; Norgren, *Cherokee Cases*, 94; ASP: PL, vol. 1: 125; John Clark to John C. Calhoun, 26 November 1821, Georgia Executive Letter Books, reel 2, pp. 2–3.

70. *Johnson v. McIntosh*, 572, 591–92; Berman, "Concept of Aboriginal Rights," 645. While Marshall clearly believed that the national interest was more important than philosophical theory, he was quite willing, when it was helpful, to use natural law to justify his conclusions.

71. *Johnson v. McIntosh*, 588–90.

72. Slaughter, *History of St. Mark's Parish*, 107–8; Marshall, *Life of George Washington*, vol. 3: 246–47; Jean Edward Smith, *Definer of a Nation*, 45–51.

73. McClung, *Sketches of Western Adventure*, 194–97; Baker, *John Marshall*, 84–86.

74. Jean Edward Smith, *Definer of a Nation*, 103–4; John Marshall to Joseph Story, 29 October 1828, *Proceedings of the Massachusetts Historical Society* 34: 337–38.

75. Burke, "Cherokee Cases," 502.

CHAPTER FOUR. THE SUPREMACY OF STATE JURISDICTION

1. *Acts of the General Assembly*, 26 December 1827, 99–101; "Resolutions," 19 December 1827, NASP: IA, vol. 9: 52–62; LR: OIA, vol. 72: 432. McLoughlin, *Cherokee Renascence*, 411–12.

2. *Acts of the General Assembly*, 20 December 1828, 87–89. The bill passed by voice vote in both the state house and senate. *Journal of the House of Representatives*, 12 December 1828, 265; *Journal of the Senate*, 17 December 1828, 209. In 1829, the legislature amended this provision to allow Indians to testify against whites who resided within the Indian nations. *Acts of the General Assembly*, 19 December 1829, 98. Perhaps the legislature hoped to use Indian testimony to prosecute white missionaries who opposed removal. Some, however, rejected the principle of using Indian testimony against whites. Twenty-three representatives signed a protest of this action, saying that the amendment was "calculated to corrupt the stream of justice at its fountainhead, to prostrate the sacred rights of personal liberty, personal security and private property, at the feet of savage ignorance." *Journal of the House of Representatives*, 12 December 1829, 271. Mary Young argued that the state was not just interested in land or gold. In addition, she said, the Georgia leadership sought to create a transportation and communication infrastructure that connected the Tennessee River to the state's Atlantic ports, that Georgians did not want to live near or with what they believed to be an inferior race, and that the state's politicians feared that if the federal government interfered with Georgia's relations with the Cherokee that it might also become interested in the civil liberties of its slaves. Young, "Exercise of Sovereignty in Cherokee Georgia." For a discussion of Georgia's attack on the Creeks, the fraudulent Treaty of Indian Springs, and its replacement, the Treaty of Washington, see Michael D. Green, *Politics of Indian Removal*, 69–125.

3. *Cherokee Phoenix*, 17 June, 1 July, and 21 October 1829; John Ross to the Senate and House of Representatives, 27 February 1829, Congress Serial Number 187, House Document 145, 1–3. On October 13, 1828, Ross provided the first enunciation of what would come to be the Cherokee defense against Georgia's usurpations. "Annual Message," 13 October 1828, RP, vol. 1: 142–44; *Cherokee Phoenix*, 13 October 1828.

4. Andrew Jackson's First Annual Message, Richardson, ed., *Messages and Papers of the President*, vol. 2: 456–59.

5. *Acts of the General Assembly*, 19 December 1829, 98–101.

6. Ibid., 270; *Journal of the House of Representatives*, 11 December 1829, 247; *Journal of the Senate*, 16 December 1829, 269; *Georgia Messenger*, 20 October 1830; George R. Gilmer to Augustine S. Clayton, 7 June 1830, in Gilmer, *Settlers of Upper Georgia*, 276. The extension act passed by a seventy to forty-eight vote in the state house and by voice in the senate. There were opponents of the extension statutes in the state legislature. For example, on November 23, 1830, Representative William Schley criticized the assembly's provocative actions: "The Indians have a natural right to the occupancy of all the lands within their boundaries, and that they may enjoy that right undisturbed until they shall voluntarily relinquish it, or another people, not having a sufficiency of land for their support, may lay claim to it. . . . The Indians have not only this natural right, but also a legal right established by the constitution of the state of Georgia, and the compact of 1802." *Georgia Messenger*, 27 November 1830; Michael D. Green, *Politics of Indian Removal*, 96–97.

7. "Memorial of John Ross and Others, Representatives of the Cherokee Nation

of Indians," NASP: IA, vol. 9: 139–41; *Niles' Register,* 14 November 1829, vol. 37: 189–90; *Cherokee Phoenix,* 20 January 1830.

8. *Niles' Register,* 20 March 1830 and 24 April 1830, vol. 38: 77, 165; *Statutes at Large,* vol. 4: 411–12; NASP: IA, vol. 9: 51–62, 142–50; Prucha, *American Indian Policy,* 239–43. For extensive arguments in favor of removal, see the Senate and House committee reports on the Indian Removal Act of 1830 at NASP: IA, vol. 9: 142–50, 151–76.

9. Prucha, *Great Father,* 201–6; Lumpkin, *Removal of the Cherokee Indians,* 47. The William Penn essays are collected in Evarts, *Essays on the Present Crisis.* For a study of the southern press's reaction to the removal debate, see Leutbecker, "Some Public Views."

10. *Niles' Register,* 1 May 1830 and 29 May 1830, vol. 38: 179–80, 265–66; John Ross, "Message to the General Council," *Cherokee Phoenix,* 17 July 1830; Satz, *American Indian Policy,* 9–63. The voting in the Senate was even more section-alized. According to Kenneth Penn Davis's allocation of the votes, southern senators approved the bill fourteen to three, the West by nine to three, and the Northeast rejected it by a thirteen to five margin. Davis included Tennessee and Kentucky in the West and Maryland and Delaware in the South in his analysis. Davis, "Ousting the Cherokees from Georgia," 49–50, n. 19.

11. *Cherokee Phoenix,* 24 July, 14 August, and 4 September 1830; William Wirt to John Ross, 4 June 1830, RP, vol. 1: 189–90; William Wirt to Judge Carr, 21 June 1830, in Kennedy, ed., *Memoirs of the Life of William Wirt,* 253–55; Norgren, *Cherokee Cases,* 49–60.

12. (U.S. Dept. Justice) 1 Op. Att'y Gen. 465, 645 (1821, 1824); 2 Op. Att'y Gen. 110 (1828); *Niles' Register,* 25 September 1830, vol. 38: 81; U.S. Constitution, art. 1, secs. 8 and 10; *Statutes at Large,* vol. 2: 139–46; Wirt to John Ross, 4 June 1830 and 15 November 1830, RP, vol. 1: 189, 205–6; IA: LT, 31. Wirt's opinion was influenced by the William Penn essays, the congressional speeches against removal, Marshall's opinion in *Johnson v. McIntosh,* and Chancellor Kent's interpretation of Indian rights in the Tommy Jemmy case and his *Commentaries on American Law.*

13. U.S. Constitution, amend. 11; U.S. Constitution, art. 3, sec. 2; Burke, "Chero-kee Cases," 512; John Ross to Hugh Montgomery, 20 July 1830, RP, vol. 1: 193–94; *Cherokee Phoenix,* 31 July 1830.

14. William Wirt to George R. Gilmer, 4 June 1830; Gilmer to Wirt, 19 June 1830, in Gilmer, *Settlers of Upper Georgia,* 270–75; Wirt to John Ross, 4 June 1830, 22 September 1830, and 15 November 1830, RP, vol 1: 197–99; Burke, "Cherokee Cases," 510–11.

15. William Wirt to John Ross, 9 August 1830, RP, vol. 1: 196; *Georgia Messen-ger,* 13 November 1830; *Georgia v. Tassels,* 229; McRay, "The Hanging of George 'Corn' Tassel Here," 7 August 1977, the *Daily Times* (Gainesville, Ga.); Abbot, *Cherokee Indians of North Georgia,* 42. Scholarly works that mention the Tassel case generally plead an ignorance of the circumstances of the murder, and there con-tinues to be a great deal of local interest in and considerable confusion about Tassel. Consequently, in the following notes, I have attempted to fill in as many details as

possible, describe the points of contention over the facts, and clarify some of the misconceptions about the case. I find no contemporary record describing the murder in the Hall County court records or the regional newspapers. Accounts of the Tassel controversy begin soon after his hanging and do not describe the circumstances of his crime.

The absence of a clear-cut record in the case has engendered a number of questions about these specifics. Tassel's name, for example, has been reported in a number of ways. In the Georgia Supreme Court reporter, he is identified as George Tassels. In the stay order from the United States Supreme Court, he is referred to as "George Tastle, alias George Tassles, alias George Tassel, alias George Tarsle, alias George Tasalle." *Augusta Chronicle*, 29 December 1830. He is often referred to as "Corn Tassel" by twentieth-century local historians such as Sybil McRay and was, in fact, referred to by that name in one of Principal Chief John Ross's annual messages and in at least two letters. McRay, "The Hanging of George 'Corn' Tassel Here," the *Daily Times* (Gainesville, Ga.), 7 August 1977; John Ross, "Annual Message," 11 October 1830, RP, vol. 1: 201–2, 210. Evidently, the defendant called himself "George Tassel." A Cherokee named George Tassel was a member of a delegation to Washington in 1825, which included John Ross, George Lowery, and Elijah Hicks, to negotiate on how the annuity funds from an 1804 treaty would be distributed between the eastern and western Cherokees. At the foot of that letter, this individual signed his name "George Tassel." It is also interesting that this Tassel is listed as a member of the "Delegation from Cherokees West of the Mississippi River." I am not sure that this is the same George Tassel accused in the 1830 murder; if it is, I have not found any evidence explaining what he was doing back in the East in the summer of 1830. The two letters of Ross that mention "Corn Tassel" imply a familiarity with him. The George Tassel who Georgia arrested may therefore have been the same person who signed the 1825 letter. Cherokee Delegation to Thomas L. McKenney, 11 March 1825, RP, vol. 1: 104; LR: OIA, M-234, 71 pp. 512–13. The defendant is also referred to as George Tassel in the *Cherokee Phoenix*, 8 January 1831. Based on this evidence, I will refer to the defendant as George Tassel except when referring to the state court opinion denominated *Georgia v. Tassels*.

According to Dudley, the state court reporter, Tassel was accused of killing "another native Cherokee Indian." For some reason, however, one local history states that Tassel "murdered a white man trespassing in Cherokee country." Bates, "Gainesville's First 150 Years," 14. I find no contemporaneous evidence that contradicts the court reporter's statement. It is possible that apologists may have changed the reported identity of Tassel's victim to a white man to help excuse the state for its subsequent actions. Some subsequent reports also changed Tassel's racial character. In "State Rights: The Hanging of George Tassel," L. L. Knight described Tassel as a "half-breed." No other record suggests that Tassel was of mixed ancestry. However, under Georgia's racial laws and social code, a person of white and Cherokee ancestry would have been considered an Indian. Thus, there is no reason to completely discount Knight's description. Moreover, the Cherokees would have considered a mixed-blood man of maternal Cherokee ancestry a Cherokee citizen. *Georgia's Landmarks, Memorials, and Legends,* 787.

Abbot's account states that the victim was "Sanders, Talking Rockford" and pinpoints the locus of the murder in modern Pickens County, some forty to fifty miles west of the Hall County courthouse. I suspect that this meant the deceased might have been a Cherokee named Sanders from Talking Rock Ford. Talking Rock is in Pickens County. There are a few Sanders named in the Ross papers and other contemporaneous Cherokee documents, but I find no convincing evidence that any of them was the victim. To make matters even more confusing, W. J. Cotter's account identifies the victim as Andrew Fallon, "a good Indian, the son, I think of Aunt Katie Fallon." *My Autobiography,* 33. I find no record of a Fallon family in the Cherokee Census of 1835. "Index to the 1835 Census of the Cherokee Indians East of the Mississippi River." The identify of the victim, I think, remains inconclusive. Another report in the *Hampshire Gazette* indicates that Tassel was drunk on illegal whiskey when he allegedly committed the crime. 12 January 1831. However, I find no evidence from the contemporary newspapers in Georgia to corroborate that fact.

16. By the time of Sherwood's *Gazetteer* in 1837, the town was populated by "200 whites and 90 blacks." "This was a place of considerable resort during the summer season," Sherwood wrote. "[T]wo lime-stone and chalybeate (containing iron compounds) spring[s], are frequently visited . . . and there are gold mines in this county, quite near to the Courthouse." By the time of Sherwood's report, the town was comprised of "31 dwelling houses, 8 stores, 4 law offices, 3 doctor[s], and 5 mechanic shops, Courthouse and Jail." Sherwood, *Gazetteer of the State of Georgia*; McRay, the *Daily Times* (Gainesville, Ga.), 11 February 1993; Bates, "Gainesville's First 150 Years," 14.

17. Underwood was, like so many southern lawyers of this period, originally from Virginia. He practiced out of Elberton, about seventy miles from Gainesville, and had been judge of the state supreme court for the western circuit from 1825 to 1828. Northen, *Men of Mark in Georgia,* vol. 3: 102; *Georgia Official and Statistical Register,* 866.

18. *Cherokee Phoenix,* 8 January 1831; *Georgia Messenger,* 13 November 1830; McRay, "The Hanging"; U. B. Phillips, "Expulsion of the Cherokees," 7. The newspaper accounts indicate that Tassel's jury trial was in November under the direction of Augustin S. Clayton; Belle K. Abbot's account from the 1880s places Tassel's trial in September before Judge Charles Dougherty. The *Southern Banner* and the *Cherokee Phoenix* both clearly identify Clayton as the presiding judge. Dougherty did not succeed Clayton until November of 1831. *Georgia Official and Statistical Register,* 866; Welborn, "Augustin Smith Clayton," in *Dictionary of Georgia Biography,* 196–98. Clayton did not identify the case in which he had already "solemnly determined this question and published it to the world." From what I can tell, Clayton was referring to an unpublished opinion at the superior court level. At the time of Tassel's case, the state authorities also had at least three other Cherokees in jail. In Hall County, the sheriff had arrested one man on the charge that he violated an injunction that Clayton had issued prohibiting the Cherokees from mining in the area.

He had also locked up John Sanders, a judge of the Cherokee court, for adjudging and punishing a white man for the crime of horse theft in the nation. In adjoining Gwinnett County, Ross reported, the sheriff had recently jailed a Cherokee woman on a debt collection case. Apparently all of these actions were suspended until the convention of judges ruled on the jurisdiction issue. John Ross, "Annual Message," *Cherokee Phoenix,* 16 October 1830; Peters, *Case of the Cherokee Nation,* 22–27; John Ross to Thomas W. Harris, 27 August 1830; Ross to William H. Underwood, 3 September 1830; both in RP, vol. 1: 197–99.

Before the appeal, Wirt asked Ross about Underwood's character and allegiance to the nation. "Tricks," Wirt said, "may be played to draw from your counsel the whole course of [the defense in another Cherokee defendant's case] in order to deflect it." William Wirt to Ross, 22 September 1830, RP, vol. 1: 199.

19. *Tassels,* 229–30, 237. In 1830, the judges of the superior courts of Georgia, the original trial level courts in the state, began meeting semiannually to consider appeals on questions of law. The judges and court reporters referred to this meeting as "the convention of judges." It was this convention of judges that issued the opinion in *Georgia v. Tassels.* In 1845, the state legislature reformed the convention and established Georgia's supreme court. See *Georgia Reports* 2 (Dudley 1837), unnumbered preface; 1 (Kelly 1846), vii–xii.

20. *Tassels,* 230. For Kent's interpretation of Native American rights, see his *Commentaries on American Law,* vol. 2: 242–43 and vol. 3: 307–19; "Appendix No. 1," in Peters, *Case of the Cherokee Nation,* 225–49. For Spencer's opinion in the Tommy Jemmy case, see *Jackson v. Goodell.* For Kent's reversal, see *Goodell v. Jackson.*

21. *Tassels,* 229–37.

22. *Tassels,* 230, 238; *Georgia Messenger,* 13 November 1830; Burke, "Cherokee Cases," 508–9, 512. According to the Dudley reports, the convention of judges was comprised of William Law, William H. Crawford, William W. Holt, L. Q. C. Lamar, Charles Daugherty, C. B. Strong, G. E. Thomas, L. Warren, John W. Hooper, and H. Warner. However, I find no way of determining how many of the convention heard the *Tassels* case or who authored their opinion. Burke suggested that Crawford, an outspoken opponent of Cherokee sovereignty, prepared the opinion. For secondary discussions of *Georgia v. Tassels,* see Barsh and Henderson, *The Road,* 50–52; Beveridge, *Life of John Marshall,* vol. 4: 542–43; Burke, "Cherokee Cases," 512–13; Christianson, "Removal," 222; McLoughlin, *Cherokee Renascence,* 438–39; Perdue, *Cherokee Editor,* 25, 120–21, 144; Perdue and Green, *Cherokee Removal,* 68, 133; Thurman Wilkins, *Cherokee Tragedy,* 215–16; and Wunder, *"Retained by the People,"* 25–26. For legal analyses, see Harring, *Crow Dog's Case,* 25–30; Norgren, *Cherokee Cases,* 41–62, 87, 95–98. The *Tassels* opinion is reprinted at the last cite at 155–64.

23. *Tassels,* 234.

24. Ibid., 232–33; Prucha, *Great Father,* 59–60.

25. *Tassels,* 231–32, 237–38.

26. *Territorial Papers,* vol. 5: 142–46.

27. *Tassels,* 232; *Fletcher,* 142–43; Prucha, *Great Father,* 59–60; Barsh and Henderson, *The Road,* 51.

28. U.S. Constitution, art. 1, sec. 9; *Tassels,* 231–34.

29. *Tassels,* 233–35.

30. Ibid., 235–36. In *Cherokee Nation v. Georgia* a few months later, John Marshall would use similar language to describe the Indian polities as "domestic, dependent nations."

31. Ibid., 235–36.

32. Several historians have attempted to locate the trial record. Unfortunately, we have all been unsuccessful. However, the records might not have been destroyed. It is also possible, as the *Cherokee Phoenix* implied, that the trial judge refused to prepare, certify, or release a copy of the record to the U.S. Supreme Court. When Tassel was executed, all efforts to procure a copy of the trial record perhaps ceased. *Cherokee Phoenix,* 8 January 1831; McRay, "Hanging of George 'Corn' Tassel," the *Daily Times* (Gainesville, Ga.), 7 August 1977.

33. More than likely, this was the case of *Georgia v. Kannetoo* that Ross described as a victory for the Cherokees in his 1831 annual message. The popular uproar against the decision ended Clayton's career as a judge. Clayton, however, quickly rebounded when he was elected to Congress to replace Wilson Lumpkin, who had left Washington to run for governor. John Ross to William H. Underwood, 22 June 1834; "Annual Message," 24 October 1831; both in RP, vol. 1: 228, 296–97; "Clayton," in Welborn, *Dictionary of Georgia Biography,* 197.

34. John Ross to George R. Gilmer, 20 December 1830, "Cherokee Indian Letters, Talks, Treaties"; *Georgia Journal,* 8 December 1830; the *Athenian,* 28 December 1830; *Augusta Chronicle,* 29 December 1830; *Southern Banner,* 27 September 1839.

35. *Acts of the General Assembly,* 21, 22, and 23 December 1830; the *Athenian,* 28 December 1830; *Georgia Messenger,* 11 December 1830; *Augusta Chronicle,* 22 December 1830. The enabling act of the lottery gave Georgia citizens who had resided in the state for four years the right to a draw for a parcel of Cherokee land; for eighteen dollars the winners could purchase forty-acre lots in the gold region and 160-acre tracts elsewhere.

36. Hugh Montgomery to John Ross, 3 September 1829, Bureau of Indian Affairs, Record Group 75; LS: OIA, vol. 6: 110–11; the *Athenian,* 14 September 1830; *Savannah Georgian,* 17 December 1830; *Augusta Chronicle,* 15 and 22 December 1830; *Georgia Messenger,* 20 October 1830 and 8 November 1830; George R. Gilmer to General Sanford, 27 January 1831, Gilmer, *Settlers of Upper Georgia,* 297–98. For histories of the gold rush in Georgia, see Coulter, *Auraria;* David Williams, *Georgia Gold Rush;* and Dorsey, *Hall County,* 23–38.

37. *Augusta Chronicle,* 29 December 1830.

38. *Augusta Chronicle,* 29 December 1830; *Georgia Messenger,* 8 January 1831; *Gainesville Eagle,* 11 May 1888; Dorsey, *Hall County,* 39; Langdon, *Law Enforcement in Hall County,* 108. Tassel is supposedly buried in the middle of what is now South Bradford Street, now a thoroughfare through the town. Soapstone hill is now

the site of Alta Vista, Gainesville's large public cemetery. One overly enthusiastic chronicler of the case claimed that he saw Tassel's skeleton, twenty years after the hanging, "with coagulated blood about his neck." Cotter, *My Autobiography*, 33. Such are the legends that developed around the Tassel hanging in north Georgia. Evidence of the more credible specifics of Tassel's hanging are limited to relatively contemporaneous accounts in the *Athenian*, 22 and 28 December 1830; *Cherokee Phoenix*, 8 January 1831. Purported eyewitness accounts include that of W. J. Cotter in *My Autobiography* and that of an observer named C. W. A., both of which were published over fifty years after the fact. See also the report of an unnamed observer published in Belle K. Abbot's *Cherokee Indians of North Georgia*, 42; the 1839 account of "Chestatee" in the *Southern Banner*, 27 September 1839; and Knight, "State Rights: The Hanging of George Tassel," in *Georgia's Landmarks, Memorials, and Legends*, 787–88. Unfortunately, no newspapers were published in Hall County until well after the trial and hanging. Dorsey, *Hall County*, vi. There are serious disagreements about the size of the crowd that witnessed the hanging. Abbot's account is based on a newspaper article published in the 1880s and places the Cherokee crowd at the hanging at five hundred, while the *Athenian* estimated the Cherokees in attendance, four days after the hanging, at a more realistic "eighteen to twenty."

39. The *Athenian*, 28 December 1830.

40. *Georgia Messenger*, 22 January 1831. Tassel's execution was widely reported across the country. For examples of southern support for Georgia's actions, see the *Columbia Times and Gazette*, 3 January 1831; the *Richmond Enquirer*, 6 January 1831. For support among the Jacksonian papers in New York, see the *New York Enquirer and Guardian*, 4 January 1831. The writer identified as "Chestatee," who claimed to have witnessed Tassel's execution, subsequently asserted that Sheriff Eberhart did not receive the state's order until "the Indian was about to mount the gallows." December 24 was the date set for the hanging, he said, and Tassel would have been executed regardless of the state's resolution. More than likely, Chestatee did not observe the hanging. No other account mentions a gallows, and his letter was published as an attempt to absolve a fellow Whig, Judge McDonald, of voting against Georgia's last-minute execution order. Democratic papers in Georgia had accused McDonald of being sympathetic to the Indians and endangering the state's sovereignty. Chestatee attempted to downplay the significance of the state order. His man McDonald, Chestatee implied, was all for the hanging of George Tassel. *Southern Banner*, 6 and 27 September 1839.

41. "Memorial of a Delegation from the Cherokee Indians," 18 January 1831, NASP: IA, vol. 9: 7; *Cherokee Phoenix*, 8 January 1831. Louis Turner Griffith and John E. Talmadge note that the *Cherokee Phoenix* was the only paper in Georgia to condemn the state's actions in the Removal Crisis. *Georgia Journalism*, 33.

42. *Niles' Register*, 8 January 1831, vol. 39: 338–39; Charles Francis Adams, *Memoirs of John Quincy Adams*, vol. 8: 262–63. For other examples of national criticism of Georgia's execution of Tassel, see the *United States Telegraph*, 3 January 1831; the *National Intelligencer* (Washington, D.C.), 10 January 1831.

43. *Memoirs of Georgia*, vol. 2: 280; David Williams, *Georgia Gold Rush*, 134 n. 19.

CHAPTER FIVE. DOMESTIC DEPENDENT NATIONS

1. John Ross to David L. Child, 11 February 1831; John Ross to Thomas W. Harris, 11 March 1831 and 27 April 1831; John Ross, "To the Cherokees," 14 April 1831; Ross to William Wirt, 10 May 1831; Wirt to Ross, 18 July 1831; all in RP, vol. 1: 214–15, 217–22.

2. Peters, *Case of the Cherokee Nation*, 2. Richard Peters, the Supreme Court's reporter, believed the case to be of national importance. To preserve the history of the proceedings, he compiled the significant documents of the action into a single volume. Peters's work included the bill that the Cherokee Nation filed, transcripts of the oral arguments of William Wirt and John Sergeant, all of the opinions of the justices, portions of the federal-Cherokee treaties, the Georgia extension statutes, the Trade and Intercourse Acts of 1802, the Compact of 1802, and Chancellor Kent's opinion that Wirt solicited when he was trying to decide how to proceed in the case. As a whole, the record of the case provoked considerable public support for the Cherokees in the North. Burke, "Cherokee Cases," 518.

3. In *Chisholm v. Georgia*, the Supreme Court allowed two citizens of South Carolina to sue the state in a federal court. In response to the protest of the states, who complained that the ruling encroached on their sovereignty, Congress passed the Eleventh Amendment. Ratified in 1795, it prohibited the federal courts from accepting jurisdiction in cases "commenced or prosecuted against one of the United States by Citizens of another State, or by Citizens or Subjects of any Foreign State." However, it did not prohibit a foreign state from bringing an action in a federal court against a state in the Union. This is why Wirt made the nation, rather than an officer of the nation, the plaintiff in the action. U.S. Constitution art. 3, sec. 2, cl. 1 and 2, and amend. 11; Cohen, *Handbook of Federal Indian Law*, 316 n. 279, 328–29; Peters, *Case of the Cherokee Nation*, 28–29.

4. Peters, *Case of the Cherokee Nation*, 7–9, 12–13, 15.

5. Ibid., 3–7, 16, 42.

6. Ibid., 5–7, 16–19, 22–27; *Cherokee Nation v. Georgia*, 10–11. On April 18, 1829, John Eaton, Jackson's secretary of war, had written to the Cherokees explaining the president's position. The 1827 declaration of Cherokee sovereignty inside the boundaries of Georgia was illegal, Eaton said, and there was nothing Jackson could or would do to prevent the state from exerting its jurisdiction. Constitutionally, he added, the president could not interfere with Georgia's internal affairs. The Cherokees, therefore, had a choice. They could submit to Georgia law or remove to the West. 18 April 1829, LS: OIA, M-21, 5, pp. 408–10.

7. Peters, *Case of the Cherokee Nation*, 10–12; *Cherokee Nation v. Georgia*, 6; Dickson, "Judicial History," 290–93.

8. Peters, *Case of the Cherokee Nation*, 18–21.

9. George R. Gilmer to Andrew Jackson, 20 June 1831; George R. Gilmer to [Augustin] S. Clayton, 7 June 1830; both in Gilmer, *Settlers of Upper Georgia*, 316.

10. Peters, *Case of the Cherokee Nation*, 22–27, 32–35; *Acts of the General Assembly*, 21 December 1830, 114–18, 127–43. George Gilmer subsequently admitted that the state was intent on seizing the Cherokees' gold mines. "The immediate possession of that part of the territory is also particularly desirable to the State, on account of the gold mines which it contains," he wrote to the secretary of war. "I would, therefore, request that the enrolling officers be directed by you to make their first efforts to remove the Indians from it." Gilmer to Lewis Cass, 20 August 1831, Gilmer, *Settlers of Upper Georgia*, 320.

11. Peters, *Case of the Cherokee Nation*, 5–7, 12–16, 28–29; *Cherokee Nation v. Georgia*, 10–11; William Morel Strickland, "Rhetoric of Cherokee Indian Removal," 125.

12. Peters, *Case of the Cherokee Nation*, 149; Norgren, *Cherokee Cases*, 100; Burke, "Cherokee Cases," 513.

13. Peters, *Case of the Cherokee Nation*, 42–43, 52–53, 62.

14. Peters, *Case of the Cherokee Nation*, 69–73; Vattel, *Law of Nations*, 2–3.

15. Wirt noted that the treaty of Holston required non-Cherokee visitors to obtain a passport to enter into the nation and authorized United States citizens to use the Tennessee River as a road through the nation. If the Cherokee Nation was not a sovereign state, Wirt argued, no such permission would have been necessary. Peters, *Case of the Cherokee Nation*, 74–75, 83, 90, 102–9, 240–47.

16. Ibid., 109–10, 130–31.

17. Ibid., 112–15.

18. Ibid., 92, 95–96.

19. Ibid., 97.

20. Ibid., 153–56.

21. Ibid., 156–59.

22. Joseph C. Burke suggested that if the Court had proceeded to the merits of the case, the justices would have come down four to two in favor of the Cherokees with Baldwin and Johnson in dissent. Burke, "Cherokee Cases," 516–17. Justice Gabriel Duvall was absent and did not vote.

23. *Cherokee Nation v. Georgia*, 15; Burke, "Cherokee Cases," 512–14. John Hurley wrote, "This case, in the unrelenting belligerence of the state of Georgia, the repeated attempts of the Cherokee Nation to obtain from the instituted authorities the protection of their rights, solemnly enshrined in formal treaties, and the ultimate rejection of their suit by the Supreme Court for lack of jurisdiction, presents all the ingredients of an authentic tragedy. Marshall C. J. was alive to this fact." Hurley, "Aboriginal Rights," 424.

24. *Cherokee Nation v. Georgia*, 15–16, 32–33, 39, 53. Baldwin defended Andrew Jackson in Congress when the latter invaded Florida and executed two British officers in the First Seminole War. Jackson repaid Baldwin for his support by appointing him to the Court. "Henry Baldwin," in Cushman, ed., *Supreme Court Justices*,

106–11; "Henry Baldwin," in Friedman and Israel, eds., *Justices of the United States Supreme Court,* 313–23.

25. *Cherokee Nation v. Georgia,* 44.

26. *Cherokee Nation v. Georgia,* 35, 39–40; JCC, vol. 32: 340–41.

27. *Cherokee Nation v. Georgia,* 16.

28. Ibid., 16, 32–33, 47–48.

29. Peters, *Case of the Cherokee Nation,* 135–39; *Cherokee Nation v. Georgia,* 59–63, 66.

30. Ibid., 18–20, 63–65.

31. Thompson agreed that some tribes had surrendered their sovereignty. Included were those "who have become mixed with the general population of the country; their national character extinguished, and their usages and customs in a great measure abandoned; self-government surrendered; and who have voluntarily, or by the force of circumstances which have surrounded them, gradually become subject to the laws of the states within which they are situated." *Cherokee Nation v. Georgia,* 52–56, 59–60.

32. Ibid., 67; *Jackson v. Goodell,* 713–14; "Smith Thompson," in Cushman, *Supreme Court Justices,* 91–92, 95; Roper, "Justice Smith Thompson," 119–39. Thompson's opinion in *Cherokee Nation* is generally regarded by legal scholars as his greatest work. Gerald T. Dunne, for example, called it "a felicitous example of . . . humanitarian leavening." "Smith Thompson," in *Justices of the United States Supreme Court,* Friedman and Israel, eds., 284–85.

33. *Cherokee Nation v. Georgia,* 16–18.

34. *Cherokee Nation v. Georgia,* 17; Norgren, *Cherokee Cases,* 103. Barsh and Henderson also succinctly described Marshall's purpose behind the use of the phrase "domestic, dependent nations": "As foreign nations, tribes' external sovereignty could not be restricted except by their consent; as domestic subdivisions they could not be saved from the police power of the states unless they were states of the Union themselves. Marshall tried to suggest the best of both principles: that tribes are so far foreign as to be immune from the internal sovereignty of the states, but so far domestic as to be limited by the internal sovereignty of the United States." Barsh and Henderson, *The Road,* 54.

35. *Cherokee Nation v. Georgia,* 17–18; Hurley, "Aboriginal Rights," 426–29; Cohen, *Handbook of Federal Indian Law,* 220–28.

36. *Cherokee Nation v. Georgia,* 39–40, 44–50.

37. Ibid., 20–24.

38. Ibid., 21–30. John Ross had contacted Johnson about how he would react to a Cherokee challenge to the Georgia extension laws, now arguably a violation of judicial ethics. (Wirt had also contacted Marshall *ex parte* about the case.) Judging from his opinion, if the South Carolina justice gave Ross an answer, it was not an encouraging one. Burke, "Cherokee Cases," 512.

39. *Cherokee Nation v. Georgia,* 25–30.

40. Ibid., 17, 53–59, 67–68.

41. Johnson was ill during the hearing of *Worcester v. Georgia.* Based on his

comments in *Cherokee Nation*, we can only surmise that he would have dissented to Marshall's holding in that case and upheld Georgia's right to extend state jurisdiction over the Cherokees. Burke, "Cherokee Cases," 524.

42. Belz, "South and the American Constitutional Tradition," 23–28; "The South and the American Constitution," in Hall and Ely Jr., eds., *Uncertain Tradition*, 6; Freehling, *Prelude to Civil War*, 113–15.

43. *Elkison v. Deliesseline*; Finkelman, "States' Rights," 131–32; Kelly, Harbison, and Belz, *American Constitution*, vol. 1: 250; Herbert A. Johnson, "Constitutional Thought of William Johnson," 134–39.

44. Loth, *Chief Justice*, 320; O'Neall, *Biographical Sketches*, 78; Morgan, *Justice William Johnson*, 268 n. 39.

45. Peters, *Case of the Cherokee Nation*, 122; *Cherokee Nation v. Georgia*, 58–59.

46. For example, see the list of cases that Cherokees filed in the North Carolina state courts in Bridgers's, "Legal Digest of North Carolina Cherokees," 21–22.

47. Burke, "Cherokee Cases," 514; Berutti, "Cherokee Cases," 302; Norgren, *Cherokee Cases*, 102; Swindler, "Politics as Law," 13; Washburn, *Red Man's Land*, 68.

48. Burke, "Cherokee Cases," 518 n. 110.

49. *Cherokee Nation v. Georgia*, 20; Norgren, *Cherokee Cases*, 102–5. Story commented on the pressure that faced Marshall and called the proposed judiciary act an attempt by Congress to "tread down the power on which [the Court's] very existence depends." Justice Thompson warned that the effort to limit federal judicial authority could transform the federal government "into the national imbecility of the old confederation." William F. Swindler has suggested that Marshall's poor health at the time may have prevented him from putting up a fight against Jackson and the states. Joseph Story to George Ticknor, January 22, 1831, Story, *Life and Letters of Joseph Story*, vol. 2: 45, 48; John Quincy Adams, 29 and 30 January 1831, Adams, *Memoirs of John Quincy Adams*, vol. 8: 303; Swindler, "Politics as Law," 11–13; Burke, "Cherokee Cases," 510–16.

50. *Cherokee Phoenix*, 9 April 1831.

51. Gilmer, *Settlers of Upper Georgia*, 294–96.

52. John Ross, Public Letter "To the Cherokees," 14 April 1831; Ross to Thomas W. Harris, 27 April 1831; both in RP, vol. 1: 215–19; McLoughlin, *Cherokee Renascence*, 439.

53. *Cherokee Phoenix*, 9 and 16 April 1831.

CHAPTER SIX. THE SOUTHERN RESPONSE TO MARSHALL

1. Southerland and Brown, *Federal Road through Georgia*; Abernethy, *Formative Period in Alabama*, 164; Merrell, "Declarations of Independence," 200; Michael D. Green, *Politics of Indian Removal*, 26.

2. Michael D. Green, *Politics of Indian Removal*, 126–46; *Alabama Journal*, 12 June 1829.

3. *Records of the States of the United States of America, Alabama, B. I. 1823–1833,* 223–25. The act also nominally endowed Indians in the state with the same civil liberties as those held by white Alabamians, required white land purchases from Indians to be in writing and for "valuable consideration," and authorized a continuing relationship between the Indian nations and the federal government. Without any record of the debate preceding the legislation, I can only assume that this provision was added to mollify specific opponents of the extension act.

4. Tuskinihahohaw to Eaton, 21 February 1831; Tuckabatchee Hadjo and Octeachee Emathla to Eaton, 1, 18, and 20 February 1831; Creek headmen to Eaton, 8 April 1831; all in LR: CRA, reel 222. The letter of February 1 included a list of property that whites had allegedly stolen from Creeks. The document included over 140 instances of livestock theft. The names of Fushatchee Yoholo and James Caldwell do not appear on this list.

5. Creek headmen to Eaton, 12 May 1831, LR: CRA, reel 222; Trial Record, January 1832, Minute Book J, Alabama Supreme Court Records, 236–37; James Caldwell, Petition for Pardon, undated, Gayle Papers. Based on the little evidence that remains, it is impossible to determine the motive for the shooting. We also know very little about Caldwell. He is found in Conecuh County, to the south of Shelby, in the Census of 1820. By the time of the 1830 count, he and his family had moved into Shelby County. In December 1831, the Creeks hired a white surveyor to document the number of white settlers in the Creek Nation. The list contains over seventy-five names, but the Caldwell family is not among them. The surveyor, however, noted that his assistant from near Shelby County had not completed his investigation in time for the report. Therefore, it is possible that Caldwell was one of the squatters the Creeks complained of in their letters to the federal government. "List of White Intruders Living in Creek Nation," 15 December 1831, Office of Indian Affairs, LR: CRA, reel 222.

6. Trial Record, 236–38. Not long after the trial, Shortridge was elected to the bench in Tuscaloosa, where he reportedly served with "firmness, patience, and integrity." Unfortunately, Shortridge's bright future as an Alabama politician was snuffed out by alcoholism. Garrett noted with more than a little sadness, "He was truly social, and the most entertaining of company. Conviviality ripened into habit, and the strong man—the prince of orators—the best of judges—gradually languished, and then his light perished in the ruin." Watrous went on to serve in the Alabama House and Senate for sixteen years. Like many of the lawyers and judges in this case, he was not content in Alabama. He moved on to Texas in 1856. The judge, Crenshaw, was a native of South Carolina, graduated from Columbia College, and moved to Alabama early in his life. Crenshaw was reputed to be a moderate Whig and a popular judge with a nonpartisan temperament. Garrett, *Reminiscences,* 266–67, 384; Deland and Smith, *Northern Alabama,* 233; Owen, *History of Alabama,* vol. 4: 1730.

7. Baldwin, *Flush Times of Alabama and Mississippi,* 58; Trial Record, 236–38; Ayers, *Vengeance and Justice,* 1–33; Prucha, *American Indian Policy,* 188–212; Gosse, *Letters from Alabama,* 250–51; Tocqueville, *Journey to America,* 108.

According to Jack K. Williams, who examined jury tendencies in cases of violence, jury convictions for murder were rare during this period in Alabama. Williams, "Crime and Punishment," 25.

8. Howington, *What Sayeth the Law*, 89–97.

9. Trial Record, 238–39.

10. Ibid., 236, 239.

11. Ibid., 239–40; *Caldwell v. Alabama*, 327–28, 343–44. Caldwell's lawyers continued to contend that their client should have been awarded a new trial because of the misconduct of the jury, but the state supreme court never addressed this issue in its opinion.

12. Arthur Pendleton Bagby presented the state's case on appeal. However, there are no extant appellate briefs or transcripts of the oral arguments. Consequently, it is impossible to determine whether the specific arguments denying the existence of Creek sovereignty were devised by Bagby or the Alabama Supreme Court.

13. Anderson, "Supreme Court of Alabama," 122–23; McMillan, "Alabama Constitution of 1819," 268–69; Owen, *History of Alabama*, vol. 4: 1052, 1488, 1651; Garrett, *Reminiscences*, 91.

14. At a public dinner in April 1831, several speakers made toasts honoring Georgia governor Gilmer and United States senator George Troup for their attacks on the Supreme Court. *Alabama Journal*, 15 and 22 April 1831; *Cherokee Nation v. Georgia*, 20.

15. The case reporter noted that the issue of Creek sovereignty had "long disturbed the country, and created much diversity of opinion." At the time, the Choctaw, Chickasaw, and Cherokee Nations all claimed portions of Alabama. *Caldwell*, 327–28, 382.

16. *Caldwell*, 329, 341, 344, 418–19. The *Alabama Journal* of May 13, 1831, also criticized "those philanthropists of the North who have been so busy in getting up petitions to Congress." The paper's editor sarcastically urged Indian supporters to spend their time and money providing donations to the Creeks who had already removed to the West. As the case progressed, the Alabama Creeks continued to suffer. On October 13, an assembly of headmen wrote the recently appointed secretary of war, Lewis Cass, that "base white people [are] daily practicing fraud upon our people." Again they complained that whites were stealing their stock and confiscating their land and houses. Creek headmen to Lewis Cass, 13 October 1831, LR: CRA, reel 222.

17. *Caldwell*, 346. Each justice issued his own opinion. Chief Judge Lipscomb wrote fifteen pages, Saffold thirty-eight, and Taylor, the most vitriolic and prolific of the three, sixty-four. Many of their arguments, however, were repeated in each opinion, and there was little disagreement among them on the points of law.

18. Ibid., 334, 403, 407, 416, 424–25, 435.

19. Ibid., 333–34, 367, 399–402, 441–43.

20. Ibid., 333–35, 407–8.

21. Ibid., 434, 441–43.

22. Ibid., 332–33, 344–45.

23. This line of thinking putatively justified the expansion of American sovereignty over the undefeated tribes in the West. With the discovery of the North American continent came, Taylor contended, the conquest of all Indians on the landmass. Even those who had ceded land by treaty had been conquered in law. For if any Indian nation had refused peaceful land negotiations, it would have been conquered in fact. Ibid., 332–33, 344–45, 393, 396, 408, 413–16.

24. Ibid., 335–36, 339, 384–87, 411–13.

25. Ibid., 358, 388–95, 397, 403–6, 413.

26. Ibid., 348, 402–3, 426.

27. Ibid., 338, 342–43, 348, 409–10. Taylor quoted John Marshall's opinion in *Johnson v. McIntosh,* saying that the Indians, even if they had been independent nations in the past, had fallen into a state of "subjection," "perpetual protection," and "pupilage."

28. Ibid., 333–37, 341, 373–74.

29. Ibid., 431–33.

30. IA: LT, vol. 2: 265–66; *Caldwell,* 353–54, 361–64.

31. *Caldwell,* 330–31, 359–61, 369–71, 375–77. Another example of the court's loose construction, to put it generously, was its handling of the Tommy Jemmy precedent. The Alabama judges cited the New York lower court opinion, which allowed New York to expand its jurisdiction over the Iroquois, as if it were the final ruling of law on the case. Kent's court had overturned this decision on appeal. The Alabama judges ignored this relevant fact. *Jackson v. Goodell,* 189–94; *Goodell v. Jackson,* 713–17.

32. *Caldwell,* 331, 372.

33. Ibid., 429–30.

34. *Caldwell,* 331, 340–42, 351–53, 359–61, 370, 409–10.

35. "Northwest Ordinance," in Commager, *Documents of American History,* 128–32; *Caldwell,* 441–42.

36. Taylor simply ignored Marshall's opinion and referred to Justice Baldwin's dissent in the case as if it were the official holding of a majority. He quoted Baldwin's statement that treating Indian nations as independent sovereign polities would "reverse every principle on which our government has acted for forty-five years." *Cherokee Nation v. Georgia,* 16, 49; *Caldwell,* 329, 355, 371–73, 380–81, 441–42.

37. *Caldwell,* 359, 435.

38. Taylor's argument accepted a permanent Indian territory in North America and a continuation of the American civilization policy. The nation, he said, should confine itself to "just bounds." He wrote, "Leave an ample territory to these nomadic tribes to subsist upon by becoming cultivators of the soil, and . . . furnish them with necessary supplies by their usual pursuits, until they can effect the necessary change in their mode of life." Saffold, in contrast, suggested that the Alabama tribes could be incorporated into the state. However, Indians would not obtain equal citizenship. Full citizenship would only be granted "progressively." *Caldwell,* 364–65, 375, 386, 425, 435.

39. James Caldwell, Petition for Pardon, Gayle Papers.

40. Garrett, *Reminiscences*, 458–59. If later actions mean anything, John Gayle was disposed to side with white settlers squatting on Creek lands. In response to several Creek complaints of settler atrocities after the Treaty of Cusseta, Andrew Jackson threatened to send in federal troops to remove white troublemakers from the nation. In the treaty, the federal government had agreed to remove white intruders until the nation was surveyed for allotment. Gayle, the legislature, and the settlers did not think that Jackson would go to the trouble of removing the squatters. In 1833, Jackson ordered the secretary of war, Lewis Cass, to send in a large federal force to quell the violence that erupted when a detachment of troops under a federal marshall killed a settler while trying to remove him from Creek lands in Russell County. Gayle made the killing a states' rights issue, abruptly turned against Jackson, and used the press to try to get Jackson's intruder policy reversed. After the dispute was peacefully resolved, Gayle tried to push a resolution through the legislature denouncing the attempted removal of the white settlers and praising his defiance of Jackson. Gayle's opponents, seeing this as unnecessarily provocative toward the federal government, shot down the motion. Owsley Jr., "Francis Scott Key's Mission," 181–92.

41. Letter from Creek delegation to Lewis Cass, Secretary of War, 19 March 1832, LR: CRA, reel 223.

42. Letter from Creek delegation to Lewis Cass, Secretary of War, 19 March 1832, LR: CRA, reel 223. For a study of this period in the history of Alabama and the Creeks, see Young, *Redskins, Ruffleshirts, and Rednecks*, 73–98; Michael D. Green, *Politics of Indian Removal*, 174–86.

CHAPTER SEVEN. SOVEREIGN NATIONS

1. Hutchins, "Trial of Reverend Samuel A. Worcester," 356–58; Burke, "Cherokee Cases," 519; Perdue, *Cherokee Editor*, 15, 62 n. 36. For a biography of Worcester, see Bass, *Cherokee Messenger*. For a study of the missionaries in the Cherokee Nation, see McLoughlin, *Cherokees and Missionaries*.

2. *Acts of the General Assembly*, 11 and 20 December 1830; *Cherokee Phoenix*, 1 January 1831; Gilmer, *Settlers of Upper Georgia*, 301; Young, "Exercise of Sovereignty," 52; McLoughlin, *Cherokee Renascence*, 440–42; Lumpkin to the House of Representatives, 2 December 1831, in Lumpkin, *Removal of the Cherokee Indians*, 95–102.

3. *Cherokee Phoenix*, 30 [sic] February 1831.

4. "Resolution and Statement of the Missionaries," *Missionary Herald* 27 (March 1831): 80–84; McLoughlin, *Cherokees and Missionaries*, 260; McLoughlin, *Cherokee Renascence*, 442–43.

5. McLoughlin, *Cherokees and Missionaries*, 257–60.

6. The missionaries did not raise the defense of federal authority; Clayton brought it up on his own. Underwood and Harris actually hoped for a conviction so that they could challenge the constitutionality of the statute. *Cherokee Phoenix*, 19 and 26 March 1831; *Boston Courier*, 3 January 1832, reprinted in *Journal of Cherokee Studies* 4 (1979): 89–90; Burke, "Cherokee Cases," 519–20; Swindler, "Politics as

Law," 15; Hutchins, "Trial of Reverend Samuel A. Worcester," 365–66; Beveridge, *Life of John Marshall*, vol. 4: 547; McLoughlin, *Cherokees and Missionaries*, 260; Reed, "Ross-Watie Conflict," 30.

7. George R. Gilmer to John H. Eaton, 20 April 1831; Gilmer to William T. Barry, 19 April 1831; Gilmer to Col. John W. A. Sanford, 14 May 1831 and 17 June 1831; Gilmer to John Thompson, 16 May 1831; Gilmer to Samuel Worcester, 16 May 1831; and Gilmer to Rev. John Howard, 1 September 1831; all in Gilmer, *Settlers of Upper Georgia*, 302–8, 313–14, 322–23.

8. *Missionary Herald* 27 (May 1831): 166. Worcester, Butler, and the missionaries were not the only victims of the new law. White women were not prohibited from residing in the Cherokee Nation under the Georgia statute. Consequently, the departing missionaries left their wives behind to conduct the affairs of their schools and churches. Unfortunately, as William G. McLoughlin has pointed out, these women have not received the scholarly attention or credit due them for their work during the Removal Crisis. McLoughlin, *Cherokees and Missionaries*, 260 n. 40.

9. Samuel A. Worcester to the editor, "Jail at Camp Gilmer," 11 July 1831, *New York Spectator*, 23 August 1831, reprinted in *Journal of Cherokee Studies* 4 (1979): 83–84; Samuel A. Worcester, J. J. Trott, Elizur Butler, and Samuel Mayes to Col. Ch. C. Nelson, and C. H. Nelson in response, 15 July 1831, reprinted in *Journal of Cherokee Studies* 4 (1979): 85–86; *Niles' Register*, 8 and 29 October 1831, vol. 41: 102, 174–76; *Cherokee Phoenix*, 9 and 16 July 1831; John Ross, "Annual Message," 24 October 1831, RP, vol. 1: 224–31. Governor Gilmer later investigated the charges of brutality that had been leveled against the guard. In response, C. H. Nelson, commander of the guard, offered his resignation. Gilmer refused to accept it and told Nelson that he was probably doing the best he could in a difficult and thankless task. Gilmer to Col. John W. A. Sanford, 3 September 1831, and Gilmer to Col. Charles H. Nelson, 5 September 1831, in Gilmer, *Settlers of Upper Georgia*, 324–26.

10. *Missionary Herald* 27 (October 1831): 333; Inferior Court Minutes, Gwinnett County, County Collection, 23 July 1831, drawer 165, reel 130, p. 304.

11. *Missionary Herald* 27 (November 1831): 363; *Niles' Register*, 8 and 29 October 1831, vol. 41: 102, 174–76; *Cherokee Phoenix*, 1 October 1831; George R. Gilmer to Maj. Philip Cook, Keeper of the Penitentiary, 22 September 1831; Gilmer to Inspectors of the Penitentiary, 22 September 1831; and Gilmer to Col. John W. A. Sanford, 23 September 1831; all in Gilmer, *Settlers of Upper Georgia*, 329–30; McLoughlin, *Cherokees and Missionaries*, 262.

12. "Imprisonment of the Missionaries to the Cherokees," *Vermont Telegraph*, 13 December 1831, reprinted in *Journal of Cherokee Studies* 4 (1979): 86; *Niles' Register*, 24 December 1831, vol. 41: 307–12.

13. *Missionary Herald* 27 (November and December 1831): 363, 395–96; *Boston Courier*, 3 January 1832, reprinted in *Journal of Cherokee Studies* 4 (1979): 86–91.

14. Worcester, 515; *Georgia Journal*, 28 November 1831; *Niles' Register*, 24 and 31 December 1831, vol. 41: 313, 335–36; Wilson Lumpkin to the Senate and House of Representatives, 25 November 1831, in Lumpkin, *Removal of the Cherokee Indians*, vol. 1: 93–94; Wilson Lumpkin to the Legislature, 30 November 1832, State of Georgia Executive Minute Books, file 50, reel 50, p. 81; David Williams,

"Cherokee Gold Lottery," 41–58. Judge Clayton again refused to certify the record of the missionaries' case to the Supreme Court, forcing, it must be assumed, Wirt and Sergeant to proffer their own documents from the trial decision. *Worcester v. Georgia.*

15. Ronald A. Berutti said that Ross's hiring of Wirt in *Cherokee Nation* "can best be described as suicidal to their case." He contended that Wirt's retention gave Jackson incentive to ignore the Court's decision in *Worcester:* "Surely Jackson was not going to execute in Wirt's favor any Supreme Court mandate which could prove harmful to Jackson's administration." Berutti, "Cherokee Cases," 300–303. These comments are wrong minded. Perhaps no other lawyer in the country could have presented an argument as convincing and comprehensive as could Wirt. Moreover, Wirt persuaded the Supreme Court to the Cherokee side in *Worcester.* There is also no evidence that Jackson would have acted any differently in regard to the Cherokees if Wirt had not been their lawyer. And as Joseph C. Burke has shown, the *Worcester* situation never got to the point where Jackson was forced to defy the Court's ruling.

16. *Cohens v. Virginia;* Thurman Wilkins, *Cherokee Tragedy,* 227–28.

17. *Worcester,* 534–35, 542.

18. *New York Daily Advertiser,* 27 February 1832; Joseph Story to Mrs. Joseph Story, 26 February 1831, Story, *Life and Letters of Joseph Story,* vol. 2: 84; Burke, "William Wirt," 261; Burke, "Cherokee Cases," 521–22.

19. *Worcester,* 562; Jean Edward Smith, *John Marshall,* 512–14, 517–18. The *Richmond Enquirer* reported that Baldwin wrote a long dissent to the majority's decision. In the official report of the case, Richard Peters, the Court's reporter, noted that Baldwin never delivered the opinion to him. *Richmond Enquirer,* 30 March 1832. *Niles' Register* reported later that it had a copy of the opinion but that "it is a long article, and presented at an inconvenient season." Apparently, it was never published by the weekly. *Niles Register,* 31 March 1832, vol. 42: 78.

20. Joseph C. Burke suggests that Marshall's opinion was a reply to Baldwin's argument in *Cherokee Nation.* The chief justice, Burke holds, may have been "disturbed" by Baldwin's heavy-handed interpretation of the chief justice's opinion in *Johnson v. McIntosh,* by the Jacksonian press's belief that the decision had vindicated Jackson's Indian policy, and by the "rumors that the decision had so discouraged the Cherokees that they were preparing to treat with Jackson." Without Baldwin's brazen states' rights interpretation, Burke maintains, Marshall could not have produced the opinion that he did in *Worcester.* Burke, "Cherokee Cases," 522. Dozens of articles and monographs have discussed the legal meaning of the *Worcester* case in varying degrees of detail, including Barsh and Henderson, *The Road,* 56–61; Berman, "Aboriginal Rights," 662–67; Berutti, "Cherokee Cases," 303–6; Beveridge, *Life of John Marshall,* vol. 4: 547–52; Burke, "Cherokee Cases," 519–31; Deloria Jr. and Lytle, *Nations Within,* 16–17; Frickey, "Marshalling Past and Present," 393–440; Hurley, "Aboriginal Rights," 429–34; Norgren, *Cherokee Cases,* 117–30; Swindler, "Politics as Law," 14–17; Walters, "Review Essay," 127–44; Washburn, *Red Man's Land,* 68–69; and Wilkinson, *American Indians, Time, and the Law,* 26, 30–31, 33–37, 55–56, 59–62, 68, 95–96 passim.

21. *Worcester,* 536.

22. Ibid., 541, 565–69.

23. Ibid., 542–43, 559.

24. Ibid., 542–45.

25. Ibid., 544–46. Justice McLean did not join Marshall's opinion, but he agreed in substance with most of what Marshall decided on the merits. His opinion also expanded on the chief justice's recognition of the Court's jurisdiction.

26. Ibid., 546–49.

27. Ibid., 549–50.

28. Ibid., 552–54, 560–61; Vattel, *Law of Nations,* 2–3.

29. *Worcester,* 556–60.

30. Ibid., 560, 584–86, 590–91, 595. In addition, in 1776, one of Georgia's delegates to the Continental Congress, George Walton, urged the confederation to take centralized authority over Indian affairs. Georgia, he said, did not have the funds to make presents to the Indians, "which will be necessary to keep them at peace." JCC, vol. 6: 1078.

31. *Worcester,* 557–59, 573.

32. Barsh and Henderson called *Worcester* a triumph of "treaty federalism" over "constitutional federalism." Congress, they argued, was limited, under Marshall's interpretation of the Commerce Clause, to regulate "commerce" in no greater degree than it might a foreign nation. "All redefinition of the tribes' political relationship to the United States must follow the same course," they wrote, that is, by "mutual agreement." Barsh and Henderson and William Walters have been extremely critical of Felix Cohen's interpretation of *Worcester.* "Where, in all of this, is the theory of 'conquest' so often attributed to Marshall by modern commentators, and popularized by Felix Cohen in his *Handbook of Federal Indian Law?*" Barsh and Henderson asked. In *Worcester,* Marshall revealed the discovery and conquest doctrines to be irrational fictions that gave legal justification to the seizure of Indian lands. For Cohen or any future court to have relied on theories of discovery and conquest to circumscribe the sovereignty of a tribal nation, as dozens of subsequent decisions have, Barsh and Henderson suggested, was a misreading of the Cherokee cases. *The Road,* 59–60, particularly n. 36.

33. Although it is rather clear from Marshall's words that this was the interpretation that he intended, all three of the theories have been used in cases at one time or another to explain the unique and complex relationship between the Indian nations and the United States. Walters, "Preemption, Tribal Sovereignty, and *Worcester,*" 132–36. Walters's excellent explanation of the impact of *Worcester* on federal Indian law complains that the editors of the most recent edition of Cohen's *Handbook of Federal Indian Law* use the theories interchangeably, a fact that confuses and distracts judges and lawyers from the true intent of Marshall's ruling. See also Frickey, "Marshalling Past and Present," 408–11.

34. *Worcester,* 569–72.

35. Ibid., 569–72, 580–81, 592–93.

36. Ibid., 571–72, 576–79. Section 19 of the Trade and Intercourse Acts of 1802 provided that the federal government did not have authority to regulate "trade or

intercourse with Indians living on lands surrounded by settlements of the citizens of
the United States, and being within the ordinary jurisdiction of any of the individual
states." Georgia argued that this provision allowed the state the authority to regulate
commerce and, by extrapolation, the right to extend its civil and criminal jurisdiction
over the Indian nations within its borders. McLean rejected this interpretation of
Section 19. This article applied to "those fragments of tribes which are found in
several of the states," not the expansive and populous Cherokee Nation. At the time
of the passage of the act, the Cherokees were not "surrounded by settlements of the
citizens of the United States," nor were they "within the ordinary jurisdiction" of the
state. In that same section, he added, Congress had provided for the upkeep of a road
that ran through the nation, had reserved the right of navigation on the Tennessee
River, and had negotiated for the right to travel on the road from Knoxville to Price's
Settlement, "provided the Indians should not object." These reservations all applied
to the Cherokee Nation, McLean said, and they signified Congress's recognition that
the lands being discussed were not in Georgia or Tennessee, but within the borders
of the Cherokee Nation. Ibid., 588–89.

37. Ibid., 582–83.

38. Ibid., 589–90.

39. Ibid., 595.

40. Ibid., 579–80, 593–94; John Ross to William Wirt, 8 June 1832, RP, vol. 1:
244–45.

41. *Worcester*, 562.

42. Barsh and Henderson, *The Road*, 60–61; Frickey, "Marshalling Past and
Present," 405 n. 107. William F. Swindler wrote that Marshall's opinion "was essen-
tially a retraction of much that had been central to the *Cherokee Nation* opinion."
"Politics as Law," 15.

43. *Cherokee Phoenix*, 12 May 1832; John Ross to the Cherokee Delegates, 30
March 1832, RP, vol. 1: 241; Elias Boudinot to Stand Watie, 7 March 1832, quoted
in Luebke, "Elias Boudinot, Cherokee Editor," 270–71.

44. For Georgia's official position on the missionaries' case, see "Report of the
Committee on the State of the Republic," 15 December 1831, in Gilmer, *Settlers of
Upper Georgia*, 335–43; Lumpkin, "Annual Message," 6 November 1832, *Removal
of the Cherokee Indians*, 103–7.

45. *Macon (Ga.) Advertiser*, 13 March 1832; George M. Troup, "The Sovereignty
of the States: An Open Letter to the Georgia Journal," 5 March 1832, in *Niles'
Register*, 31 March 1832, vol. 42: 78; Gilmer, *Settlers of Upper Georgia*, 313. Gilmer
apparently never felt remorse for his role in the removal of the Cherokees. In his
memoirs he wrote, "All now admit that the public men of Georgia showed their
wisdom in what they did, and their slanderers their folly. . . . It is a source of pride
and pleasure to those who were responsible for the conduct of Georgia towards the
Cherokees, to know that what they did has tended to the good both of the Indians
and Georgians." Gilmer wrote that after he left office he was traveling through North
Carolina. He stopped to eat dinner at a roadhouse between Charlotte and Salisbury.
When the landlord discovered that Gilmer was from Georgia, he "abused very freely

the tyranny of the Governor of Georgia for his conduct in putting ministers of the gospel into the penitentiary for preaching." Gilmer attempted to explain why the governor had acted as he did, but the landlord refused to accept his explanation for the government's prosecution of the missionaries. "The old man . . . would not believe me until I told him that I was the person he had been abusing, and knew all about the matter." Gilmer reported, "His face would have made a good picture just then, for the confounded." Gilmer added, "It was very painful to know that I was an object of dislike to great numbers of my fellow-beings." In trying to explain in his memoirs his actions during the Removal Crisis, Gilmer wrote that John Ross had said the Cherokees "had as much confidence in me as any other public man." He also listed the acts of kindness he had made on behalf of the Cherokees. For example, he wrote that he helped return a kidnapped Cherokee infant to its mother. These acts, he argued, showed that he had always had the Cherokees' best interests in mind. Gilmer, *Settlers of Upper Georgia*, 330, 332–33.

46. *Alabama Journal*, 17 March 1832; Lumpkin, "Annual Message," in *Removal of the Cherokee Indians*, 1832, 124–25.

47. Joseph Story to Mrs. Joseph Story, 4 March 1832; Story to George Ticknor, 8 March 1832; both in Story, *Life and Letters of Joseph Story*, vol. 2: 83–84. Story was occasionally quite cynical about the Court's treatment of nonwhite interests. Finkelman, "Story Telling on the Supreme Court," 247–94.

48. *Cherokee Phoenix*, 7 and 29 July 1832; John Ross to Richard Taylor, et al., 28 April 1832; Elias Boudinot to John Ross, 1 August 1832; both in RP, vol. 1: 242–43, 247–48; Perdue, *Cherokee Editor*, 25–26; Thurman Wilkins, *Cherokee Tragedy*, 228–31.

49. Greeley, *American Conflict*, vol. 1: 106; Norgren, *Cherokee Cases*, 123–24; Miles, "After John Marshall's Decision," 519–44.

50. Burke, "Cherokee Cases," 524–27; Satz, *American Indian Policy*, 48–50; Andrew Jackson to John Coffee, 7 April 1832, in *Correspondence of Andrew Jackson*, vol. 4: 430. Wirt proposed a series of amendments to the Judiciary Act that would have required Jackson to enforce the decision of the Court. For a discussion of the historiography of Jackson's general attitude toward Indians, see Satz, "Rhetoric versus Reality," 29–54. For competing interpretations, see, among many others, Prucha, "Andrew Jackson's Indian Policy," 527–39; Remini, *Legacy of Andrew Jackson*, 45–82. Ironically, both Jackson's opponents and friends condemned the president's reluctance to act in the weeks after the Court's decision. George Gilmer wrote, "Even Gen. Jackson, with his thorough knowledge of the subject and bold, fearless spirit, had to be stirred up, and coaxed into the humor to do any thing worth doing." The president, he complained, was more interested in removing the Cherokees from Tennessee than he was in satisfying the promises made to Georgia in the federal compact thirty years before. Gilmer, *Settlers of Upper Georgia*, 319.

51. Burke, "Cherokee Cases," 524–26; Richardson, *Messages and Papers of the Presidents*, vol. 3: 576; Act of 2 March 1833, *Statutes at Large*, vol. 4: 632–34; Miles, "After John Marshall's Decision," 526–27.

52. Miles, "After John Marshall's Decision," 535–36; McLoughlin, *Cherokees*

and Missionaries, 297–98; Burke, "Cherokee Cases," 530; *Acts of the General Assembly,* 12 December 1832, 107.

53. *Missionary Herald* 29 (March 1833): 112; Samuel A. Worcester and Elizur Butler to Wilson Lumpkin, 8 January 1833, in Kilpatrick and Kilpatrick, *New Echota Letters,* 117–18; Lumpkin to Charles C. Mills, Principal Keeper of the Penitentiary, 14 January 1833, State of Georgia Governor's Executive Minute Books, vol. 50: 118.

54. McLoughlin, *Cherokees and Missionaries,* 298–99; McLoughlin, *Cherokee Renascence,* 445–47; Norgren, *Cherokee Cases,* 128–29. William G. McLoughlin, a historian of the Cherokees, was especially critical of the missionaries' surrender: "There seemed to be in this complex reasoning a greater emphasis upon prudence and political expediency (not to mention defeatism) than had been evident in their former pronouncements; spiritual righteousness and national honor had somehow been displaced by practical necessity, national security, and 'changing circumstances.' " McLoughlin, *Cherokees and Missionaries,* 298–99.

55. *Niles' Register,* 2 February 1833, vol. 43: 382–83; Miles, "After John Marshall's Decision," 533–44; Berutti, "Cherokee Cases," 306–7.

CHAPTER EIGHT. THE LAW OF THE LAND

In the Cherokee census of 1835, and in almost every other mention of his name in the court records, the defendant James Foreman's last name is spelled with an "e." In the published report of the decision, however, the court reporter spelled the defendant's name "Forman." In this chapter I use "Foreman" except when referring to Tennessee's appellate decision.

1. *Niles' Register,* 27 October 1832, vol. 43: 131; Young, "Exercise of Sovereignty," 53–55; Thurman Wilkins, *Cherokee Tragedy,* 245, 249–52.

2. John Ross to "My Friends," 9 August 1833, John Ross Folder, Georgia Department of History and Archives; Wilson Lumpkin to Benjamin F. Curry, 13 December 1834, in Georgia Executive Letter Books; McLoughlin, *Cherokee Renascence,* 449–51; Perdue, "Conflict Within," 486–89; Thurman Wilkins, *Cherokee Tragedy,* 236–43. Wilkins's history of the crisis is the best account of the Ridge party's actions and is sympathetic to their motives. He concluded that the "accusations of bribery lodged by the Ross faction and their sympathizers [against the Ridges and Boudinot] were based on groundless suspicion." It was also unlikely, he said, that Ross did anything financially untoward during the Removal Crisis. Wilkins, *Cherokee Tragedy,* 251 note *. However, the Ridges and Boudinot did obtain benefits from Georgia for their position. When they expressed their support for removal, Georgia governor Wilson Lumpkin exempted their property from the state's land lottery. Theda Perdue has argued that much of the animosity that developed between the Ridges and Ross was based on class jealousy. The Ridges, she said, represented an emerging middle class of affluent slave-holding planters who envied the political power of Ross and became frustrated by their inability to crack the highest echelon of Cherokee society. Perdue, *Cherokee Editor,* 26–27; Perdue, *Slavery and the Evolution of Cherokee Society,* 66–67.

3. Elias Boudinot, "To the Editor of the *Cherokee Phoenix*," in Perdue, *Cherokee Editor,* 170–74; Thurman Wilkins, *Cherokee Tragedy,* 256–57; Perdue, *Cherokee Editor,* 25–26.

4. King and Evans, "Death of John Walker, Jr.," 4. The Meigs family disapproved of the wedding, and Walker and Emily ran away to Bristol, Virginia, to get married. Her father and brother gave chase in an effort to prevent their intentions, but the couple was married before they could catch them. Chandler, *Associate Justice John Catron,* 23 n. 15.

5. *Cherokee Phoenix,* 12 May 1832; 23rd Congress, 1st sess., Sen. Doc. 512, Serial 248, 412–16; Will of John Walker Jr., John Walker Jr. file; King and Evans, "Death of John Walker," 6–7.

6. John Ross, et al. to Lewis Cass, 26 February 1833; John Ross to Benjamin F. Currey, 23 October 1834; and John Ross to the General Council, 28 October 1834; all in RP, vol. 1: 265, 310–11; Cong. Serial 268, Sen. Doc. 71, 1–2; Serial 292, Sen. Doc. 286, 133–40; King and Evans, "Death of John Walker," 7–8.

7. John Ross to William H. Underwood, 12 August 1834, RP, vol. 1: 300; Benjamin F. Currey to Lewis Cass, 15 September 1834, LR: CAE, group 75, reel 76, pp. 135–45; Ehle, *Trail of Tears,* 268–69; Thurman Wilkins, *Cherokee Tragedy,* 242. I was unable to determine the kinship relationship between Tom and James Foreman, although they both lived near the Amohee mission on the Ocoee River.

8. Currey to Cass, 15 September 1834.

9. Ibid., 15 September 1834; Thurman Wilkins, *Cherokee Tragedy,* 263; King and Evans, "Death of John Walker," 10. Hicks's petition also called for David Vann, an affluent member of the Treaty Party, to resign.

10. Currey to Cass, 15 September 1834; Grand Jury Indictment, 31 October and 1 November 1834, *State v. Forman,* Tennessee Supreme Court Records, file box 245; Thurman Wilkins, *Cherokee Tragedy,* 263; Chandler, *Associate Justice John Catron,* 23 n. 15; Byrum, *McMinn County,* 16.

11. Andrew Jackson to Benjamin F. Currey, 3 September 1834, *Correspondence of Andrew Jackson,* vol. 5: 288; King and Evans, "Death of John Walker," 13.

12. John Ross to John Ridge, 12 September 1834, RP, vol. 1: 302–3.

13. John Ross to Andrew Jackson, 15 September 1834; "Annual Message to the General Council," 11 October 1834; both in RP, vol. 1: 304–5, 307. Thurman Wilkins, perhaps the scholar most likely to believe Ross guilty of treachery, does not draw any conclusion about Ross's culpability in Walker's killing. Duane H. King and E. Raymond Evans believe that Ross was likely involved: "The fact that John Ross did not disassociate himself with the murderers, but rather raised a defense fund for them, adds some support to Major Walker's contention that Ross was the principal instigator of his son's murder." "Death of John Walker," 14. Ross's admirers have usually portrayed the principal chief as an intelligent and crafty politician. I wonder if we can also attribute Ross with skill at "plausible deniability." In his letters to Ridge and Jackson, he does perhaps protest a bit too much.

14. The 1835 Cherokee census lists Springston as a "half-blood" and Foreman as a "full blood" Cherokee, an example of how dangerous it is to generalize polit-

ical affiliation from racial ancestry. According to one family history, Foreman and Springston were also closely related to their victim. Hoskins, *Cherokee Land Valuations;* Tyner, *Those Who Cried,* 184; Franks, *Stand Watie,* 85–86; King and Evans, "Death of John Walker," 4–5; "Chronology, Dromgoode Family," E. G. Fisher Public Library, McMinn County, Tennessee.

15. Grand jury indictment. King and Evans contend, contrary to the grand jury report, that Foreman fired the lethal shot. "Death of John Walker," 14.

16. The Tennessee legislature had considered passing an extension law in 1829 and 1832. *Journal of the House of Representatives of the State of Tennessee, 1829,* 65; *Journal of the Senate of the State of Tennessee, 1829,* 333; *Journal of the Senate of the State of Tennessee, 1832,* 133. One historian has suggested that Georgia leaders pressured Tennessee officials into passing its extension statute. Corlew, *Tennessee, A Short History,* 152.

17. In 1817 Congress had claimed criminal jurisdiction over Indians who committed crimes against whites in the Indian territory. In *United States v. Bailey,* however, the federal circuit court in Knoxville ruled the act unconstitutional and void on the grounds that the Commerce Clause did not provide Congress with criminal jurisdiction. *Statutes at Large,* vol. 3: 383; U.S. Constitution art. 1, sec. 8; Prucha, *Great Father,* 104; *United States v. Bailey.*

18. *Public Acts Passed at the First Session of the Twentieth General Assembly of the State of Tennessee, 1833,* 10–12; Record of Plea, undated, *State v. Forman,* Tennessee Supreme Court Records, file box 245. The state house committee report on the bill specifically criticized John Marshall's holding in *Worcester v. Georgia. Journal of the House of Representatives of the State of Tennessee, 1833,* 42.

19. Record of Arraignment, Plea, and Demurrer by the Attorney General, undated, *State v. Forman,* Tennessee Supreme Court Records, file box 245.

20. Order, *State v. Forman,* file box 245; *Nashville Republican,* 20 November 1834. Unlike the partisan papers in Georgia, the *Nashville Republican* was generally detached in its reporting of the case. The *Republican,* the editor said, would withhold an opinion on the case until it was completely resolved. Coincidentally, Judge Keith had studied law with John Marshall's brother Charles in Virginia. Byrum, *McMinn County,* 13–14.

21. Circuit Court Minutes, 4–6 November 1834, *State v. Forman,* file box 245; *Nashville Republican,* 20 November 1834.

22. John Ridge to Benjamin Currey, November 1834, LR: CAE, M-234, reel 76, p. 206; John Ross to Andrew Jackson, 28 March 1834; and John Ross to Lewis Cass, 14, 25, and 29 February 1835; all in RP, vol. 1: 282–84, 321–27.

23. John Ross to Lewis Cass, 14, 25, and 27 February 1835; Ross to Friedrich Ludwig Von Roenne, 5 March 1835; Ross to Joaquin Maria del Castillo y Lanzas, 22 March 1835; all in RP, vol. 1: 330, 334–35; Andrew Jackson to the Cherokees, 16 March 1835, LS: CAE, reel 15, p. 169; Thurman Wilkins, *Cherokee Tragedy,* 266–69.

24. *Nashville Republican,* 10 September 1835; *Tennessee v. Forman,* 255–57, 353.

25. The *Nashville Republican* published Yerger's argument on September 10,

1835. It was also included as an appendix to the judges' opinions. Yerger was the official court reporter and must have been impressed with his argument. For a biography of Yerger and a brief discussion of his role in the *Forman* case, see John Green, "Four Attorneys-General and Reporters," 1–4.

26. *Nashville Republican*, 10 September 1835.

27. Ibid.

28. Ibid.

29. Ibid.

30. Ibid.

31. Contrary to the courts in Alabama and Georgia, the Tennessee Supreme Court had a long history of decisions dealing with the sovereignty and rights of Native Americans. Those rulings were wildly divergent. In 1805, the court held that judgment creditors could execute their judgments against land in the Indian country. The jurisdiction of the state, the court said, was coextensive with its territorial limits, even if part of that territory was in the federally denominated Indian country. *Glasgow's Lessee v. Smith and Blackwell*, 144, 164–67. On the other hand, in 1823, the same year that the Supreme Court ruled in *Johnson v. McIntosh*, the Tennessee court held in *Holland v. Pack* that a white man could not bring an action in a Tennessee court against a Cherokee innkeeper in the Cherokee Nation for the theft of his horse. To obtain redress, the court said, the plaintiff would have to file suit in a Cherokee national court. Though the Cherokees retained only a right of usufruct to their land, the court declared, they comprised an independent nation and were governed by their own laws. In *Pound v. Pullen's Lessee* (1832), the court reversed its position in *Glasgow's Lessee* and held that a Tennessee sheriff could not, on behalf of Tennessee creditors, levy executions or sell any real property lying within the Indian country.

32. *Forman*, 369–70.

33. John W. Green, "Jacob Peck," *Lives of the Judges*, 80–86; *Forman*, 353–59, 363–68.

34. *Forman*, 357–62; U.S. Constitution, art. 6.

35. *Forman*, 356–59, 363–66. Peck suggested that the federal government could bring a separate criminal action against Springston and Foreman in its local district court.

36. *Forman*, 345, 347–53. Nathan Green was another Virginia transplant. Most of his acquaintances remembered him as an excellent lawyer but a dour colleague. One of his biographers wrote, "In everything he did, earnestness, sincerity and power were manifest. As an advocate he possessed almost none of the graces, but was rich in substantial qualities. Physically, he lacked symmetry, but he spoke with vehemence, and it need not be said that he reasoned with power. His methods were straightforward and direct. He was wanting in wit, humor and fancy, but never in logic." At least two of his biographers mention that Green lost most of his legal fees in card games during the early years of his career. Over time, though, Green steadied his life and reportedly became one of the best lawyers in Tennessee. After his death, his colleagues memorialized him as "patient, laborious, conscientious, large-

minded, learned in the truest and best learning." Green was, they said, "the pillar of the judicial system, the keystone of its arch." Joshua W. Caldwell, *Bench and Bar of Tennessee*, 139–43; John W. Green, "Nathan Green," *Lives of the Judges*, 92–95.

37. *Forman*, 339–40, 343–45, 350–52.

38. Ibid., 337, 346–53.

39. Ibid., 337, 339–40, 343–53, 364–65.

40. Ibid., 258. In 1824, Catron was elected to the supreme court of Tennessee; in 1830 he became the court's first chief judge. Catron was a native of Pennsylvania. According to one biographer, he "showed a lack of culture and refinement and was gruff, blunt, and plainspoken." A student of Catron's work summarized the contemporary descriptions of the Tennessee chief justice: "He was not an orator, did not have a pleasing voice, or graceful gestures, did not present an especially methodical argument, but was earnest and resourceful, and his tenacity was without limit. In appearance, John Catron was a commanding figure, more than six feet tall, and of large frame. He had penetrating black eyes, ample dark hair, a large nose, and a square jaw." Chandler, *Associate Justice John Catron*, 3. For a discussion of Catron's career on the bench, see Huebner, *Southern Judicial Tradition*, 40–69.

41. *Forman*, 271, 278.

42. *Forman*, 311–12; Huebner, *Southern Judicial Tradition*, 59.

43. *Cornet v. Winston's Lessee*, 143, 150; *Forman*, 287; Huebner, *Southern Judicial Tradition*, 56–58.

44. *Blair v. Pathkiller*, 407, 413.

45. *Blair v. Pathkiller*, 413; *Forman*, 333–34.

46. *Tennessee v. Ross*, 74.

47. Huebner, *Southern Judicial Tradition*, 57–58, 62.

48. Flattering accounts of the judge's life hold that he was with Jackson at the Battle of New Orleans. See, for example, Joshua W. Caldwell, *Bench and Bar of Tennessee*, 86–87. However, Walter Chandler's more reliable biographical sketch confirms that Catron admitted that he fell ill during the Creek campaign from "hardships and privations" and "was brought back to Tennessee in a wagon." Chandler, *Associate Justice John Catron*, 2, 23 n. 6.

49. Jackson to Currey, 3 September 1834. Near the end of his term, Jackson convinced Congress to increase the number of justices on the Supreme Court from seven to nine. His appointment of Catron was one of his last official acts as president. Along with the *Forman* decision, Jackson also rewarded Catron for his support in managing Martin Van Buren's Tennessee campaign. Van Buren faced considerable difficulty in Tennessee, for the Whig candidate was Hugh Lawson White, a well-regarded favorite son. Catron's wife, Matilda Childress, certainly believed that Jackson owed her husband an appointment. In his *Diary of an Old Lawyer*, John Hallum wrote that after Matilda heard that there were openings on the Supreme Court, she immediately ordered her husband to speed from Nashville to Washington. Reportedly, upon their arrival Mr. and Mrs. Catron went directly to the White House, pushed aside the doorman, and rushed into Jackson's bedroom. The president, still in his nightgown, was smoking his morning pipe when Matilda barged in and asked Jackson to appoint

Catron to the Court. Jackson supposedly responded, "By the eternal, he shall have it!" Five days after Jackson's nomination and immediately after taking office, Van Buren reaffirmed Catron's selection.

Catron served twenty-eight years on the high court. Joshua W. Caldwell noted that despite his affiliation with Jackson, most of the Tennessee justice's opinions reflected a "manifest leaning toward Federalist principles in construing the Constitution." Edmund C. Gass, conversely, suggested that Catron "showed a pronounced adherence to the principles of Andrew Jackson." Based on the wild disparity of his opinions, it is difficult to detect exactly where Catron stood ideologically. While on the Court, Catron wrote opinions defending the states' interests in the police power and slavery. Despite these views and the rabidity of his states' rights opinion in *Forman*, Catron vehemently disagreed with Calhoun's theory of nullification and subsequently opposed Tennessee's secession from the Union. In fact, he remained a Unionist throughout the Civil War. When he returned to Nashville after hostilities began, his friends, worried for the justice's safety, persuaded him to leave the city. After a brief exile, he returned after the Union captured Nashville and presided over the federal district court. Gass, "Constitutional Opinions of Justice John Catron," 54–59; Chandler, *Associate Justice John Catron*, 1, 12, 20, 25 n. 29; Joshua W. Caldwell, *Bench and Bar of Tennessee*, 86–92; Huebner, *Southern Judicial Tradition*, 58–60, 63–65.

50. *Forman*, 258–85, 287, 332–35.

51. Ibid., 259–61, 264, 278, 332–33.

52. Ibid., 265–66, 277–78.

53. Ibid., 280–83.

54. Ibid., 280–83, 343–45.

55. Ibid., 266–67, 70. Catron adopted Vattel's quote directly from Yerger's argument. See *Nashville Republican*, 10 September 1835.

56. *Cornet*, 144–45.

57. *Forman*, 271–72, 282–84.

58. Ibid., 270–72, 277–78.

59. Ibid., 287–88.

60. Ibid., 270–72, 277–78, 282–85, 287–88, 319.

61. Ibid., 301–6.

62. Ibid., 285–88, 294–95.

63. U.S. Constitution, art. 2, sec. 2 and art. 6; *Forman*, 307–8.

64. George Washington, 17 September 1789, in De Pauw, ed., *Documentary History*, vol. 2: 40–43; *Forman*, 308–10.

65. Washington, 17 September 1789, in De Pauw, ed., *Documentary History*, vol. 2: 42–43; *Forman*, 310.

66. *Forman*, 301–4, 332–33.

67. John Catron to Newton Cannon, 2 November 1835, *Messages of the Governors of Tennessee*, vol. 3: 94–98.

68. Byrum, *McMinn County*, 18; King and Evans, "Death of John Walker," 13; Chandler, *Associate Justice John Catron*, 23–24, n. 15; Bradley County Circuit Court, Loose Records of State Cases.

69. John Ridge to Benjamin Currey, November 1834, LR: CAE, M-234, reel 76, p. 206; Ross to the General Council, 22 October 1835; Ross to John F. Schermerhorn, 23, 27, 28, and 30 October 1835; Ross to the National Committee and National Council, 24 October 1835; James J. Trott to Ross, 6 January 1836; Walter S. Adair to Ross, 8 January 1836; Ross to Lewis Cass, 14 January and 9 February 1836; Major Ridge, et al. to Ross, 6 February 1836; all in RP, vol. 1: 360–62, 363–64, 366–70, 371–72, 380, 382–86. See also Schermerhorn to Ross, 30 October 1835 (two letters of the same date), LR: OIA, reel 76, pp. 953–58.

70. The Treaty Party portrayed the killings as political assassinations. Ross's followers insisted that the attacks were legal executions to carry out the nation's prohibition against selling national lands. The penalty for that act was death. Ironically, the Ridges had been forceful advocates for the adoption of the law. Major Ridge had killed the Cherokee chief Doublehead for violating the statute in 1807. Tyner, *Those Who Cried*, unnumbered introduction; LCN, 136–37; Franks, *Stand Watie*, 55–56, 85–86; Foreman, "Murder of Elias Boudinot," 19–24; Rennard Strickland, *Fire and the Spirits*, 77. For the best history of the continuing conflict among the Cherokees in the West, see McLoughlin, *After the Trail of Tears*.

71. Paschal, "Trial of Stand Watie," 318.

72. Reports of the attacks on Springston and Foreman conflict. Some suggest that Springston died of his wounds, but evidence shows that he lived on until 1866. John G. Ross's letters imply that Stand Watie's shot missed Foreman and that Foreman died from the stab wounds. Witnesses at Watie's trial testified that Foreman was killed by a gunshot. Ross's accounts also contend that Foreman was unarmed and do not mention the whipping. John G. Ross to John Ross, 19 May 1842; John Ross to Lucy A. Butler, 20 July 1842; both in RP, vol. 2: 126–27, 143–44; John Rollin Ridge to Stand Watie, 7 November 1844, Parins, *John Rollin Ridge*, 37, 47–48; McLoughlin, *After the Trail of Tears*, 41–43; Franks, *Stand Watie*, 64–66, 80–88; Paschal, "Trial of Stand Watie," 313–17.

EPILOGUE

1. Russell Thornton, *Population History*, 73–76; Russell Thornton, *American Indian Holocaust and Survival*, 113–18; Woodward, *The Cherokees*, 217–18, 316–28. Ross, per usual, persevered with determined optimism. He led his people through the travails of their forced exile, through the bloody and bitter tribal civil war, and through the renewed divisions produced by the American Civil War. Through it all, through challenges, recovery, and prosperity, Ross retained the confidence of the Cherokee people. Reelected time and again by his constituents, John Ross finally died in office in 1866, almost forty years after his initial campaign for principal chief.

2. *Caldwell v. Alabama*, 337.

3. Sturtevant, ed., "John Ridge on Cherokee Civilization in 1826," 79–91; Perdue, *Cherokee Editor*, 20; *Niles' Register*, 18 August 1838.

4. Tocqueville, *Democracy in America*, 308–12.

5. John Ross to the General Council, 13 May 1833; John Ross to Lewis Cass, 14 February 1835; both in RP, vol. 1: 268, 321; Beveridge, *Life of John Marshall*, vol.

4: 552 n. 5; Norgren, *Cherokee Cases,* 132–33. In at least one case, a lower state court followed *Worcester* and recognized the sovereignty of the Cherokees. In the early 1830s, a trial court judge in St. Clair County, Alabama, ruled that the state did not have jurisdiction over a Cherokee who was accused of murdering another tribal citizen within the territorial limits of the Cherokee Nation. The judge based his decision on *Worcester,* declared the extension laws of the state unconstitutional, and dismissed the prosecution. John Ross, "Annual Message," 15 October 1833, RP, vol. 1: 271.

6. Harring, *Crow Dog's Case,* 34 n. 40; *Nevada v. McKenney.* In the following cases, state courts upheld the extension statutes of their state legislatures: *Kansas v. John Ward; People of the State of California v. Juan Antonio; United States v. George Stahl (Kansas); North Carolina v. Ta-Cha-Na-Tah;* and *Wisconsin v. Doxtater.* The Minnesota Supreme Court also specifically mentioned the southern cases in *Minnesota v. Campbell* but refused to extend the state's criminal jurisdiction over the Indians within that state.

7. *United States v. Rogers,* 571–72; *Dred Scott v. Sandford,* 403–4; *Cherokee Nation v. Southern Kansas Railway Company,* 653.

8. Pevar, *Rights of Indians and Tribes,* 119–20; *United States v. Cisna; United States v. McBratney; Utah and No. Ry. v. Fisher; Ward v. Race Horse.*

9. *Ex parte Crow Dog; United States v. Kagama;* Harring, *Crow Dog's Case,* 53–56; David E. Wilkins, *American Indian Sovereignty,* 67–81. For the Major Crimes Act, see 18 U.S.C.A., sec. 1153.

10. *Lone Wolf v. Hitchcock;* Norgren, *Cherokee Cases,* 146; Clark, *Lone Wolf v. Hitchcock;* Prucha, *Great Father,* 659–757.

11. 18 U.S.C. sec. 1162 (a); 28 U.S.C. sec. 1360 (a); Pub. L. 83–280, secs. 6, 7; 25 U.S.C. secs. 1322, 1326. In 1968 Congress amended Public Law 280 to require tribal consent to any future state extension legislation and provided legal mechanisms to allow a state to retrocede all or part of its jurisdiction to a tribal nation. Nebraska, Washington, Minnesota, Nevada, Wisconsin, and Oregon subsequently retroceded their jurisdiction over some or all of the Indian territory in their states.

12. Wilkinson, *American Indians, Time, and the Law,* 56–60; *Williams v. Lee; Fisher v. District Court; Oliphant v. Suquamish Indian Tribe;* Harring, *Crow Dog's Case,* 290–91; David. E. Wilkins, *American Indian Sovereignty,* 35; *Vermont v. Elliot;* Norgren, *Cherokee Cases,* 150–51.

13. David E. Wilkins, *American Indian Sovereignty,* 275–76; Cohen, *Handbook of Federal Indian Law,* 117; *County of Yakima v. Yakima Indian Nation; Brendale v. Confederated Yakima Tribes.*

14. Barsh and Henderson, *The Road,* 60–61; *Kagama,* 384. For succinct analyses of the cases considering state legislative encroachments on tribal rights, see Cohen, *Handbook of Federal Indian Law,* 259–79, 348–80; Pevar, *Rights of Indians and Tribes,* 119–25.

BIBLIOGRAPHY

COURT CASES

Blair v. Pathkiller, 10 Tenn. (2 Yerg.) 407 (1830).
Brendale v. Confederated Yakima Tribes, 492 U.S. 408 (1989).
Caldwell v. Alabama, 6 Stew. & P. 327 (Ala. 1831).
Calvin's Case, 77 Eng. Rep. 377 (1608).
Campbell v. Hall, 1 Cowp. 204 (1774).
Cherokee Nation v. Georgia, 30 U.S. (5 Peter) 1 (1831).
Cherokee Nation v. Southern Kansas Railway Company, 135 U.S. 641 (1890).
Chisholm v. Georgia, 2 U.S. 419 (1793).
Cohens v. Virginia, 19 U.S. 264 (1821).
Cornet v. Winston's Lessee, 10 Tenn. (2 Yerg.) 143 (1826).
County of Yakima v. Yakima Indian Nation, 502 U.S. 251 (1992).
Danforth's Lessee v. Thomas, 14 U.S. 155 (1816).
Dartmouth College v. Woodward, 17 U.S. 518 (1819).
Dred Scott v. Sandford, 60 U.S. 393 (1857).
Elkison v. Deliesseline, 8 Federal Cases 493 (Case 4,366) (Cir. Ct. S.C. 1823).
Ex Parte Crow Dog, 109 U.S. 556 (1883).
Fisher v. District Court, 424 U.S. 382 (1976).
Fletcher v. Peck, 10 U.S. 87 (1810).
Georgia v. Tassels, 1 Dud. 229 (Ga. 1830).
Gibbons v. Ogden, 22 U.S. 1 (1824).
Glasgow's Lessee v. Smith and Blackwell, 1 Tenn. (1 Overt.) 144 (1805).
Goodell v. Jackson (Tommy Jemmy), 20 Johns. 693 (N.Y. 1822).
Holland v. Pack, 7 Tenn. 151 (1823).
Jackson v. Goodell (Tommy Jemmy), 20 Johns. 188 (N.Y. Sup. Ct. 1822).
Jackson v. Hudson, 3 Johns. 375 (N.Y. 1808).
Johnson v. McIntosh, 21 U.S. 543 (1823).
Kansas v. John Ward, 1 Kansas 601 (1863).
Lone Wolf v. Hitchcock, 187 U.S. 553 (1903).
Marbury v. Madison, 5 U.S. 137 (1803).
Marshall v. Clark, 8 Va. 208 (1791).
Martin v. Hunter's Lessee, 14 U.S. 304 (1816).
McCulloch v. Maryland, 17 U.S. 316 (1819).
Minnesota v. Campbell, 55 N.W. 553 (Minn. 1893).
Nevada v. McKenney, 2 Pac. 171 (Nev. 1883).
New Jersey v. Wilson, 11 U.S. 164 (1812).
North Carolina v. Ta-Cha-Na-Tah, 64 N.C. 614 (1870).
Oliphant v. Suquamish Indian Tribe, 435 U. S. 191 (1978).

People of the State of California v. Juan Antonio, 27 Cal. 404 (1865).

Pound v. Pullen's Lessee, 11 Tenn. (3 Yerg.) 338 (1832).

Preston v. Browder, 14 U.S. 115 (1816).

Prigg v. Pennsylvania, 41 U.S. 539 (1842).

South Carolina ex rel. John Marsh v. Managers of Elections for the District of York, 17 S.C.L. (1 Bailey) 215 (1829).

Strother v. Cathey, 5 N.C. 162 (1807).

Tee-Hit-Ton Indians v. United States, 348 U.S. 272 (1955).

Tennessee v. Forman, 16 Tenn. (8 Yerg.) 256 (1835).

Tennessee v. Ross, 15 Tenn. (7 Yerg.) 74 (1834).

Thomas v. Adams, 2 Port. 188 (Ala. 1835).

United States v. Bailey, Fed. Cas. No. 14,495, (C.C. Tenn.) (1834).

United States v. Cisna, 25 Fed. Cas. No. 14,795 (C.C. Ohio) (1835).

United States v. George Stahl, 1 Kansas 606 (1868).

United States v. Hudson and Goodwin, 11 U.S. 32 (1812).

United States v. Kagama, 118 U.S. 375 (1886).

United States v. McBratney, 104 U.S. 621 (1882).

United States v. Rogers, 45 U.S. 567 (1846).

Utah and No. Ry. v. Fisher, 116 U.S. 28 (1885).

Vermont v. Elliot, 616 A. 2d 210 (Ver. 1992).

Ward v. Race Horse, 163 U.S. 504 (1896).

Williams v. Lee, 358 U.S. 217 (1959).

Wisconsin v. Doxtater, 47 Wis. 278 (1879).

Worcester v. Georgia, 31 U.S. 515 (1832).

RECORDS FROM THE NATIONAL ARCHIVES

Records of the Bureau of Indian Affairs, National Archives Record, Group 75 (microfilm): Letters Received by Secretary of War Relating to Indian Affairs, 1800–1823 (microfilm series M271. 4 reels).

Correspondence of the Office of Indian Affairs and Related Records, National Archives: Letters Received, 1824–81 (microfilm series 234. Cherokee and Creek Agencies. Reels 71, 72, 76, 222). Letters Sent (microfilm series 21. Reels 5, 6).

Office of the Secretary of War, National Archives: Letters Sent by the Secretary of War Relating to Indian Affairs, 1800–1824 (microfilm series M15. 6 reels).

SPECIAL COLLECTIONS

Alabama State Archives, Montgomery: Alabama Supreme Court Records; Governor's Pardons; John Gayle, Personal Papers; Shelby County Court Records

Bradley County Library-Historical Branch, Cleveland, Tennessee: Bradley County Court Records; John Walker Jr. file; Loose Records of State Cases (microfilm); Walker Family Genealogical Files

Chestatee Regional Library, Gainesville, Georgia: Cherokee File; Gainesville History File; Genealogical Files; Hall County Court Records (microfilm); Hall County History Files

E. G. Fisher Public Library, McMinn County, Tennessee: Dromgoode Genealogical Files; McMinn County Court Records (microfilm)

Georgia Department of Archives and History, Atlanta: "Cherokee Indian Letters, Talks, Treaties"; Georgia Executive Letter Books (microfilm); Hall County Court Records (microfilm); "Index to the 1835 Census of the Cherokee Indians East of the Mississippi River"; County Collection, Gwinnett County, Inferior Court Minutes (microfilm); John Ross folder; State of Georgia Executive Minute Books (microfilm)

Gilcrease Institute of American History and Art, Tulsa, Oklahoma: John Ross papers

Tennessee State Library and Archives, Nashville: Circuit Court Minutes, *State v. Forman,* file box 245; John Catron papers; McMinn County Court Records (microfilm); Tennessee Supreme Court Records

OTHER SOURCES

Abbot, Belle K. *The Cherokee Indians of North Georgia.* University, Ala.: Confederate Publishing, n.d.

Abernethy, Thomas Perkins. *The Formative Period in Alabama, 1815–1828.* Montgomery: Brown Printing Company, 1922.

———. *Western Lands and the American Revolution.* New York: Russell and Russell, 1959.

Acts of the General Assembly of the State of Georgia. 1823–33. Milledgeville, Ga.: Camak and Ragland, 1824–34.

Acts of the Privy Council of England, Colonial Series. 6 vols. Hereford, England: Anthony Brothers, 1908–12.

Adams, Charles Francis, ed. *Memoirs of John Quincy Adams, Comprising Portions of His Diary from 1795 to 1848.* 12 vols. Philadelphia: J. B. Lippencott and Company, 1874–77.

Adams, Henry. *History of the United States.* New York: Charles Scribner's Sons, 1889.

Alabama Census Returns 1820 and an Abstract of Federal Census of Alabama 1830. Baltimore: Genealogical Publishing, 1996.

Althusius, Johannes. *The Politics of Johannes Althusius.* Translated by Frederick S. Carney. London: Eyre and Spottiswoode, 1965.

American Indian Lawyer Training Program, Inc. *Indian Tribes as Sovereign Governments: A Sourcebook on Federal-Tribal History, Law, and Policy.* Oakland, California: American Indian Lawyer Training Program, Inc., 1988.

American State Papers: Foreign Relations. 6 vols. Washington, D.C.: Gales and Seaton, 1832–61.

American State Papers: Indian Affairs. 2 vols. Washington, D.C.: Gales and Seaton, 1832–34.

American State Papers: Public Lands. 8 vols. Washington, D.C.: Gales and Seaton, 1832–61.

Anderson, John C. "The Supreme Court of Alabama: Its Organization and Sketches of Its Chief Justices." *Alabama Historical Quarterly* 1 (1930): 122–23.

Annals of the Congress of the United States, 1789–1824. 42 vols. Washington, D.C.: Gales and Seaton, 1834–56.

Arber, Edward, ed. *The First Three English Books on America: Being Chiefly Translations, Compilations, etc. by Richard Eden*. Westminister: Constable, 1895.

Aristotle. *The Nicomachean Ethics*. Translated by H. Rackham. Cambridge: Harvard University Press, 1962.

———. *"The Art" of Rhetoric*. Translated by John Henry Freese. Cambridge: Harvard University Press, 1967.

Aron, Raymond. *Peace and War: A Theory of International Relations*. Translated by Richard A. Howard and Annette Baker-Fox. New York: Frederick A. Praeger, 1967.

Ayers, Edward L. *Vengeance and Justice: Crime and Punishment in the Nineteenth-Century American South*. New York: Oxford University Press, 1984.

Bailyn, Bernard. *The Ideological Origins of the American Revolution*. Cambridge: Belknap Press of Harvard University Press, 1967.

Baker, Leonard. *John Marshall: A Life in Law*. New York: Macmillan Publishing Co., Inc.; London: Collier Macmillan Publishers, 1974.

Baldwin, Joseph G. *The Flush Times of Alabama and Mississippi: A Series of Sketches*. New York: D. Appleton & Co., 1858.

Ball, Milner. "Constitution, Court, Indian Tribes." *American Bar Foundation Research Journal* 1 (1987): 1–140.

Barbour, Philip L. *The Jamestown Voyages under the First Charter, 1606–1609*. London: Hakluyt Society, 1969.

Baritz, Loren. *City on a Hill: A History of Ideas and Myths in America*. New York: Wiley, 1964.

Barkum, Michael. *Law without Sanctions: Order in Primitive Societies and the World Community*. New Haven: Yale University Press, 1968.

Barsh, Russell Lawrence, and James Youngblood Henderson. *The Road: Indian Tribes and Political Liberty*. Berkeley: University of California Press, 1980.

Bass, Althea. *Cherokee Messenger: A Life of Samuel Austin Worcester*. Norman: University of Oklahoma Press, 1936.

Bates, Mrs. James E. "Gainesville's First 150 Years." *Georgia Magazine* (May 1971): 14.

Belz, Herman. "The South and the American Constitutional Tradition at the Bicentennial." In *An Uncertain Tradition: Constitutionalism and the History of the South*, edited by Kermit L. Hall and James W. Ely Jr., 17–59. Athens: University of Georgia Press, 1989.

Bennett, Gordon I. "Aboriginal Title in the Common Law: A Stony Path through Feudal Doctrine." *Buffalo Law Review* 27 (1978): 617–23.

Berkhofer, Robert F. *The White Man's Indian: Images of the American Indian from Columbus to the Present*. New York: Random House, 1978.

Berman, Howard R. "The Concept of Aboriginal Rights in the Early History of the United States." *Buffalo Law Review* 27 (1978): 637–67.

Berutti, Ronald A. "The Cherokee Cases: The Fight to Save the Supreme Court and the Cherokee Indians." *American Indian Law Review* 17 (1992): 291–308.

Beveridge, Albert J. *The Life of John Marshall.* 4 vols. Boston: Houghton Mifflin Company, 1916–19.

Blackstone, William. *Blackstone's Commentaries on the Laws of England.* Oxford: Clarendon Press, 1766–69.

Bodin, Jean. *On Sovereignty: Four Chapters from "The Six Books of the Commonwealth."* Edited and translated by Julian H. Franklin. Cambridge: Cambridge University Press, 1992.

Boldt, Menno, and J. Anthony Long, eds. *The Quest for Justice: Aboriginal Peoples and Aboriginal Rights.* Toronto: University of Toronto Press, 1985.

Braund, Kathryn E. Holland. *Deerskins and Duffels: Creek Indian Trade with Anglo-America, 1685–1815.* Lincoln: University of Nebraska Press, 1993.

Bridgers, Ben Oshel. "A Legal Digest of North Carolina Cherokees." *Journal of Cherokee Studies* 4 (1979): 21–43.

Brown, John P. *Old Frontiers.* Kingsport, Tennessee: Southern Publishers, 1938.

Bryan, George. *The Imperialism of John Marshall: A Study in Expediency.* Boston: Stratford Company, 1924.

Bull, Hedley. *The Anarchical Society.* London: Macmillan Press, 1977.

———. *Systems of States.* Leicester: Leicester University Press, 1977.

Burke, Joseph Charles. "The Cherokee Cases: A Study in Law, Politics, and Morality." *Stanford Law Review* 21 (1969): 500–531.

———. "William Wirt: Attorney General and Constitutional Lawyer." Ph.D. diss., Indiana University, 1965.

Byrum, C. Stephen. *McMinn County.* Memphis: Memphis State University Press, 1989.

Caldwell, Charles. *Thoughts on the Original Unity of the Human Race.* New York: E. Bliss, 1830.

———. *Autobiography of Charles Caldwell, M.D.* New York: DeCapo Press, 1968.

Caldwell, Joshua W. *Sketches of the Bench and Bar of Tennessee.* Knoxville: Ogden Brothers and Company, 1898.

Canny, Nicholas P. *The Elizabethan Conquest of Ireland: A Pattern Established, 1565–1576.* Hassocks, Sussex: Harvester Press, 1976.

Carmichael, Virgil F. "The James Foreman Murder Case." *Chronicles of Bradley* 2 (1982): 1–17.

Carson, James Taylor. "Searching for the Bright Path: The Mississippi Choctaws from Prehistory to Removal." Ph.D. diss., University of Kentucky, 1996.

Carter, Clarence E., ed. *The Territorial Papers of the United States.* 26 vols. Washington, D.C.: United States Government Printing Office, 1934–62.

Caughey, John Walton. *McGillivray of the Creeks.* Norman: University of Oklahoma Press, 1938.

Chambers, Reid Peyton. "Judicial Enforcement of the Federal Trust Responsibility to Indians." *Stanford Law Review* 27 (1975): 1213–48.

Champagne, Duane. *Social Order and Political Change: Constitutional Governments among the Cherokee, the Choctaw, the Chickasaw, and the Creek.* Stanford: Stanford University Press, 1992.

Chandler, Walter. *The Centenary of Associate Justice John Catron of the United States Supreme Court: Address of Walter Chandler at the Fifty-Sixth Annual Session of the Bar Association of Tennessee at Memphis, Friday, June 11, 1937.* Memphis: S. C. Toof, 1937.

Christianson, James R. "Removal: A Foundation for the Formation of Federal Indian Policy." *Journal of Cherokee Studies* 10 (1985): 215–25.

Churchill, Ward. *From a Native Son: Selected Essays on Indigenism, 1985–1995.* Boston: South End Press, 1996.

Clark, Blue. *Lone Wolf v. Hitchcock: Treaty Rights and Indian Law at the End of the Nineteenth Century.* Lincoln: University of Nebraska Press, 1994.

Clinton, Robert. *Marbury v. Madison and Judicial Review.* Lawrence: University of Kansas Press, 1989.

Clinton, Robert N., Nell Jessup Newton, and Monroe E. Price. *American Indian Law: Cases and Materials.* Charlottesville, Va.: Michie Press, 1991.

Cohen, Felix S. *Handbook of Federal Indian Law.* Washington, D.C.: United States Government Printing Office, 1942. Revised reprint, Charlottesville, Va.: Michie Company, 1982.

Colonial Records of the State of Georgia. Edited by Allen D. Candler. 39 vols. Atlanta: Franklin Printing, 1904–16.

Commager, Henry Steele, ed. *Documents of American History.* New York: Appleton-Century-Crofts, 1968.

Conser, Walter H., Jr. "John Ross and the Cherokee Resistance Campaign, 1833–1838." *Journal of Southern History* 44 (1978): 191–212.

Corkran, David H. *The Cherokee Frontier, 1740–1762.* Norman: University of Oklahoma Press, 1962.

———. *The Creek Frontier, 1540–1783.* Norman: University of Oklahoma Press, 1967.

Corlew, Robert Ewing. *Tennessee, A Short History.* Knoxville: University of Tennessee Press, 1981.

Corn, James Franklin. *Red Clay and Rattlesnake Springs: A History of the Cherokee Indians of Bradley County, Tennessee.* Cleveland, Tennessee: n.p., 1959.

Cotter, W. J. *My Autobiography.* Nashville: Publishing House of the M. E. Church, South, 1917.

Cotton, Joseph P., Jr. *The Constitutional Decisions of John Marshall.* 2 vols. New York: G. P. Putnam's Sons, 1905.

Coulter, E. Merton. *Auraria: The Story of a Georgia Gold-Mining Town.* Athens: University of Georgia Press, 1956.

Crane, Verner Winslow. *The Southern Frontier, 1670–1732.* Durham: Duke University Press, 1928.

Cronon, William. *Changes in the Land: Indians, Colonists, and the Ecology of New England.* New York: Hill and Wang, 1983.

Cushman, Clare, ed. *The Supreme Court Justices, 1789–1993.* Washington, D.C.: Congressional Quarterly, Inc., 1993.

Davis, Kenneth Penn. "Ousting the Cherokees from Georgia." M.A. thesis, Georgia State College, 1968.

Debo, Angie. *The Rise and Fall of the Choctaw Republic.* Norman: University of Oklahoma Press, 1934.

Deland, T. A., and A. Davis Smith, eds. *Northern Alabama: Historical and Biographical Illustrated.* Chicago: Donahue and Henneberry, 1888.

Deloria, Vine, Jr. *Of Utmost Good Faith.* San Francisco: Straight Arrow Books, 1971.

———. "Self-Determination and the Concept of Sovereignty." In *Economic Development in American Indian Reservations,* edited by Roxanne Dunbar Ortiz. Albuquerque: University of New Mexico Native American Studies, 1979.

———. *American Indian Policy in the Twentieth Century.* Norman: University of Oklahoma Press, 1985.

———. *Behind the Trail of Broken Treaties: An Indian Declaration of Independence.* Austin: University of Texas Press, 1985.

Deloria, Vine, and Clifford M. Lytle. *American Indians, American Justice.* Austin: University of Texas Press, 1983.

———. *The Nations Within: The Past and Future of American Indian Sovereignty.* New York: Pantheon Books, 1984.

DeLupis, Ingrid. *International Law and the Independent State.* New York: Crane, Russack and Co., 1974.

De Milford, Louis LeClerc. *Memoir or a Cursory Glance at My Different Travels & My Sojourn in the Creek Nation.* Translated by Geraldine De Courcy. Edited by John Francis McDermott. Chicago: Lakeside Press, 1956.

De Pauw, Linda Grant, ed. *Documentary History of the First Federal Congress of the United States of America, March 4, 1789–March 3, 1791.* 14 vols. Baltimore: Johns Hopkins University Press, 1974.

DeRosier, Arthur H., Jr. *The Removal of the Choctaw Indians.* Knoxville: University of Tennessee Press, 1970.

De Vorsey, Louis. *The Indian Boundary in the Southern Colonies, 1763–1775.* Chapel Hill: University of North Carolina Press, 1966.

Dewey, Donald O. *Marshall versus Jefferson: The Political Background of Marbury v. Madison.* New York: Alfred A. Knopf, 1970.

Dickson, John Lois. "The Judicial History of the Cherokee Nation from 1721 to 1835." Ph.D. diss., University of Oklahoma, 1964.

Dobyns, Henry. *Their Number Become Thinned: Native American Population Dynamics in Eastern North America.* Knoxville: University of Tennessee Press, 1983.

Dorsey, James E. *The History of Hall County, 1819–1900.* Gainesville, Ga.: Magnolia Press, 1991.

Dowd, Gregory Evans. *A Spirited Resistance: The North American Struggle for Unity, 1745–1815.* Baltimore: Johns Hopkins University Press, 1992.

Downes, Randolph C. *Council Fires on the Upper Ohio: A Narrative of Indian Affairs in the Upper Ohio Valley until 1795*. Pittsburgh: University of Pittsburgh Press, 1940.

Duursma, Jorri. *Fragmentation and the International Relations of Micro-States: Self-Determination and Statehood*. Cambridge: Cambridge University Press, 1996.

Eccles, William J. *France in America*. New York: Harper and Row, 1972.

Edmunds, R. David. *American Indian Leaders: Studies in Diversity*. Lincoln: University of Nebraska Press, 1980.

Ehle, John. *Trail of Tears: The Rise and Fall of the Cherokee Nation*. New York: Anchor Books of Doubleday Press, 1988.

Evarts, Jeremiah. *Essays on the Present Crisis in the Condition of the American Indians*. Boston: Perkins and Marvin, 1829.

Farand, Max, ed. *Records of the Federal Convention of 1787*. 3 vols. New Haven: Yale University Press, 1911.

Faulkner, Robert Kenneth. *The Jurisprudence of John Marshall*. Princeton: Princeton University Press, 1968.

Fehrenbacher, Don E. *The Dred Scott Case: Its Significance in American Law and Politics*. New York: Oxford University Press, 1978.

Fenwick, Charles G. "The Authority of Vattel." *American Political Science Review* 7 (1913): 370–424.

Filler, Louis, ed. *The Removal of the Cherokee Nation*. Boston: D. C. Heath and Company. Reprint Malabar, Fla.: Robert E. Krieger Publishing, 1988.

Finkelman, Paul. "States' Rights North and South in Antebellum America." In *An Uncertain Tradition: Constitutionalism and the History of the South*, edited by Kermit L. Hall and James W. Ely Jr., 125–58. Athens: University of Georgia Press, 1989.

———. "Story Telling on the Supreme Court: *Prigg v. Pennsylvania* and Justice Joseph Story's Judicial Nationalism." *Supreme Court Review* (1994): 247–94.

———. *Slavery and the Founders: Race and Liberty in the Age of Jefferson*. Armonk, N.Y.: M. E. Sharpe, 1996.

Foreman, Grant. "The Murder of Elias Boudinot." *Chronicles of Oklahoma* 12 (1934): 19–24.

Fowler, Michael Ross, and Julie Marie Bunck. *Law, Power, and the Sovereign State: The Evolution and Application of the Concept of Sovereignty*. University Park, Pa.: Pennsylvania State University Press, 1995.

Franks, Kenny A. *Stand Watie and the Agony of the Cherokee Nation*. Memphis: Memphis State University Press, 1979.

Freehling, William W. *Prelude to Civil War: The Nullification Controversy in South Carolina, 1816–1836*. New York: Oxford University Press, 1965.

Frickey, Philip P. "Marshalling Past and Present: Colonialism, Constitutionalism, and Interpretation in Federal Indian Law." *Harvard Law Review* 107 (1993): 381–440.

Fried, Morton. *The Notion of Tribe*. Menlo Park, N.J.: Cummings Publishing, 1975.

Friedman, Leon, and Fred L. Israel, eds. *The Justices of the United States Supreme Court: Their Lives and Major Opinions*. New York: Chelsea House, 1995.

Galloway, Patricia. "'The Chief Who Is Your Father': Choctaw and French Views of the Diplomatic Relation." In *Powhatan's Mantle: Indians in the Colonial Southeast*, edited by Peter H. Wood, Gregory A. Waselkov, and M. Thomas Hatley, 254–78. Lincoln: University of Nebraska Press, 1989.

Garrett, William. *Reminiscences of Public Men in Alabama*. Atlanta: Plantation Publishing Company's Press, 1872.

Gass, Edmund C. "The Constitutional Opinions of Justice John Catron." *East Tennessee Historical Society's Publications* 8 (1936): 54–73.

Gearing, Fred. *Priests and Warriors: Social Structures for Cherokee Politics in the Eighteenth Century*. American Anthropological Association Memoir No. 93. Menasha, Wis.: American Anthropological Association, 1962.

Georgia Facts and Figures. Athens: University of Georgia Press, 1946.

Georgia Official and Statistical Register. Atlanta: Georgia Department of Archives and History, 1978.

Gibson, Arrell M. *The Chickasaws*. Norman: University of Oklahoma Press, 1971.

Gilmer, George R. *Sketches of Some of the First Settlers of Upper Georgia*. Baltimore: Genealogical Publishing, 1965.

Gosse, Philip Henry. *Letters from Alabama (U.S.) Chiefly to Natural History*. London: Morgan and Chase, 1859.

Gossett, Thomas F. *Race: The History of an Idea in America*. 1963. Reprint, Oxford: Oxford University Press, 1997.

Greeley, Horace. *The American Conflict*. 2 vols. Hartford: O. D. Case, 1864–66.

Green, John. "Four Attorneys-General and Reporters." *Tennessee Law Review* 19 (1945–47): 1–4.

Green, John W. *Lives of the Judges of the Supreme Court of Tennessee, 1796–1947*. Knoxville: Archer & Smith, 1947.

Green, L. C., and Olive P. Dickason. *The Law of Nations and the New World*. Edmonton: University of Alberta Press, 1989.

Green, Michael D. "Alexander McGillivray." In *American Indian Leaders: Studies in Diversity*, edited by R. David Edmunds, 41–63. Lincoln: University of Nebraska Press, 1980.

———. *The Politics of Indian Removal: Creek Government and Society in Crisis*. Lincoln: University of Nebraska Press, 1982.

Green, Raleigh Travers. *Genealogical and Historical Notes on Culpeper County, Virginia*. Culpeper, Va: R. T. Green, 1900.

Griffith, Louis Turner, and John E. Talmadge. *Georgia Journalism, 1763–1950*. Athens: University of Georgia Press, 1951.

Grotius, Hugo. *The Law of War and Peace (De Jure Belliae Pacis Libri Tres)*. Translated by Francis W. Kelsey. Indianapolis: The Bobbs-Merrill Company, Inc., 1962.

Hall, Kermit L., and James W. Ely Jr., eds. *An Uncertain Tradition: Constitutionalism and the History of the South*. Athens: University of Georgia Press, 1989.

Hall, Thomas D. *Social Changes in the Southwest, 1350–1880.* Lawrence: University of Kansas Press, 1989.

Haller, John S. *Outcasts from Evolution: Scientific Attitudes of Racial Inferiority, 1859–1900.* Urbana: University of Illinois Press, 1971.

Hallum, John. *The Diary of an Old Lawyer, or, Scenes behind the Curtain.* Nashville: Southwestern Publishing House, 1895.

Hanke, Lewis. *Aristotle and the American Indians: A Study in Race Prejudice in the Modern World.* Chicago: H. Regnery Co., 1959.

———. *All Mankind Is One: A Study of the Disputation between Bartoleme' de Las Casas and Juan Gines de Sepulveda in 1550 on the Intellectual and Religious Capacity of the American Indians.* Dekalb, Ill.: Northern Illinois University Press, 1974.

Harring, Sidney L. *Crow Dog's Case: American Indian Sovereignty, Tribal Law, and United States Law in the Nineteenth Century.* Cambridge: Cambridge University Press, 1994.

Harrington, James. *The Commonwealth of Oceana.* Edited by J. G. A. Pocock. 1656. Reprint, Cambridge: Cambridge University Press, 1992.

Haskins, George L., and Herbert A. Johnson. *Foundations of Power: John Marshall, 1801–15. History of the Supreme Court of the United States,* vol. 2. New York: Macmillan Co., 1981.

Hatley, Tom. *The Dividing Paths: Cherokees and South Carolinians through the Era of Revolution.* New York: Oxford University Press, 1993.

Henderson, James Y. "Unraveling the Riddle of Aboriginal Title." *American Indian Law Journal* 5 (1977): 75–102.

———. "The Doctrine of Aboriginal Rights in the Western Legal Tradition." In *The Quest for Justice: Aboriginal Peoples and Aboriginal Rights,* edited by Menno Boldt and J. Anthony Long. Toronto: University of Toronto Press, 1985.

Henry, William Wirt. *Sketches of the Life and Character of Patrick Henry.* 3 vols. New York: Charles Scribner's Sons, 1891.

Hewatt, Alexander. *An Historical Account of the Rise and Progress of the Colonies of South Carolina and Georgia, 1779.* 2 vols. London: A. Donaldson, 1779.

Hinsley, F. H. *Sovereignty.* New York: Basic Books, 1966.

Horsman, Reginald. *Expansion and American Indian Policy, 1783–1812.* East Lansing: Michigan State University Press, 1967.

———. "American Indian Policy and the Origins of Manifest Destiny." In *The Indian in American History,* edited by Francis Paul Prucha, 20–28. Hinsdale, Ill.: Dryden Press, 1971.

———. *Race and Manifest Destiny: The Origins of American Racial Anglo-Saxonism.* Cambridge: Harvard University Press, 1981.

Hoskins, Shirley Coats, ed. *Cherokee Land Valuations in Tennessee in 1836.* N.p.: Shirley Coats Hoskins, 1984.

Howington, Arthur F. *What Sayeth the Law: The Treatment of Slaves and Free Blacks in the State and Local Courts of Tennessee.* New York: Garland Publishing, 1986.

Hoxie, Fred E. *A Final Promise: The Campaign to Assimilate the Indians, 1880–1920*. Lincoln: University of Nebraska Press, 1984.

Hudson, Charles. *The Southeastern Indians*. Knoxville: University of Tennessee Press, 1976.

Huebner, Timothy S. *The Southern Judicial Tradition: State Judges and Sectional Distinctiveness, 1790–1890*. Athens: University of Georgia Press, 1999.

Hurley, John. "Aboriginal Rights, the Constitution and the Marshall Court." *Revue Juridique Themis* 17 (1982–83): 403–43.

Hutchins, John. "The Trial of Reverend Samuel A. Worcester." *Journal of Cherokee Studies* 2 (1977): 356–74.

Jackson, Andrew. *Correspondence of Andrew Jackson*. Edited by John S. Bassett. 7 vols. Washington, D.C.: Carnegie Institute, 1926–35.

James, Alan. *Sovereign Statehood: The Basis of International Society*. London: Allen and Unwin, 1986.

Janis, M. W. "Jeremy Bentham and the Fashioning of International Law." *American Journal of International Law* 78 (1984): 405–18.

Jefferson, Thomas. *The Writings of Thomas Jefferson*. Edited by Albert Ellery Bergh. 20 vols. Washington, D.C.: The Thomas Jefferson Memorial Association, 1903–5.

———. *The Papers of Thomas Jefferson*. Edited by Julian P. Boyd. 25 vols. Princeton: Princeton University Press, 1950–92.

———. *Notes on the State of Virginia*. Edited by William Peden. Chapel Hill: University of North Carolina Press, 1955.

Jennings, Francis. "Virgin Land and Savage People." *American Quarterly* 23 (1971): 519–41.

———. *The Invasion of America: Indians, Colonialism, and the Cant of Conquest*. New York: W. W. Norton, 1975.

———. *The Founders of America: How Indians Discovered the Land, Pioneered in It, and Created Great Classical Civilizations; How They Were Plunged into a Dark Age by Invasion and Conquest; and How They Are Reviving*. New York: W. W. Norton and Company, 1993.

Jensen, Merrill. *The Articles of Confederation: An Interpretation of the Social-Constitutional History of the American Revolution, 1774–1778*. Madison: University of Wisconsin Press, 1940.

Johnson, Herbert A. "The Constitutional Thought of William Johnson." *South Carolina Historical Magazine* 89 (1988): 132–45.

Johnson, Herbert A., et al. *The Papers of John Marshall*. 8 vols. Chapel Hill: University of North Carolina Press, 1974–95.

Johnson, Joseph. *Traditions and Reminiscences Chiefly of the American Revolution in the South: Including Biographical Sketches, Incidents, and Anecdotes*. Charleston: Walker and Jones, 1851.

Jordan, Winthrop D. *White over Black: American Attitudes toward the Negro, 1550–1812*. Chapel Hill: University of North Carolina Press, 1968. Reprint, New York: W. W. Norton, 1977.

Journals of the Continental Congress. 34 vols. Washington, D.C.: U.S. Government Printing Office, 1907–34.

Journal of the House of Representatives of the State of Georgia. 1828–34. Milledgeville, Ga.: Camak and Ragland, 1829–34.

Journal of the Senate of the State of Georgia. 1824–34. Milledgeville, Ga.: Camak and Ragland, 1824–35.

Journal of the House of Representatives of the State of Tennessee. 1829–35. Nashville: Allen A. Hall and F. S. Heiskell, 1829–35.

Journal of the Senate of the State of Tennessee. 1829–35. Nashville: Allen A. Hall and F. S. Heiskell, 1829–35.

Kappler, Charles Joseph. *Indian Affairs: Laws and Treaties.* 4 vols. Washington, D.C.: United States Government Printing Office, 1903–29.

Kelly, Alfred H., Winfred A. Harbison, and Herman Belz. *The American Constitution: Its Origins and Development.* 2 vols. New York: W. W. Norton and Company, 1991.

Kennedy, John P., ed. *Memoirs of the Life of William Wirt.* 2 vols. Philadelphia: Lea Blanchard, 1849.

Kent, James. *Commentaries on American Law.* 4 vols. New York: O. Halsted, 1826–30.

Kilpatrick, Jack F., and Anna G. Kilpatrick. *New Echota Letters: Contributions of Samuel A. Worcester to the Cherokee Phoenix.* Dallas: Southern Methodist University Press, 1968.

King, Duane H., and E. Raymond Evans. "The Death of John Walker, Jr.: Political Assassination, or Private Vengeance?" *Journal of Cherokee Studies* 1 (1976): 4–16.

Kingsbury, S. M., ed. *The Records of the Virginia Company.* Washington, D.C.: Library of Congress, 1933.

Knight, L. L. *Georgia Landmarks, Memorials, and Legends.* Atlanta: Byrd Printing, 1913.

Knudson, Jerry W. "The Jeffersonian Assault on the Federalist Judiciary, 1802–1805." *American Journal of Legal History* 14 (1970): 55–75.

Kohn, Richard H. *Eagle and Sword: The Federalists and the Creation of the Military Establishment in America, 1783–1802.* New York: Free Press, 1975.

Korman, Sharon. *The Right of Conquest: The Acquisition of Territory by Force in International Law and Practice.* New York: Oxford University Press, 1996.

Lamplugh, George R. *Politics on the Periphery: Factions and Parties in Georgia, 1783–1806.* Newark: University of Delaware Press, 1986.

Langdon, Willard J. *Law Enforcement in Hall County, 1818–1980.* Lakemont, Ga.: Copple House, 1981.

Large, Donald W. "This Land Is Whose Land? Changing Concepts of Land as Property." *Wisconsin Law Review* (1973): 1034–83.

de Las Casas, Bartolomé. *The Tears of the Indians: Being a Historical and True Account of the Cruel Massacres and Slaughters Committed by the Spaniards . . .* Translated by John Phillips. New York: Oriole Editions, 1972.

Laski, Harold J. *The Foundations of Sovereignty and Other Essays.* New York: Harcourt, Brace and Company 1921. Reprint: Freeport, N.Y.: Books for Libraries Press, Inc., 1968.

Laws of the Cherokee Nation, Adopted at Various Periods, Printed for the Benefit of the Nation. Tahlequah, Cherokee Nation: Cherokee Advocate office, 1852. Reprint, Wilmington, Delaware: Scholarly Resources, 1973.

Leutbecker, Mark R. "Some Public Views on Indian Removal in the South." M.A. thesis, Louisiana State University, 1973.

Levin, A. J. "Mr. Justice William Johnson and the Common Incidents of Life." *Michigan Law Review* 44 (1945): 243–93.

———. "Mr. Justice William Johnson, Jurist in Limine: The Judge as Historian and Maker of History." *Michigan Law Review* 46 (1947): 131–86.

———. "Mr. Justice William Johnson, Jurist in Limine: Views on Judicial Precedent." *Michigan Law Review* 46 (1948): 481–520.

———. "Mr. Justice William Johnson, Jurist in Limine: Dissent and the Judging Faculty." *Michigan Law Review* 47 (1949): 477–536.

Lillich, Richard B. "The Chase Impeachment." *American Journal of Legal History* 4 (1960): 49–72.

Llewellyn, Karl, and E. Adamson Hoebel. *The Cheyenne Way: Conflict and Case Law in Primitive Jurisprudence.* Norman: University of Oklahoma Press, 1941.

Locke, John. *Two Treatises of Government.* 1690. Reprint, Indianapolis: Hackett Publishing Co., 1980.

Loth, David. *Chief Justice: John Marshall and the Growth of the Republic.* New York: W. W. Norton and Company, Inc., 1949.

Luebke, Barbara Francine. "Elias Boudinot, Cherokee Editor: The Father of American Indian Journalism." Ph.D. diss., University of Missouri, 1981.

Lumpkin, Wilson. *The Removal of the Cherokee Indians from Georgia.* New York: Dodd Mead, 1907. Reprint, New York: Arno Press, 1969.

Lunenfield, Marvin. *1492: Discovery, Invasion, Encounter.* Lexington, Mass.: D. C. Heath and Company, 1991.

Lurie, Nancy Oestreich. "Indian Cultural Adjustment to European Civilization." In *Seventeenth Century America: Essays in Colonial History,* edited by James Morton Smith. Westport, Conn.: Greenwood Press, 1959.

Lyons, Chief Oren, and John Mohawk, eds. *Exiled in the Land of the Free: Democracy, Indian Nations, and the U.S. Constitution.* Santa Fe: Clear Light Publishers, 1992.

Madison, James. *Papers of James Madison.* Edited by Robert Allen Rutland and Rachel W. Rutland. Chicago: University of Chicago Press, 1973.

Magrath, Peter C. *Yazoo: Law and Politics in the New Republic.* Providence: Brown University Press, 1966.

Marshall, Charles Burton. *The Exercise of Sovereignty: Papers on Foreign Policy.* Baltimore: Johns Hopkins University Press, 1965.

Marshall, John. *The Life of George Washington.* 5 vols. Philadelphia: C. P. Wayne, 1805–7.

―――. "John Marshall to Joseph Story." 29 October 1828. *Proceedings of the Massachusetts Historical Society* 34: 337–38.

Martin, Joel. *Sacred Revolt: The Muskogees' Struggle for a New World*. Boston: Beacon Press, 1991.

McClung, John A. *Sketches of Western Adventure*. Maysville, Ky.: Collins, 1832. Reprint, New York: Garland Publishing Co., 1975.

McLoughlin, William G. "Cherokee Anomie, 1794–1810: New Roles for Red Men, Red Women, and Black Slaves." In *Uprooted Americans: Essays in Honor of Oscar Handlin*, edited by Richard Bushman and Stephan Thernstrom. Boston: Little, Brown Publishers, 1979.

―――. *Cherokees and Missionaries, 1789–1839*. New Haven: Yale University Press, 1984.

―――. *Cherokee Renascence in the New Republic*. Princeton: Princeton University Press, 1986.

―――. *After the Trail of Tears: The Cherokees' Struggle for Sovereignty, 1839–1880*. Chapel Hill: University of North Carolina Press, 1993.

McLoughlin, William G., Walter H. Conser Jr., and Virginia Duffy McLoughlin. *The Cherokee Ghost Dance: Essays on the Southeastern Indians, 1789–1861*. Macon, Ga.: Mercer University Press, 1984.

McMillan, Malcolm Cook. "The Alabama Constitution of 1819: A Study of Constitution-Making on the Frontier." *Alabama Review* 3 (1950): 263–85.

McNeil, Kent. *Common Law Aboriginal Title*. Oxford: Clarendon Press, 1989.

Medham, Marchamont. *The Case of the Commonwealth of England Stated etc.* Edited by Philip A. Knachel. 1650. Reprint, Charlottesville: University of Virginia Press, 1969.

Memoirs of Georgia. 2 vols. Easley, S.C.: Southern Historical Press, 1895.

Merrell, James H. "Declarations of Independence: Indian-White Relations in the New Nation." In *The American Revolution: Its Character and Limits*, edited by Jack P. Greene, 197–223. New York: New York University Press, 1987.

Messages of the Governors of Tennessee, 1835–1845. 10 vols. Nashville: Tennessee Historical Commission, 1954.

Miles, Edwin A. "After John Marshall's Decision." *Journal of Southern History* 39 (1973): 519–44.

Mitchell, John. *The Present State of Great Britain and North America, with Regard to Agriculture, Population, Trade, and Manufactures, Impartially Considered*. 1767. Reprint, New York: Research Reprints, 1970.

Mooney, James. *James Mooney's History, Myths, and Sacred Formulas of the Cherokees*. Asheville, N.C.: Historical Images, 1992.

More, Thomas. *Utopia*. Edited by George M. Logan and Robert M. Adams. 1516. Reprint, Cambridge: Cambridge University Press, 1989.

Morgan, Donald G. *Justice William Johnson, The First Dissenter: The Career and Constitutional Philosophy of a Jeffersonian Judge*. Columbia: University of South Carolina Press, 1954.

―――. "Mr. Justice William Johnson and the Constitution." *Harvard Law Review* 57 (1957): 328–61.

————. "William Johnson." In *The Justices of the United States Supreme Court 1789–1969: Their Lives and Major Opinions,* edited by Leon Friedman and Fred L. Israel, 4 vols. 1: 355–72. New York: Chelsea House Publishers, 1969.

Morris, Thomas D. *Southern Slavery and the Law, 1619–1860.* Chapel Hill: University of North Carolina Press, 1996.

Mosse, George L. *The Struggle for Sovereignty in England: From the Reign of Queen Elizabeth to the Petition of Right.* East Lansing: Michigan State College Press, 1950.

————. *The Crisis of German Ideology: Intellectual Origins of the Third Reich.* New York: Grosset and Dunlap, 1964.

Moulton, Gary E. *John Ross: Cherokee Chief.* Athens: University of Georgia Press, 1978.

Muldoon, James, ed. *The Expansion of Europe: The First Phase.* Philadelphia: University of Pennsylvania Press, 1977.

New American State Papers: Indian Affairs. Edited by Loring B. Priest. 13 vols. Wilmington, Del.: Scholarly Resources, 1972.

Newton, Nell Jessup. "At the Whim of the Sovereign: Aboriginal Title Reconsidered." *Hastings Law Journal* 31 (1980): 1215–85.

Norgren, Jill. *The Cherokee Cases: The Confrontation of Law and Politics.* New York: McGraw Hill, Inc., 1996.

Northen, William J. *Men of Mark in Georgia.* 7 vols. Atlanta: A. B. Caldwell, 1907–12.

Nussbaum, Arthur. *A Concise History of the Law of Nations.* New York: Macmillan Publishing, 1947.

O'Donnell, James H., III. *Southern Indians in the American Revolution, 1775–1783.* Knoxville: University of Tennessee Press, 1973.

O'Neall, John Belton. *Biographical Sketches of the Bench and Bar of South Carolina.* Charleston: Courtenay, 1859.

Onuf, Peter, and Nicholas Onuf. *Federal Union, Modern World: The Law of Nations in an Age of Revolutions, 1776–1814.* Madison, Wis.: Madison House, 1993.

Ortiz, Roxanne Dunbar, ed. *Economic Development in American Indian Reservations.* Albuquerque: University of New Mexico Native American Studies, 1979.

Otis, D. S. *The Dawes Act and the Allotment of Indian Lands.* Norman: University of Oklahoma Press, 1973.

Owen, Thomas M. *History of Alabama and Dictionary of Alabama Biography.* 1921. Reprint, Spartanburg, S.C.: Reprint Company, 1978.

Owsley, Frank L., Jr. "Francis Scott Key's Mission to Alabama in 1833." *Alabama Review* 23 (1970): 181–92.

————. *Struggle for the Gulf Borderlands: The Creek War and the Battle of New Orleans.* Gainesville: University Presses of Florida, 1981.

Padover, Saul K., ed. *The Complete Jefferson.* Freeport, N.Y.: Books for Libraries Press, 1969.

Parins, James W. *John Rollin Ridge: His Life and Works.* Lincoln: University of Nebraska Press, 1991.

Paschal, George. "The Trial of Stand Watie." *Chronicles of Oklahoma* 12 (1934): 305–39.

Pearce, Roy Harvey. *The Savages of America: A Study of the Indian and the Idea of Civilization.* Baltimore: John Hopkins University Press, 1953.

———. "A Melancholy Fact: The Indian in American Life." In *The Indian in American History,* edited by Francis Paul Prucha. Hinsdale, Ill.: Dryden Press, 1971.

Perdue, Theda. "Rising from the Ashes: The Cherokee Phoenix as an Ethnohistorical Source." *Ethnohistory* 24 (1977): 207–18.

———. *Slavery and the Evolution of Cherokee Society, 1540–1866.* Knoxville: University of Tennessee Press, 1979.

———. "Southern Indians and the Cult of True Womanhood." In *The Web of Southern Social Relations: Women, Family, and Education,* edited by Walter J. Fraser Jr., R. Frank Saunders Jr., and Jon L. Wakelyn, 35–51. Athens: University of Georgia Press, 1985.

———. "Cherokee Women and the Trail of Tears." *Journal of Women's History* 1 (1989): 14–30.

———. "The Conflict Within: The Cherokee Power Structure and Removal." *Georgia Historical Quarterly* 73 (1989): 467–91.

———. *Cherokee Women.* Lincoln: University of Nebraska Press, 1999.

———, ed. *Cherokee Editor: The Writings of Elias Boudinot.* Knoxville: University of Tennessee Press, 1983.

Perdue, Theda, and Michael D. Green, eds. *The Cherokee Removal: A Brief History with Documents.* Boston: Bedford Books of St. Martin's Press, 1995.

Persico, V. Richard, Jr. "Early Nineteenth-Century Cherokee Political Organization." In *The Cherokee Indian Nation: A Troubled History,* edited by Duane H. King, 92–109. Knoxville: University of Tennessee Press, 1979.

Peters, Richard, ed. *The Case of the Cherokee Nation against the State of Georgia: Argued and Determined at the Supreme Court of the United States, January Term 1831.* Philadelphia: John Grigy, 1831.

Pevar, Stephen L. *The Rights of Indians and Tribes: The Basic ACLU Guide to Indian and Tribal Rights.* Carbondale and Edwardsville: Southern Illinois University Press, 1992.

Phillips, Ulrich B. "Georgia and States' Rights: A Study of the Political History of Georgia from the Revolution to the Civil War with Particular Regard to Federal Relations." *Annual Report of the American Historical Association* 2 (1902): 3–224.

———. "The Expulsion of the Cherokees." In *The Removal of the Cherokee Nation,* edited by Louis Filler. Boston: D. C. Heath and Company, 1962. Reprint, Malabar, Fla.: Krieger Publishing, 1977 and 1988.

Pindar, George A. *Georgia Real Estate Law and Procedure.* Atlanta: Harrison Company, 1971.

Porter, Henry Culverwell. *The Inconstant Savage: England and the American Indian, 1500–1600.* London: Duckworth Press, 1979.

Posey, Walter Brownlow. *Frontier Mission: A History of Religion West of the Southern Appalachians to 1861.* Lexington: University of Kentucky Press, 1966.

Preso, Timothy Joseph. "A Return to Uncertainty in Indian Affairs: The Framers, the Supreme Court, and the Indian Commerce Clause." *American Indian Law Review* 19 (1994): 443–72.

Priest, Loring Benson. *Uncle Sam's Stepchildren: The Reformation of United States Indian Policy, 1865–1887.* New Brunswick: Rutgers University Press, 1942.

Prucha, Francis Paul. *American Indian Policy in the Formative Years: The Indian Trade and Intercourse Acts, 1790–1834.* Cambridge: Harvard University Press, 1962.

———. "Andrew Jackson's Indian Policy: A Reassessment." *Journal of American History* 56 (1969): 527–39.

———. *The Indian in American History.* Hinesdale, Ill.: Dryden Press, 1971.

———. *American Indian Policy in Crisis: Christian Reformers and the Indian, 1865–1900.* Norman: University of Oklahoma Press, 1976.

———. *The Great Father: The United States Government and the American Indian.* Lincoln: University of Nebraska Press, 1984.

———. *American Indian Treaties: The History of a Political Anomaly.* Berkeley: University of California Press, 1997.

———, ed. *Documents of United States Indian Policy.* Lincoln: University of Nebraska Press, 1990.

Public Acts Passed at the First Session of the Twentieth General Assembly of the State of Tennessee, 1833. Nashville: Allen A. Hall and F. S. Heiskell, 1833.

Pufendorf, Samuel von. *De Jure Naturae Libri Octo.* Translated by Charles Henry Oldfather, William Abbot Oldfather, and Walter Simmons. Oxford: Clarendon Press, 1934.

Purchas, Samuel. *Hakluytus Posthumus or Purchas His Pilgrimes.* Glasgow: MacLehose, 1906.

Quinn, David Beers. "Ireland and Sixteenth Century Expansion." *Historical Studies* 1 (1958): 20–58.

Records of the States of the United States of America. Alabama. B. I. 1823–33.

Reed, Gerald Alexander. "The Ross-Watie Conflict: Factionalism in the Cherokee Nation, 1839–1865." Ph.D. diss., University of Oklahoma, 1967.

"Reflections on the Institutions of the Cherokee Indians." *Analectic Magazine* 38 (1818): 41–42.

Reid, John Phillip. *A Law of Blood: The Primitive Law of the Cherokee Nation.* New York: New York University Press, 1970.

———. *A Better Kind of Hatchet: Law, Trade, and Diplomacy in the Cherokee Nation during the Early Years of European Contact.* University Park: Pennsylvania State University Press, 1976.

Remini, Robert. *The Legacy of Andrew Jackson: Essays on Democracy, Indian Removal, and Slavery.* Baton Rouge: Louisiana State University Press, 1988.

Richardson, James D., ed. *A Compilation of the Messages and Papers of the Presidents.* 20 vols. New York: Bureau of National Literature, 1897.

Richter, Daniel K. *Ordeal of the Longhouse: The Peoples of the Iroquois League in the Era of European Colonization.* Chapel Hill: University of North Carolina Press, 1992.

Robinson, W. S., and Alden T. Vaughan, eds. *Early American Indian Documents: Treaties and Laws, 1607–1789,* ed. Alden T. Vaughan. Vol. 4, Virginia Treaties, 1607–1722. Washington, D.C.: University Publications of America, 1979.

Robinson, W. Stitt. *The Southern Colonial Frontier, 1607–1763.* Albuquerque: University of New Mexico Press, 1979.

Rogers, William Warren, Jr. "Alabama and the Presidential Election of 1836." *Alabama Review* 35 (1982): 111–26.

Rogin, Michael Paul. *Fathers and Children: Andrew Jackson and the Subjugation of the American Indian.* New York: Alfred A. Knopf, 1975.

Romans, Bernard. *A Concise Natural History of East and West Florida.* 1775. Reprint, Gainesville: University of Florida Press, 1962.

Roper, Donald M. "Justice Smith Thompson." *New York Historical Society Quarterly* 51 (1967): 119–39.

———. *Mr. Justice Thompson and the Constitution.* New York: Garland Publishing Co., 1987.

Ross, John. *The Papers of Chief John Ross.* Edited by Gary E. Moulton. 2 vols. Norman: University of Oklahoma Press, 1985.

Rountree, Helen. *Pocahontas's People: The Powhatan Indians of Virginia through Four Centuries.* Norman: University of Oklahoma Press, 1990.

Rousseau, Jean-Jacques. *The Social Contract and Discourses.* Translated by G. D. H. Cole. 1762. Reprint, London: Dent Press, 1973.

Ruddy, Francis Stephen. *International Law and the Enlightenment: The Background of Emmerich de Vattel's "Le Droit des Gens."* Introduction by Clive Perry. Dobbs Ferry, N. Y.: Oceana Publications, Inc., 1975.

Satz, Ronald E. *American Indian Policy in the Jacksonian Era.* Lincoln: University of Nebraska Press, 1975.

———. "Rhetoric versus Reality: The Indian Policy of Andrew Jackson." In *Cherokee Removal: Before and After,* edited by William L. Anderson, 29–54. Athens: University of Georgia Press, 1991.

Saye, Albert Berry. *A Constitutional History of Georgia, 1732–1968.* Athens: University of Georgia Press, 1948. Revised reprint, 1970.

Schroeder, Oliver, Jr. "The Life and Judicial Work of Justice William Johnson, Jr." *University of Pennsylvania Law Review* 95 (1946): 164–201.

———. "The Life and Judicial Work of Justice William Johnson, Jr., Part II." *University of Pennsylvania Law Review* 95 (1947): 344–86.

Sheehan, Bernard W. "Indian-White Relations in Early America: A Review Essay." *William and Mary Quarterly* 3d Ser. 26 (1969) 267–87.

———. *Seeds of Extinction: Jeffersonian Philanthropy and the American Indian.* Chapel Hill: University of North Carolina Press, 1973.

Sherwood, Adiel. *A Gazetteer of the State of Georgia.* Washington, D.C.: Force, 1837.

Shortt, Adam, and Arthur G. Doughty, eds. *Documents Relating to the Constitutional History of Canada, 1759–1791.* Ottawa: J. De L. Tache, 1918.

Silverberg, Robert. *Mound Builders of Ancient America: The Archeology of Ancient America.* Greenwich, Conn.: New York Graphic Society, 1968.

Slattern, Brian. "The Land Rights of Indigenous Canadian Peoples as Affected by the Crown's Acquisition of Their Territories." Ph.D. diss., University of Oxford, 1979.

Slaughter, Phillip. "History of St. Mark's Parish." In Raleigh Travers Green, *Genealogical and Historical Notes on Culpeper County, Virginia.* Culpeper, Va.: R. T. Green, 1900.

Smith, Jean Edward. *John Marshall: Definer of a Nation.* New York: Henry Holt and Company, 1996.

Smith, Joseph Henry, ed. *Appeals to the Privy Council from the American Plantations.* New York: Columbia University Press, 1950.

Sosin, Jack M. *Whitehall and the Wilderness: The Middle West in British Colonial History, 1760–1775.* Lincoln: University of Nebraska Press, 1961.

Southerland, Henry DeLeon, Jr., and Jerry Elijah Brown. *The Federal Road through Georgia, the Creek Nation, and Alabama, 1806–1836.* Tuscaloosa: University of Alabama Press, 1989.

Stannard, David E. *American Holocaust: Columbus and the Conquest of the New World.* New York: Oxford University Press, 1992.

Statutes at Large of the United States of America, 1789–1873. 17 vols. Washington, D.C.: U.S. Government Printing Office, 1850–1873.

Stites, Francis N. *John Marshall: Defender of the Constitution.* Boston: Little, Brown and Company, 1981.

Story, William Wetmore, ed. *Life and Letters of Joseph Story.* 2 vols. Boston: Charles C. Little and James Brown, 1851.

Strickland, Rennard. *Fire and the Spirits: Cherokee Law from Clan to Court.* Norman: University of Oklahoma Press, 1975.

Strickland, Rennard, and William M. Strickland. "Beyond the Trail of Tears: One Hundred Fifty Years of Cherokee Survival." In *Cherokee Removal: Before and After,* edited by William L. Anderson, 112–38. Athens: University of Georgia Press, 1991.

Strickland, William Morel. "The Rhetoric of Cherokee Indian Removal from Georgia, 1828–1832." Ph.D. diss., Louisiana State University, 1975.

Sturtevant, William C. *The Development of Political Organization in Native North America.* 1979 Proceedings of the America Ethnological Society. Edited by Elisabeth Tooker. Washington, D.C.: American Ethnological Society, 1983.

———, ed. "John Ridge on Cherokee Civilization in 1826." *Journal of Cherokee Studies* 7 (1981): 79–91.

Swanton, John R. *The Indians of the Southeastern United States.* Washington: Smithsonian Institution Press, 1946. Reprint 1979.

Swindler, William F. "Politics as Law: The Cherokee Cases." *American Indian Law Review* 3 (1975): 7–20.

Takaki, Ronald. " 'The Tempest' in the Wilderness: The Racialization of Savagery."
    Journal of American History 79 (1992): 892–912.
Taylor, E. G. R., ed. *The Original Writings and Correspondence of the Two Richard
    Hakluyts.* 2 vols. London: Hakluyt Society, 1935.
Thornton, J. Mills, III. *Politics and Power in a Slave Society: Alabama, 1800–1860.*
    Baton Rouge: Louisiana State University Press, 1978.
Thornton, Russell. "Cherokees Losses during the Trail of Tears: A New Perspective
    and a New Estimate." *Ethnohistory* 31 (1984): 289–300.
———. *American Indian Holocaust and Survival: A Population History Since 1492.*
    Norman: University of Oklahoma Press, 1987.
———. *The Cherokees: A Population History.* Lincoln: University of Nebraska
    Press, 1990.
Tocqueville, Alexis de. *Democracy in America.* Edited by J. P. Mayer and Max
    Lerner. 1835. Reprint, New York: Harper and Row, 1966.
———. *Journey to America.* Edited by J. P. Mayer. Translated by George Lawrence.
    New Haven: Yale University Press, 1960.
Turner, Kathryn. "Federalist Policy in the Judiciary Act of 1801." *William and Mary
    Quarterly* 22 (1965): 3–33.
Tyner, James W. *Those Who Cried: The 16,000.* N.p.: Chi-ga-u Inc., 1974.
United States Department of Justice. *Official Opinions of the United States Attorney
    General.* 13 vols. Washington, D.C., Government Printing Office, 1873–.
U.S. Congress. "Report on Cherokee Proposals on Disputed Lands." 18th Cong., 1st
    sess., H. R. 136. Serial 102.
U.S. Congress. "Report on Indian Land Title Dispute with Georgia." 19th Cong.,
    2nd sess., H. R. 98. Serial 161.
Usner, Daniel H. *Indians, Settlers, and Slaves in a Frontier Exchange Economy: The
    Lower Mississippi Valley before 1783.* Chapel Hill: University of North Carolina
    Press, 1992.
Van Doren, Mark, ed. *Travels of William Bartram.* Philadelphia: James and Johnson,
    1791. Reprint, New York: Dover Publications, Inc., 1955.
Vattel, Emmerich. *The Law of Nations or the Principles of Natural Law Applied
    to the Conduct of Affairs of Nations and Sovereigns.* Translated by Charles G.
    Fenwick. Washington, D.C.: The Carnegie Institution of Washington, 1916.
Vaughan, Alden T. " 'Expulsion of the Savages': English Policy and the Virginia
    Massacre of 1622." *William and Mary Quarterly* 3rd Ser., 35 (1978): 57–84.
Victoria, Francisco. *De Indis et de Ivre Belli Reflectiones.* Edited by E. Nys. Trans-
    lated by J. P. Bate. New York: Oceana Press, 1917.
Vipperman, Carl J. "Forcibly If We Must: The Georgia Case for Cherokee Removal,
    1802–1832." *Journal of Cherokee Studies* 3 (1978): 103–10.
Wallace, Anthony F. C. "Revitalization Movements: Some Theoretical Considera-
    tions for Comparative Study." *American Anthropologist* 58 (1956): 264–81.
———. *Jefferson and the Indians: The Tragic Fate of the First Americans.* Cam-
    bridge: Harvard University Press, 1999.

Wallerstein, Immanuel. *The Modern World System: Capitalist Agriculture and the Origins of the European World Economy in the Sixteenth Century.* New York: Academic Press, 1974.

Walters, William. "Review Essay: Preemption, Tribal Sovereignty, and *Worcester v. Georgia.*" *Oregon Law Review* 62 (1983): 127–44.

Warren, Charles. *The Supreme Court in United States History.* 2 vols. Boston: Little, Brown, 1928.

Washburn, Wilcomb E. *Red Man's Land/White Man's Law: A Study of the Past and Present Status of the American Indian.* New York: Charles Scribner's Sons, 1971.

Welborn, Robert H. *Dictionary of Georgia Biography.* Edited by Kenneth Coleman and Charles Stephen Gurr. Athens: University of Georgia Press, 1983.

Werther, Guntram F. A. *Self-Determination in Western Democracies: Aboriginal Politics in Comparative Perspective.* Westport, Conn.: Greenwood Press, 1992.

White, G. Edward, and Gerald Gunther. *The Marshall Court and Cultural Change, 1815–1835.* Volumes 3 and 4 of *History of the Supreme Court of the United States.* New York: Macmillan Publishing Company and London: Collier Macmillan Publishers, 1988.

White, Richard. *Roots of Dependency: Subsistence, Environment, and Social Change among the Choctaws, Pawnees, and Navajos.* Lincoln: University of Nebraska Press, 1983.

Wilkins, David E. *American Indian Sovereignty and the U.S. Supreme Court.* Austin: University of Texas Press, 1997.

Wilkins, Thurman. *Cherokee Tragedy: The Ridge Family and the Decimation of a People.* New York: Macmillan, 1970. Reprint, Norman: University of Oklahoma Press, 1986.

Wilkinson, Charles F. *American Indians, Time, and the Law: Native Societies in a Modern Constitutional Democracy.* New Haven: Yale University Press, 1987.

Williams, David. "The Cherokee Gold Lottery and Georgia's Gubernatorial Campaign of 1831." *Journal of Cherokee Studies* 15 (1990): 41–58.

———. *The Georgia Gold Rush: Twenty-Niners, Cherokees, and Gold Fever.* Columbia: University of South Carolina Press, 1993.

Williams, Jack K. "Crime and Punishment in Alabama, 1819–1840." *Alabama Review* 6 (1953): 14–30.

Williams, Robert A. *The American Indian in Western Legal Thought: The Discourses of Conquest.* New York: Oxford University Press, 1990.

———. *Linking Arms Together: American Indian Treaty Visions of Law and Peace, 1600–1800.* New York: Oxford University Press, 1997.

Williams, Samuel Cole, ed. *Lieut. Henry Timberlake's Memoirs.* Johnson City, Tenn.: Watauga Press, 1927.

———, ed. *Early Travels in the Tennessee Country, 1540–1800.* Johnson City, Tenn.: Watauga Press, 1928.

———, ed. *Adair's History of the American Indians.* Johnson City, Tenn.: Watauga Press, 1930.

Williams, Walter L. "From Independence to Wardship: The Legal Process of Erosion of American Indian Sovereignty, 1810–1903." *American Indian Culture and Research Journal* 7 (1983): 5–32.

Wilms, Douglas C. "Cherokee Land Use in Georgia before Removal." In *Cherokee Removal: Before and After*, edited by William L. Anderson, 1–28. Athens: University of Georgia Press, 1991.

Wolff, Christian. *Jus Gentium Methodo Scientifica Pertractatum.* Translated by Joseph H. Drake. Oxford: Claredon Press, 1934.

Wood, Gordon S. *The Radicalism of the American Revolution.* New York: Knopf, 1992.

Wood, Peter H., Gregory A. Waselkov, and M. Thomas Hatley. *Powhatan's Mantle: Indians in the Colonial Southeast.* Lincoln: University of Nebraska Press, 1989.

Woodward, Grace Steele. *The Cherokees.* Norman: University of Oklahoma Press, 1963.

Worcester, Samuel A. "Jail at Camp Gilmer." *New York Spectator,* 11 July 1831 and 23 August 1831. Reprinted in *Journal of Cherokee Studies* 4 (1979): 83–84.

Worcester, Samuel A., J. J. Trott, Elizur Butler, and Samuel Mayes to Col. Ch. C. Nelson, 15 July 1831. Reprinted in *Journal of Cherokee Studies* 4 (1979): 85–86.

Wunder, John R. *"Retained by the People": A History of American Indians and the Bill of Rights.* New York: Oxford University Press, 1994.

Young, Mary Elizabeth. *Redskins, Ruffleshirts, and Rednecks: Indian Allotments in Alabama and Mississippi, 1830–1860.* Norman: University of Oklahoma Press, 1961.

———. "Women, Civilization, and the Indian Question." In *Clio was a Woman: Studies in the History of American Women,* edited by Mabel E. Deutrich and Virginia C. Purdy, 97–110. Washington, D.C.: Howard University Press, 1980.

———. "The Cherokee Nation: Mirror of the Republic." *American Quarterly* 33 (1981): 502–24.

———. "Racism in Red and Black: Indians and Other Free People of Color in Georgia Law, Politics, and Removal Policy." *Georgia Historical Quarterly* 73 (1989): 492–518.

———. "The Exercise of Sovereignty in Cherokee Georgia." *Journal of the Early Republic* 10 (1990): 43–63.

INDEX

LaVergne, TN USA
18 January 2011
212998LV00003B/31/P